THE MIDDLE AGES SERIES

Ruth Mazo Karras, General Editor
Edward Peters, Founding Editor

A complete list of books in the series
is available from the publisher.

Text and Territory

Geographical Imagination in the European Middle Ages

Edited by
Sylvia Tomasch and Sealy Gilles

PENN

University of Pennsylvania Press

Philadelphia

Copyright © 1998 University of Pennsylvania Press
All rights reserved
Printed in the United States of America on acid-free paper

10 9 8 7 6 5 4 3 2 1

Published by
University of Pennsylvania Press
Philadelphia, Pennsylvania 19104-4011

Library of Congress Cataloging-in-Publication Data
Text and territory : geographical imagination in the European Middle Ages / edited by Sylvia Tomasch and Sealy Gilles.
p.   cm. — (The Middle Ages series)
Includes bibliographical references and index.
ISBN 0-8122-3422-7 (cloth : alk. paper). — ISBN 0-8122-1635-0 (pbk. : alk. paper)
1. Geography, Medieval.   I. Tomasch, Sylvia.   II. Gilles, Sealy.
III. Series.
G89.T49 1997
910—dc21   97-35675
                                                                      CIP

Contents

List of Illustrations   vii

Acknowledgments   ix

Introduction: Medieval Geographical Desire
Sylvia Tomasch   1

I
CENTERS AND MARGINS

1. "Nel mezzo del cammin di nostra vita": The Palpability of *Purgatorio*
Mary Baine Campbell   15

2. Defining the Earth's Center in a Medieval "Multi-Text": Jerusalem in *The Book of John Mandeville*
Iain Macleod Higgins   29

3. Against Gog and Magog
Scott D. Westrem   54

II
PLACE AND THE POLITICS OF IDENTITY

4. Territorial Interpolations in the Old English Orosius
Sealy Gilles   79

5. Making History English: Cultural Identity and Historical Explanation in William of Malmesbury and Laȝamon's *Brut*
Robert M. Stein   97

6. Too Close for Comfort: Dis-Orienting Chivalry in the
Wars of Alexander
Christine Chism | 116

III
GENDER, SEXUALITY, GEOGRAPHY

7. City Air Makes Men Free and Women Bound
Jo Ann McNamara | 143

8. Land-Taking and Text-Making in Medieval Iceland
Margaret Clunies Ross | 159

9. Courted in the Country: Woman's Precarious Place in the Troubadours' Lyric Landscape
Gale Sigal | 185

10. Assault from Behind: Sodomy, Foreign Invasion, and Masculine Identity in the *Roman d'Enéas*
Vincent A. Lankewish | 207

IV
THE TERRITORY OF TEXTS

11. Judecca, Dante's Satan, and the *Dis*-placed Jew
Sylvia Tomasch | 247

12. The ABC of Ptolemy: Mapping the World with the Alphabet
Kathleen Biddick | 268

Bibliography | 295
List of Contributors | 321
Index | 323

Illustrations

1. Detail from Hereford map, circa 1280	2
2. Andreas Walsperger's world map, 1448	4
3.1. Johann of Udine's *mappa mundi*, circa 1455	63
3.2. Anonymous *mappa mundi*, circa 1450	64
11.1. Detail of roll of the Issues of the Exchequer, 1233	252
11.2. Taddeo di Bartolo, detail from Hell fresco, circa 1320	256
12.1a. Mohammed ben Al-Saal's Toledo astrolabe, 1029	272
12.1b. Detail from Mohammed ben Al-Saal's Toledo astrolabe	273
12.2. Astrolabe from Chaucer's lesson on telling time	280
12.3. Letter "M" from Marie de Bourgogne's alphabet	282
12.4. Letter "A" from Damiano da Moille alphabet	283
12.5. Alphabetical register of places and coordinates from *Claudius Ptolomaeus Cosmographia*, 1513	286
12.6. Anonymous engraving of the ritual murder of Simon of Trent, 1475	289

Acknowledgments

TEXT AND TERRITORY HAS, FROM THE beginning, been a collaborative effort. The idea was born in sessions at the 1992 Medieval Academy meeting and the 1994 International Congress on Medieval Studies. We are grateful for the responses and encouragement received from audiences and panelists at both sessions. It has been a pleasure and an education working with the individual contributors, who cheerfully revised and reformatted as the volume took shape.

We are grateful to Dartmouth College's Humanities Computer Center for the use of its impressive facilities and to the Research Foundation of the City University of New York for a generous publication subvention. In particular, we thank Jerome Singerman for shepherding the volume through its initial submission to the Press; Peter Travis for indispensable advice and encouragement at every point; and especially Timothy Gilles, without whose word processing skills and midnight computer forays this volume would still be in typescript.

Finally, the editors acknowledge the pleasures and the pains of collaborative editing, a textual endeavor that we wouldn't have missed for all the world's territory.

This volume is dedicated to Sadie and Morris Tomasch and to Eleanor, Duncan, Alison, Hadiya, and Erica.

Introduction: Medieval Geographical Desire

SYLVIA TOMASCH

> Immediately there came into view a distinguished-looking lady, holding a geometer's rod in her right hand and a solid globe in her left. . . . "I am called Geometry because I have often traversed and measured out the earth, and I could offer calculations and proofs for its shape, size, position, regions, and dimensions. There is no portion of the earth's surface that I could not describe from memory."
>
> —Martianus Capella,
> *The Marriage of Philology and Mercury*
> (fifth century)

In book 6 of Martianus Capella's *The Marriage of Philology and Mercury*, the "celestial senate" of the gods and the liberal arts listens intently to Lady Geometry's extended explication of the "precepts of her discipline" (218). On the one hand, hers is a descriptive, or geo-graphical, discipline dedicated to the empirical and verbal depiction of the contours of the earth; on the other, hers is also a mathematical discipline dedicated to rationalizing those contours into perfect geo-metrical forms. The interlocking of these two characteristics is expressed by the icons of her craft: the solid globe, a sign of Geometry's possession of complete knowledge of the earth's surface; and the geometer's rod, a symbol of intellectual order, whereby the earth's irregularities are rationalized by the instruments of human mensuration.

A servant brings to Geometry a third instrument, an "abacus board," which, we are told, "can represent the entire circumference and the circles of the universe, the shapes of the elements, and the very depths of the earth; you will see there represented anything you could not explain in words" (217–18).[1]

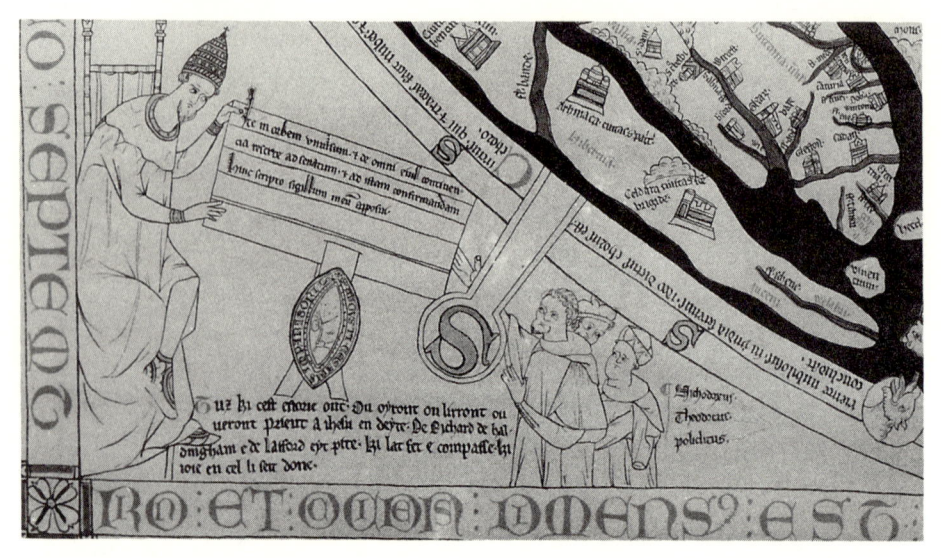

Figure 1. Detail (northwest [bottom left corner]) from the Hereford map, attributed to Richard of Haldingham, circa 1280; oriented to the east. Hereford Cathedral. By permission of the Dean and Chapter of Hereford Cathedral.

A perfectly performing signifier, the abacus bridges the gap between itself and its signified, an operation, this text acknowledges, in which language inevitably fails. As a mechanism of absolute representation, the abacus performs tasks visible and invisible, superficial and profound; in revealing the "shape, size, position, regions, and dimensions" as well as the unseen "depths of the earth," it uncovers the hidden and exposes the concealed.

Jupiter, one of Geometry's divine auditors, exhibits a particular enthusiasm for the discovery powers of the geographical art: "Jupiter as well was eager to investigate all the hiding places on earth—for the reason, I suppose, that no beautiful girl of that epoch, either, might escape that lecher of many transformations" (220). Though the narrator's sly joke is directed at Jupiter's eroticization of the geographical process, it also implicates all who share the general desire to "know" the earth and to experience earth's innermost secrets. Lady Geometry is indeed a patron of the quest for geographical knowledge, but, Martianus here suggests, that knowledge always enjoys an element of control, of conquest, even of ravishment. Thus her art is one that is far from disinterested in its search for truth, for what is it she is asked, and is eager, to do? Not only to partake of the joys of abstraction and to smooth surface irregularities, but to penetrate interior enigmas, to master and possess. In short: to gratify geographical desire.[2]

In the Middle Ages, geographical desire appears in a variety of forms;

here, two examples will have to suffice. Richard of Haldingham's Hereford map provides an instance of optimism, perhaps even hubris, about the possibility of achieving geographical satisfaction. On this thirteenth-century *mappa mundi* appears the whole of the terrestrial world, laid out in its historical, fabulous, and contemporary multiplicity. Above the circle of the earth, Christ in majesty decrees the separation of the saved from the damned; below the earth's circle, as if analogously set, the Roman emperor Augustus hands a scroll to three surveyors, ordering them to take the earth's measure (Figure 1).[3] By means of these counterpointed scenes of division and allocation, the map declares the importance of geographical activity. It asserts the significance of empirical investigations in making the world secure for secular kingdoms as well as for the Christian imperium. This map informs its viewers that acts of territorial assessment and spiritual valuation are not alternative possibilities; each is necessary to secure the temporal realm as well as the eternal. So too the geometer's art involves not only the establishment of boundaries but also the estimation, and the achievement, of merit. Thus, in its representation of the dual ideologies of perfect knowledge and absolute possession, this particular "abacus board" performatively claims for itself the gratification of geographical desire.

In contrast, the 1448 map of Andreas Walsperger (Figure 2) exhibits great anxiety about achieving a precise alignment of secular and sacred mensuration.[4] Although it employs the same T-O form as the Hereford map, a form that has little concern with accuracy of position, this map includes a prominently placed, inaccurate, and utterly unusable mileage scale. Although traditional T-O maps are oriented toward the east, this map puts south on top, in the fashion of medieval Arabic maps, and incorporates up-to-date information gained from Arabic and Portuguese Atlantic and African coastal navigations.[5] The resulting clash of cartographic conventions—combining the vestiges of an earlier, unified, christianized vision with new technologies and empirical information—pushes the map off-center, both literally and figuratively.[6] Jerusalem is dispossessed of the cartographic midpoint and moved "up," toward the Arabic south; Africa, the southern continent, continues somewhere off the page, beyond the control of its European cartographer. Furthermore, because one of Walsperger's stated aims is to distinguish between Christian cities (colored red) and those of the infidel (colored black),[7] he is forced to acknowledge contemporary political realities: he must color Jerusalem black. Unlike the neatly framed Hereford circle, the world Andreas draws is disunified rather than multiplicitous, resistant to the regularizing art of mapping. This cartographic construction marks not the satisfaction but the thwarting of geographical desire.

Longings for geographical satisfaction have a lengthy history in West-

Figure 2. World map of Andreas Walsperger, drawn in Constance, 1448; oriented to the south. Rome, Biblioteca Apostolica Vaticana, Pal. lat. 1362b. By permission of the Vatican Library.

ern thought, even though, as in the examples above, the degrees of self-implication are often only partially expressed. A short parable by Jorge Luis Borges captures the paradoxes inherent in the cartographic ambition to measure and secure the contours of the world. In "Of Exactitude in Science," Borges writes of a culture whose College of Cartographers constructed "a Map of the Empire that was the same Scale as the Empire and that coincided with it point for point." However, succeeding generations found this great achievement of Perfection "cumbersome," and the map was left to disintegrate, "abandoned... to the rigors of sun and Rain," so that finally "no other relic is left of the Discipline of Geography" (141).[8] Borges's bittersweet satire focuses attention on issues of representation and domination inherent in any geographical practice. It warns against the intellectual hubris of reifying the image with such precision that no space remains between the signifier and the signified, between the simulacrum and the thing itself—between, that is, the text and the territory.[9] By linking scientific construction with construction of the realm, the tale reveals the double delusion of geographers: to achieve exactitude and to replicate empire ("empirical" being the buried pun here). It thereby also reminds us of the political investment of any geographical undertaking, medieval or modern.

The contributors to this volume, conscious of the perennial attractions and the inevitable dangers of the subject, take as their collective task an investigation of medieval geographical desire. Building upon the insights of recent studies—particularly Gillian Overing and Marijane Osborn's *Landscape of Desire*, Mary Campbell's *The Witness and the Other World*, and the essays in *Discovering New Worlds*, edited by Scott D. Westrem—the writers here expand the range of medieval studies by employing feminist, queer, cultural, and postcolonial theories in specifically geographical ways. As literary scholars and historians, the contributors emphasize the inscriptive foundation of all geographical endeavor: "writing" is stressed as much as "earth"; "geo-" is completed by "-graphy." Hence our title, *Text and Territory*, which suggests a revalorized definition of "geography" as "the writing of the world." For it is the reciprocal interaction of two associated processes—the textualization of territories and the territorialization of texts—that perhaps most clearly illustrates the pervasiveness and potency of geographical desire. Through these processes, land is re-presented as territory, and works are surveyed, explored, located, and bounded; they become, as it were, texts.[10]

In their analyses of the reciprocal process of textualization and territorialization, the contributors to this volume evoke and extend the disparate facets of geographical desire already encountered. As in Martianus's paideic epic, the essays are concerned with the romance of discovery and the eroticization of the empirical; like the *mappae mundi*, they are interested in the politics of empire, the construction of signifiers of mapping, the relationship between centers and peripheries, and the problematics of alterity; and, as does Borges's fable, they explore the construction of texts that purport to embody their territories, as well as the discipline of geography itself. It may be helpful at this point to arrange these diverse concerns according to four concepts borrowed from Derek Gregory's *Geographical Imaginations*: "representation," "articulation," "spatialization," and "authorization." These concepts, Gregory argues, are not only crucial "in the conduct of any critical project" but are particularly urgent "within the contemporary reconfiguration of human geography and the other humanities and social sciences" (103–4).[11]

The first concept, "representation," has two important components: First, it "draws attention to the different ways in which the world is made present, re-presented, discursively constructed" (104). Second, it "has a related, more directly political meaning that has to do with giving voice to the concerns and situations of others" (104). This process of "othering" is never neutral, however, and always works through "grids of power" (104). The writers of the first three essays in Part 1 confront the complexities of discursive representation in travel narratives, pilgrim accounts, and maps. Attending specifically to the implications of positionality, they explicate verbal and visual constructions of periphery and center.

In "'Nel mezzo del cammin di nostra vita': The Palpability of *Purgatorio*," Mary Baine Campbell considers Dante's representation of the defining center, the "middleness" of images at the center of the central *cantica* of the *Divine Comedy*. In an analysis that recalls Martianus's Jove, she discusses the "erotic lure of geographical topics" in *Purgatorio*, a text that is simultaneously a love story and a travel account. Maintaining that its middleness is an aspect both of space and of narrative seduction, Campbell believes that the central canticle thereby fulfills what seems to be Dante's purpose in this portion of his text: "the journey between."

In "Defining the Earth's Center in a Medieval 'Multi-Text': Jerusalem in *The Book of John Mandeville*," Iain Macleod Higgins focuses on the diverse representations of Jerusalem in written as well as visual texts. Through his study of *The Book*'s numerous redactions, Higgins argues that this travelogue is analogous to late medieval *mappae mundi* that also imagine Jerusalem as the geographical and theological midpoint of the *oikoumene*. Like that of the Hereford map, Mandeville's geography is both textual and territorial, working to "claim" a Christian "domain." Higgins ends his essay by considering the ease with which the middle can be overlooked when reading a linear, end-oriented text—a situation that requires "compensation" to achieve "a fuller experience of the center."

Scott D. Westrem's essay, "Against Gog and Magog," is directly concerned with representational "grids of power" in the form of cartographic "othering." Surveying the "literal vagary" of Gog and Magog, Westrem argues that the unexpected cartographic juxtaposition of Gog and Magog with Asian Jews is a consequence of theologically inflected political events, such as the twelfth-century movement of the Mongols from the East. European territorial anxieties, combined with a Christian hermeneutics, lead, he believes, to the identification of Gog and Magog as an internal danger, rather than simply as a remote threat. Thus the center, the "transcendental point of reference,"[12] finds itself endangered by its own margins.

Part 2 explores the problematics of what Gregory calls "articulation," a notion "intended to challenge the sedimented division between the economic, the political, the social and the cultural" (105). To accomplish this, articulation "requires an identification of the modalities through which time and space are bound into the constitution of social life" (105). Each of the Old and Middle English texts under consideration in this part is directly concerned with discursive presentations of time (histories, chronicles, and genealogies) that simultaneously constitute their subjects in space (nations, kingdoms, and empires). These narratives of trade, colonialism, and conquest are each, in turn, situated firmly within a cultural, political, and psychological matrix.

In "Territorial Interpolations in the Old English Orosius," Sealy Gilles analyzes the Cotton Tiberius Bi manuscript to disclose the "cultural agenda" that authorizes the incorporation of geographical materials. However, in critical response to the tenets of contemporary anthropological theory, she argues that neither the alterations to Orosius's *History* nor the interpolated travel accounts of Ohthere and Wulfstan should be read according to programmatic expectations. When the Anglo-Saxon compilers contextualize the travelers' reports of alien geographies, they do not define the others as either exotic or demonic. Rather, the remote north and the customs of its inhabitants are neither recuperated nor marginalized but naturalized in the service of writing culture.

In contrast, Robert M. Stein, in "Making History English: Cultural Identity and Historical Explanation in William of Malmesbury and Laʒamon's *Brut*," shows that these later English writings, like Walsperger's map, reveal great geographical anxiety—in this case, concerning the post-Conquest amalgamation of diverse peoples and regions into one, English, whole. He links their apprehensions to their discourses of embodiment: the king's two bodies, the fragmented body politic, the translated relics of saints. William's aim, Stein argues, is to simplify "contested space" so that "geographical diversity is rewritten under the pressure of ideological purity." Laʒamon rewrites succession narratives as alliance narratives in order to transfer the notion of "identity of [royal] blood" "from time to space"; the poet thereby associates "legitimate sovereignty with a racially pure territory."

Christine Chism's essay, "Too Close for Comfort: Dis-Orienting Chivalry in the *Wars of Alexander*," fulfills Gregory's prescription to "challenge the sedimented division" between the cultural, the political, and (to add a term to

Gregory's list) the psychological. In the *Wars*, Alexander's battles necessarily juxtapose time and space: not only are his "conflicts of identity" transformed "into familial, political, and ideological ones," but his "genealogical conquests against his predecessors are reenacted as spatial and geographical ones." Chism also argues that the territorial anxieties within the text are linked to the specific spatial and temporal context of the English North West Midlands which provides for the production of the text itself. This translation of the deeds of the ancient (oriental) hero must therefore be understood within the context of contemporary, conflicted constructions of English chivalric identity.

In Part 3, the contributors pay particular attention to the concept of "spatialization." "Spatialization," according to Gregory, "refers to those ways in which social life literally 'takes place': to the opening and occupation of different sites of human action and to the differences and integrations that are socially inscribed through the production of place, space, and landscape" (104). A "double valency" of "space" is thereby implied: it is "coded in both physical and social terms" (104). The essays in Part 3 are specifically concerned with gendered and sexualized spatializations as a means and consequence of setting territorial boundaries; analyses of civic records, Icelandic sagas, Occitan lyrics, and a French romance reveal the complications of patriarchal geography.[13]

Jo Ann McNamara, in "City Air Makes Men Free and Women Bound," contends that urbanization in the later Middle Ages was an important force in the overall tendency to further restrict legal, economic, and spiritual opportunities for women. As towns became thoroughly spatialized according to increasingly rigid notions of gender, "anthropomorphized institutions," such as universities, "effectively barred women." According to McNamara, the enclosure of women was a general trend in many European cities; this trend, she maintains, is consistent with an ideology that "imaged a broad womanless space." Ultimately, therefore, the city can be understood as a paradoxical "instrument for the freedom of men and the containment of women."

Similarly, Margaret Clunies Ross, in "Land-Taking and Text-Making in Medieval Iceland," asserts that initial acts of settlement of Iceland and subsequent textual justifications are both differentially gendered. A new, sexualized social space is created through the processes of migration and colonization. In sagas and legal texts, space is coded as female ("domestic"), male ("public"), or sacred. Land is feminized, and female possession of land is accomplished communally, "through marriages and alliances." Land is also spiritualized, so that male territorial dominance is expressed not only individually, through "phallic display" and the symbolic "threat of homosexual rape," but also through "assertions of divinely sanctioned authority."

Gale Sigal also explores gendered territories in "Courted in the Country: Woman's Precarious Place in the Troubadours' Lyric Landscape," maintaining that the dichotomy between the lady of the *canso* and the shepherdess of the *pastourelle* is as equally dependent upon geographical space as it is upon social place. Only in the court is the *domna* protected, but there she is also silenced, for "inside castle walls, ladies don't talk back." Only in the country is the shepherdess free to speak, yet there she is vulnerable to verbal or physical violence. Thus it is the locations in troubadour lyrics where women are found (i.e., discovered, invented, and rooted) that determine their status, mobility, and voice.

In "Assault from Behind: Sodomy, Foreign Invasion, and Masculine Identity in the *Roman d'Enéas*," Vincent A. Lankewish argues for the primacy of territory not only in this text but in "medieval marriage practices" and "medieval constructions of gender and sexuality" as well. He links the conquest of territory to an expanded notion of "sodomy" (imputed to the Trojan invader by the queen of Latium), which includes military assaults, gender battles, and homosocial activities, all of which entangle the characters in conflicts of passivity, identity, and power. Eneas's newly conquered territory is thereby fully "eroticized," becoming the means to reinscribe male bonds, re-imagine sexual relations, and transform the space of desire.

Part 4 is directly concerned with issues of "authorization," as set out by Gregory: "authorization is an attempt to make [the political] dimension more explicit by raising a series of questions about the inscription of subjectivity and the operation of power-knowledge: about the privilege of position, and about authorship and authority, representation and rights" (105). The final two essays explicitly examine the territories claimed in and created through—that is, authorized by—texts themselves. Analyses of Dante, Mandeville, and Ptolemy reveal that the politics of textual production, inscription, and reception are firmly linked to ideologies of representation, articulation, and spatialization.

My essay, "Judecca, Dante's Satan, and the *Dis*-placed Jew," examines the inscription of "Judecca," the previously unquestioned reception of Jews in the *Divine Comedy*, and the ways in which Dante articulates the conjunction of Jews and Satan in temporal and spatial terms. Asserting that Dante's paradoxical (non)placement of Jews at the midpoint of hell has been matched by their subsequent neglect by generations of *dantisti*, I argue that the reinforcement of exclusionist territories, both within and without the text, is part of an ongoing christianist hermeneutics that demands attention from medievalists today.

In the final essay of the collection, "The ABC of Ptolemy: Mapping the

World with the Alphabet," Kathleen Biddick shows how cartographic practices are dependent upon "technologies of temporality," which include astrolabical calculations, alphabetizations, and apocalyptic speculations. Texts as diverse as Ptolemaic maps, Hebrew-Christian disputations, and *Mandeville's Travels* ensure the "translation" of Jews "from time into space" so that they are "detemporalized" and "reterritorialized" as "old talmudic" phantasms. The fulfillment of Christian, European geographical desire results in a form of "colonization" by which, "guaranteed of origin, cartographic space could become timeless" and "cleansed."

As all of these essays show, geographical desire encompasses an extraordinary array of notions constitutive of Western thought. Geographical desire is revealed as eroticized (Campbell, Lankewish), gendered (McNamara, Clunies Ross, Sigal, Lankewish), and enclosed space (McNamara, Sigal, Tomasch); as narratives of centers (Campbell, Higgins, Tomasch), anti-Semitism (Westrem, Tomasch, Biddick), travel (Campbell, Higgins, Gilles, Clunies Ross), and conquest (Stein, Chism, Lankewish, Biddick); as strategies of cartography (Higgins, Westrem, Gilles, Biddick), genealogy (Stein, Chism, Clunies Ross), and temporality (Tomasch, Biddick); as crises of individual (Chism), urban (McNamara, Sigal), English (Gilles, Stein, Chism), and Christian identity (Tomasch, Biddick). However, perhaps the most salient point about geographical desire is that, as this multiplicity of versions illustrates, it can never be completely or finally gratified. In every case, the signifying fragment of desire "becomes an index of inaccessibility to totalization, or wholeness, the desire for which it repeatedly motivates" (Lowe, 98).[14]

But if "the very trajectory of desire [is] the push toward necessary failure" (Butler, "Desire," 374),[15] how then can "geography" ever be a satisfactory (if not a fully satisfied) "writing of the world"? It is my belief that only through the acknowledgment of inevitable failure will we be able to produce substantial textual/territorial inquiry. Modern scholarship—no less than the medieval texts it studies—has too often been motivated by the Jovian conjunction of discovery, dominion, and domination. By participating in such "empirical" constructions, however, medievalists may find themselves arriving at the same end as the geographers in Borges's story: loss of relevance, loss of value, and even perhaps loss of the discipline itself.

Like other cartographic productions, medievalists' mappings of the Middle Ages are necessarily fundamentally flawed. Judith Butler suggests that to desire is "to err, but to err necessarily and, perhaps, never fully with intention or guilt" ("Desire," 385). Perhaps, then, the best we can do is to create many, competing versions of the medieval world, for, as Borges cautions, no one map can encompass space-time "point for point." Faced with irreconcilable demands and expectations of politics and ideality, a totally successful "writing of the world" is simply not possible. Despite cartographers' best efforts, therefore, there will always be land unknown. Yet, at the same time, it is only through the mediation between text and territory that we can begin to take the measure of the earth. Recognizing the complexities and contradictions of geographical desire, the contributors to this volume do not pretend to fix textual territories, to create an empire of medievalism. Instead we attend (to borrow Borges's phrases once again), "not without Irreverence," to the "Fragments of the Map" that we call "the Middle Ages."

Notes

1. Such measureless claims are echoed in Alan of Lille's *Anticlaudianus*, in his hyperbolical characterization of Geometry's art as "the art which spreads abroad the knowledge of mensuration and teaches its use, confines the boundless, restrains the wide-spreading, reaches the small, measures the great, examines the deep, dwells in valleys, scales heights" (113).

2. Other discussions of desire include Butler, "Desire," whose focus is on the psychosexual construction of desire; Young, who emphasizes the collective social constitution of Western desire; and Deleuze and Guattari, who analyze desire within the operations of global capitalism. In medieval geographical studies, see Overing and Osborn, who do not, however, theorize the concept.

3. On the Hereford map, see Cross, *The World Map of Richard of Haldingham*, and "New Light on the Hereford Map"; also Bevan and Phillott. On medieval maps in general, see von den Brincken, *Fines Terrae*; and Woodward. On T-O maps in particular, see Tomasch.

4. On Walsperger's map, see Gallez; Kretschmer; Durand; von den Brincken, *Fines Terrae*.

5. On the Arabic tradition of world maps for the period corresponding to the European Middle Ages, see Tibbetts; and Ahmad.

6. Walsperger's contemporary, Fra Mauro, "rationalize[d] his placing of Jerusalem away from the center" of his 1459 map "by stating that he [was concerned to show] the center of population" (Woodward, 317 n. 147). Cartographic historians have speculated about the off-centeredness that characterizes both of these transitional, mid-fifteenth-century maps, as well as those by Pirrhus de Noha and Andreas Bianco. Suggestions include economics (i.e., it was more important to depict significant trade relations than accurate coastlines) and stemmatics (i.e., Andreas deliberately or inadvertently deviated from the cartographic model on which he based his map). I intend to discuss the ideological implications of such off-centeredness at greater length in my forthcoming book, *The Medieval Geographical Imagination*.

7. The relevant part of the legend reads: "The earth is indeed white, the seas of a green color, the rivers blue, the mountains variegated, likewise the red spots are cities of the Christians, the black ones in truth are the cities of the infidels on land and sea" (quoted from Woodward, 325); see also von den Brincken, "Die Ausbildung konventioneller Zeichen."

8. The tale in full, from ellipsis to fictional citation:

OF EXACTITUDE IN SCIENCE

... In that empire, the craft of Cartography attained such Perfection that the Map of a Single province covered the space of an entire City, and the Map of the Empire itself an entire Province. In the course of Time, these Extensive maps were found somehow wanting, and so the College of Cartographers evolved a Map of the Empire that was of the same Scale as the Empire and that coincided with it point for point. Less attentive to the Study of Cartography, succeeding Generations came to judge a map of such Magnitude cumbersome, and, not without Irreverence, they abandoned it to the Rigors of sun and Rain. In the western Deserts, tattered Fragments of the Map are still to be found, Sheltering an occasional Beast or beggar; in the whole Nation, no other relic is left of the Discipline of Geography.—from *Travels of Praiseworthy Men* (1658), by J. A. Suarez Miranda

I am grateful to Carlos Hortas for bringing this story to my attention.

9. Or, as Butler writes, "[f]ulfillment of desire would be its radical self-cancellation" ("Desire," 381).

10. On the textuality of geographical constructions and the geographicality of texts, see Higgonet; Smith and Katz; Duncan and Ley, "Introduction: Representing the Place of Culture"; and the essays in Barnes and Duncan.

11. For the purposes of my discussion, I have changed the order of Gregory's terms. Other important interrogations of the discipline of geography can be found in Keith and Pile; and Soja. For feminist critiques of geography, see Massey; Rose; and the essays in Blunt and Rose.

12. In *Travel as Metaphor*, Van Den Abbeele describes the *oikos* as "the transcendental point of reference that organizes and domesticates a given area by defining all other points in relation to itself" (xviii).

13. On the connections between gender, sexuality, and geography, see Massey; Rose; Blunt and Rose; Higonnet and Templeton; and Parker et al.

14. In *Critical Terrains*, Lowe's focus is on fragments of orientalism, but I believe the same case holds for geography as well.

15. Although Butler is speaking specifically of Plato's notions of desire in language, it is clear that the case can be made more generally.

I
CENTERS AND MARGINS

I

"Nel mezzo del cammin di nostra vita"

The Palpability of *Purgatorio*

MARY BAINE CAMPBELL

PURGATORIO, CANTO 33: DANTE AND Beatrice are standing by a spring in a fragrant, breezy garden at the summit of a mountain about three thousand miles high. Beautiful angels hover respectfully nearby. The lovers have not seen each other in ten years, and one of them is dead. They are talking, among other things, about topography.

    The erotic lure of geographical topics (especially, but not exclusively, in their narrative form, the travel tale) should come as no surprise to the well-read (or the well-traveled). When Odysseus returns to Penelope after twenty years, the gods delay sunrise so he can give her a geography lesson. The *Purgatorio* itself, like the Greek romances, is either a travel account or a love story, as an electron is either a particle or a wave, depending on what you are measuring. Dante's excruciating climb to the summit of this three thousand-mile-high mountain (*Purg.* 2.69) is motivated by a destination more erotic than geographical, but his account of it is punctuated, like most secular travel accounts of its era, with discourses on stars, on botany, on meteorology, on the cultural practices of the natives. It is possible to read the *Divine Comedy* as the only medieval account of travel that fully understands its genre and fully exploits the correspondences between travel, love, and narrative itself.

    Those correspondences are most salient in the poem's middle canticle, which I will be reading as in fact its center of gravity. It is in the middle of any narrative that we are closest to earth, to life as we know it—unfolding in time, distant from the shaping horizons of Chapter One and death, concerned with facts, sensations, places and our motions between them, possessed of memory and anticipation, ignorant of meaning, blind as yet to the Big Picture. In the middle of *To the Lighthouse*, Virginia Woolf places a short section called "Time Passes"—an act of formal genius in which the "baggy monster" of novelistic middles is replaced by a generic description of pure matter and the pure time that measures its infinitesimal decay—the world without gods, time without a climax. A suspension.

Dante isolates his middle too by the firmly formal division of the poem into three equal canticles. As I hope to show, he puts his weight there, in that segment of narrative which is the narrative territory of travel literature, in the middle book concerning the middle (and material) realm of the Other World, to which he traveled "in the middle of the journey of our life." Suspended there at high noon between heaven and hell with a veiled and untouchable Beatrice in the Earthly Paradise, Dante achieves the pinnacle of suspense. This suspension is in part a concrete adumbration of the *mente . . . sospesa* (*Par.* 33.97) of Dante in the Beatific Vision at the end of the *Paradiso*—which phrase follows immediately the image of Neptune gazing at the shadow of the world's first ship. Even to depict that moment of transfixing stillness and consummation, at the very end of his *Comedy*, Dante invokes the image of journey and the experience of suspension. For the earthly reader, love is desire and desire is characteristically experienced as suspense.

Grown-up readers of Dante love the *Purgatorio*, and most love it best of the canticles. This might seem to contradict an axiom of reading, that we are pulled through the matter of a narrative by an increasing and finally overwhelming desire for climax, where the "real" "pleasure of the text" must be found. If this is the case, then the last canto of the *Paradiso* should be the most satisfying moment in literary history, since its narrative object or end is imagined as a consummation absolute, transcendent, and eternal. There should be no *tristesse* after the Beatific Vision, for the Beatific Vision is infinite.

For some, no doubt, it *is* the most satisfying moment in literature. But in fact, for some, it is not. Taking issue with the emphasis of recent narrative theorists, from Walter Benjamin to Peter Brooks, on climax and closure as readerly goals, I would like to read the poem as responding more satisfactorily to our need for and identification with *medias res*, the material and open-ended space and time of "life as we know it" and as journey literature generically presents it.[1] I would like to imagine here for a while the pleasures of the middle and the importance of the palpable, in the material world at the heart of Dante's perfect narrative. This emphasis, on the corporeality of Dante's traveler and his landscape, and on its function as a medium for eros as well as punishment (even in the Afterlife, even in a dream)—this emphasis is clearest when we read the *Purgatorio* in the light of other contemporary journey literature. It is, for the moment then, a travel book we are reading, and a geography lesson that, as the *Odyssey* puts it, "holds the long night back at the outward edge" (23.243).

Dante's *Comedy* and the *Purgatorio* especially find a literary context among three closely related genres of their period: (1) the Other World narrative of which *St. Patrick's Purgatory* is the most famous exemplar (Morgan; Zaleski);[2] (2) the Holy Land *itineraria*, among which John Demaray has identified the ascents of Mount Sinai as a model for the ascent of Mount Purgatory;[3] and (3) the account of secular or at least nonpilgrimage travel to exotic lands beyond Palestine—all of which forms flourished in the thirteenth century (Campbell, *Witness*, chap. 3). We will attend to important differences between them, but it should be noted first that they are varieties of a single generic type, the *itinerarium* written from firsthand experience. As such their means and ends are similar and offer similar baffles to the writer: how to convey the radically alien in the tongue of the *patria*, how to render space and its objects in a narrative medium, and, most important for our purposes, how to do without or artificially manufacture a climax from essentially anticlimactic material. Travel's constitutive preposition is "between," and its destination is not a true analogue to the marriage or catastrophe that pulls down closure upon comic and tragic fictions. Even the most narratively prefigured of real world journeys, the Holy Land pilgrimage that "ends" in Jerusalem, offers the traveler a false climax. It is easy to wonder whether the traditional tears of the pilgrims as they enter the Holy City are not the tears of *tristesse*: "That is not it. / That is not it at all." The pilgrim arrives at a representation, an antique, an empty tomb. There is nothing to do but go home.[4]

The solutions to the problem of climax are not merely rhetorical because the problem is not merely rhetorical either. If travel were summed up in arrival we would go everywhere in airplanes and write shorter travel books. The characteristic solution of Other World journey narratives offers readers the sensational repetitiveness of pornography—the work unfolds a nonstop series of graphic, sensational tortures (heaven was rarely or briefly visited)—so the absence of trajectory is hidden in the numbing presence of a continuous excitement. The Holy Land guidebooks and *itineraria*, at the other extreme, busy themselves transcending the material landscape. As Demaray noticed years ago, writing at the American University in Beirut after making many pilgrimages himself over the traditional routes, Dante's intensely ritualized and liturgical stations on the way up the mountain mimic precisely the ritual punctuation of pilgrim travel. At every stop along the axis of the route through space, prayers and readings from Scripture mold the pilgrim's experience into a contact on the temporal axis with the sacred past, memorialized physically in chapels and shrines and administered by monks who as often as not grant indulgences like Dante's angels. Every one of these sacramental moments, you might say, constitutes a climax. The account gives little or no sense of "rising action" or trajectory, and the visit to Jerusalem itself can appear at almost any point in the narrative: in Adamnan's *De locis sanctis* it comes first.

To take a random example of place description in the *itineraria*, here is the Garden of Gethsemane from a fourteenth-century guidebook:

Then you come to the Garden of Gethsemane, under the foot of Mt. Olivet, in the Valley of Jehosephat, where our Lord is to judge the quick and the dead. And there is the place where the Lord Jesus was taken captive by the Jews, where Judas Iscariot kissed him, saying, "Hail, Master"; and there the Jews before him "went backwards and fell to the ground" at the voice of Christ, when he said "I am he," according to John [John 18.6]. And there is an indulgence for seven years and seven Lenten seasons. (*Guidebook to Palestine*, 17)[5]

Gethsemane, like any place in this extraordinary territory, is a place where something happened long ago. To visit it is to remember the old story, and the meaning of the visit is measured penitentially ("an indulgence for seven years"). What does Gethsemane look "like"? It looks like John 18.6. Sometimes this equation is stunningly overt—the fourth-century pilgrim Egeria tires quickly of describing the Tombs of Lust and tells her readers to look them up in "the holy books of Moses" (Egeria, 5.8). So Dante flags in describing the Beasts of the Apocalypse in his Earthly Paradise, sending us instead to a previous text in Scripture (Ezek. 10.4–14): "ma leggi Ezechiel . . . / e quali i trouverai ne le sue carte, tali eran quivi" [read Ezekiel . . . and as thou shalt find them on his pages such they were here] (*Purg.* 29.100, 103–4).[6]

To the experienced reader of *peregrinationes*, Dante's gesture here comes as a little joke—a joke that gets better when he advises us to consult John (Apoc. 4.6–8), rather than Ezekiel, on the *wings* of the Beasts. Did the wings *change* between Ezekiel and John's Apocalypse, or did Ezekiel get it wrong in the first place? At any rate, our new authority is to be the eyewitness travel writer, that is, Dante. The joke points many ways. Here in the midst of the most strenuous, not to say exhausting passage of *descriptio* in the whole canticle, the sudden moment of writerly sloth is charmingly unconvincing—sixteen more tercets of detailed description are still to come in this canto. Best of all, this direct echo of the pilgrim style is positioned in the midst of a description of a purely *allegorical* phenomenon. This is one way of marking Dante's rhetorical difference from the *peregrinatio* of this world. If it is real world topography that wearies the writer on Palestine's places, it is during the composition of allegorical detail that Dante abdicates. As the rhetorical aim of the

Holy Land *itinerarium* is the sublimation of Palestine, Dante's counterobjective is the somatizing of Purgatory, an incarnation that mimics the history of the concept itself, which developed from an adjective into a noun before finally becoming an article of Christian dogma in the century before Dante.[7]

The Dante of the *Purgatorio* is a magical realist. Not because the a priori imaginary realm needs to be made "believable" to the reading imagination, but because, as the site of a love story and a journey, it needs to be made palpable. The Other World of the Sinai pilgrimage or the Holy City is all too palpable, reachable, present—its holiness requires a distancing, which is provided by a shifting of temporal register into the time of scriptural history or ritual and sacrament. Jerome's protégée Paula looks at the manger, at Calvary, at the Jordan, and she "remembers" (Jerome [Paula], 12). Egeria arrives at Sinai and requires prayers and readings; she arrives at last at Jerusalem to describe not places but liturgies and offices. Dante structures his pilgrim's journey up the mountain in the same way, as a series of stations marked by prayers, hymns, and absolutions, but his pilgrim has, emphatically, a body, and so does his mountain. And so, in her way, does Beatrice, his destination—a "shadowy body" [corpo fittizio] (26.12) explained to us in rigorous detail as the pilgrim climbs to the final cornice of Lust.

Of course the emphasis on the body and kinds of body is a feature of the *Comedy* generally, as is a continuous attention to topography and cosmography; this suffusion of experienced corporeality distinguishes the *Comedy* from the *peregrinationes*, at least as far as Dante's time, and even from Other World narratives (where tortures are visited only upon anonymous souls who do not speak to us—they are edifying spectacles, not suffering persons). But the emphasis is clearest and most significant in the *Purgatorio*, where space and time are constitutive. Purgatory is not eternal, and the body is in a special sense the medium of its definitive function.[8] (This is of course a very vexed issue— to see how vexed, look at Aquinas trying to figure it out in the supplement to part 3 of the *Summa theologica* [qu. 70, art. 3]. Aquinas is emphatic: "the fire . . . is not called so metaphorically, nor an imaginary fire, but a real corporeal fire." We'll return later to his explanation of how such a fire can harm a noncorporeal entity like a soul—he says the fire confines or "defines" (*definiat*) the soul, "*detains*" it in fact (*detineat*), as the flesh had in life, and that the apprehension of detainment is for a naturally mobile entity like a soul a kind of harm.[9]) These data are articles of faith. But the Church has decided few of the details. Dante must invent them—and his limiting conditions are literary as well as theological.

The secular travel account provides another model for Dante here, in its comprehensiveness, its encyclopedic capacity for digression, its interlace of natural history and narrative motion, its dependence on a readerly interest in the structure and contents of space. Dante would be dead thirty years by the time *Mandeville's Travels* combined again the models of sacred and secular travel to describe an entire World, and Mandeville's World is the earth. But the two works point to each other across the decades by means of a shared feature, the territorial and ontological limit of both their Worlds, a towering mountain crowned by an Earthly Paradise ringed round with flames. Great lords who, like Dante's Ulysses, have tried to approach the island of the Earthly Paradise "weren perisscht and loste withinne the wawes, so that no mortell man may approche to that place withouten specyall grace of god. And therefore"—no Aeneas, Mandeville, no Paul—"I schall holde me stille And retournen to that that I haue seen" (Hamelius, 34.204). If the *Travels* could be said to have a climax, it lies in this failure to visit the Earthly Paradise, in the impossibility of our ultimate earthly destination—the first, best home of the human race. You can't get there from here. That is the real world meaning of the Earthly Paradise, and as such has generated the forbidding topography of its surround.

But that can't be the meaning of the Earthly Paradise on Dante's journey, since he does get there. It is the meaning he counterpoints by a structural emphasis on the presence and palpability of his body, a body that not only casts shadows and falls asleep but also senses its surroundings with a vividness strangely out of sync with their at least partly "shadowy" nature.

This vivid surround and palpable body would have been shockingly emphatic to a medieval reader, even a reader of secular travelogues, that most mundane and unmoralized of medieval genres. I know of only one medieval traveler who regularly mentions his body, the thirteenth-century missionary William of Rubruck, whom Dante is unlikely to have read. (William goes so far as to mention frostbite in "the tips of our toes," but such minutiae is rare.) Canto 1 of the *Purgatorio* mentions Dante's eyes three times, his face twice, his breast, legs, brow, and cheeks; and the eyes are mentioned not only as vehicles of sight but as organs that can feel pain and get dirty. The preoccupation is really with the tactile. He needs to clear his lungs, wash his face; his eyes too have been "afflicted" by the "dead air" of Hell [l'aura morta / che m'avea contristati li occhi e 'l petto] (1.17–18).

The visual and aural as vehicles of iconographic, liturgical, and literary messages will of course be primary here, as elsewhere in the *Comedy*, but the tactile stands out as unusually present, and the tactile is the body's most pointed metonymy. When Dante walks through the barrier of flame on the cornice of lust and says "in un bogliente vetro / gittato mi sarei per rinfrescarmi, / tant' era lui lo 'ncendio sanza metro" [I would have flung myself into molten glass to cool me, so without measure was the burning there] (27.49–51), our first impulse is not to interpret but to scream. It is a measure of the importance of Dante's material body that those who have been standing in these flames for centuries observe the shadow he casts upon them, and one is distracted enough to ask about it. (Wonderfully, the poet's last experience in Purgatory is "the sweet drink" of Eunoe [lo dolce ber] and a refreshing dip in its "santissima onda" [33.138, 142].)

The landscape is not only minutely sensed, but minutely moved in: "I turned to the right" [I' mi volsi a man destra] (1.22), "[I withdrew] my gaze, turning a little to the other pole" [Com'io da loro sguardo fui partito, / un poco me volgendo a l'altro polo] (1.28–29). Dante kneels, rises, draws close to Virgil, turns his eyes upon him, makes his "way across the solitary plain" [Noi andavam per lo solingo piano] (1.118) to some dewy grass, reaches his face toward Virgil, comes to "the desert shore" [lito diserto] (1.130) where Virgil picks a rush.

It is dawn: Venus is up in the sign of Pisces along with what may or may not be the Southern Cross, and the Big Dipper has gone down. Dante and Virgil are on an island with a mountain at its center surrounded by a soft, muddy shore, where rushes grow and a slight breeze preserves the dew from the sun, which rises opposite the side of the mountain behind the pilgrims.

This is not simply the obligatory scene-setting of a narrative opening. Mounting to Ante-Purgatory in Canto 4 we find just as much attention to body and landscape. Even Dante's temporary abstraction from his body, as he listens to Manfred speak (about *his* body), is measured spatially: "Che ben cinquanta gradi salito era / io sole, e io non m'era accorto" [full fifty degrees the sun had climbed and I had not perceived it] (4.16). Dante's and Virgil's movement up the cleft rock occupies the first fifty-odd lines of the canto and is followed by a geography lesson of another fifty. Their meeting with Belacqua is full of references to Dante's material body and to the position and posture of Belacqua's shadowy one, and the canto ends with another brief spurt of cosmography: "vedi ch'e tocco / meridian dal sole, e a la riva / cuopre la notte gia col pie Morrocco" [see, the meridian is touched by the sun, and on the shore night now sets its foot on Morocco] (4.137–39). Even night has a body and is traveling in a landscape, setting foot on Morocco as earlier today Dante set foot on the shore of Purgatory.

The ultimately distinctive feature of a material being, here in this realm where so many kinds of immaterial body and sensation are possible, is falling asleep. (The souls in Purgatory do not sleep.) Dante's three eventful bouts of sleeping also distinguish Purgatory from Heaven and Hell—where he does not sleep, since he is in places where there is no alternation between day and night, light and dark. Sleep is, among other things, the body's response to the diurnal motion of the sun, and Dante's sleep confirms the continuity of Purgatory with our diurnal world, just as his reaction to purgatorial sunset and sunrise confirm his capacity for bodily sensation and response.[10]

The middle night falls in the middle canto, after Dante has a vision that ends "as sleep is broken" [come si frange il sonno] (17.40). The two pilgrims are climbing to the middle cornice of Purgatory, the Cornice of Sloth, where Dante falls asleep for real and dreams of the "sweet Siren" [dolce serena] who had distracted Ulysses before him, in the middle of *his* journey to the right woman [Io son . . . dolce serena/ che' marinari in mezzo mar dismago] (19.19). We are in the middle of middles here, and the dream is a dream of the body. I am not interested in the allegorical meaning of the dream: it is important to the consideration of the "mezzo" because it is *nel mezzo* of the journey of the poem, and because it is *about* the *mezzo*, the medium, of that middle.[11] The body of the Siren, Dante's landscape for the moment, is as continuous with, as interdependent with, Dante's gaze as is Dante's sleep with the sun, or Dante's body with the topography of Purgatory. As he gazes at the maimed body of the witch,

> . . . come 'l sol conforta
> le fredde membra che la notte aggrava,
> cosi lo sguardo mio le facea scorta
> la lingua, e poscia tutta la drizzava
> in poco d'ora, e lo smarrito volto,
> com' amor vuol, cosi le colorava
> (19.10–15)

[even as the sun revives cold limbs benumbed
by night, so my look made ready her tongue
and then in but little time set her full
straight, and colored her pallid face even as
love requires]

To break the spell, a dream-Virgil must show him her womb ("l' ventre" [the middle of her body]), and it is the stench of that womb that wakes the dreamer for another morning's climb. Dante's senses here create this body: the sight and smell of *her* body is evidence of his.

Awfully vertiginous: for this central dream on the middle of the mountain in the middle of the middle canticle of the poem is after all the dead center of a larger and longer dream that began in another dawn, a few days back on Good Friday. We are deep asleep here, in an allegorical dream inside an allegorical dream inside an allegorical poem. The emphatic image at the center of it all is an image of the flesh. But it is also, and equally emphatically, an image, and a symbolic image at that. It must mean something other than itself. Sleep may be the sign of bodily reality, but what appears to us in sleep is definitively, ipso facto, nonbodily, even in a poem which claims some kind of body for ghosts and rainbows. This flesh is not the thing itself, but ideas about the thing—and as such, the most immaterial object in the poem.

Ideas about the flesh and in particular the womb reappear, of course, in Statius' famous lecture on embryology in Canto 25, where the pilgrims are climbing up to the Cornice of Lust and Dante's encounter with purgatorial flame. Dante has wanted to know (perhaps because he is hungry—he sleeps but he never eats!) how supposedly incorporeal souls can become "lean," and this question, asked in the proximity of the very corporeal sin of Lust, opens a Pandora's box of medieval doctrine on the soul's experience of the Other World. By this time the reader is perhaps comfortable with, enculturated in, the extreme physicality of Dante's vision, but we are so close to Beatrice and the leap to Paradise that interrogation of the paradox can no longer be avoided—the decorum is about to change.

The short answer to Dante's question—that souls are figurative, literally *fittizio*, their forms express "desires and other affections"—is consistent with the (inverse) function of the Siren's dream-body, which expresses not her own but Dante's "desires and other affections," first lust, then revulsion. The "shadowy bodies" of the souls in the afterlife are then just exactly what they are in Dante's poem: figures of speech, metaphors.

But this short answer arrives as the payload of Statius' long and medically quite respectable speech about embryology: what is *that* doing here? It adds a philosophical density to the otherwise slightly airy analogy of the rainbow, and thus helps to connect the earthly and eternal careers of the self who experiences both embodied and disembodied existence. Aha, I see: the spiritual genotype, as we might call it, that organized my physical body out of fetal matter can also organize a fictitious one out of air, as light does in a rainbow. In fact, a serious seventeenth-century text on optics by the Bohemian Marcus Marci of Kronland also makes the connection between optics and embryology, likening the formative virtue in the fetus to a ray of light passing through the center of a prism and breaking into not the spectrum of visible light but the various limbs and organs of the developing embryo (Needham, 80–81).

But of course, however plausible in its way, the explanation is itself *fittizio*, for there is nothing to explain, outside of Dante's fictional world—as far as we know, the separated souls don't *have* "shadowy bodies," and it is perhaps even doubtful that there is any "air" to make them out of in the Great By and By. What we do know is that the *fire* is, as Aquinas says, "a real, corporeal fire"—and as such it should burn the pilgrim Dante's body, emphasized as corporeal once again by its noticeable shadow as he nears the edge of the flame ("e io facea con l'ombra più rovente / paper la fiamma" [26.7–8]).

Curiously, the fire stimulates the dreamer into intense tactile hallucination, but, as Virgil promises, it doesn't make him "bald of a single hair" [non ti potrebbe far d'un capel calvo] (27.27). In his promise Virgil refers to the fire's womb, its *alvo*, where he says Dante could safely "stay a thousand years." This fire is the final womb of the *Purgatorio*, reminding us of Aquinas's explanation of how damage is done to a soul by so unlike a thing as a "corporeal fire"; the fire *becomes* the body of that otherwise immaterial and undetainable spirit, entrapping it in a *place*: "The fire of its nature is able to have an incorporeal spirit united to it as a thing placed is united to a place . . . as the instrument of Divine justice it is enabled to detain it enchained as it were, and in this respect the fire is really hurtful to the spirit, and thus the soul seeing the fire as something hurtful to it is tormented by the fire" (3 [suppl.], qu. 70 art. 3).

Which brings us back around to the issue of narratives and middles, the issue so central to the discourse of places. Placing the Siren and her stinking womb amid the spectrum of enclosing wombs in this poem, we can see her as the *malum* image of arrest (the kidnapper). Whatever she may mean, the Siren *functions* here as she does in the *Odyssey*—as the threat of narrative entropy. The chief taboo in the *Odyssey* is inertia, represented by sleep, forgetfulness, satiation—a satiation always followed by *tristesse* (seven years of it in one case). It is a taboo so strong it permeates even the poem's licit destination, the bedding of Odysseus and Penelope. When they go to bed at last, they do not sleep. They stay up all night, talking about travel, and Odysseus even tells his wife about the next journey he must make. We understand: the bones piled up on the island of the Sirens have already told us that desire satisfied is the end of everything, and indeed, the satisfaction of Odysseus' desire on Ithaca has taken its first form in a massacre.

Dante is committed by religion to an intense rejection of such psychological realism. But he is "curbed by art" in more than one way: he is writing a travelogue, and the travelogue is the genre of deferral, of the middle, of an experience constitutively and doubly bodily—the body's motion in a material world—and of the triumph of fact over meaning, motion over destination. The final tantrums of Homer's hero record a terror of the final, of *finis*. It is the terror of the genre itself. Many medieval travel narratives end by requesting the reader to pray for the writer's soul—as does that other great medieval travel poem, the *Canterbury Tales*.

All ends are "the end," of course, but traditionally and normatively narrative uses them as consummations. Peter Brooks speaks of the "passion for meaning . . . the active quest of the reader for those shaping ends that . . . promise to bestow meaning and significance on the beginning and the middle" (19). In the travel book, the middle is what matters, and the tension between middle and end dramatizes the primacy of the middle—one rushes backward toward it from the end as one does, no doubt, in real death. Alluding to a great line from Walter Benjamin's "The Storyteller," "Death is the sanction of everything that the storyteller can tell" (94), Brooks claims that we require from the storyteller "that knowledge of death which is denied to us in our own lives" (19)—that is, closure. But that is just what the Siren offers—"For we know everything that the Argives and Trojans did and suffered in wide Troy," they sing to Odysseus (*Odyssey*, 12.189–90). "I am the sweet Siren who leads mariners astray *in the middle* of the sea," sings Dante's Siren [io son dolce serena, / che' marinari in mezzo mar dismago] (19.19–20).

One might say that the placement of this hideous, deathly, *immaterial* image of the flesh in the middle of Dante's *mezzo* belies the primacy of the middle for him, if the middle is life, the body, motion, space—all that characterizes natural experience in the material world, suspended between heaven and hell, birth and death. But in fact the Siren is an image of the *end*, too. "Qual meco s'ausa / rado sen parte; si tutto l'appago" [whoever abides with me rarely departs, so wholly do I satisfy him] (19.23–24). She appears as a phantom of erotic, geographical, and narrative satisfactions—as a potential lover, but the wrong one, an abortive end to the journey, a singer who knows how the story comes out.[12] The Siren is the Storyteller who tells you your whole life when you're only in the middle of it, offering that "knowledge of death"—that closure—that means it's over. The Siren is premature—as any know-it-all storyteller would be in the middle of things. She appears on the Cornice of Sloth because death is the greatest image of Sloth, the "end" of narrative entropy. Death is not what Dante is looking for in the afterlife: "That is not it. / That is not it at all." Like any traveler, he is desperately fleeing it (does Dante the poet know he is writing close to the end of his own life?). Like anyone fleeing anything, he runs right into what he is fleeing—after all, "in the *midst* of life there is death." But it was only a dream, he made it up. It can't happen here, not *nel mezzo del cammin di nostra vita*, or what's a middle for?

Coda

I first read the *Purgatorio* in an undergraduate course taught by John Gardner. When someone complained in class that the *Purgatorio* was boring, Gardner smiled distantly and said "Ah, you don't like long, boring books. I do." Middles *are* boring—they have none of that morbid pizzazz of closure that gives the end its jolt. But as a twentieth-century siren said in one of his *Dream Songs* (#14), "Life, friends, is boring." And in fact Benjamin liked it that way, though he thought we were losing our talent for it (and died, like Dante, Gardner, and John Berryman, more toward the middle of the journey). "If sleep is the apogee of physical relaxation, boredom is the apogee of mental relaxation. Boredom is the dream bird that hatches the egg of experience. His nesting places . . . are already extinct in the city and are declining in the country as well. With this the gift for listening is lost and the community of listeners disappears" (91).

I quote Benjamin's wonderful passage on good boredom not simply to defend my appreciation of a "long, boring book" but also to connect the theme of the Storyteller's anonymous, fecund boredom to my interests—and Dante's—in popular literature and the corporeality of folk theology. Whatever high-philosophical subsuming Dante had in mind for his middle canticle, its matter and structure both owe allegiance to the folkloric imagination that first inserted the middle term of purgatory into the stark dichotomy of the Fathers' eschatology and that supported, against growing ecclesiastical disfavor, the concrete piety of pilgrimage.[13] Purgatory is a place in what Jacques Le Goff calls "this world"—Ireland or Sicily or Iceland; its fires are corporeal and inflicted on the "not very good" and "not very bad"—the ethically ambivalent, the characteristic population of folk narrative. The *Purgatorio*'s structural model in pilgrimage is the concrete, "real world" mimesis of the spiritual journey toward God; this ambitious eschatological poem is composed in the vernacular language of farming, commerce, travel books, and love songs. These identifications of the poem with the realm of the Storyteller—the material, the literal, the ambivalent, the *heimlich* and the *un*—seem to me either insufficiently felt by much of Dante's professional readership or at any rate not articulated as a point of view. And yet much of the spell cast over us by this *Comedy* is rooted in the poem's deep materiality. Nowhere is it closer to home than in the *Purgatorio*, from which one might see the rest of the *Divine Comedy* radiating like spectral rays from the glass body of the prism, or limbs and organs from the heart of the analogous fetus, whose growth we hear so much about as we climb to the Cornice of Lust.

From the folkish point of view, where the corporeality of purgatorial fire bothers no one but Aquinas and his crowd, the *Purgatorio* is easily a love story, because Dante is a man and Beatrice is a woman and Dante seeks the woman out in marvelous and dangerous territories, exerting himself boldly for love. Thousands of oral and vernacular stories hang on this plot, so oddly parallel with the plot of pilgrimage. Dante of course "transcends" the earthly eros of his plot and his setting by moving onward and upward from his encounter in the Earthly Paradise into a barely sensible Paradise of light.[14] Feminist readings of his poem might part company with him here, as Costanza does in the beginning of *Paradiso*, who "singing, vanished, *like a weight* through deep water" (3.122–23).

Notes

I would like to thank several people for their helpful responses to an earlier version of this essay: Laurence Breiner, Peter Hawkins (who invited me to write it in the first place), Iain Higgins, Rachel Jacoff, Richard Lansing, Judith Tabron (my research assistant), Diana Bishop, and the Medieval Seminar at Harvard University's Center for Literary and Cultural Studies, which Jan Ziolkowski kindly put at my disposal for a fruitful afternoon in the fall of 1991.

1. On closure, see Benjamin; Herrnstein Smith; Kermode; and Winnett. A politically inflected examination of "ends" is missing from this list. Why?

2. The classic study of the setting in literature and folklore remains Patch; Gardiner has recently edited a collection of translations.

3. See also Kaske. According to Davis, the studium at S. Maria Novella, one of three schools Dante is likely to have attended in or near Florence, included a principal lector in theology named Riccoldus of Montecroce, "who went on a missionary journey to the Orient and wrote a fascinating book about his travels" (347). We can't know exactly what travel literature Dante read, but it seems clear that he had access to some of it and perhaps studied with a travel writer.

4. See Sumption, 95–97, for a discussion of the early medieval Irish holy men who wandered without destination, dramatizing their distaste not only for the materialism and literalism of pilgrimage, but even for the concept of "home."

5. The Latin original of this work is not available to me; the sole manuscript is MS D.4.7 in the library of Trinity College, Dublin. According to the Palestine Pilgrim's Text Society translator, Bernard, it is "based, in the main, on the account of the Holy Land given by Philippus Brusserius Savonensis" (circa 1290). See Bernard's "Introductory Note" to the translation for locations of materials out of which this "guidebook" was compiled (v).

6. All quotations and translations are cited from Singleton's edition; my modifications are noted or marked with brackets. The emphases, "in the middle" and "like a weight," are mine.

7. See Le Goff for passage of the concept from adjectival to nominal status. He also discusses a sermon of Innocent III, dividing the afterlife into three realms, including a purgatorial one, though he doesn't use the word "purgatorium" (see appendix 2, "Purgatorium: The History of a Word").

8. This at least is what I extrapolate from Le Goff's discussion of several writers on purgatorial fire of the twelfth and early thirteenth centuries; see esp. chap. 4.

9. In the response to obj. 1, explaining a quotation from Augustine, Aquinas says: "the fire as apprehended is the proximate cause of [the soul's] distress, whereas

the corporeal fire which exists outside the soul is the remote cause" [ignis ergo apprehensis est proximum affligens, sed ignis corporeus extra animam existens est affligens remotum] (3 [suppl.], qu. 70 art. 3).

10. For *purgatorium* in real world places see Le Goff, chap. 6, "Purgatory between Sicily and Ireland."

11. In his note to *Purg.* 1.14–15, "nel sereno aspetto / del mezza," Singleton says: "Some commentators take 'mezzo' to mean 'center' or 'zenith.' More probably it means the 'air,' or 'atmosphere,' which is said to be serene and pure." He quotes Dante's use of the word with this meaning of "medium" from the *Convito*: "Pero puote parere cosi per lo mezzo che continuamente si transmuta. Transmutasi questo mezzo di molta luce in poca luce, si come a la presenza del sole e a la sua assenza" (3.9.12). Note "sereno" in the line from Canto I: Dante's peculiar spelling of his word for Siren, "serena," may function as a multiple pun. The words "sereno" and "mezzo" appear together a third time at the end of the poem: "luna per sereno / di mezza notte nel suo mezzo mese" (29.53–54). "Mezza" is used in something like this sense in relation to another episode of bodily transformation in a female figure: "O folle Aragne, si vedea io te / gia mezza ragna" (12.43–44).

12. The reader will think of Dido here, and her prophetic prayer that Aeneas die "ante diem mediaque" (*Aeneid* 4.620).

13. For ecclesiastical dislike of pilgrimage, see Sumption; for folk resistances to dichotomy and idealism, see Gurevich; and, of course, Bakhtin.

14. For another account of the sensational and particular in the *Purgatorio*, see Bleeth, who focuses on "the dramatic function of [the] blend of symbolic and realistic description in the Earthly Paradise cantos" (32). In this reading, the transfer from naturalistic description to allegorical pageantry in those cantos "anticipates a life beyond nature" (47) and thus mimics formally the spiritual trajectory of the poem's protagonist.

2

Defining the Earth's Center in a Medieval "Multi-Text"

Jerusalem in *The Book of John Mandeville*

IAIN MACLEOD HIGGINS

> ... that famous Traveller Sir John Mandevile, whose Geographie Ortelius commendeth, howsoever he acknowledgeth his Worke stuffed with Fables.
> —Samuel Purchas, *Purchas His Pilgrimes* (1625)

The "Foremost Peculiarity" of Medieval Geography

A little more than a hundred years ago, in 1867, a young American journalist and aspiring writer calling himself Mark Twain sailed from New York on an "Excursion to the Holy Land, Egypt, the Crimea, Greece, and Intermediate Points of Interest." During this updated and upscale version of the medieval mass pilgrimage, Twain sent back to several U.S. newspapers a series of letters describing his journey. These Quaker City Letters, as they were called (after the cruise ship), proved to be popular enough that he soon republished them in book form as *The Innocents Abroad, or the New Pilgrims' Progress* (1869). Like any good reporter, innocent or not, Twain followed his fellow travelers wherever they went, including Jerusalem, whose sites he described in almost as much detail as one finds in typical medieval pilgrims' guides.

At the center of his account of the sacred city stands a description of the Church of the Holy Sepulchre, the Christian shrine to which "one naturally goes first" (293). Surveying the memorial sites located within this famous church, Twain paid particular attention to the Greek chapel, "the most roomy, the richest, and the showiest" of any. Yet it was not its appearance as such that he chose to single out for notice. Rather, it was the presence there of a physical sign recalling a long-lived belief characteristic of what may be called imaginative—or more specifically, theological—geography: that is, a way of thinking about the earth whose unfamiliar distinctiveness Twain attempted to capture with a pair of anecdotes that ultimately derive from topographical proofs discussed by several medieval writers.

> The feature of the place is a short column that rises from the middle of the marble pavement of the chapel, and marks the exact *centre of the earth*. The most reliable tradition tells us that this was known to be the earth's centre ages ago, and that when Christ was upon earth he set all doubts upon the subject at rest for ever, by stating with his own lips that the tradition was correct. . . .
> To satisfy himself that this spot was really the centre of the earth, a sceptic once paid well for the privilege of ascending to the dome of the church to see if the sun gave him a shadow at noon. He came down perfectly convinced. The day was very cloudy and the sun threw no shadows at all; but the man was satisfied that if the sun had come out and made shadows it could not have made any for him. Proofs like these are not to be set aside by the idle tongues of cavillers. To such as are not bigoted, and are willing to be convinced, they carry a conviction that nothing can ever shake. (295–96, original emphasis)

Twain is of course writing here as a satirist of popular belief, and not as an anthropologist or historian attempting to understand alien or archaic modes of thought. For that we have to turn to a couple of his English contemporaries, the Reverend W. L. Bevan and the Reverend H. W. Phillott, who in 1873 published a booklet entitled *Mediaeval Geography: An Essay in Illustration of the Hereford Mappa Mundi*. Like Twain, they drew explicit attention to "the opinion that Jerusalem occupied the central point of the habitable world," remarking that such a view had to be placed "foremost among the peculiarities of mediaeval geography" (xiii). Unlike the American satirist, though, the two English churchmen attempted to render this curious element of Christian topography less rather than more peculiar by pointing out that a similar conception of a sacred or mythical center could be found in many cultures, and they thus arrived at a simple conclusion: "It was not unnatural that the Jews, and still more the Christians, should attribute the same property to Jerusalem, which for centuries had been the focus of their aspirations, their anxieties, and their most devoted exertions" (xiii).

Yet different as these apologetic observations are in tone and attitude from Twain's comments, the two sets of remarks reveal their authors to be making a similar assumption about the belief they are referring to. Specifically, the three writers assume that, throughout the millennium of the Middle Ages, Christian pilgrims and geographers must always have given credence and significance to the idea of a literally central Jerusalem. Satirist and scholar alike presuppose that belief in this traditional idea was never subject to variation—or even to being ignored altogether—as a consequence of any number of contextual factors (such as the historical moment and the particular aims of the text in which mention of it is or is not made). In short, these authors assume that the medieval conception of Jerusalem's earthly location lacks a history of its own.

So far as I know, that history remains to be written. Although it is not my aim to attempt its writing here, I intend to contribute toward its reconstruction by examining what is in my view the single most interesting and elaborate—as well as the most widely circulated—medieval account of Jerusalem as the earthly center, and to do so in the context of other references to the belief made in related writings from the fourth century through to the fifteenth. I proceed therefore by briefly tracing those other references, which, despite the comments of Twain and Bevan and Phillott, I show to be both unexpectedly few and surprisingly brief, even insignificant, in most instances. I then turn to discuss the account in question in order not only to show the different kinds of evidence that its author brings to bear on the subject of Jerusalem's place in the world, but also to suggest why he takes the idea far more seriously than do most medieval writers working in the same basic genres. Those genres are the guides and memoirs produced either by or for Latin Christian pilgrims, and the particular account I have in mind occurs in *The Book of John Mandeville*, a virtually unique fusion of the pilgrims' report with a description of the Eastern world beyond the Holy Land. As an eminent historian of medieval geography long ago observed, this work "has unquestionable value as illustrating the fourteenth-century layman's idea of the world" (Kimble, 95)[1]—rather than just that of the Near East, especially since its "layman's idea" largely coincides with both the learned geographer's and the pious theologian's. Indeed, as I suggest in closing, *The Book of John Mandeville*, more than any other medieval travel book, can be thought of as a verbal analogue to those encyclopedic medieval world maps that represent the earth not merely geographically as a physical arrangement of lands and waters but theologically as the site of salvation history.

Moreover, as I show in the following introductory section, *The Book* likewise has unquestionable value as a work illustrating the remarkably dynamic transmission of texts in the medieval world and therefore the problem of reading any verbal construct characterized by what Paul Zumthor has called "mouvance," or continuous recreation in transmission (*Essai de poétique*, 507; also 43–46, 126).[2] Accordingly, it is also part of the task of the present essay to explore an especially striking instance of what I would call medieval "multitextuality."

The Book of John Mandeville as a Medieval "Multi-Text"

Exactly when, where, or under whose shaping hand *The Book of John Mandeville* was first sent into the world is uncertain.[3] All that is known for sure is that the work was originally set down in French a decade or so before 1371, possibly on the Continent, by someone calling himself John Mandeville, knight, of St. Albans, England. Purporting to be the memoirs of a traveler whose journeys *outre mer* out-Poloed Polo's, as it were, *The Book* is in fact an innovative compilation of others' writings, including several produced by genuine far travelers. Praised by some scholars as "a book of wonder and high romance" (J. W. Bennett, 16) and dismissed by others as a "mendacious romance" (Hodgen, 103), the actual composite text is much more, and more interesting, than either term would suggest.[4] In my view, *The Book* represents a new kind of travel account that attempts to entertain, divert, teach, chastise, challenge, and console its late-fourteenth-century audience by providing them with an even more comprehensive and "theologically correct" vernacular account of the East than Marco Polo had done just half a century earlier (Polo's *Description of the World*, which was also originally set down in French, is conspicuously absent from the list of *The Book*'s known sources). By way of providing this description, the *Mandeville*-author's compilation extends the territorial reach of Polo's select ethnogeography and natural history to cover northern Africa and Asia from Constantinople to the Earthly Paradise, and it combines this extended work with a guide for genuine and vicarious pilgrims to Jerusalem and the Holy Land.

Such a book could hardly have failed to be popular with medieval audiences, and it was not long before it had been translated, either directly or indirectly, into nine other languages: Czech, Danish, Dutch, English, German, Irish, Italian, Latin, and Spanish. All told, close to three hundred manuscripts have survived, the bulk of them in French, English, German, and Latin. With the advent of printing, *The Book* received a new lease on life, being issued in eight of its ten languages between about 1480 and 1515 (only the Danish and Irish Versions remained unprinted), and since the early sixteenth century it has lived on in three or four languages, above all in English and German. More than most medieval books, *The Book of John Mandeville* has been persistently successful, surviving the dismantling not only of its conceptual and geographical worlds in the sixteenth century, but also of its textual and authorial integrity in the nineteenth.

As a consequence of its remarkable medieval success, *The Book* can be regarded not as a single, invariant work, but as a multinodal network, a kind of rhizome, whose French "radical" gave rise to a discontinuous series of related offshoots in several languages, each of which can vary quite considerably from the others while being *The Book* itself to certain readers. In transmitting this popular work, in other words, the *Mandeville*-author's medieval intermediaries handled their particular source text(s) with that remarkable combination of freedom and fidelity typical of medieval translation. In most cases, the resulting version proves to be freely faithful, distinguished by its somewhat shorter length and various small interpolations and rearrangements that confirm, qualify, or supplement individual details, anecdotes, and the like, but in several notable cases the ensuing redaction is rather less faithful and more free, distinguished by major omissions, additions, and/or rearrangements. Taken together, *The Book*'s textual isotopes, or (to use still a third metaphor) its topological transformations, present us with two major and some half-dozen minor variations on the postulated French original. Clearly, *The Book* is more than several books at once, both in its origins and generically; it is textually multiple as well, characterized by its typically medieval intertextuality, and by what might be called its *intra*textual multiplicity, or its "multi-textuality."

Since there is no space here to sketch even the outlines of *The Book*'s complicated early textual history,[5] I confine myself simply to noticing the relationship between the two versions to which, because of their radically different positions on Jerusalem's centrality, I chiefly refer in the subsequent discussion, showing how one attempts to support and the other to refute the belief. These are the so-called Vulgate Latin and Continental (French) Versions. The latter version, along with another closely related French text known as the Insular Version, may to all intents and purposes be considered to represent the *Mandeville*-author's original compilation. Between them, the two French versions account for some fifty—that is, about one-sixth—of all the extant manuscripts. The other principal text mentioned here, the Vulgate Latin Version, represents a significant condensation and free reworking of a third French text, the Interpolated Continental or Liège Version, itself a curious redaction distinguished by a number of striking changes, including a series of interpolations about the exploits of the Carolingian hero Ogier the Dane—a figure who made his first literary appearance in the *Chanson de Roland*. Unlike its idiosyncratic French source, which survives in only seven manuscripts, the Vulgate Latin Version circulated widely and has survived in some forty-one manuscripts. On the strength no doubt of its learned language, it was to this reworked Latin text that many late medieval and Renaissance geographers turned when they consulted the "English Knight's memoirs," and it was this version that Richard Hakluyt, for example, chose to print in the first edition of his *Principall Navigations* (1589).

Jerusalem as the Center of the Earth from St. Jerome to Felix Fabri

Like the origins of most such ideas, those of the medieval belief in Jerusalem's geographical centrality are obscure, but that the idea existed should come as no revelation, given that many cultures have viewed their most sacred place as an earthly *omphalos* (Eliade, chap. 1). Likewise unremarkable is the fact that this belief was found to be supported by scriptural authority, whether or not Scripture itself originally helped give rise to it, since the sacred page could be advanced in favor of all sorts of beliefs. Of the biblical texts cited in support of the idea, the most important were Psalm 73(74).12 and Ezekiel 5.5, and these were explicitly connected in an important gloss offered by Jerome in his early-fifth-century *Commentary on Ezekiel*:

Ps. 73(74).11–12. Deus autem rex noster ante saecula, / Operatus est *salutem in medio terrae* [For God our king before the ages worked *salvation in the middle of the earth*].
Ezek. 5.5. Haec dicit Dominus Deus: Ista est Hierusalem; *in medio gentium* posui eam et in circuitu eius terras [Thus says the Lord God: This is Jerusalem: I have set it *in the midst of peoples* and the lands round about it].
Jerome. *Jerusalem is situated in the middle of the world* [Jerusalem in medio mundi sitam]. This is affirmed by the Prophet, showing it to be the navel of the earth [umbilicum terrae], and by the psalmist expressing the birth of the lord: "Truth," he says, "rose from the earth"; and next the passion: "[God] worked," he says, "*salvation in the middle of the earth* [salutem in medio terrae]." From the eastern parts of course it is surrounded by the area that is named Asia; from the western parts, by that which is called Europe; from the south, Libya and Africa; from the north Scythia, Armenia and also Persides and by all the nations of the Black Sea. *It is therefore situated in the midst of the peoples* [In medio igitur gentium posita est]. (PL 25. cols. 52b)[6]

As one might expect, given Jerome's central place among the church fathers, this gloss was echoed by later writers. One of the most influential was Isidore of Seville, whose early-seventh-century encyclopedia, the *Etymologiae*, remained in use until the fourteenth century. In it Isidore follows biblical and patristic precedent in referring to Jerusalem as the "navel of the entire area" [umbilicus regionis totius] (*Etym.* 14.3.21; cited in Bevan and Phillott, xiv). Isidore's reference was itself echoed some two centuries later by Rabanus Maurus (12.4; cited in Bevan and Phillott, xiv), whose early-ninth-century *De rerum naturis* (or *De universo*) was a more elaborate if also a less popular encyclopedia than his predecessor's.

Yet somewhat unexpectedly, few such echoes occur in the pilgrimage writings that survive from these five centuries—the very centuries in which the practice of Christian pilgrimage was being established. It is presumably no surprise that both the anonymous Bordeaux pilgrim, the first Latin Christian to leave a written account of the Jerusalem pilgrimage, and the nun Egeria, the first to leave more than a list of places and distances, neglect to make any reference whatsoever to the centrality of Jerusalem. After all the former traveled to Palestine in 333, before Jerome was born, while the latter made her journey probably in the 380s, before Jerome wrote his commentary.[7] But it is surprising to find only a single reference to the belief in those writings of the fifth through the ninth centuries collected in the Library of the Palestine Pilgrims' Text Society. *The Epitome on Certain Holy Places* (c. 440) attributed to Eucherius, Bishop of Lyons, *The Breviary of Jerusalem* (c. 530), Theodosius's *Topography of the Holy Land* (c. 530), the *Itinerary* of Antoninus Martyr (c. 570), the Venerable Bede's treatise *On the Holy Land* (early eighth century), the *Hodoeporicon* based on St Willibald's pilgrimage (c. 754), and the *Itinerary* of Bernard the Wise (870) — not one of these texts mentions the centrality of Jerusalem. The sole text that does is Adamnan's *On the Holy Places*, a treatise based on the account dictated to him by a pilgrim known as Arculf, who traveled to Palestine late in the seventh century.[8]

After Adamnan's treatise the next such references to a central Jerusalem do not appear for some four hundred years — until the crusading period, in other words. At that point they become commonplace, at least for a time. A recent collection of writings relating to the Jerusalem pilgrimage in the years 1099 to 1185, for instance, contains ample evidence of this. Of the fourteen texts produced by Latin Christians, slightly more than half (nine in all) note that Jerusalem is the center of the world.[9]

The same assertion is somewhat harder to find in thirteenth- and fourteenth-century writings, but it can still be found. Jacques de Vitry's early-thirteenth-century *History of Jerusalem* (*LPPTS*, 11.32), one of the many texts produced by this crusading propagandist and bishop of Acre in Palestine, makes it explicitly, although another text which presents itself as deriving from Jacques's *History*, Burchard of Mount Sion's *Description of the Holy Land* (*LPPTS*, vol. 12), omits the assertion altogether. Oddly enough, a reference to the belief turns up in Friar William of Rubruck's mid-thirteenth-century letter to Louis IX in which he recounts his extraordinary journey to the Mongol court in central Asia ("Journey," 214). The idea is also mentioned in both a mid-fourteenth-century guidebook to Palestine (*LPPTS*, 6.4) and a text produced slightly earlier in the same century, Marino Sanudo's *Secrets for True Crusaders* (*LPPTS*, 12.40–41).

So far I have been referring to Latin works, but the situation is apparently little different if we turn to vernacular writings from the same period. A collection, for instance, of fourteen French itineraries and descriptions from the eleventh to thirteenth centuries contains only three texts that mention Jerusalem's centrality (Michelant and Raynaud, 132–33, 164, 230). One of them is a mid-thirteenth-century continuation of William of Tyre's late-twelfth-century history of deeds done beyond the sea, while the second is a late-thirteenth-century account of pilgrimages and pardons in Acre (the third text, by Matthew Paris, stands somewhat apart, and will be discussed below). In addition, Philippe de Mézières's late-fourteenth-century allegorical *Le Songe de vieil pelerin*, though belonging to a somewhat different genre—the dream voyage—likewise reminds its readers of Jerusalem's place in the world (1.233).

Knowing what we do about the recycling of received material in medieval thought, we should expect to find that most of these references to Jerusalem's centrality take roughly the same form and offer much the same information. And that is almost exactly what we do find. But we also find something perhaps more noteworthy: virtually all of the references are characterized by both their extreme brevity and their lack of significance in context (i.e., in relation to the world picture of the particular work in which it is found). From Jerome on, in other words, few writers in either Latin or the vernacular give this geographical peculiarity more than passing mention, and those mentions are often qualified with a rhetorical disclaimer like "they say." In one case, that of William of Rubruck, Jerusalem's centrality is mentioned not by the friar himself, but by an Armenian bishop during a conversation, and William neither confirms nor contradicts him. Clearly, a good many authors were content to fulfill the presumed expectations of their readers about the nature of sacred geography, leaving their own views unstated.

Theoderich's well-known and widely used *Booklet on the Holy Places* (*Libellus de locis sanctis*, c. 1172), for example, an account written expressly for those unable to make the Jerusalem pilgrimage, has much to say about the city, but little about its centrality. The sole reference comes in the detailed description of the Chapel of St. James in the *Templum Domini*, and takes some of the sting out of Twain's later satire: "As we return from it [the chapel] by the same door, on the left hand, behind the jamb of the door, there is a place five feet in length and breadth on which our Lord stood when he was asked where he was in Jerusalem, which *they assert* is situated in the middle of the world, and he answered, 'This place is called Jerusalem'" (*Guide*, 28, emphasis added; *LPPTS*, 5.28). Theoderich is obviously having it both ways here, making the assertion, yet neither endorsing nor refuting it. Less circumspect than Theoderich is Saewulf, whose concise but compelling Latin narrative of his own difficult journey in 1101–2 (or 1102–3) reveals that Jerome's gloss was still being cited eight centuries after it was first made. Saewulf's account, unlike Theoderich's, also reveals that Twain's satire was not pure fabrication, since the medieval English pilgrim thought it helpful to bring Jesus himself in as a witness, in this case to highlight the typological reading of history implicit in the concept of Jerusalem's centrality: "Outside the Church of the Holy Sepulchre but within its surrounding walls, not far from the place of Calvary, is the place called 'Compas', where our Lord Jesus Christ with his own hand marked and measured the centre of the world, as the Psalmist bears witness: *But the Lord our King has before the ages worked salvation in the centre of the earth*'" (Wilkinson, 103; *LPPTS*, 4.12 [English trans.], 39 [Latin]).[10]

Only one pre-fourteenth-century writer, so far as I know, goes farther than Saewulf in attempting to support his assertion that Jerusalem is the center of the earth. That writer is Adamnan, who, as mentioned above, set down Arculf's recollections in Latin late in the seventh century. Adamnan gives us Arculf's account in three books, the first of which is devoted entirely to Jerusalem and contains the sole reference to its centrality. The passage is interesting enough to quote in full, in part because it looks like the seed for Twain's second anecdote, but also because it was omitted from another text based on Adamnan's—Bede's treatise *On the Holy Land* (recall that Burchard of Mount Sion likewise omitted reference to the belief in borrowing from Jacques de Vitry):

A summary account must be given of a very high column which stands in the centre of the city to the north of the holy places facing the passers-by. It is remarkable how this column (which is situated in the place where the dead youth came to life when the cross of the Lord was placed upon him) fails to cast a shadow at midday during the Summer solstice, when the sun reaches the centre of the heavens. When the solstice is passed, however . . . , after an interval of three days, as the day gradually grows shorter it casts a brief shadow at first, then as the days pass a longer one. And so this column, which the sunlight surrounds on all sides blazing directly down on it during the midday hours (when at the Summer solstice the sun stands in the centre of the heavens), proves Jerusalem to be situated at the centre of the world. Hence the psalmist, because of the holy places of the passion and resurrection, which are contained within Helia itself, prophesying sings: 'God our king before the ages hath wrought our salvation in the centre of the earth', that is Jerusalem, which is said to be in the centre of the earth and its navel.[11] (*De locis*, 57, 56 [Latin]; *LPPTS*, 3.16–17)

In this last remark we can hear one of the clearest medieval echoes of Jerome, whose various writings along with the Bible and several other texts are thought to have been among Adamnan's sources (*De locis*, 13–14 [Meehan's intro.]). More interesting than that echo, though, are the way in which it is introduced and the context in which it occurs. Like Saewulf, Adamnan saves the received scriptural evidence for last, using it to sum up the brief account by placing sacred topography firmly in relation to salvation history.

Unlike Saewulf, he offers his readers evidence not only from history and Scripture but also from nature—in the form of a marvelous physical phenomenon explicitly connected with a miracle, as though an ordinary empirical proof would be insufficient. Thus, although he does not claim that Arculf himself saw the natural evidence, Adamnan presents the belief in a central Jerusalem as grounded *in rerum natura*, in the very order of things, and therefore available to the prophesying psalmist not as a mere literary trope but as a geographical fact. Oddly, given the elaborate character of this combined natural, historical, and scriptural proof of Jerusalem's centrality, Adamnan has not previously mentioned this belief in his text.

This last point is important. Although Adamnan has rather more to say about Jerusalem's centrality than almost any other writer, he still does not go so far as to make its place in the world any more important to the aims of his own account of the holy places than other pilgrimage writers do. Like them, he mentions the belief only in passing. Even the garrulous friar Felix Fabri, who late in the fifteenth-century made two trips to the Holy Land in order to gain a clearer insight into Scripture, and who wrote at greater length than Adamnan about the earth's center, does not make the centrality of Jerusalem especially prominent in his Latin account. He does however discuss the question at greater length than previous writers, perhaps because it was during his lifetime that most European cartographers were decentering Jerusalem as they adapted their world maps to accord with the recently rediscovered and increasingly influential geographical conceptions of Ptolemy.[12]

Thus, after mentioning Jesus' supposed confirmation of the earthly center's exact location—a claim which he attributes to "the Eastern Christians"—Fabri turns his attention to the famous column that casts no shadow: "Ancient histories also tell us that before the building of this temple [of the Holy Sepulchre] a tall marble pillar was set up in this place by philosophers, which pillar at the summer equinox threw no shadow at mid-day, as the sun stood directly over it" (*LPPTS*, 7.374–75). Having mentioned the pillar, he goes on to recount a remarkable anecdotal proof that closely resembles the one Twain satirized:

A certain knight who was a pilgrim in my company wished to prove this by experiment, and having obtained leave . . . he ascended with some of his comrades above the vaulted roof of the choir, which . . . has steps by which it can be ascended. On the topmost part of the roof is a high place cunningly built of stone, whereon a man may stand without peril and look round about him. To this place that knight ascended at mid-day, to see whether his body would cast any shadow. He declared to us that in very truth he saw no shadow proceeding from his body, for he stood directly above that place round which we stood, because *the dome is so built as to stand above that place, in order that the experiment may be made there.* (7.375, emphasis added)

More remarkable than this anecdotal proof, however, is Fabri's complex response to it. He thinks it no proof at all, and cites a number of authorities, including several of Ptolemy's maps, that describe the same phenomenon elsewhere in the world, before concluding with an anthropological reflection on the human need to think of oneself as being at the center:

But I do not see that the fact that the sun shines at mid-day so directly above men's heads that their bodies cast no shadow is any true and certain proof that the spot where it does so is the middle of the world.... Ptolemy, too, in his third and fourth map of Africa brings in many regions where the noonday sun stands directly overhead: and what is more than this, in the same map many places are noted where twice in the year the sun stands overhead without casting any shadow.... Howbeit, the opinion of the vulgar is that any place is the middle of the world. (7.375–76)

This last reflection leads Fabri into a brief discussion of a more controversial question than that of the location of Jerusalem: whether the antipodes exist or not. The reader is thus quite surprised when the friar suddenly rounds on himself, and, shaking off the authority of science, takes a position little different from Jerome's a millennium earlier, declaring that Jerusalem is the world's center, since Scripture alone can suffice as proof:

But the infallible truth of Holy Scripture proves by its testimonies that Jerusalem is in the middle of the world. However, many say that Jerusalem is indeed the middle of the habitable world, but is not in the middle of the entire scheme of the universe. Whichever of these opinions is true, we must believe the Holy Scripture, which declares that Jerusalem lies in the midst of the earth, and tells us that our Saviour worked out our salvation in the midst of the earth. (7.376–77)

In support of this unexpected assertion Fabri proceeds to quote not only the familiar passages from Ezekiel and the Psalms alluded to here, but also three other biblical texts and St. Hilarius. From Hilarius he takes a claim that the *Mandeville*-author also used in the previous century: that the crucifixion necessarily occurred at the center "in order that all men might have equal opportunities of obtaining knowledge of God" (7.377). The three biblical texts are Genesis 2.9, Deuteronomy 7.21, and Leviticus 26.11, not one of which says anything about the location of Jerusalem, but all of which the friar interprets allegorically as proving his geographical belief. Like Arculf and Saewulf centuries before him, then, Fabri ends his account of Jerusalem's location by quoting Scripture, but, unlike them, he offers more than just the received texts as evidence—a sign perhaps that belief in Jerusalem's centrality was collapsing in the wake of new developments in geography and cartography, and could only be shored up by the kind of faith that Twain was to mock some four hundred years later.[13]

Jerusalem in *The Book of John Mandeville*

Yet as we have seen, surprisingly few medieval pilgrim writers left any evidence of such faith; instead, the vast majority give the notion of Jerusalem's centrality only qualified credence, and none of them, apart possibly from Fabri, makes it a significant part of his work's argument about the nature of the world. The only writer known to me who does accept the idea without qualification and who gives it genuine significance in his account is the *Mandeville*-author, whose vernacular book, I have already observed, is virtually unique among medieval travel writings in expanding the pilgrims' guide with a survey of the world beyond the Holy Land. Commenting on this highly unusual combination, two critics have recently argued that the extension of *The Book*'s world into the Far East necessarily signals a break with the Jerusalem pilgrim's view of the world. Christian K. Zacher, for instance, claims that "Mandeville's book effectively subordinates pilgrimage to a form of travel motivated by love for this world" and "decentralizes Jerusalem . . . because his mental map of the world is much larger and his reasons for travel are other than spiritual" (140). Similarly, Stephen Greenblatt asserts that the move beyond Jerusalem implies "an abandonment of the dream of a sacred center upon which all routes converge and a turning instead towards diversity, difference, the bewildering variety of 'marvellous things'" (29). There is something to be said for these two views, since *The Book* does in fact promote curious travel and celebrate the world's marvelous diversity, but both are in my opinion a little too neat, since they assume, rather than demonstrate, that the pilgrim's world alone is transvalued in its new context—as though the significance of the Far Eastern world were not reciprocally affected—and they both ignore the kind of contrary textual evidence I cite below. So too does the claim made by John Block Friedman, who suggests on the basis of a single remark in *The Book*'s "original" prologue that "Mandeville tried to see the problem [of Jerusalem's centrality] as a metaphor" (*Monstrous Races*, 22, n. 23).

In the Continental as in the Insular Version, Jerusalem's literal—and not metaphorical—centrality is affirmed on three separate occasions: in the prologue, in the account of the holy city itself, and in a later passage making the case for the earth's spherical shape, the possibility of circumnavigation, and the existence of an inhabited antipodes. Of the three discussions the first and the third are especially striking, since both offer memorable "proofs" of the belief. Only the second is more commonplace, if still a little more elaborate than its antecedents, and it alone derives from any of *The Book*'s known sources, although not from the principal source for the Holy Land, William of Boldensele's early-fourteenth-century *Liber de quibusdam partibus ultra-*

marinis [book about certain overseas regions]. In contrast, neither of the other two passages, taken in their entirety, can be traced to any previous text, and so each represents a largely independent composition by the *Mandeville*-author.[14]

It is worth noting here, incidentally, that *The Book* does not neglect to provide its audience with a conventionally geographical account of Jerusalem's location as well, a fact which implies that the *Mandeville*-author regarded physical, historical, political, and theological conceptions of geography as compatible with one another, rather than contradictory. Thus, toward the end of its trip through the Holy Land, the French text defines the precise extent and location of the territory in which Jerusalem is the principal attraction, taking care even to specify the system of measurement: "The land of promise begins there [at the source of the Jordan river] and lasts until Beersheba in length going from the north to the south; and it contains a good 9,000 leagues. . . . that is, leagues of our country or of Lombardy, which are small. These are not the leagues of Gascony, Provence, or Germany, where they are large leagues" (*MT*, 2.293; cf. *Buke*, 58).[15] Similarly, as soon as it arrives at the holy city itself, the text attempts to situate the place by way of several kinds of loosely geographical information:

And on the way [from Bethlehem] there are many Christian churches through which one goes then to Jerusalem the holy city, [which is] well situated between two mountains; and there are no rivers or wells there, but the water comes by conduits from Hebron. . . . [Here follows an explanation of the historical origins of the sacred city's name.] Around Jerusalem is the realm of Syria; and next to it is the land of Palestine. . . . Jerusalem is in the realm of Judea. . . . And it borders in the east on the realm of Arabia, in the south on the land of Egypt, in the west on the great sea [the Mediterranean], and in the north on the realm of Syria and the sea of Cypress. (*MT*, 2.267–68; cf. *Buke*, 37)

Between these two unexceptional geographical descriptions, in the account of the Church of the Holy Sepulchre, the text makes its least emphatic and most typical reference to Jerusalem as *omphalos*, or sacred center. Within the church, the reader is told, there exists a white rock called Calvary, "where our Lord was placed on the cross," and that rock is cracked, the crack itself being Golgotha, the place of the skull:

There in that crack Adam's head was found after Noel's [*sic*] flood, a sign that the sins of Adam would be pardoned or redeemed in that very place. And on that same rock Abraham made his sacrifice to our lord, and there is an altar there. And before that altar lie Godfrey of Bouillon and other Christian kings, who were kings of Jerusalem. And there by the side where our lord was crucified this is written in Greek, *Etheos et basileon ysmon proseonas erogaze sochias et mosotis gis*. That is in Latin, *Hic Deus rex nos-*

ter ante secula operatus est salutem in medio terre. Also on the rock where the cross was placed is written in the rock, *Cyos nist basys ys tou pysteos thoy chesmosy*. That is in Latin, *Quod vides est fundamentum totius fidei huius mundi* [What you see is the ground of this world's entire faith]. (*MT*, 2:269–70; cf. *Buke*, 40)[16]

Also in the middle of the body of the church there is a compass where Joseph of Arimathea laid the body of our lord, when he had removed him from the cross, and right there he washed his wounds. And *they say* [*dist on*] that this compass is right in the middle of the world. (*MT*, 2.271, emphasis added; cf. *Buke*, 40)

What is interesting about these two passages in the present context is the oblique way in which they assert the fact of Jerusalem's centrality. The first does so entirely indirectly, citing but not translating or glossing the important verses from Psalm 74, which means that the reader has to know Latin as well as the tradition deriving from Jerome's interpretation, while the latter passage qualifies the assertion by attributing it to received opinion, perhaps because the *Mandeville*-author was himself uncertain about the exact location of the earthly center's own center. Whatever the reason for his reticence, he nevertheless appears to have thought it useful to bring together here several different kinds of evidence, all of them testifying to both the symbolic and the potentially literal centrality of Jerusalem in Christian thought: not just Scripture, which is cited in both Latin and (garbled) Greek, but also the physical nature of the place itself, relics, oral tradition, and the events of history, whether recent or biblical (the latter presented according to the standard typological reading).

If this were the sum total of what the text had to say about Jerusalem's centrality, *The Book* would hardly stand apart from other pilgrimage writings, but, as I have noted already, it is not. Of the two other statements, the more elaborate comes in the text's most prominent and rhetorically effective place: the privileged space of the prologue, which serves to call text, author, and audience into being while also establishing the reader's expectations and foreshadowing the ethos of the work as a whole. By way of doing these things, *The Book*'s opening section first praises the Holy Land and the life and death of Jesus Christ, then exhorts Christians to worship and serve both their lord and their overseas territorial inheritance, and finally criticizes the ruling estate for being more concerned with fighting among themselves than with leading a new crusade—and only then gets around to explaining what the text will contain (that is, a detailed description of the ways to Jerusalem and other holy places in and around Palestine combined with an account not only of those places but of others still farther east).

By opening as it does with fulsome praise of "the land overseas, that is the holy land, the land of promise," *The Book* begins by situating this at once foreign and familiar territory in physical, historical, and theological space. Separated by the Mediterranean from Europe, the Holy Land lies far away, yet is near in significance, for it has been blessed above all other lands, the text claims, by the presence and suffering of Jesus Christ, whose domain is asserted to be the entire universe: "he who was King of the heavens and earth, of air and sea, and of all things contained in them"—including, as *The Book* eventually makes clear, all of humanity, whether Christian or not. This faraway place, moreover, is "the best, the most virtuous and the most worthy in the world; for it is *the heart and middle of all the land of the world*, and thus, as the philosopher says, *Virtus rerum in medio consistit* [the virtue/excellence of things lies in the middle]." As such, the Holy Land alone is the proper place for the central event of history, the event that links the expulsion from Paradise with the return to it (a typological reading of history returned to in the account of Golgotha quoted above):

In that very worthy land would the heavenly King . . . suffer passion and death for love of us, in order to redeem and deliver us from the pains of hell and perpetual death, which was ordained for us for the sin of our first father Adam, and for our very own sins as well. . . . And well would the King of glory in that land more than in any other suffer passion and death. For *whoever wants to make something public* [qui veult aucune chose publier], such that everyone might know it, *must have it cried and announced in the town center*, such that the thing be known in all parts. Therefore the creator of all the world would suffer death for us in *Jerusalem, which is in the middle of the world, so that the thing would be made public and known in all regions of the world.* . . . (*MT*, 2.229–30, emphasis added; cf. *Buke*, 1–2)

One might suppose that this philosophical as well as "common sense" proof, along with the empirical, historical, and scriptural testimony cited in the city itself, would suffice to substantiate the claim that Jerusalem lies at the center of the world. Yet this is not the case. The *Mandeville*-author appears to have thought a third, quite different proof necessary. In the latter part of *The Book*, as the text is surveying the world between Palestine and the Earthly Paradise, the audience is given a sketch of the false paradise of Lamory (Sumatra?), perhaps in anticipation of the Eden still to be described. One of the most striking features of Lamory—apart from the local people's habits of going naked, holding property, spouses, and children in common, and eating human flesh—is that there one loses sight of the North Star and gains sight of the South. Such heavenly symmetry proves of course that the earth is a circumnavigable sphere, and, as the text goes on to argue, both of these things prove that the earth is everywhere inhabited, including at the antipodes.

Yet before the text gets to the latter and, for medieval thinkers, troubling question, the *Mandeville*-author follows the abrupt shift from cannibalism to circumnavigation by having the English Knight make one of his infrequent but striking appearances as an actor on the stage of "his own memoirs" (*The Book*'s "I," as Donald Howard has noted, is mainly "an impersonal Everyman" retailing information [2]). In case anyone should doubt the text's claims about the earth's shape—which are borrowed chiefly from John of Holywood's textbook *De Sphera*—Sir John provides the measurements that he himself made with his astrolabe, and in case anyone should doubt the measurements, he tells the story of a young man who without knowing it almost circled the globe, only to stop short; not until he returned the long way round did the fellow realize what he had done. In between the measurements and the memorable anecdote, immediately following the first of two assertions that the antipodes are inhabited, comes *The Book*'s third and final proof of Jerusalem's centrality:

And know that, according to what I can perceive and understand, the land of Prester John, emperor of India, is beneath us. For *in going from Scotland and England towards Jerusalem one is continually climbing*. For our land is in the low regions of the earth towards the west, and the land of Prester John is in the low region towards the east. And they have day there when we have night, and also conversely they have night when we have day. For the earth and the sea are of round form, as I told you before, and as you climb to one spot you descend to the other. *Now you have heard it said before that Jerusalem is in the middle of the world; and that is shown by a spear fixed in the earth at the hour of noon, which casts no shadow in any direction, and that it be in the middle of the earth David testifies, where he says, Et operatus est salutem in medio terre etc.* (MT, 2.332–33, emphasis added; cf. *Buke*, 91)

Arculf's seventh-century proof is now advanced in an entirely different context: one that links the internally divided Latin Christendom of the fourteenth century with the ideal Christian empire of Prester John's land, which in *The Book* is depicted as a realm characterized by a sort of apostolic simplicity and an easy harmony between the spiritual and temporal realms. And the link is made by way of an umbilical Jerusalem, which, however, is no longer in Christian hands, a consequence, according to the text, of the egregious sins of Latin Christians. In its new context, then, the traditional proof of Jerusalem's geographical centrality becomes part of an implicit demonstration that the entire symmetrical earth is potentially Christian both near and far.

Recognizing this, we can now see why the *Mandeville*-author takes the idea of Jerusalem's centrality so much more seriously than his predecessors did. He does so because it accords with one of the larger concerns of his multi-faceted compilation. Writing some seventy years after the fall of Acre, the last Latin Christian foothold in Palestine, in the wake of intermittent and mainly failed attempts by the papacy to establish not only effective bishoprics within the extensive Mongol empire, but also a military alliance with the Mongols against Islam, and during a protracted crisis within Latin Christendom (not only had the papacy been displaced to Avignon, but England and France were at war, the European economy was in a bad way, and the plague had recently swept across the entire region, devastating the population and leaving behind social disarray and labour unrest)—writing in such troubled circumstances, the *Mandeville*-author appears to have set himself the task of renewing belief in the possibility of a universal Christendom and using it as an enticement to Latin Christians to reform themselves (Higgins, "Imagining Christendom"). If so, then *The Book*'s emphasis on Jerusalem's centrality can be read as both a consolation offered to a much shrunken Christendom and a challenge laid down to those Christians who, as the Prologue puts it, have the wherewithal to undertake a holy voyage overseas.

Whether *The Book*'s medieval intermediaries read the text as I have done is hard to know for sure, but one thing is clear: of those versions translated directly from the Continental or the Insular Version, the majority keep the three "original" discussions of Jerusalem's centrality, leaving them virtually unchanged even as they otherwise transform the text in transmission. These include several of the most widely circulated or historically important redactions: that is, Michel Velser's German and the English Cotton, Defective, and Egerton Versions, respectively. In this context, I would draw attention to a striking interpolation found at the close of the three interrelated English redactions, all of them made early in the fifteenth century, as well as in one Insular Latin manuscript copied later in the same century. Not only does this interpolation reveal the freedom with which medieval redactors intervened in their source texts, it also illustrates the way in which some of them read *The Book* as both a geographically and a theologically orthodox account of the world—or perhaps alternatively, it shows the way in which they were anxious to ensure that the text be read as such.

The precise wording as well as the exact placement of the interpolation varies somewhat in all four instances, but its specific point does not. In each version, as the English Knight is taking leave of his audience by way of some closing reflections on the content and aims of his "memoirs," the added passage has him assert that since not everyone will credit things they have not seen for themselves, he has visited Rome on his return to Christendom in order to submit his book for papal approval. Although the papacy was located in Avignon at the time of Sir John's ostensible return (the mid-1350s—such matters of historical fact seem to have been of no concern to *The Book*'s Insular intermediaries here), the pope nevertheless confirmed the submitted "recollections" against another larger book. According to the three English redactions, it was from this larger book that the (Hereford?) *mappa mundi* was made, while in the Latin manuscript the authorizing book is said to have provided the information depicted on a kind of globe shown to Sir John himself: "a certain spherical instrument, painstakingly and curiously made, containing in itself in the form of figures or pictures [per sculpciones vel depicturas] virtually all realms and races of people—a wonderful device which he [the pope] called the *Sphere of the World*."[17] Clearly, some of *The Book*'s fifteenth-century readers were prepared to endorse the truth claims of a text that undertook a much more literal and elaborate defense of the "foremost peculiarity" of medieval geography than most earlier pilgrim writers had been willing to offer.

Yet there was at least one roughly contemporary reader who was not prepared to do so: the Vulgate Latin redactor, who made his version of *The Book* sometime between 1396 and 1415 (*Liber Ioannis Mandevil* [*LIM*]). In addition to dispensing entirely with the first and the third of the three assertions of Jerusalem's centrality (i.e., the striking ones in the prologue and in the passage on the earth's sphericity), this unknown intermediary reworked the second, or indirect assertion, so that the English Knight explicitly refutes the traditional belief. The Latin redactor's decided independence here stands in even clearer relief if we compare him with Otto von Diemeringen, who claims to have made use of the Vulgate Latin text along with the Interpolated Continental Version for his German rendering. Unlike his learned source, von Diemeringen omits only the proof in the prologue, leaving the remaining two largely as they appear in the Continental Version, a double change which suggests that the German translator himself sided with the theologically orthodox geographical view. Oddly enough, given that he does retain the latter two proofs, von Diemeringen's revised prologue has nothing at all to say about Jerusalem, discussing instead the value of foreign travel and his own decision to translate this widely respected work "from Latin and French . . . in praise of the well-known knight, who made the book for his eternal good fame after his death."[18]

There is no question but that the Vulgate Latin redactor considered Jerusalem as significant a site as did the *Mandeville*-author, since his reworked prologue accords with the "original" exordium in its affirmation that no earthly place is worthier than "terra Hierosolimitana, terra promissionis filiorum Dei" [the Jerusalem territory, the promised land of God's sons], "especially because God the maker of heaven and earth deigned to value it so much that there he revealed his own son, Christ the saviour of the world, to humankind" (*LIM*, 25). It is simply that he refused to follow the "original" in conflating the sacred city's originary and symbolic centrality with its geographical. Yet if the Latin translator appears to be historically "in advance" of the *Mandeville*-

author on this count, he looks reluctant to follow him on the potentially unorthodox matters of the earth's circumnavigibility and inhabited antipodes. Thus, while he keeps the brief reference to the two pole stars that emerges from the account of Lamory, and even repeats practically verbatim the measurements that Sir John made with the astrolabe (though displacing them to a slightly later section), he omits everything else.

Some of that omitted material turns up elsewhere in his text, in a place where one might least expect to encounter it—just as one hardly expects to come across an "empirical" proof of Jerusalem's centrality in a discussion of polar stars, the earth's shape, circumnavigation, and the antipodes. Perhaps taking his cue here from *The Book*'s unknown author, but reversing the emphasis, the Latin translator worked a discussion of the earth's shape into his rendering of the account of the church of "the reverend and most holy sepulchre of our Lord Jesus Christ" (*LIM*, 35). The account as a whole contains much of the information originally gathered together by the *Mandeville*-author, though newly arranged according to the redactor's sense of appropriate disposition. The description of Golgotha, for instance, comes slightly later in the account, omitting only the mention of Adam's skull, while keeping both of the Greek quotations used to signal Jerusalem's centrality; and this passage is immediately followed by a slightly fuller description of the "compass" ("a place wonderfully and beautifully covered with tiles in the true shape of a circle," *LIM*, 36) which ignores the *Mandeville*-author's qualified reference to its geographical location—a juxtaposition that required the redactor to omit intervening legendary matter about, among other things, St. Helen's "invention" of the cross. At the end of this reworked account, where the Continental Version simply moves on to another church, leaving the reader to accept or reject the implied typological proof of Jerusalem's centrality, the Vulgate Latin Version raises the question explicitly, setting itself against an overtly theological conception of geographical space and eventually going so far as to call Sir John himself as witness against the very claim the Knight makes in most other versions of *The Book*:

> ... that which certain people make known or at least suppose—that Judea or even Jerusalem, or this Church stands at the center of the whole world, according to the aforesaid scripture [in medio terrae]—cannot be understood spatially [localiter] according to the measure of the earth's body. (*LIM*, 36)

In support of this counterclaim, the Vulgate Latin text proceeds to offer a strictly geographical explanation which shows that its redactor has nevertheless accepted as true a related theological element of the received Christian topography of the period:

for if we consider the earth's breadth, which they estimate between the two poles, it is certain that Judea cannot be in the middle, because then it would be at the circle of the Equator, and it would always be equinox there, and both poles would stand horizontal to it. Which in any case is not so, because to those in Judea the north star is raised very high. Conversely, if we consider the earth's length, which can be estimated from *the earthly Paradise* — that is, from *the worthier and more elevated place on earth* — towards its Nadir — that is, towards the place on the earth's Sphere opposite it — then Judea is at the Antipodes of Paradise, which it appears cannot be so, because then *for a traveler from Judea towards Paradise the distance of the route would be the same either to the East or to the West. But this is neither apparent nor true, as the experience of many attests.* (*LIM*, 36, emphasis added)

"The experience of many" includes Sir John's, of course, and this the Vulgate redactor now reinvents to confirm a loose geographical — rather than a literal and theological — interpretation of the famous verses from the Psalter, simply by shifting the focus from Jerusalem to the larger surrounding territory, since that land in fact did lie roughly in the middle of the "habitable region" then known to Latin Christendom:

To me moreover it seems that the Prophet's writing mentioned before can be explained: "in medio terrae," that is, around [circa] the middle of our habitable region, namely as Judea is around the midpoint between Paradise and the Antipodes of Paradise, being distant only 96 degrees from Paradise in the east, *as I myself have tested by the eastern route*: although from this it does not appear that complete certainty is to be easily had, since no stars remain immobile in the length of the sky as the pole stars always do in the breadth. (*LIM*, 36–37, emphasis added)

Finally, the Latin redactor turns from this simple (and fabricated) experiential proof to perfectly comprehensible "common sense," on the one hand, and unfathomable divine mystery, on the other, giving the latter pride of place in the entire revisionary account, as if he were Milton's Raphael instructing an audience of Adams to "be lowly wise" instead of inquiring too much into the secrets of the universe:

Or it can be explained thus, that David, who was King of Judea, said "in medio terrae," that is, in the principal city of his land, Jerusalem, which was the royal or priestly city of the land of Judea: or perhaps the holy spirit, which was given voice through the prophet's mouth in this phrase, wanted to be understood neither bodily nor spatially, but entirely spiritually, about which view nothing should be written at present. (*LIM*, 37, emphasis added)

What more shall I say? as Polo's amanuensis Rustichello might ask. With this passage the Vulgate Latin redactor illustrates just how far some of *The Book*'s medieval intermediaries could go both in adapting their source and in concealing their changes — as far as the *Mandeville*-author himself, in other words. Perhaps more importantly, though, the passage points up how differently two roughly contemporary medieval authors (and presumably their readers as well) could understand the same geographical concept and therefore how distinctive the *Mandeville*-author's defense of a literally central Jerusalem is in its historical context.

By Way of Conclusion: *The Book* and the Maps

This distinctiveness, I suggested at the outset, connects the *Mandeville-author*'s "original" compilation—and those of its textual isotopes that preserve the emphasis on Jerusalem's literal centrality—with a particular kind of medieval map: the Jerusalem-centered encyclopedic *mappae mundi*, or circular world maps, which are a Christianized version of a cartographic form deriving ultimately from Greco-Roman geography. It is often thought that such maps were the only kind of world map produced in the medieval period, just as it is commonly asserted that belief in Jerusalem's centrality was universal (Seymour, ed., *Mandeville's Travels*, 231 n. to 1/20). But just as the textual evidence of the pilgrims' guides fails to support the latter assertion, so the cartographic evidence reveals a fair degree of historical and contextual variety. According to David Woodward, Jerusalem began to be placed at the center of the earth on world maps only after the beginning of the Crusades, and although the practice continued even into the fifteenth century, it was not universally followed (341–42). A telling example of this variation in the *mappae mundi*, as also in local plans of Palestine, can be found in a pair of maps made by Matthew Paris to accompany his thirteenth-century *Chronica majora*. Not only does his map of Palestine place Jerusalem off center, giving pride of place to Acre, so does his circular world map, which represents the city by name only (there is no picture). This double displacement is all the more striking as Paris's pictorial representation of Jerusalem in the former map actually contains a Latin text announcing its centrality, and this text is itself placed next to a French text that does the same (the French text is the third of the three vernacular texts mentioned above).[19]

Yet in the present context there is an even more relevant negative example than that of Paris's maps: the sort of *mappae mundi* that resulted when some of the so-called Catalan-style portolans (that is, Mediterranean sea charts made for coastal navigation) expanded in "speculative" fashion into Asia, heading eastward and inland beyond the Mediterranean coastline. The most famous of the "speculative" portolans is the encyclopedic *Catalan Atlas* of 1375, a map whose correspondence with *The Book* had already been noticed in the nineteenth century, although not in the way that I suggest here. In my view, *The Book* can be be considered a verbal analogue to this famous portolan in that it extends the textual equivalent of a coastal chart—the pilgrims' guide—in the same eastward and "speculative" direction by splicing onto it a description of the world beyond the *oikoumene*.[20] Where such an analogy breaks down, however, is in relation to the fundamental "take" that each work has on the earth's territory. In contrast to the radically expanded portolan, which gives Jerusalem visual prominence but not literal centrality and so refuses to place its world under the aegis of theology even as it incorporates the circular *mappa mundi* into its cartographic form, the *Mandeville*-author's radically extended pilgrims' guide retains the "foremost peculiarity" of medieval geography even as it makes its own "speculative" expansion eastward.[21]

A better visual analogue, then, can be found in two of the most famous medieval *mappae mundi*—the Ebstorf and Hereford maps—both of which were probably made in the thirteenth century, well before *The Book*, and which clearly place Jerusalem at the center of the *orbis terrarum*.[22] In contrast to the partly related *Catalan Atlas*, these two maps explicitly depict the earth as the space of Christian history, showing this history unfolding from Paradise at the top, or east, through Jerusalem in the center, to Europe at the bottom, or west, and yet each also fills this theologically defined space with non-Christian material, such as natural marvels. They thus represent the world as *The Book* does: as God's country, so to speak, in which everything ultimately falls under his sway, whether or not it falls within the political boundaries of Latin Christendom. In this sense, *The Book* and the maps alike can be understood as theologically and historically motivated "inventories" of creation designed to offer medieval Christians a comforting vision of their earthly centrality, despite their geographical marginality.[23] This ideological analogy, I would argue, makes *The Book* in some important respects a "reactionary" document: that is, one which looks back toward an earlier synthesis of theology and geography as much as it looks ahead toward the expanded and revised physical geography that eventually undermined medieval conceptions of the earth as an uncircumnavigible sphere inhabited only above the torrid zone.[24]

Whatever their relation as analogues, though, these verbal and pictorial representations of a Jerusalem-centered earth differ in the effect that they potentially have on readers and viewers. Unlike a circular world map, a text is necessarily linear, and its readers or hearers eventually have to leave Jerusalem behind for other places. This may well explain not only why the *Mandeville*-author needs to remind his readers more than once of Jerusalem's location, but also why modern readers have generally overlooked *The Book*'s insistence on the city's centrality, often regarding its briefer account of Paradise as more important simply because it comes later in the text (Zacher, 151; Mary B. Campbell, *Witness*, 160).[25] In contrast, the viewer of a circular map can never quite lose sight of a well-marked center, since the very shape of the map keeps one's gaze circling around it. What a text must offer in compensation, therefore, is a fuller experience of the center, which *The Book* does both through its lengthy account of the city and through repetition (Jerusalem, though not its centrality, is often mentioned in the text, and, through a lengthy meditation on the Passion relics, is evoked in the opening account of Constantinople). That fuller experience was presumably part of what the *Mandeville*-author wanted to offer his readers, in order to remind them of how much they had lost with the failure of the Crusades. No other medieval text reminds its readers in quite this way of Jerusalem's significance, and to recognize this is to begin to learn to read *The Book* and its textual isotopes with the subtlety they deserve.

Notes

Earlier versions of this essay were delivered at the annual meeting of the Medieval Academy of America, Columbus, March 1992, and at the Thirtieth International Congress on Medieval Studies, Kalamazoo, May 1995.

1. Johannes Witte de Hese's *Itinerarius* provides a partial exception to my statement about *The Book*'s uniqueness; see Scott Westrem, "A Critical Edition of Johannes Witte de Hese's *Itinerarius*, the Middle Dutch Text, an English Translation, and Commentary, together with an Introduction to European Accounts of Travel to the East (1240–1400)" (Ph.D. diss., Northwestern University, 1985).

2. See also Zumthor, "Intertextualité et mouvance," and Speer, esp. 317–19.

3. For a fuller treatment of the matters discussed here, see my *Writing East*, 6–14.

4. On the authorship question, see Lejeune.

5. See my *Writing East*, 20–24. See also J. W. Bennett, app. 1 and 2; de Poerck; Seymour, "The Scribal Tradition of Mandeville's *Travels*: The Insular Version," and "The Scribal Tradition of Mandeville's Travels in England"; and Bremer.

6. The passage from Jerome is found in *Patrologia Latina* (hereafter cited as PL followed by volume and column numbers); all three passages are quoted from Arentzen, 218; my translation, emphasis added.

7. For the Bordeaux pilgrim, see *Itineraria et alia geographica*, xvii–26 (Latin), and the translated *Egeria's Travels* (153–63); for Egeria, see both *Egeria's Travels* and *Itineraria*, 27–90.

8. *Library of the Palestine Pilgrims' Text Society*, vols. 2 (*Epitome*; *Breviary*; Theodosius, *Topography*; Antoninus, *Itinerary*) and 3 (Bede, *Holy Land*; *Hodoeporicon*; Bernard, *Itinerary*; Adamnan, *Holy Places*), respectively. Texts from this collection will be cited hereafter as *LPPTS*, with volume number. For the Latin texts of the *Epitome*, the *Breviary*, Theodosius, Antoninus, and Bede, see *Itineraria et alia geographica*; for Arculf, see Adamnan's *De locis sanctis*.

9. Wilkinson, 87, 90, 92, 103, 198, 212, 233, 260 (the relevant passage from Theoderich is not included in the editor's selection; see *LPPTS*, vol. 5). The reference to Jerusalem's centrality can also be found in an Icelandic and a Russian text in this collection.

10. Saewulf here follows the received view; Theoderich's location is unusual. On the tradition of the location in the *Templum Domini*, see French 56.

11. French refers to a Jewish tradition of this anecdotal proof (52).

12. Note that although most mapmakers decentered Jerusalem, not all did; see Woodward, 317 and n. 147.

13. Arculf's proof was also used, positively, by Gervais of Tilbury in his *Otia imperialia* (see Wright, 260) and by the Icelandic pilgrim Nikulás of Ðverá (see the excerpt in Wilkinson, 217). On Fabri's account, see French, 70–75.

14. For the most recent study of *The Book*'s sources, see Deluz, 39–72 (analysis), 428–91 (a running "tableau des sources").

15. All translations from *The Book*, regardless of version, are mine; all references to Letts's edition will be given as *MT*, and to Warner's edition as *Buke*.

16. The Greek in this quotation is (mis-)taken from Peter Comestor; see *Buke*, 178–79, n. to 39/4.

17. For the Latin interpolation, see *The Bodley Version*, 175 (n. to 146/7). Scholars continue to treat this interpolation as authorial: for example, Phillips, 206.

18. I quote here from "Otto von Diemeringen: A German Version of Sir John Mandeville's 'Travels,'" ed. Edward W. Crosby (Ph.D. diss., University of Kansas, 1965), 31. A critical edition is now being prepared by Klaus Ridder. On von Diemeringen's source, see Ridder, *Jean de Mandevilles*, 187. For further discussion of von Diemeringen's handling of the account of the earth's sphericity and Jerusalem's centrality, see Ridder, 249–53.

19. On Paris's maps, see Lewis, 373, fig. 222 (world map), 350–51, figs. 214–15 (Palestine), 355 (Latin text on Jerusalem). References to Jerusalem's centrality attributed to Paris can also be found in Michelant and Raynaud, 132–33. Further evidence for the variety of conceptions underpinning medieval mapmaking in this respect comes from the cartographic representations of the holy city itself; see Arentzen, 133.

20. For the idea that Catalan-style portolans expanded east in a "speculative" fashion, see Tony Campbell, "Portolan Charts," 394. Notes on the correspondences and differences in detail (but not in conception) between the *Atlas* and *The Book*, can be found in, e.g., *Buke*, 170 (n. to 22/15), 204 (103/11), 211 (126/6), 213 (130/chap. 29), 216 (137/6), and 219 (148/15).

21. In shedding the explicitly theological world picture of the thirteenth-century *mappae mundi*, incidentally, the *Catalan Atlas* also updates their picture of the Far East; thus, whereas it contains information on Cathay (China), most of it got from Marco Polo's book, the other maps do not even mention the country. Examining twenty-one *mappae mundi* made between the fourth and the fifteenth centuries, von den Brincken found Cathay depicted on one map only ("Mappa mundi und Chronographia," 165 [Tafel 5, Asien 1]).

22. On dating the Ebstorf map, see Lindemann, 45–49; and Wolf, 51–68.

23. On the Christian topography and symbolism of the maps, see Arentzen; Woodward; von den Brincken, "Mappa mundi," and "Ut describeretur." I borrow the term "inventory" from von den Brincken, "Ut describeretur," 277–78, who uses it to gloss the medieval cartographer's "descriptio."

24. The best analogue of *The Book* as this latter kind of "mappemonde prophétique" (Deluz, 189) is Martin Behaim's 1492 globe, the earliest surviving globe, and one that explicitly cites "the worthy doctor and knight John of Mandavilla" as an authority. Deluz argues against linking *The Book* and the Hereford *mappa mundi*, simply because they do not correspond very well in geographical detail. On the globe and *The Book*, see Moseley, 89–91.

25. Cf. Greenblatt, chap. 2, who reads *The Book* as refusing all territorial possession.

3

Against Gog and Magog

SCOTT D. WESTREM

THE LAST PLACE THAT Johannes Witte de Hese visits on his fantastical journey through Asia is Amosona, whose queen bears the name of her land, and where inhabitants are either black or very white, people have two faces (one in front, one in back), and Gog and Magog live imprisoned between two mountains. Although Witte states that he rested here for eight days, his description is so imprecise that we cannot discern if he is referring to one, two, or several population groups. Nor can we calculate exactly where he is: more than a year has passed since Prester John personally gave him leave to depart India—in early 1392, judging from the account's loose internal chronology—and he has all this while been sailing east by north in nebulous territory that recalls the insular landscapes of the St. Brendan legend. Witte's movement beyond the confines of Gog and Magog is also geographically obscure; after leaving Amosona, he voyages for another three months among unnamed islands without making landfall until returning to Jerusalem, where his "pilgrimage" began and where he concludes his *Itinerarius* perfunctorily: "Everyone knows what things look like here. The end."[1]

There is little reason to believe even the minor truth claims of this narrative; that an individual named Johannes Witte, a native of the village of Hese and a priest in the diocese of Utrecht, ever left northern Europe in the late fourteenth century is highly doubtful. The treatise's pedestrian Latin does not reveal its author to have been much of a stylist or a reader, and so *any* entry in its geographical lexicon warrants attention. Witte can hardly be said to have given Gog and Magog clear definition. The inharmonious names are associated with a territory of binary oppositions, a people of extreme skin colors, a society of Januses, where this putative traveler pauses on his itinerary between an island on which sirens sing enticingly, his previous stop, and Holy Jerusalem, his destination. A place of such unsettling contraries would, for many medieval clerics, indeed be fit for a queen.

Witte's ambiguous "Gog et Magog" constitutes an apt image of medieval Europe's vague and shifting conception of an entity that has been given a name by the world's three prominent monotheistic religions, but no real habitation. So elliptical is the referent, in fact, that writers treat it variously as singular or plural. In a sense, this grammatical vagueness is also fitting, since "Gog/Magog" functions as a semantic cipher whose value has been its capacity to assume identity, or identities, as the needs of a historical moment determine. Western culture has adopted Gog or Magog or both as a pseudonym for political threats from the Goths under Alaric to the Soviets under Brezhnev.

On the one hand, this act of naming may serve a delimiting purpose, one analogous to Anthony Pagden's "principle of attachment," by means of which a social group attains "some degree of understanding . . . when confronted with the blatantly unknown" by assimilating it into "the known" (24). Individual Europeans, coming to terms with a variety of unknown enemies during the millennium between the sack of Rome in 410, and the fall of Constantinople in 1453, discovered an ample array of ethnic synonyms for Gog and Magog. In so doing, they did not so much disarm a palpable threat as bring it into a context in which the very heavens guaranteed its ultimate defeat and the namer's victory. Such identifications were neither common nor unequivocal, however; indeed, the absence of "Gog/Magog" from many texts bears noticing. On the other hand, naming Gog and Magog could have sinister implications, for what I have called a cipher also functioned as a specter. Many of Christian Europe's keenest anxieties—parricide, infanticide, cannibalism, anomie, nomadism, foreigners, peculiar languages (and character systems), inhabitants of the North, and religious dissidence—in various combinations underlie specific invocations of "Gog/Magog." This had potentially dire consequences when conjoined with a hermeneutics that denied the existence of Gog or Magog as a unique, and remote, people, identifying it instead as a dangerous element already lurking in the European social fabric. Augustine, rejecting literal readings of scriptural prophecy in his own day, lent his authority to this interpretation, which nearly a millennium later could be called into the service of anti-Semitism.

* * *

In general terms, Gog and Magog elicit language—in Jewish, Christian, and Muslim sources—that is, like the people in Witte's *Itinerarius*, black and white. It would be hard to imagine a more excoriated, more exilic figure than Magog, who appears innocently in Genesis as a son of Noah's son Japheth;

whose name is appropriated to designate the homeland of Gog, to whom the prophet Ezekiel was commanded by the Lord of Israel to thunder "I am against thee" not once but twice; and who appears in some mortal form at the end of the Revelation of St. John as half of the innumerable twin forces, with Gog, assembled by Satan from the four quarters of the earth to fight, unsuccessfully, against the saints and the beloved city of Jerusalem (20.8; also Gen. 10.2; 1 Chron. 1.5; Ezek. 38, 39). As if the opposition of Yahweh and the Triune God were not enough, the Qur'an reports Allah's antipathy for Gog and Magog, who ravage a land so remote that its people can "barely understand a word," yet who plead with Alexander the Great (called Dhul-Qarnain) to help them; he builds a rampart of iron and brass against them, which Allah will level at the end of time, when unbelievers will be cast into hell (sura 18.83–108).[2]

So far, so evil. As a result of the role they play in Christian, and less distinctly in Islamic, eschatology, however, Gog and Magog take on the oxymoronic character of a welcome enemy, for their movement from the margin to the center of the earth is the necessary prelude to the communion of saints in Paradise. Even in its terse, ambiguous formulation in holy books, the story of Gog and Magog requires ambivalent readers.

The complications of reading and defining "Gog/Magog" are not widely recognized. This is owing partly to the authority that has been granted, for more than sixty years, to Andrew Runni Anderson, whose monograph on the subject is an invaluable source for scholars, who have generally overlooked Anderson's central argument: that the "legend of Alexander's Gate and of the enclosed nations [of Gog and Magog] is in reality the story of the frontier in sublimated mythologized form" (8). According to Anderson, the opposition of Alexander and Gog and Magog epitomized the Greek ideal of a civilized *oikoumene* from which barbarians must be banned (3–4). Writing just over a decade after World War I, Anderson uses "frontier" to signify a defensive buffer zone, a kind of Maginot line, rather than territory that attracts an advancing civilization, as in the vocabulary of nineteenth-century Manifest Destiny. His image suggests an equivalence between the socially self-satisfied Greeks, who viewed mumbling *barbaroi* with disdain, and religiously confident but culturally insecure medieval Europeans, worrying over an uncertain border against unknown outsiders. This in turn has contributed to the misleading notion that "Gog/Magog" held stable or cumulative meaning during the Middle Ages.[3]

To a certain extent, this notion is understandable. As individual Europeans imagined their culture under siege, they identified a series of ethnic groups as Antichrist's allies, including Goths, Huns, Alans, Khazars, Arabians, Turks, Magyars, Parthians, Mongols, the Ten Lost Tribes, Scythians, Scandinavians, Terracontans, Essedones, and Jews (Muslim writers shared several of these interpretations and added to them Latin Christians) (Anderson, 12–14; Boorstin, 104).[4] In addition, Anderson's brief chapter on medieval *mappae mundi* suggests that European cartographers, between 1100 and 1500, more or less programmatically assigned territory to Gog and Magog (gradually shifting their haunts to the east) (Anderson, 85, 87–90, 101–4). But a moderate number of primary sources, some of them idiosyncratic and uninfluential, together with this one scholar's opinion, do not prove that "Gog/Magog" constituted a story that was either widely told or much developed during the European Middle Ages. Furthermore, Anderson almost completely overlooks the exegetical approach that treated Gog and Magog as a metaphor for enemies of the Latin church who would work to destroy it from within.

While "Gog/Magog" receives some notice in literary, cartographical, geographical, and theological texts, the common denominator of its meanings seems to be little more specific than "bogeyman" (itself a verbal orphan of uncertain etymology and shifting applications), as a brief survey will demonstrate. Evidence from maps is particularly problematic; a few well-known examples may unwisely be construed as representing a general point of view or may naively be treated as texts without contexts. In addition, turning to cartography for images of "Gog/Magog" overlooks the fact that mapping an allegorical interpretation of Gog and Magog is, by definition, impossible (although at least one chart maker proclaimed his allegiance with Augustine).

As might be expected from the Qur'anic reference, Gog and Magog play a role within the Alexander legend, an extremely dense network of stories, popular on many levels during the European Middle Ages. In the many Latin and vernacular versions of the story that descend from the *Historia de Preliis* (I[2] and I[3] recensions), for example, they appear as border people whose principal characteristic is a delight in things unnatural.[5] The Middle English *Kyng Alisaunder* describes, in some 1,200 octosyllabic lines, how the Greek hero, having defeated Darius, is introduced to the marvelous flora, fauna, and humans of India. He learns about the twenty-two realms "from Gog . . . to Magog" that include a "contreye" named Taracun whose inhabitants think human flesh "swete and good"; this place later metamorphoses into Taracuncte, chief city of Magogas, where people have a similar diet and practice every form of (heterosexual) incest (5949–6159, esp. 5952–71, 6095–6129).[6] Gog and Magog are by no means fixtures of the Alexander legend, however. The story received its most sophisticated—and in terms of literary history, its most influential—treatment by Walter of Châtillon, whose *Alexandreis* (circa 1180) survives in some two hundred manuscripts and was well known to

Dante, Chaucer, and other figures in the medieval canon. But Walter, like his prominent readers, makes no mention of Gog or Magog.

Outside the Alexander legend, "Gog/Magog" appears in medieval fiction only rarely, and usually to designate some threat within Christian Europe. The names are fused, for example, in Geomagog, or Goemagog, the giant who opposes Brutus and his fellow Trojans in the founding myth of Britain that originates in the mid-1100s with Geoffrey of Monmouth, in his *Historia regum Britanniae* (1.40), and gets retold soon thereafter in works based on it, the *Brut* of both Wace (s.1063–1168) and Laȝamon (902–66). In all three works, Geomagog leads a band of twenty giants whose monstrosity is an essential component of Brutus's land claim. Nonhumans have no right to possess territory, but nevertheless the Trojans can legitimize an appropriation of Britain only after their captain, Corineus, throws Geomagog off a cliff. The immigrants typically rename everything they see, and so they call this site Gog's Leap, which Laȝamon is careful to point out has become its permanent name in every language. In the late medieval lowbrow comic work *Rauf Coilyear*, Magog is a Saracen enemy riding a camel through northern France, whom Rauf, not one of Europe's brighter heroes, cannot distinguish from the Christian Roland (lines 804–972). This Magog owes very little to the frightening figure of Scripture: he eagerly agrees to "forsaik Mahoun and tak me to [Christ's] micht" (line 938) and even gives his orthodox opponents a lesson in proper conversion by rejecting what amounts to a bribe from Roland. A more sinister Magog ("Mergot") is figured along with Muhammad as one of several idols to which pagan sailors appeal in a storm on the Mediterranean in the *Pearl*-poet's telling of the Jonah story (*Patience*, 167).[7]

Cartographical and geographical texts that attempt to account for "Gog/Magog" do so within an Asian context, yet hardly in any regular or consistent way. In her study of Christopher Columbus's intellectual heritage, Valerie I. J. Flint maintains that "*Mappa mundi* makers loved to depict Gog and Magog and distributed them quite liberally over the globe; but by the later Middle Ages they seem firmly to be placed in Asia, and to the far east of that continent" (*Imaginative Landscape*, 13 n. 21). Flint bases her claim in part on Anderson's overview of medieval maps, but both scholars may mislead readers in several ways.[8] We simply cannot know that cartographers mentioned, or represented, "Gog/Magog" out of enthusiasm or habit, nor is there evidence that they ever wittingly located one or the other outside northern Asia. Since *mappae mundi* lack coordinates and were not drawn to scale, it is unwise to rely heavily on a toponym's "movement" from one map to another.[9] Finally, we must be wary of the temptation to compile an assortment of references to "Gog/Magog," from sources distant in time and space, based on the assumption that the presence of one informational item (such as enclosure, opposition to Alexander, or cannibalism) in one legend necessarily testifies to that mapmaker's—or that map's reader's—participation in a tradition that incorporates all the variables, including moral opprobrium. For example, the appearance of "Gog gentes" on the so-called Jerome Map (circa 1150) has been cited as an early cartographical reference to the people of the eschaton, but the map appears with treatises by St. Jerome on the Book of Genesis and Old Testament topography, and these "people" may simply represent the descendants of Japheth's son Magog mentioned in Genesis 10.2.[10] The very emptiness of "Gog/Magog" as a signifier rendered it malleable, adaptable to widely discrepant interpretations.[11]

Given the number of medieval *mappae mundi* that survive—David Woodward has counted 1,100 (286)—Gog or Magog appears in map legends with remarkable *infrequency*.[12] Once again, medieval maps must be considered in their contexts. Since many of the exemplars Woodward counts accompany classical works or Christian books that make no mention of Gog or Magog—texts by Sallust (*De bello Jugurthina*), Pomponius Mela (*De chorographia*), Lucan (*Pharsalia*), Macrobius (*In somnium Scipionis expositio*), Isidore (*Etymologiarum*), Bede (*De natura rerum*)—the general absence of an apocalyptic people should not be surprising.[13]

The content of an adjoining text may in fact explain a chart's silence. In Bibliothèque Nationale MS lat. 5510, the late-thirteenth-century map that follows William of Tripoli's *De statu Saracenorum* announces, "Here are the names of all the peoples of Asia," but neither William's book nor the map's list of forty-five ethnic groups includes Gog or Magog.[14] Matthew Paris, who compiled his *Chronica majora* in part out of a belief that Antichrist would come in the year 1250, concludes that the Mongols, who invaded Russia and eastern Europe beginning in the 1230s, were ushering in the last days; his discovery that a river named Egog flowed in their homeland only strengthened this conviction. Matthew's cartography was not clearly influenced by his eschatology, however; the people confined by a semicircular sweep of mountains in the northeast corner of his three extant maps of the Crusader Kingdom are Jews whose escape Matthew describes as a future danger.[15] If we look for Gog and Magog, who play a key role in the prophecy of Revelation 20, on maps where we might expect to find them—those that accompany Beatus of Liébana's *Commentary on the Apocalypse*—we will, as Anna-Dorothee von den Brincken has pointed out, "seek in vain" ("Die Ebstorfer Weltkarte").

A map's intellectual roots obviously affect its content as well. Arabic maps from at least the twelfth century show Yâjûj and Mâjûj (Jadjoudj and Madjoudj) along the world's rim at the lower left (in the northeast, since Arabic maps generally place south at the top). These Islamic equivalents of Gog and Magog, as peoples or lands, appear into the late eighteenth century on maps that sometimes include miniatures of scenes from the *Iskandarnâmah*, which records the heroic exploits of Alexander (Schwartzberg, 394–96 and figs. 17.1, 17.4, plate 29). Thus, the presence of Gog and Magog on Western maps oriented in the Arabic fashion—including some jewels of fifteenth-century European cartography—may be evidence that European cartographers borrowed Islamic motifs but not necessarily that they understood the Qur'anic source.[16] Even a "cartographical tradition" may not be internally consistent: in a copy of Lambert of Saint-Omer's *Liber floridus* (circa 1120) produced in 1180 (Wolfenbüttel, Herzog August Bibliothek, Codex Guelf. 1 Gud. Lat.), one map that styles itself a "Globus Terre" (fols. 59v–60r) includes the simple legend "Gog et magog" below "mare caspium," whereas a "hemisphere map" (on fols. 69v–70r) contains a legend, in a roughly analogous location, noting Alexander's having "enclosed thirty-two [sic] kingdoms" but naming none of them (von den Brincken, *Fines Terrae* 153; plates 28, 29).

The notion that medieval cartographers "loved to depict Gog and Magog" may derive some of its misleading fervor from the witness of famous *mappae mundi*, where text and image sometimes combine with dramatic force. These maps evidently served a didactic purpose, given the presence on them of significant tropological emblems, including Adam and Eve fleeing Paradise, the Tower of Babel standing vacant, Christ rising from the tomb, and souls moving to bliss or damnation at the Last Judgment. The vertical diameter of *mappae mundi* may delineate the course of human history from a Christian perspective, which, according to Augustine and Orosius, proceeded from east to west. While such historiography made the northern extremes, where "Gog/Magog" is found, into sinister territory, portrayal of the entity was by no means uniform or univalent.

The earliest appearance of "Gog/Magog" in European cartography dates from the tenth century, when the Anglo-Saxon ("Cotton") Map (British Library, MS Cotton Tiberius B.v, fol. 56v) locates "gog et magog" in a small compartment on the southern shore of a body of water probably representing the Caspian Sea. No pejorative value is conveyed by either the territorial confinement or the legend, however. The map's pictorial character is spare, with lines boxing in most "countries," and its verbal content is limited almost exclusively to simple toponyms. Approximately twenty castles mark principal towns, a dozen mountain chains appear in green, waterways (some reddish) offer vermiform contrast to the straight lines of human boundaries, and a lion nearly the size of Britain prowls the upper-left (northeast) corner of the earth, but no technical design elucidates the reference to Gog and Magog (Woodward, fig. 18.57).

On the Henry of Mainz Map of circa 1180 (Cambridge, Corpus Christi College, MS 66, p. 2; Woodward, fig. 18.59), a more ominous "Gog et magog," specifically called an "unclean people," inhabit a squarish promontory east of (above) the Caspian Sea, hemmed in by mountains on three sides and a crenellated wall to the south. Similarly, on the thirteenth-century Ebstorf Map, Gog and Magog are enclosed on the eastern shore of the Caspian, this time by two walls—a white battlement to the west and a red one to the south—with mountain barriers to the east and north that merge with the earth's rim. The artist of this cartographical behemoth—it measured ten feet on a side—had the luxury of space, and chose to display two naked humans, the one on the right with a notably beaked nose, munching on the amputated limbs of a smaller light-haired figure, apparently a child, who bleeds from all extremities; the body parts include three legs and one hand. The attending legend summarizes the terror: "Here Alexander enclosed the two unclean peoples Gog and Magog; Antichrist will control their lords. They devour human flesh and drink blood."[17]

The Henry of Mainz and Ebstorf maps give Gog and Magog characteristics that echo contemporary geographical works, although these are not much more informative, and their authors seem noncommittal. For example, Honorius Augustodunensis's *Imago mundi* (circa 1110)—a widely circulating compendium of geographical, astronomical, calendrical, and historical information about the world—reports that Gog and Magog "*are said* to have been imprisoned by Alexander" at "Mount Caspius" in Asia; they eat human flesh and raw animals. Hugh of St. Victor, in his *Descriptio mappe mundi* (1127/1128), places "*those people* Gog and Magog, about whom one reads in [John's] Apocalypse" on islands in the Northern Sea near the Amazons.[18]

Other map styles and traditions add little to what in any event is only a sketch. Nautical charts might offer an invaluable witness to "Gog/Magog" since they served the needs of merchants and sailors rather than historians and theologians, but they are almost by definition silent on the matter. Covering territory from the Atlantic to the Black Sea, they do not extend to the trans-Caspian region usually associated with Gog or Magog. The *Catalan Atlas*, a hybrid *mappa mundi*/portolano prepared on Mallorca by Abraham Cresques and in the library of France's King Charles V at his death in 1380, labels land at its northeast (upper right) corner "GOG I MAGOG" in alternating red and blue letters. Above it a legend reads: "The great lord and prince of Gog and of Magog. He will break forth during the time of Antichrist with many people." In the adjacent depiction, within a trapezoidal area surrounded by mountains, a king dressed in blue and holding a scepter rides eastward beneath a baldachin between two groups of men (nine behind him, some wearing peaked caps with brims, and at least five in front of him), each of which carries a banner displaying a black scorpion-like beast on a white field. Five trees, bearing red fruit or berries, stand along the northeast (topmost) perimeter of the territory; just outside it to the south (below) is a seated king, identified as "allexandri," and two naked figures, facing west, blowing horns.[19]

A legend outside this territory explains the elaborate depiction:

> The mountains of Caspis, within which Alexander saw trees so tall that their tops reach the clouds. And he would have died there if Satan [setanat] had not, by means of his strategem, assisted him. And by means of his strategem, Alexander enclosed here the Tartars Gog and Magog [los tartres gog e magog], and he had made for them two images of metal. . . . Item: he enclosed here many diverse races of people who have no hesitation to eat all kinds of raw meat. And this is the race from which Antichrist will come, and their end will be fire, which will come down from heaven and consume them. (Grosjean, 88)

Abraham Cresques, in placing Gog and Magog at the earth's northeast extreme, may have been influenced by Islamic cartography, or he may even have been attempting, without complete success, to transfer material from a round *mappa mundi* to a rectangular format. In a nearby legend about Alexander the Great, he expresses doubt that the Macedonian hero had in fact ventured so far into Asia. Thus, the map that offers more data than any other about Gog and Magog calls its own representation of them into question.[20]

Several fifteenth-century European maps give "Gog/Magog" a different kind of hybrid quality. Oriented to the south in the fashion of Arabic maps, they follow Islamic tradition in locating the Qur'an's apocalyptic people of Yâjûj and Mâjûj in the northeast (Schwartzberg, 394–96). Accompanying legends recall the succinct statements on European *mappae mundi*. For example, on a map by Johann of Udine, a legend at the lower-left rim, in the vicinity of Asia Minor and "Caldea," notes that "Here Gog are [sic] secluded in the Caspian mountains" (Figure 3.1).[21] The excision of Magog suggests a cartographer's rather muddled understanding of his subject. A mid-fifteenth-century map in a manuscript once in the "Studienbibliothek" at Olmütz (now Olomouc, Czech Republic, MS g/9/155; it appears to be lost) includes Gog and Magog not once but twice, a redundancy the cartographer apparently never noticed. One legend, within a box placed outside the earth's rim, reads, "Here, between the Caspian mountains, Alexander enclosed Gog and Magog, an unclean people," while "Gog and Magog" also marks a small space between two boxed areas labeled "India" in the east-southeast (at the lower left; Figure 3.2).[22] The aid of another intellectual tradition, in other words, did not promote a more coherent picture of this phenomenon.

While "Gog/Magog" may cut a pictorially and textually lurid figure in a few geographical and cartographical texts produced between 1100 and 1500,

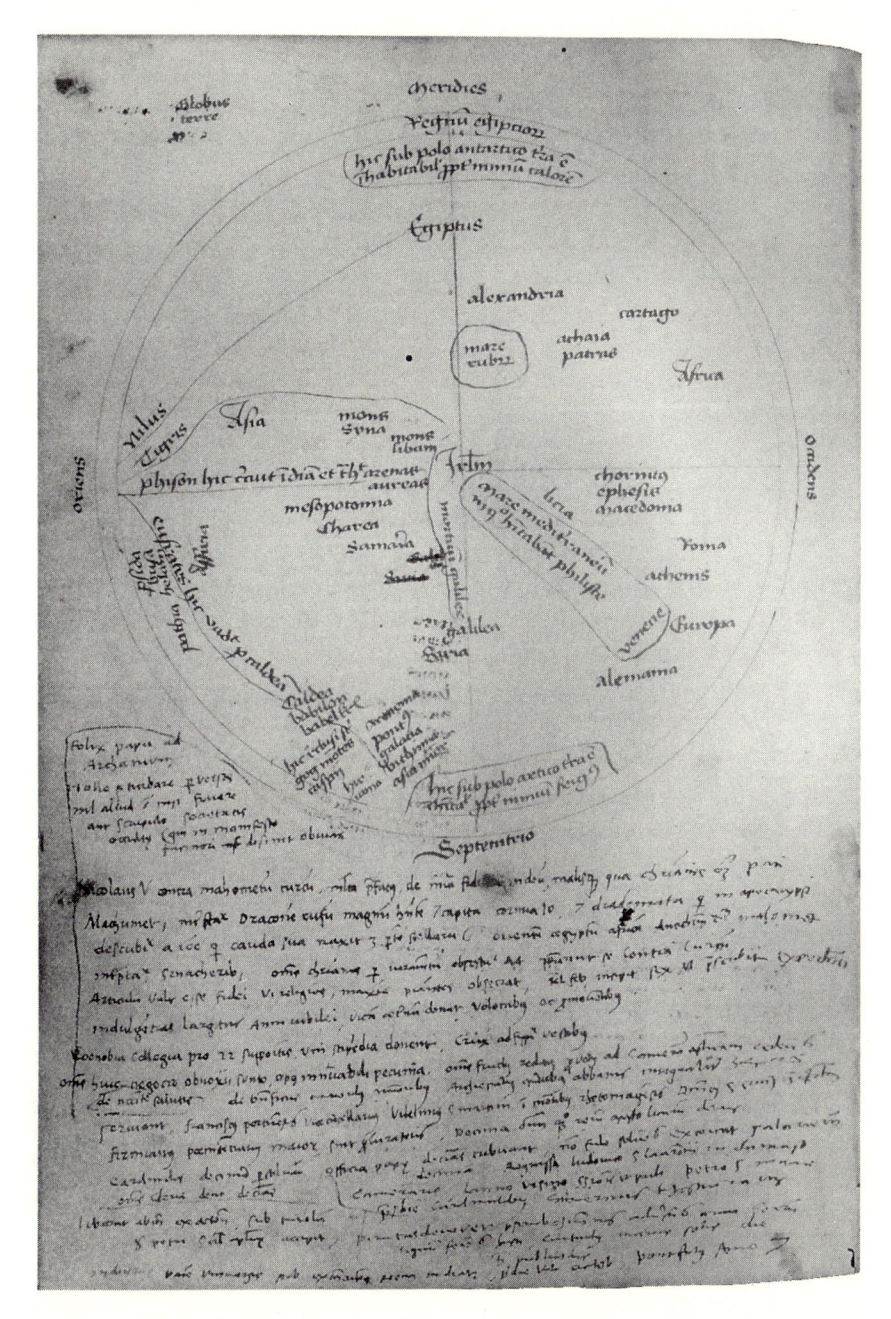

Figure 3.1. *Mappa mundi* by Johann of Udine (Johannes Utinensis), original circa 1344, this copy circa 1455. The map shows south at the top; excerpts from an anti-Muslim tract by Pope Calixtus II (1455–1458) have been added below. Stuttgart, Württembergische Landesbibliothek, MS Cod. theol. et phil. 2° 100, fol. 3v. By permission of the Württembergische Landesbibliothek.

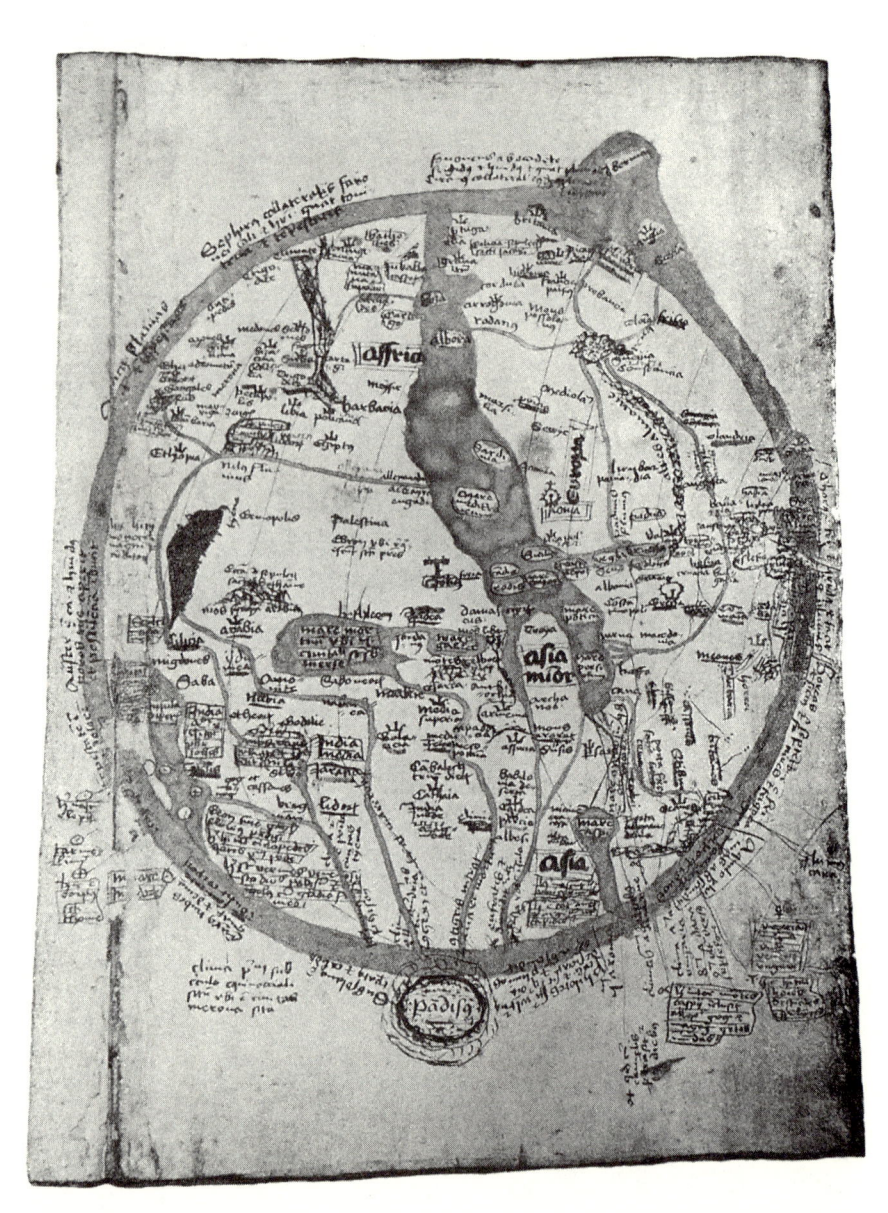

Figure 3.2. *Mappa mundi* (anonymous), circa 1450. Once Olmütz (Olomouc, Czech Republic), Studienbibliothek, MS g/9/155, lost after World War II. The map shows west at the top; the redundant legends for Gog and Magog may have resulted from the cartographer's re-orientation of an original with south or east at the top. Photo by the author from Anton Mayer, *Mittelalterliche Weltkarten aus Olmütz*, vol. 8 of *Kartographische Denkmäler der Sudetenländer* (Prague: K. André, 1932), plate 1. By permission of the Map Division, the New York Public Library, Astor, Lenox, and Tilden Foundations.

the frisson elicited should not misdirect us into considering this entity to be a consistent marker of some putative intellectual landscape. One complex of ethnic identifications, made by European writers beginning in the thirteenth century, does deserve some attention, however, because its formulation was rapid, its influence considerable, and its implications important. The Mongol invasions of Russia in the 1230s, with attacks as far west as Silesia during the next decade, elicited a terror in Europe that invited apocalyptic interpretation. Brother Julian, the Hungarian Dominican who reported the advance of Batu Khan in late 1237, appears to have been the first European to link the Mongols to Gog and Magog (Lerner, 10, 21–22, n. 26). It has already been noted that Matthew Paris made a similar connection a few years later.[23]

Given the sudden and violent appearance of the Mongols in Europe, this interpretation of history is not difficult to understand. Less obvious is the basis for the association, first made in the mid-1200s, between Mongols and Jews, setting up an anti-Semitic ethnography for "Gog/Magog." The deportation "into Assyria . . . by the river of Gozan" of the ten tribes of the kingdom of Israel had the canonical authority of 2 Kings 17.6 (repeated at 18.11), and their return was prophesied by Isaiah, Jeremiah, and Ezekiel.[24] Christian geographers as early as Orosius (418), associated captive Jews and Alexander the Great. The first person to identify a Jewish population specifically with Gog and Magog appears to be Christian of Stavelot (Stablo), also known as Christianus Druthmarus, in his *Expositio in Matthæum Evangelistam* (circa 865). In explaining one of the signs that Jesus indicated would immediately precede the end of the world—that "this gospel of the kingdom shall be preached in all the world for a witness unto all nations" (Matt. 24.14)—Christian argues that the prophecy has been fulfilled:

For we know of no people under heaven among whom Christians do not live. For even in Gog and in Magog, who are Hunnish people [Nam et in Gog et in Magog, quæ sunt gentes Hunnorum] and who are called Gazari [Khazars] after them, there is one people, which once was more powerful and is descended from those whom Alexander led away, and which is circumcised and observes all the Jewish practices [omnem Judaismum]. The Bulgari, who themselves are related to these people, are also being baptized today.[25] (PL 106: 1455–56)

Contrary to received scholarship, then, Peter Comestor (circa 1100–1178) is not the first European authority to construct a network of associations linking Alexander, confined Jews, and (by implication but *not* by name) Gog and Magog; his influence was far greater than Christian's, however, and his famous identification finds its way almost verbatim into Vincent of Beauvais's *Speculum historiale* (after 1254), although Vincent later refuted the claim, stating that Dominican missionaries to Georgia had found it baseless.[26] Jacques de Vitry, the bishop of Acre who was resident between 1216 and 1225 (at least), tacitly makes this connection. In the *Historia orientalis* he refers to several nations that are of "Jewish stock," among them those who "dwell by themselves in that part of the East where Alexander . . . is said to have shut them up below the Caspian Mountains, whence they shall be brought out in the time of Anti-christ, and led back" to Israel. Alexander, Jacques continues, also shut up "Gog and Magog, whose numbers are countless as the sands of the sea, because he loathed their abominable habits of eating human flesh and the raw flesh of unclean animals." In his next sentence he observes that "[o]thers of the Jews . . . are scattered all over the world," making implicit their identification with Gog and Magog (84, 86).

The erudite, observant Franciscan William of Rubruck is the only medieval European to my knowledge who actually claims to have seen Alexander's rampart; he does so in the context of bringing together these same three variables. Arriving at Derbent on around November 15, 1254, he observes "foundations of walls from one mountain to another," which Alexander erected to keep back "the barbarians, that is to say the nomads of the wilderness" (*Itinera*, 199–200; William of Rubruck, 116). William attributes the destruction of these walls to the Tartars and apparently thinks the people they have liberated are Semitic, because in his next sentence he notes that "There are *other* enclosures in which there *are* Jews, but I was unable to learn anything definite about them, however there are many Jews throughout all the cities of Persia" (*Itinera*, 319; William of Rubruck, 211, emphasis mine).[27] William shared the information he gathered on his trek to Karakorum and back with Roger Bacon, who urged the study of geography to prepare for the coming of Antichrist by anticipating where he and Gog and Magog might be found (Bacon, *Opus majus*, 1.322–23, 382–83; Bigalli, 32–33, 173 n. 21).

Other thirteenth-century Europeans attempted to explain the baffling, sudden appearance of the Mongols, a race unrecorded in the Bible, by making them Jewish. Reporting around 1291 on a decade of travels in Asia, the Dominican Ricold of Monte Croce referred to "the opinion of many" (they need not necessarily have been Europeans) in identifying the "Tartari" with the "Ten Tribes of Israel, who were taken captive." Ricold advances a linguistic argument: the Mongol language and script are similar to "Chaldean" (Arabic), which in turn resembles Hebrew. He also cites evidence that would seem to disprove the thesis—Mongols know nothing of the Law of Moses or the escape from Egypt, they have no Levitic priesthood, and they do not "look Jewish"—and technically he leaves the issue open ("Solucionem relinquo"). A medieval audience would have found especially persuasive one etymology

Ricold advances: the people who call themselves "Mogoli" employ a corrupt version of an original "Magogoli," proof that they are descended from Gog and Magog, a race that Pseudo-Methodius had long since identified with captive Jews (Laurent, 118–19 [10.35–49]; also Monneret de Villard, 54–56).[28] Ricold's contemporary Raymond Lull considered it equally possible—and worrisome—that the Mongols would convert to Judaism as to Islam, both religions, in his estimation, actively proselytizing among this "[i]nnumerable ... generation" (Thorndike, 126; Emmerson, 55–56).

By 1300, written sources—almost exclusively within German-speaking Europe—describe Jews of central Asia as "Rubei Iudei" [Red Jews]. Scholars have speculated that the name has its origin in Jewish physical appearance or was derived from Reuben, one of the two-and-one-half tribes that settled *east* of the Jordan, according to Numbers 32. Given the menacing tone with which the word is sometimes employed, it is more probably an anti-Semitic slur based on a secondary meaning of the Middle High German *rôt* ("deceitful" or "cunning").[29] Late medieval maps—from 1400 and later—also identify Gog and Magog with Jews; here again the examples are few, the texts brief, and the informational value to a reader difficult to measure. If "Roten Juden" did function as a racial epithet, however, its usage would bring to these cartographical references an unambiguous moral opprobrium. In any event, it is an early, however tenuous, link between "Gog/Magog" and a population group resident in Europe rather than a frightening, remote menace.[30]

So far, this discussion has proceeded as if the medieval authorities who thought about Gog and Magog assumed them to be geographically or ethnically specific. Such an assumption, which lies at the heart of most investigations of the issue—including Anderson's—ignores the fact that interpretations of Ezekiel 38–39 and Revelation 20 have pitted literalists against allegorists since the late fourth century. It was then that Ambrose's equation of Goths and Gog was challenged openly (it seems) by Jerome (*Hebraicae Quaestiones in Libro Geneseos*, 10.2 [p. 11]) and with thundering silence by St. Augustine, who undertakes, in his *City of God*, to explain how a Christian God could have permitted the sack of Rome in 410, yet who refuses to treat prophecy as a *roman à clef*. Indeed, Augustine denies that "Gog and Magog" have any national or ethnic integrity, calling them the citizenry of Satan, ubiquitous in the world and threatening the Church everywhere; his formulation makes "Gog/Magog" a concealed element within every society, one that will in the fullness of time "break forth ... to open hatred."[31] This interpretation allowed medieval Christians to locate the agent of Satan within the European community rather than anticipate an invasion from the horizon. Although it was endorsed by other authorities and had sinister repercussions, Augustine's reading of Gog and Magog warrants only a footnote in Andrew Runni Anderson's study (10 n. 1).

Though allegorical, Augustine's interpretation made its way occasionally into medieval cartography, most remarkably onto Fra Mauro's 1459 *mappa mundi* (Venice, Biblioteca Marciana). Measuring six feet on a side and crammed with designs and notations, it is the copy of a lost original commissioned by the king of Portugal, whose nation then stood at the forefront of European exploration. Near the lower-left rim of the map, which is oriented to the south, is a place for those who were "imprisoned by Alexander in this land of Hung and Mongul," and said to be "the people we call Gog and Magog." Fra Mauro himself disputes this identification ("I do not believe this opinion"), arguing in a second legend that *any* geographical location of "Gog/Magog" is wrongheaded:

Some writers claim that those people who were enclosed by Alexander of Macedon [Alexandro Macedo] live beyond the foothills of the Caspian Mountains [radice del monte caspio], but this is most obviously an error, for a great diversity of nations live there.... And some say that these people, called Ung and Mongul, but whom we call Gog and Magog [vng e mongul, i qual el uulgo dice gog e magog], are those whom the devil will use at the time of the Antichrist, but the certainty of this error is obvious to anyone who heeds the Scriptures. And so I hold to the authority of St. Augustine, who in his *De civitate Dei* disputes the opinion of those who hold that Gog and Magog are a particular race of people who give favor to Antichrist; with this idea Nicolaus of Lyra agrees, offering an interpretation based on the original Hebrew.[32]

Nicolaus of Lyra (circa 1270–1349), a Franciscan from Normandy, wrote a biblical commentary—in the form of glosses on individual verses—that circulated in hundreds of manuscripts. His interpretation of Gog and Magog at Revelation 20.8 shows him to have been greatly influenced by Augustine.[33]

Augustine's exegetical approach, rejecting an identification of "Gog/Magog" with any literal ethnic group, was not immune from intolerant applications. In identifying the enemy as "one of us," he furnished a paradigm that had nefarious implications and allowed either hermeneutical system—literal or allegorical—to make "Gog/Magog" a Jewish problem. The papal delegate at the Council of Breslau (Wrocław) in 1267 suggests how: "Since the Poles are a new plantation of the soil of Christendom, we must continually be on our guard lest the Christian population here . . . succumb to the influence of the counterfeit faith and the evil habits of the Jews living in their midst" (quoted from Richards, 97).

The most direct claim I know of that European Jews were complicit in a plot against Christians is found in *The Book of John Mandeville* (circa 1360), a text whose genial treatment of Muslims, Hindus, and animists is offset by one astonishing anecdote.³⁴ It begins by identifying Gog and Magog with the Ten Lost Tribes of Israel, which we have seen literalists in western Europe already doing in the twelfth century. In the mountains of the Caspian region, *The Book*'s author claims, "are enclosed the Iewes of the ten tribes [ligniees] whom one calls Goth and Magoth"; their incarceration was effected by Alexander, who "chased" them into a natural trap, and then, though he himself was a pagan, successfully prayed that God would miraculously cause the mountains to close. Alexander thus resembles one of *The Book*'s Brahmans, who are ignorant of Christian revelation but nevertheless demonstrate moral virtue and so win divine favor. Jews, on the other hand, are regularly excluded from this celestial Jerusalem with greater latitude. Ever one to borrow a story and then to dilate upon it, the *Mandeville*-author considers several angles of his story that are found in his known sources. He explains why the Jews could not escape by sailing across the Caspian, then lists several handicaps—their feudal obligations to the Amazon queen, rugged terrain, desert vipers—that ensure their incarceration. Their chief obstacle, however, is linguistic. Three times *The Book*'s author mentions that the people of Gog and Magog are entrapped by the Hebrew language itself. He observes first that "they know no language but their own language, and thus they cannot get out." This limitation turns out to be less absolute than it first seemed, for escape, he implies, *is* possible, although it inevitably comes to nothing: "And although some [Jews] have gotten out a few times, they know no language except Hebrew, and they cannot speak to any people." Finally, the problem is not merely resolved but becomes integral to the fundamental evil of these people. Following a fox, the Jews will burrow out from under the Gates of Alexander "in the time of Antichrist, and . . . will effect a great slaughter of the Christians." In this cataclysm they will be aided by a fifth column of supporters, with whom they share a language:

For this reason *all the Jews* who live in all lands always learn to speak Hebrew in the hope that, when those [Jews] of the mountains of Caspie get out, the *other Jews* will be able to speak to them and to lead them into Christendom to destroy Christians. For the *other Jews* say that they know well by their prophecies that those [Jews] of the Caspie will get out and spread throughout the world, and that Christians will then be in as much—and more—subjection to them as they have been in subjection to Christians.³⁵ (*Buke*, 132, emphasis mine)

With uncanny subtlety, the *Mandeville*-author has managed to turn "les Iuys" of central Asia into "other Jews" of Flanders, the Rhineland, Bohemia, and Iberia: these constitute the real danger of Gog and Magog. What they "say that they know well," even if it represents prophecy and fair play (for example, that they will someday acquire the power hitherto exercised by domineering Christians), is by definition suspect since the voices that publicly speak a European vernacular whisper privately in Hebrew code. This bizarre accusation, moreover, strongly suggests that the *Mandeville*-author, in a rare moment of true verbal independence, speaks here for himself.[36] While some of his sources and contemporaries sought answers to the literal meaning of "Gog/Magog" by looking for clues in what were for them arcane languages, "Mandeville" turns their linguistic games into an outing of conspirators. In a book directed at anyone who "gets great solace hearing [someone] speak of strange things"—presumably everyone, and not just Christian Europeans— this yoking of literal and allegorical exegesis of "Gog/Magog" is no stranger perhaps than the monstrous woman of Lango or the dog-heads of Natumeran, except, of course, that the audience for *this* story might indeed include Jews, who are its victims (*Buke*, 14).

By considering a scene of victimization on one other famous *mappa mundi*, we may see, in both image and text, a final example of how unstable, and potentially dangerous, the signifier "Gog/Magog" was in medieval Europe. The Hereford Map, a product of late-thirteenth-century England, includes one legend that names Gog and Magog specifically and has two others that mention or illustrate matters associated with them in other texts. In the Sea-Ocean that encircles the map's world, at the northern extreme of the earth and immediately offshore from the source of the river that separates Asia from Europe, lies the "island of Terraconta, which the Turks [turchi] inhabit, of the lineage of Gog and Magog [gog et magog], a barbarous and filthy people who eat the flesh of children [iuvenum] and of miscarried fetuses." Some distance to the east of (above) this island, and immediately east of the foot-shaped Caspian Sea, is a promontory ringed by mountains on the three sides that abut water and by a wall with four towers on the landward side; the entire space is filled with text describing the unnamed inhabitants of this large prison as "truculent" cannibals, cursed offspring of Cain who were confined by Alexander the Great. In open territory between and to the south (right) of these repellent regions are two knife-wielding humans who, recalling a scene on the Ebstorf Map, gnaw on the severed limbs of a nearby victim. The adjacent legend names them "Essedones of Scythia [essedones de scithia]," a race that earlier writers, including Jacques de Vitry, associated with the Ten Lost Tribes of Israel and with Gog and Magog. Their behavior is allegedly pious— they eat the bodies of deceased relatives rather than let them suffer the ignominy of decay—but the general vision of violence, and the proximity of the two other monstrous people, leaves them as if on shifting sand.[37] Clothing was a badge of personal identity long before Chaucer made it one of three things he promises "to tellen" about his pilgrims; the peaked cap of the Essedone on the left, frequently a marker of the European Jew, brings to this English image of remote dangers a racist immediacy.[38]

By presenting in so diffuse a way the names, behaviors, and features that we have seen ascribed to the matter of "Gog/Magog" in a variety of texts, the Hereford Map offers a warning about the limitations of cartographical information. Like a modern dictionary, a map may simply record information without necessarily judging it. Many surviving *mappa mundi* legends that mention Gog and/or Magog are not just morally ambiguous: they are historiographically naive—that is, we do not (and cannot) know how precisely a cartographer "conceived" his toponym or a reader/viewer "received" it. Richard of Haldingham gets "Gog/Magog" on the map in such a way that he may not only reflect contemporaneous anxieties about child-killing invaders from Asia but also accommodate future fears: one can imagine an audience in 1453 listening to a priest read out the legend on the "turchi" of Terraconta.

The scribes and printers who copied the text of Johannes Witte de Hese's *Itinerarius*, with which this discussion began, were also uncertain about how to present "Gog/Magog"; they seem to be as confused about the issue as other medieval people who chanced to think about it. Of the surviving texts—eight manuscripts and eleven early printed editions (seven of them incunables)—most relate the entire anecdote of Witte's pause in Amosona in the subjunctive voice of indirect speech, leaving the reader ultimately responsible to judge the accuracy of the anonymous testimony (three manuscripts and two printed editions more definitively employ the indicative voice). All the printed editions delete the reference to the local queen, and one printed edition uses a singular verb with the subject "gog et magog."[39] If these variants suggest that Gog and Magog were less present than dreamt of in medieval geography and cartography, they also leave them—or it, or this territory—so shapeless that individuals over many centuries could find here a name for perceived evil that would grant divine sanction to monstrous attitudes.

Notes

1. See my *Johannes Witte de Hese's "Itinerarius": An Extension of the Medieval Pilgrim's Horizon* (Cambridge, Mass.: Medieval Academy of America, forthcoming). Quotations from medieval sources are given in English in the body of this essay; I cite the original only when the text has not been published or the linguistic evidence relates specifically to my argument. All translations, unless otherwise noted, are mine. Because writers do not employ a consistent nomenclature for Gog and/or Magog, I will use the name(s) as given in each source; in speaking generally about this "entity," I will refer to "Gog/Magog."

2. The letting loose and destruction of Gog and Magog "when the true promise nears its fulfilment" is foreseen in sura 21.97.

3. In his 1933 review, Barry disputed Anderson's claim that the Alexander/Gog and Magog opposition had Greek intellectual roots, arguing instead that "the apocalyptic conception of history, originated in Jewish circles, and, developed by Christians, gave rise to the legend . . . and kept it alive almost to our own time" (270).

4. An Oviedan cleric transformed Gog *in bono* in the *Crónica profética* (883), where Gog stands for Visigothic Spain, subdued by Muslim North Africans on account of its sinfulness but repentant, so that "the kingdom of the Goths will be restored by our prince [Alfonso III]." See Williams, who calls this a "freewheeling interpretation of Ezekiel 38–39" ("Purpose and Imagery," 230).

5. On the tenth-century *Historia*, see Cary; see also David J. A. Ross, esp. 34–35. Michael (esp. 133–34) warns against simplistic readings of the Alexander legend, but his focus is on the heroism of Alexander rather than the malevolence of Gog and Magog.

6. In this story (and its French source), the evil of Gog and Magog is compromised in two ways: first, the allure of these twenty-two realms distracts Alexander from his intended assault on western Europe, and thus Gog and Magog can be said to have saved the audience's *patria* from attack (5932–37); second, Alexander observes that if the people of Gog and Magog ever sample Western food and drink, their delight will cause them to kill all the civilized Europeans—and then eat them, an indication that English cooking cannot completely tame them (6140–45).

7. A thirteenth-century French verse fragment describes a knight's battle with the giant Gogulor to prevent him from marrying a young woman against her will; see Livingston.

8. Flint may have been led astray by Anderson's page headings, "Alexander's Gate Shifted to Northern Europe" (89) and "Alexander's Gate Shifted to Asia" (93–103), which anachronistically endorse twentieth-century geographical knowledge and taxonomy. Boorstin also reads cartographers' minds when he claims that "[l]ocating the people and the place of Gog and Magog became a favorite pastime of Christian geographers" (104).

9. Discussions that suggest a conscious "movement" of "Gog/Magog" on various maps do not apply the same principle of accuracy to other toponyms, such as the Red Sea, another "shifting" feature of Asian geography.

10. The Jerome Map, of Asia, is in London, British Library, Add. MS 10049, fol. 64r; reproduced in Woodward, fig. 18.1. A second "Jerome" map, on fol. 64v, focuses on Palestine but extends east of the Caspian Sea, where it locates unnamed ferocious people; detail reproduced in Woodward, fig. 18.31. Jerome mentions Gog and Magog in *Hebraicae Quaestiones in Libro Geneseos*, 10.2 (p.11).

11. For map legends that specifically mention Gog and Magog, see von den Brincken, *Fines Terrae* 26, 61–62, 70, 93, 115, 118, 119, 136, 146, 153, and 156. These few references do not, in my opinion, justify treating "Gog/Magog" as a stable "concept" (but see von den Brincken, 17, 20, 89, 167–68).

12. Von den Brincken's thoroughness (*Fines Terrae*) should call attention to their relative absence from maps.

13. Isidore names Magog, son of Japheth, as scion of the Scythians and Goths (9.2.27); in his discussion of Asian geography he makes "Gothia" a synonym for

Scythia (14.3.31). The fifteenth-century "Geneva Sallust" Map (Geneva, Bibliothèque Publique et Universitaire, MS lat. 54, fol. 34v) goes beyond the associated text's focus on Africa and assigns separate territorial compartments in Asia to Magog, Gog, and "enclosed Jews."

14. William's book is found on fols. 99r–117v, with the map on fol. 118r; Jacques de Vitry's *History of Jerusalem* follows on fols. 162v–198r (see below).

15. Matthew's map is, admittedly, sketchy and does not extend east of the Caspian. The legend on his Crusader Kingdom (also known as Palestine) map reads in part: "The enclosure of the Caspian mountains. Here dwell the Jews whom God locked up at the request of King Alexander, who will go forth on the eve of the Day of Judgment and will massacre all manner of peoples." In his *Historia Anglorum*, Matthew states that Alexander enclosed "Gog and Magot" in northeast Asia; see Lewis, 348–49, 507 nn. 63, 65; also 9, 103, 138.

16. Among these are the Walsperger, Borgia, Zeitz, and Fra Mauro maps (see below). Pseudo-Methodius's *Revelations* (*De consummatione saeculi*), written in Greek circa 675 and translated into Latin by circa 700, underlies the Alexander/Gog and Magog connection in both the Qur'an and the Alexander legend.

17. "Hic inclusit alexander duas gentes immundas gog et magog, quas comites habebit antichristus. Hii humanis carnibus vescuntur et sanguinem bibunt." The map was destroyed in 1943, but old photographs survive. A second reference to Gog and Magog, as Turks, appears to the west (below), in an unillustrated legend on an island in the surrounding Sea-Ocean; see Arentzen, 161–62, 180–82. The beaked nose of one of the cannibals is reminiscent of medieval caricatures of Jews; see Blumenkranz, *Juden und Judentum* 27, 48, and plates 21, 22, 56.

18. "Gog et Magog, gentes ferocissime a magno Alexandro incluse *feruntur*, que humanis carnibus vel crudis bestiis vescuntur" (Flint, "Honorius Augustodunensis," 53 [emphasis mine]). According to Hugh, the Amazons reside in "Albania inferior," not far from "gentes ille Gog et Magog" (Dalché, 144–45 [lines 310–16], 170–71 n. 40). On a related twelfth-century map from northern France, now Munich, Bayerische Staatsbibliothek, Clm. 10058, fol. 154v, two protuberances on a rectangular surface in the northern ocean bear the names "gog" and "magog"; see Dalché, 82.

19. For a facsimile, with transcriptions and German translation, see Grosjean, 92. The royal banner is very similar to one used during the 1300s by portolan chart makers to designate Mongol harbor towns.

20. In designing the *Catalan Atlas*, Cresques used Marco Polo's *Divisament dou monde* (circa 1298), but not here. Only seven days' journey from Cathay (and not in northern Asia), Marco finds "the place which we call in our language Gog and Magog [Gogo et Magogo]; the natives call it Ung and Mungul. . . . [I]n Ung lived the Gog, in Mungul the Tartars" (Latham, trans., 106; Benedetto, ed., 61).

21. "[H]ic reclusi sunt [s't] gog montes caspij"; the abbreviation might also be expanded with a more cautious subjunctive "sint." Johann of Udine prepared the original map around 1344; one fourteenth- and three fifteenth-century copies are known, the largest (shown here) dated circa 1455.

22. The first legend reads: "Hic inter montes caspÿ inclusit allexander gog et magog gentes immundas"; the second, "gog et magog." I am indebted to Šárka Daňková and to Dr. Pumprla, of the Státní Vědecká Knihovna of Olomouc, for invaluable assistance in trying to locate this map. See Mayer.

23. See Guzman, 31–54, esp. his notes, 54–68, for a review of scholarship.

24. Ezekiel's vision of the gathered "dry bones" of all Israel (37.1–14) immediately precedes his furious condemnation of Gog.

25. *Patrologia Latina*, cited hereafter as PL, followed by volume and column numbers. Christian's reference to Gog and Magog follows his interpretation of the verse "And then shall many be offended" (Matt. 24.10) as a reference to Jews "who will become enraged when they come to see everyone believe in Christ, for it is an offense to the Jews to hear of God incarnate" (see Chekin).

26. See *Historia scholastica*, PL 198: 1498 (in Peter's commentary on the Book of Esther); and Andrew Runni Anderson, 65. Vincent's borrowing from Peter and his retraction are at 4.43 (p. 129b) and 29.89 (p. 1215b).

27. William mentions Alexander's gate on his eastward journey (*Itinera*, 199–200; William Rubruck, 116). Eight years earlier, John of Plano Carpini reported that the Mongols had attempted to defeat "inhabitants hemmed in by the Caspian Mountains," but had been hindered by a cloud; this may be the only record of people trying to break *in* on "Gog/Magog" (*Itinera*, 61–62; John of Plano Carpini, 24).

28. In 1348, a German traveler in Asia maintained that the Mongol khan once "ruled all the places in India that the Romans held, . . . and ruled even the [territory] within the mountains where Alexander enclosed the Jews; and they are carefully guarded so that they do not escape" (Röhricht and Meisner, 58).

29. On Andrew Runni Anderson's view that red hair is a reliable marker of Jewish identity, see 68, 72–74. On the Middle High German adjective *rôt*, see *Matthias Lexers Mittelhochdeutsches Taschenwörterbuch*, 36th ed. (Stuttgart: Hirzel, 1981), 171. This essay was written before the appearance of Gow, who argues that the portrayal of "Red Jews" represented the "most virulent form of antisemitic apocalypticism, in which other-worldly dread and this-worldly loathing combine to form a potent and toxic cocktail" (3). He shows "Red Jews" to be an anti-Semitic designation that began in the thirteenth century (67–69, 185, 189–293), though he adds that some cartographers viewed the "Red Jews," as well as Gog and Magog, with "a sceptical attitude" (170). Witte de Hese locates "Red Jews" in "the land of the Urchaldees," but they are neither confined nor menacing.

30. Munich, Bayerische Staatsbibliothek, Clm. 14583 contains cosmographical tables and what appear to be map legends (but not an actual map) locating Red Jews near the "hirsen mer" (fol. 225r), as well as near the Caspian (fol. 268v); see Durand, 182, 197, and plate 10, where "Roten Juden Lant" is in "Gegonageg, in the enclosed land." A map by Andrea Bianco (fl. 1436–1451) obscurely refers to "Gog Magog of the tribes of the Jews, which Alexander once closed up in [behind?] boulders"; the legend spills over from land ("Alisandro. Gog Magog. de tribus iudeoron") to the adjacent rim of Sea-Ocean ("chest Alasander gie ne roccon ecartaira"). The Walsperger Map (1448) (Rome, Biblioteca Apostolica Vaticana, MS Pal. lat. 1362b), also identifies Gog and Magog with "the land of the Red Jews, enclosed within the Caspian mountains" ("gog et magog. terra rufforum iudeorum conclusorum inter montes caspios"). The Borgia Map (1452) makes Gog a province in which enclosed Jews are found ("provincia Gog, in qua fuerunt Judei inclusi"); Magog is mentioned separately as a single word. The Zeitz Map (circa 1470) (Zeitz, Stiftsbibliothek, MS Lat. Hist., fol. 497), treats "Gog and Magog" as the *territory* within which Jews are enclosed ("Gog et magog. Judei ruffi hic sunt inclusi").

"Gog/Magog" seldom appears in the Ptolemaic tradition, one exception being the Johan Ruysch *mappa mundi*, printed 1508, which shows "Ivdei inclvsi," hemmed in by a semicircle of mountains and a seashore, in northeastern Asia adjacent to Greenland and at a longitude nearly coincident with the edge of a scroll that functions as the west coast of South America ("Terra Sancte Crvcis"); below the "enclosed Jews" are large labels for the separate territories of Gog and Magog. "De Locis ac Mirabilibus Mundi," which appears as an appendix in Johann Reger's edition of Ptolemy (Ulm, 1486), mentions the land of "gothia," named after Japheth's son "magoth," where the people eat human flesh and drink blood (sig. A3rb). Hanns Rüst's woodcut world map, printed circa 1480, includes the legend "Caspian mountain. Gog Magog enclosed" [berg caspÿ. verschlossen gog magog]; see Tony Campbell, *Earliest Printed Maps*, 79–84. The territory "Gog" appears in European cartography as late as Rumold Mercator's polar map of 1595 and Matthäus Merian's world map of 1638.

31. Augustine's argument begins: "these nations which [John] names Gog and Magog are not to be understood of some barbarous nations in some part of the world, whether the Getæ and Massagetæ, as some conclude from the initial letters, or some other foreign nations not under the Roman government." His subsequent etymology—"The meaning of these names we find to be, Gog, 'a roof,' and Magog, 'from a roof'"—becomes a marker of Augustinian influence in medieval exegesis (*The City of God*, [20.11], 729, 730).

32. For a facsimile and the text, see Leporace, 61, 56 (tables XXXVIII, 52 and XXXIII, 77). Fra Mauro seems familiar with Marco Polo.

33. In his gloss on the verse "And fire shall descend from God [*sic*]" (Rev. 20.9), Nicolaus writes: "It seems that John is not speaking here of the Tartars, as some would claim, for the Tartars did not find the city of Jerusalem inhabited by Christians, nor did fire from heaven descend on them to devour their army" (sig. 69.1ra). He suggests that Muslims are linked to the persecutions of the last days, but additional glosses by Paul, bishop of Burgos (1441), argue that Muslims permit Christians to live and worship in their territory and thus cannot be the people of Antichrist (Gog and Magog are not specifically named); see *Additiones ad postillam* (in *Postillae perpetuae*), sig. t6vb.

34. Translations (my own) are from the best version of the French original, *The Buke of John Maundeuill* 131 (ed. Warner). Among his many anti-Semitic comments, the author's accusation of Jews as poisoners is most odd since he claims to know about one such deed from a deathbed confession, a scene at which it is difficult to imagine either a Jew or a knight and one that suggests clerical authorship (94). Such claims are especially pernicious given the swift, polylingual circulation of the text in manuscript and early printings; see Higgins, *Writing East*, 6, 8, 20–24.

35. See DiMarco, esp. 69–71, 78–79.

36. This passage may also reflect Qur'anic influence: according to sura 18, the people walled up by Alexander "barely understand a word."

37. For transcriptions of these legends, see Bevan and Phillott, 58–59, 50–51, 61.

38. On the "pileum cornutum," see Blumenkranz, *Juden und Judentum*, 34–35 and plates 31–34; Trachtenberg, 44–46. Jews were banished from England in 1290, at about the time this map was made.

39. The variants are recorded at the end of my forthcoming edition (nn. 1180–81, 1184–85); two manuscripts have the spelling "goch et magoch."

II
PLACE AND THE POLITICS OF IDENTITY

4
Territorial Interpolations in the Old English Orosius

SEALY GILLES

THE RECENT SURGE OF INTEREST in the Age of Exploration and in the impact of European incursions on native peoples has led to renewed work on early maps and geographical treatises. Conferences on subjects such as "Imagining New Worlds: Factual and Figural Discovery during the Middle Ages" and "The Expansion of Europe: 1250–1492,"[1] and books such as *The Witness and the Other World* by Mary Campbell and *Discovering New Worlds*, edited by Scott Westrem, have encouraged us to look to the Middle Ages for the roots both of European expansionism and European treatment of indigenous peoples. Medieval histories and geographies can, however, provide us with more than an understanding of subsequent cultural and political phenomena. Like the diaries and travelogues of the Renaissance, medieval geographies, and literary and historical texts that use geography, chart their own space even as they record and imagine the territory of others. In these texts we see images of indigenous selves as well as those defined as alien. In the way that they fix their people in space, geographers tell us something about who they are, how they see themselves, and what place they occupy in the world. By limning the territory of others, both contiguous to native folk and on the edges of the knowable world, geographers tell us whom they fear and what they desire.

A similar situating of selves and others happens in historical texts. The chronicles of the Middle Ages give us the genealogies, the defining events, and the political alliances of their people. They define time as local, unique, and specific. They identify enemies, strangers, and ancestors. When geography is coupled with history, the producers of the amalgam become anchored, or anchor themselves, in time as well as in space.

The British Library's manuscript Cotton Tiberius Bi, from the middle of the eleventh century, presents us with just such a temporal and spatial matrix. The first 111 folios consist of a translation of Orosius's *History against the Pagans*, which includes a detailed world geography; folios 112–164 begin with a calendar of holy days and a collection of gnomic sayings, followed by a version of the *Anglo-Saxon Chronicle*.[2] It is the first, geographical section that I will focus on here. In this opening book, the codex commits itself not only to a rendition of geographical and historical facts but also to an exploration of the margins, spatial and temporal, of the society that produced it. By juxtaposing global and local terrain, human and cosmic time, in a dizzying, and very medieval, attempt to encompass the known world and to locate its producers spatially and temporally, it creates a multidimensional record of Anglo-Saxon culture, seen from an eleventh-century West Saxon point of view. Unlike earlier historical texts, this compilation does not translate the national past into a larger eschatological scheme; moreover, unlike many travel itineraries, it does not exoticize or demonize its others. Lacking an explicit ideological program, it is curiously awkward in its moves to incorporate and couple unlike materials, and yet that very awkwardness encourages us to look more closely at the process through which one society textualizes its own past and the past of others, its own mores and the ways of others, its own territory and the lands of others.

Ambitious attempts to catalog human knowledge or encompass human history are a characteristic feature of late classical and early medieval literary productions. Unlike the work of great encyclopedists such as Isidore of Seville and Vincent of Beauvais, the Cotton codex is not the work of one man or even of one workshop. It is instead a collection of texts drawn from three centuries, the ninth, tenth and eleventh, and based in two linguistically distinct cultures, the Anglo-Saxon and the Latin. Our reading of the codex must therefore be complicated not only by the mix of genres but also by the diversity of (anonymous) authorship and provenance, as well as by questions of compilation. A brief summary of the manuscript's contents will illustrate its heterogeneity: Cotton Tiberius Bi begins with a ninth-century Old English translation and adaptation of the fifth-century Orosius's world geography and history, into which are inserted two purportedly eyewitness travelogues, also from the ninth century;[3] this history is followed by a calendar of church festivals and saints' days (known inaccurately as the *Menologium*), a collection of maxims (*Maxims II*), and the "C" version of the *Anglo-Saxon Chronicle*. Although these last three works are in a mid-eleventh-century hand (Plummer, xxx), the composition of the *Menologium* and of *Maxims II* has been placed in the tenth century (Dobbie in *Anglo-Saxon Minor Poems*, lxvii). The *Chronicle* concludes with a brief, interrupted account of the Battle at Stamford Bridge, in a twelfth-century hand.

Although each of the manuscript's pieces has been thoroughly studied, the collection is seldom treated as a whole, and in fact there is substantial codicological evidence that the *Chronicle* grouping (which includes *Menologium* and *Maxims II*) and the translation of Orosius were bound together some time after their inscription and original gathering. Nevertheless, this essay, although necessarily limited in scope, treats the early folios of Cotton Tiberius Bi as part of an aggregate. At some point, perhaps in the twelfth century, the various pieces of Cotton Tiberius Bi were seen as belonging together, and I am suggesting that, far from being a careless collection of disparate texts, this *compilatio* can and should be read as a complex act of cultural definition, spanning several centuries and engaging numerous scribes, book-owners, translators, chroniclers, poets, and compilers. What may have begun as a simple and dutiful translation of Orosius's popular apologetic becomes the initial chapter in a complex inscription of a culture, the lineaments of which shift and reconfigure themselves as materials are gathered, translated, interspersed, and expanded. This essay focuses on the very beginning of that inscription because it is here, in the rewriting of Orosius's geographical book, that the canonical text is reshaped to incorporate northern tribes and territories, lands and peoples neglected or censured by Orosius but of compelling interest to the Anglo-Saxons, a people whose Germanic heritage was crucial to their most profound sense of themselves.

Translation, Text, and Territory

For an understanding of the production of the Old English Orosius we must rely heavily upon the work of Janet Bately and Elizabeth Liggins. In consecutive issues of *Anglia*, Liggins and Bately effectively demolish claims that King Alfred authored the translation of Orosius's *History against the Pagans*, although the translator may well have been part of Alfred's circle of scholars and churchmen. Bately also points out that it is impossible to tell with any precision how closely the Old English follows the Latin version as we cannot identify the manuscript which served as the exemplar for the Anglo-Saxon translator ("Latin Manuscripts"). Nevertheless, there is no question that substantial changes have been made in Orosius's text and that through these changes Latin continental history is made to serve insular needs.

In her discussion of translation in the late Middle Ages, Rita Copeland argues that "translation dramatizes the most central problems of historical and textual mediation in the Middle Ages" and that it is "intrinsic to an understanding of textual production" because it contains within it both "reception and appropriation" ("Rhetoric and Vernacular Translation," 41–42). Even as the translator performs the rhetorical act of *inventio* by exploiting another text, he or she also interprets and paraphrases (52–53). Thus a supratext is created—a text which is part paraphrase, part gloss, part rhetorical analysis, and which sounds like a faithful translation even as it takes great liberty with its sources. The translator, in relationship to the source, is thus both disciple and adversary, student and appropriator; in contesting and expanding the source, he or she also shapes the vernacular culture and the vernacular text.[4] Although Copeland is speaking largely of later medieval texts, much of what she says is relevant to the Old English Orosius as well.

Although there is no translator's preface, no announcement of principles and procedures such as we find in many Middle English translations and adaptations, the translator of Orosius notes his distance from, and reminds his readers of his debt to, the original with frequent repetition of the phrase "Orosius cwæð" [Orosius said]. This introductory formula distinguishes the Old English version from the Latin and, even as it reassures us that we are hearing the substance of Orosius's history, it also admits the possibility that there are points at which the ninth-century translator is speaking, not the fifth-century Spanish priest. In many places, although not consistently, the translator serves his English audience well. For example, in a nod to the ancestors, he edits out the condemnation of Germanic tribes (7.35).[5] He provides explanations for references not readily accessible to Anglo-Saxon readers, so that the stories of Medea, Lucretia, and the rape of the Sabine women, merely alluded to in the Latin, are considerably expanded in the Old English (Bately, "Those Books," 58). The Anglo-Saxon heroic ethos is reflected in revisions which deemphasize the outcome of a battle in favor of the strategies and heroic behavior of its generals; thus, in the Old English, Caesar's mercifulness and Hannibal's tactical abilities are emphasized over their military win-loss records.[6] The translator also deflects the eschatological thrust of his source by not focusing on wickedness and its effects. He omits the first part of book 1 in which Orosius asserts that the history of the world and its calamities is the history of sin and the punishment of sin and that the human race is "ardentem malis . . . face cupiditatis incensum" (1.1.16) [burning with evils, set afire with the torch of greed (7)].

The Old English translator of Orosius does not engage in Alfredian musings on his own method, but, like Alfred, he appears to translate "hwilum word be worde, hwilum andgit of andgi[e]te" [sometimes word for word, sometimes sense for sense] (Alfred, 7.19–20, my translation), often, as we have seen, eliding, altering, or expanding the sense to serve his own cultural agenda. In the territorial interpolations discussed below he goes even further and incorporates material entirely alien to his original, material that is both temporally and geographically anomalous. The additions to book 1, a ninth-century geography of northern Europe and two exploration narratives, are the most drastic of the Anglo-Saxon translator's alterations. Here, geography and ethnography demarcate physical and cultural territories unavailable to the Latin historian. The amplifications ensure that the resulting text is not simply the popularization of a "Great Book." Rather, they can be seen as the beginnings of an attempt to appropriate a Pan-European history in the service of an emerging national culture.

The Political Geography of the Old English Interpolations

In his *History against the Pagans*, Orosius begins with a geographical survey in which he divides the world into the usual three continents: Asia, Europe, and Africa. This panoramic opening so impressed insular historians that it was imitated by Gildas (chap. 3), Bede (bk. 1, chap. 1), and Geoffrey of Monmouth (chap. 1, pt. 2), although they "translated" the introduction by placing an expanded description of Britain at its center. Such a territorial survey, after all, was well suited to an island people for whom geography so often determined history.[7] But Orosius's Anglo-Saxon translator takes a different approach to the problem of situating his audience vis-à-vis his material. Rather than beginning with a portrait of Britain itself, he expands the section of Orosius's second chapter in which the regions and rivers of northern Europe are briefly cataloged into a detailed account of the ninth-century tribes of northern Europe, tribes which Orosius only mentions in passing: "deinde Germania est ubi plurimam partem Suebi tenent: quorum omnium sunt gentes LIIII" (1.2.52) [then there is Germania where the Suebi possess the largest part. Among all these there are fifty-four peoples (13)].[8]

In addition, someone responsible for the Old English version, either our translator or a compiler,[9] has added two accounts of voyages into northern waters. The first is a Norseman's account of his voyage up the coast of Norway and around the Kola Peninsula into the White Sea. The second is an Englishman's description of a journey through the Baltic to Estonia and of the customs of the people found there. The former narrative, Ohthere's, is firmly placed in King Alfred's ninth-century court, and the second voyager bears an Anglo-Saxon name, Wulfstan; both, therefore, like the tribal geography, are at temporal odds with their fifth-century Latin host. This anachronism is reinforced by geographical and generic anomalies. Spatially and temporally specific, these interpolations narrate in the midst of catalogic description, and, in spite of the Pan-European scope of their Latin host, they insist on the local and the specific. Together, these disjunctions create an insistent and disruptive English context for reading, or hearing, global history, a context that foreshadows the chronicle found in the codex's second half.

The Englishing of Orosius begins in the adaptation of book 1's geographical survey. Bately maintains that the changes from Orosius are "so radical that it is possible to consider the whole section as rewritten to conform to the ninth-century situation as known to the author of [the Old English Orosius] or his immediate source" (*Old English Orosius*, lxvii). Of all the European territories, Spain and Italy alone are unaffected by the translator's revisions.

In the revisions, the translator does more than simply add geographical details. He changes the criteria that define a region; that is, his geography is tribal, or political, rather than physical. Lands are defined not so much by rivers, mountains, and towns as by the people who inhabit them. Each tribe is located through its relationship to contingent peoples,[10] although its territorial boundaries are often first fixed by its proximity to the sea or to a river (Malone, 71):

Þonne wið norþan Donua æwielme & be eastan Rine sindon Eastfranc[an], & be suþan him sindon Swæfas, on oþre healfe þære ie Donua, & be suþan him & be eastan sindon Bægware, se dæl þe mon Regnesburg hætt, & ryhte be eastan him sindon Bæme, & eastnorþ sindon Þyringa[s], & be norþan him sindon Ealdseaxan & be norþanwestan him sindon Frisan.[11] (12)

[Then to the north from the wellspring of the Danube and to the east of the Rhine are the East Franks, and to the south of them are the Swabians (or Suebi), on the other side of the river Danube, and to the south of them and the east are the Bavarians, that part which its people call Regensburg, and due east of them are the Bohemians, and to the northeast are the Thuringians; and to the north (of them) are the Old Saxons, and to the northwest of them are the Frisians.]

The Old English redactor has taken his method of pivotal placement from Orosius himself, who frequently uses it to locate cities and islands, but not tribes. Orosius's geography is entirely physical, and one constellation is linked to another intermittently at best.[12] His Anglo-Saxon translator, on the other hand, consistently subordinates physical to political geography and carefully delineates the juxtaposition of peoples.

Even as the Latin text's physical geography of northern Europe is given a political cast, there is also an English emphasis in its configuration. Peoples historically important to the English, such as the Saxons and the Danes, are made geographical centers. Moreover, the chapter as a whole evinces the consciousness of ancestry which Nicholas Howe sees as prevalent in early English histories (*Migration* and *Catalogue Poems*; also Lerer). Indeed, the recasting of the first book of the *Historia adversum paganos* evokes other Anglo-Saxon histories that incorporate geography, genealogy, and an interest in northeastern Europe. For instance, Bede's geographical account of origins in *Historia ecclesiastica* 1.15 dominates and supplants its chronological context. According to Howe,

> By placing each tribe in one region on the continent and one on the island, [Bede] draws a dramatic and memorable map of the migration. Geography replaces chronology as the measure of history because it better contains the dynamic of this event. The map of tribal movements establishes as well that the adventus was from the start communal in nature. (*Migration*, 59–60)

A crucial element noted by Howe in other texts is missing here, however. Unlike Bede or Archbishop Wulfstan or the poet of *Exodus*, the Anglo-Saxon translator eschews judgments and threats. His tribes are neither the scourge of God nor the chosen people, and his language is matter-of-fact, not hortatory. Nevertheless, the catalog has an impact. The lists are circular, rather than linear, and insist on multiple points of reference. They seem to *cover* ground, not just traverse or mark it. Orosian territory is masked and reconfigured, but never quite obliterated, by the Old English amplifications.

Ohthere's Voyage to the White Sea

The other two interpolations into book 1 break entirely with Orosius's text. Rather than overwriting or amplifying the Latin, these additions intrude themselves into the *Historia* with a bare nod at the stylistic conventions of their host. In an associational shift reminiscent of the paratactic structures of gnomic poetry, the tribal geography is immediately followed by an account of Ohthere the Norseman's visit to the ninth-century court of King Alfred, in which the traveler describes several northern voyages. This itinerary is succeeded in turn by an account of Wulfstan's travels in the Baltic Sea in which he recalls encounters with the Estonians. The anachronistic placement of two ninth-century Anglo-Saxon accounts in a history written by a fifth-century Spanish priest is emphasized by the explicit grounding of the former in King Alfred's court: "Ohthere sæde his hlaforde, Ælfrede cyninge, þæt he ealra Norðmonna norþmest bude" (13) [Ohthere told his lord, King Alfred, that he lived northmost of all the Northmen].

Although we have no external evidence for the historicity of Ohthere, or of the Englishman, Wulfstan, who follows him in the manuscript, both narratives purport to be garnered from the explorers themselves, and within each account the source insists on the veracity of his story. Moreover, not only is the content of each tale grounded in an individual experience, but the first, and perhaps the second, is represented as an oral performance in a very specific arena, in the presence of Alfred, the king under whose aegis the translation of Orosius may have been made.

Ohthere (Scandinavian Ottarr) is from Halgoland in northern Norway and, according to a self-effacing narrator, tells Alfred a tale of a sea voyage north into the White Sea. Ohthere says that "he ealra Norðmonna norþmest bude" (13)—he lived northmost of all the Norsemen. Nevertheless, the land he visited "sie swiþe lang norþ þonan" [is much further north from there]. And in that northernmost land "hit is eal weste" or uninhabited wasteland, except for a few Lapps who hunt in winter and fish in the summer (14). Ohthere at first seems to have sailed north simply out of curiosity: he "wolde fandian hu longe þæt land norþryhte læge" and "hwæðer ænig mon be norðan þæm westenne bude" (14) [he wished to discover how far the land lay to the north and whether any human lived north of the wasteland]. He traveled north, with wasteland on his starboard and open sea on his larboard or port side, for three days. He was "swa feor norþ swa þa hwælhuntan firrest faraþ" (14) [as far north as the whalehunters fare furthest], yet he pushed on for three more days. When the land bent eastward, or the sea into the land, "he nysse hwæðer" [he knew not which], he waited for a west wind a little from the north and sailed eastward for four days. The land bent southward—or the sea into the land; again "he nysse hwæþer" (14).

Catching a due north wind Ohthere sailed south for five days. He saw inhabitants on the other side of a great river (he was probably now sailing along the southern edge of what is now called the Kola Peninsula) but, fearful of "unfriþe" [hostility], he did not land. At some point, Ohthere and his companions must have made contact with the inhabitants of these northern regions because he learned "fela spella" (14) [many stories] from the Beormas, as he calls the more settled tribes (also known as Northern Karelians [A. S. C. Ross, *Terfinnas*, "Ohthere's Cwenas," 337]). Conscious once again of the configuration of peoples, the narrator says the stories Ohthere heard were "ægþer ge of hiera agnum lande ge of þæm landum þe ymb hie utan wæron" (14) [both of their own land and of the lands which lay around them]. In a conscientious moment typical of this sober and straightforward account, the narrator says Ohthere cannot judge the truth of the Beormas' tales because he did not see for himself ["he nyste hwæt þæs soþes wæs, for þæm he hit self ne geseah" (14)]. Thus he tells us about none of them, leaving the Beormas voiceless.

Up to this point, Ohthere seems to be that rarity, an explorer motivated solely by curiosity, but soon we find that he is also interested in economic gain.

Swiþost he for ðider, toeacan þæs landes sceawunge, for þæm horshwælum, for ðæm hie habbað swiþe æþele ban on hiora toþum—þa teð hie brohton sume þæm cyninge—& hiora hyd bið swiðe god to sciprapum. (14–15)

[He mostly went there, as well as to see this land, for the walruses, because they have very fine bone in their teeth (they brought some teeth to show the king) and their hide is very good for ship's ropes.]

Several features of Ohthere's *Voyage* construct the account as both transparent and authentic, especially when it is read in isolation. Ohthere impresses us with his precision and clarity. He is scrupulous about evidence and tells his audience only what he sees firsthand. Despite the sparse nature of the narrative and its brevity, we get the flavor of a personality. This northernmost of Norsemen is at once adventurous, able to sail the dangerous northern seas with impunity, and cautious, not about to risk unnecessary hostilities. He is curious and mercenary. He extracts tribute from the Laplanders. He is enough of an anthropologist to distinguish between nomadic and agricultural peoples, and enough of a linguist to note kinship of languages.

Ne mette he ær nan gebun land siþþan he from his agnum ham for, ac him wæs ealne weg weste land on þæt steorbord, butan fiscerum & fugelerum & huntum, & þæt wæron eall Finnas. . . . Þa Finnas, him þuhte, & þa Beormas spræcon neah an geþeode. (14)

[Nor did he come earlier across any inhabited land after he left his own home, but it was all wasteland (i.e., uninhabited) on the starboard, except for fishermen and fowlers and hunters, and those were all Lapps. . . . The Lapps, he thought, and the Beormas spoke nearly one language.]

Ohthere's relatively straightforward and simple account offers several versions of marginal peoples. First are the Lapps, whose nomadic habits place them in a lower class of some sort: their land is defined as "weste" or wasteland and they pay tribute to Ohthere and presumably other Norsemen.[13] Next come the Beormas, who are not entirely to be trusted. Nevertheless, both peoples are recognizably human. The third, and perhaps most intriguing, marginal other is Ohthere himself, an outsider, negotiating the space between the society he addresses and those cultures he "discovers," or rather uncovers, for the English. He is not indigenous to the land from which this text is produced, and to which the narrator, he who retells the Norseman's tale, presumably belongs. Ohthere's story, therefore, embodies two kinds of encounters—his own visit to Alfred's court and his interactions with peoples unfamiliar to the English. His narrative is, in effect, a tale told to King Alfred *by* a stranger *about* strangers. That narrative and his material offerings emphasize both his alterity and his usefulness, for he brings Alfred practical information about trading routes and exploitable natural resources, as well as a tangible gift of walrus teeth—a gift that vouches for his information. His credibility is further reinforced, and his reception assured, by his standing in his own community—a standing that is carefully explained by the Anglo-Saxon interpolator. We are assured that, by Norse standards, he is a wealthy man, both because he extracts tribute from the Lapps and because he owns livestock:

He wæs swyðe spedig man on þæm æhtum þe heora speda on beoð, þæt is on wildrum. He hæfde þagyt, ða he þone cyningc sohte, tamra deora unbebohtra syx hund. Þa deor hi hatað hranas; þara wæron syx stælhranas, ða beoð swyðe dyre mid Finnum, for ðæm hy foð þa wildan hranas mid. He wæs mid þæm fyrstum mannum on þæm lande; næfde he þeah ma ðonne twentig hryðera & twentig sceapa & twentig swyna, & þæt lytle þæt he erede he erede mid horsan. (15)

[He was a very wealthy man in those things in which wealth lay for them, that is in wild animals. He had still, when he sought out the king, six hundred tame animals not yet bought. Those animals they call "reindeer"; of those six were decoy deer, these are very valuable among the Lapps, because through them they catch the wild reindeer. He was the first man among them in that land; even though he had no more than twenty cattle and twenty sheep and twenty swine, and the little that he plowed he plowed with horses.]

The Anglo-Saxon narrator here seems to be concerned not only that his audience respect Ohthere but also that we understand the difference between Anglo-Saxon and Norse cultures. He measures the disparity in material assets but he points out that the value of those assets is determined differently in different societies. Although there is a note of condescension here, the foreign visitor is neither incomprehensible nor threatening. He translates well.

Wulfstan's Encounter with the Estonians

Ohthere's commitment to geographical specificity, his own presence as a foreigner, and the narrator's interest in measuring status and wealth are all paralleled in Wulfstan's account of the Estonians and their burial practices. Here, the narrator also begins with a specific travel itinerary, measuring out the physical stages of a journey. The regions Wulfstan traverses were probably more familiar to King Alfred's court than the far northern seas explored by Ohthere. There are known points of departure and of arrival: the towns Hedeby and Truso. The coastlines along which Wulfstan voyages are identified as being under the jurisdiction of first the Danes, then the Swedes, and the rivers are described by name, by course, and by origin. Such geographical specificity lends credibility to Wulfstan's subsequent anthropological account. Although we are told less about Wulfstan than about Ohthere, he seems far more willing (or able) than the Norseman to engage the culture he encounters. We hear nothing of the caution that Ohthere exhibits, but this of course may simply be a result of the greater accessibility of the Estonian region and mores.

In Estonia, Wulfstan finds many towns and a king in each: "Þæt Estland is swyðe mycel, & þær bið swyðe manig burh, & on ælcere byrig bið cyningc" (17) [Estonia is very big, and there are a great many towns, and in each town is a king]. He briefly records some general cultural characteristics before moving on to discuss Estonian funeral customs with some specificity. The Estonians drink mare's milk if they are wealthy and mead if they are slaves or poor folk. There is much conflict among them (17). A dead man is honored by a wake of a month or more in which the body remains "unburnt" and exposed within the house while those who mourn him drink and compete in games. When his corpse is finally carried to the pyre, his possessions are divided into parts and laid out at intervals along a five- or six-mile-long route, the most valuable share being the farthest from town. The mourners then assemble on horseback and race toward the dead man's loot, claiming shares as they reach them:

Ðonne sceolon beon gesamnode ealle ða menn ðe swyftoste hors habbað on þæm lande, forhwæga on fif milum oððe on syx milum from þæm feo. Þonne ærnað hy ealle toweard þæm feo; ðonne cymeð se man se þæt swift(ost)e hors hafað to þæm ærestan dæle & to þæm mæstan, & swa ælc æfter oðrum, oþ hit bið eall genumen; & se nimð þone læstan dæl se nyhst þæm tune þæt feoh geærneð. & þonne rideð ælc hys weges mid ðan feo & hyt motan habban eall, & for ðy þær beoð þa swiftan hors ungefoge dyre. (17)

[Then must all the men who have the swiftest horses in the land come together, at least within five or six miles from (the dead man's) property. Then they all race toward the property; then the man who has the swiftest horse comes to the first share and to the greatest (share), and thus one after another, until it is all taken; and he gets the least share who reaches that part nearest the town. And then each rides on his way with that property and might have it all, and because of this swift horses are extraordinarily valuable.]

Wulfstan's account of Estonian funeral customs continues with several other anthropological notes and again the goal seems to be an understanding of the foreign culture and an assessment of its assets. Along with the value of a swift horse, we hear of the consumption—through celebration or by fire—of all the substance and the body of a man. Not a possession remains unclaimed. Not a single bone may rest unburnt. Finally, the ability of one tribe actually to produce cold is remarked upon, in a curious internalization of climate:

& þær is mid Estum an mægð þæt hi magon cyle gewyrcan, & þy þær licgað þa deadan men swa lange & ne fuliað, þæt hy wyrcað þone cyle hine on, & þeah man asette twegen fætels full ealað oððe wæteres, hy gedoð þæt oþer bið oferfroren, sam hit sy sumor, sam winter. (17–18)

[and there is among the Estonians a tribe which is able to create cold, and among them dead men lie so long and do not decay, because they create the cold in them, and if one set out two barrels full of ale or water, they will make both freeze over, just the same if it be summer or winter.]

In his celebration of the exotic and the familiar together, Wulfstan accepts an alien culture even as he authenticates his own. The cremation of the dead, the funeral as the measure of a man, drink as a facilitator of communal activity, the horse race as a celebratory contest, and the fluidity of material possessions: each also has its place in Old English poetry. Wulfstan's account of pagan customs persisting on the margins of European Christendom is reminiscent of the ancient customs of the English themselves, customs celebrated in texts as diverse as *Beowulf*, *Maxims I* and *II*, and *The Seafarer*. As such, his exploration of a Baltic people authenticates his own heritage and blunts the thrust of Orosius's Christian apologetic, explicitly written "adversum paganos."

Neighboring Strangers

Although Ohthere and Wulfstan's accounts both speak to issues crucial to students of travel literature, ethnography, and geography, neither fits neatly into any of these genres. They do not quite satisfy Mary Campbell's definition of a travel book "as a kind of first-person narrative, or at least a second-person [guide]" (*Witness*, 5), and they are, of course, brief and fragmentary in comparison with the accounts of Egeria or Marco Polo. Nevertheless, a barely submerged first person drives the narrative as we are told what Ohthere and Wulfstan saw, thought, and said, and at times the detachment of third-person narration cracks when the transcriber slips into the first person; at such points we are encouraged to "hear" an oral occasion behind the written account: "þonne Burgenda land wæs us on bæcbord" (16) [then the Burgundians' land was on our port side]. However, when we consider the issues raised by Campbell, we are forced to distinguish Wulfstan, Ohthere, and their recorder from the travel writers she studies. She identifies "moments of discovery in travel accounts since Columbus by a certain rhetoric—by a subject-centered burst of landscape description" ("'The Object,'" 4), whereas early medieval travel writers such as Egeria focused on "the divine and human," on event, not physical description. In between the two lie the elaborate and fantastic accounts of *Wonders of the East* and Marco Polo. In all of these texts, to a greater or lesser extent, "the limit of geographical knowledge, wherever located, was a point commonly charged with moral significance and, even in pre-Christian times, with divine dangerousness" (*Witness*, 53). In the Anglo-Saxon interpolations, however, the dangers Ohthere recounts are of a practical, immediate nature, not loaded with moral, or eschatological, significance, and Wulfstan simply seems unconcerned, moving from the familiar to the exotic without discomfort or anxiety.

Anxieties about geographical limits are, of course, closely linked to the fear of, or need to master, human others. Campbell sees the medieval narratives she studies as "written by the ignorant for the parochial," as texts which use the grotesque and the parodic to place those who are feared or suspected on the margins of the known world (*Witness*, 2). Similarly, Johannes Fabian speaks of modern ethnographers as driven to "place" their subjects in another time—a prior time—so that they may be defined as inferior, as primitive. The anthropologist denies his subjects coevalness in order to distance and categorize them (Fabian, 50, 143–44, 147–48). Ohthere and Wulfstan, and their Anglo-Saxon amanuensis, recognize and are fascinated by alterity, but, rather than inscribing it as grotesque, exotic, or primitive, they seem driven to translate the foreign into the vernacular, to naturalize it.

This inclination to incorporate rather than marginalize may result from a sense that there are *degrees* of otherness, degrees of distance, in both time and space. As Wulfstan and Ohthere mark the ports and the landmarks they pass, they mark also increments of distance from home, sovereignty over land, and possibilities for trade. By articulating the stages of their outward journeys in such detail, they make it possible for all of us to return to port over and over again, by reading backward, or replaying, the northward- or northeastward-bound itinerary. Thus, even as Ohthere and Wulfstan push back the edges of the known world in their accounts of northern seas, shores, and peoples, they remain firmly grounded in the economy and traditional values of their Anglo-Saxon audience. Even exotic qualities, such as the production of cold, are given explanations and uses that fit the Anglo-Saxon sense of things. The effect is not one of extreme alterity, but rather of acceptable liminality—an edge, not a precipice. The two travel narratives, themselves interlopers in their textual landscape, refuse to render their foreign subjects as either primitives or exotics. Foreign territories and alien peoples have relevance and familiar uses. They can be evaluated and made to fit, and, rather than threatening the text's host culture and its values, they are used to expand and enrich it.

All Translation Is Local

In the first 111 folios of Cotton Tiberius Bi, the translation of difference occurs in several spheres: linguistic, geographical, and ethnographic. Orosius's Latin is rendered into English; his geography and, to a lesser extent, his history are recast for an Anglo-Saxon audience. Northern seas are described as potential economic resources. Estonian mores are cast in Germanic terms. Such translation of alien lands, peoples, and languages into the idiom of an English court can be seen as a hallmark of Alfred's reign. D. J. V. Fisher notes that Ohthere's visit to England shows international contacts at the end of the ninth century, when Viking attacks are lessening (196). At this time Alfred is also recruiting European churchmen such as Grimbald from Flanders, who may have been responsible for an earlier manuscript of the Old English Orosius produced at Winchester (Parkes, 163–66). In a venerable metaphor, Asser, King Alfred's contemporary and biographer, says that the king, like a bee seeking honey, "turned the gaze of his mind afar and sought from abroad that which he had not at home, that is, in his own kingdom" (57). The king applied himself "with all his heart" to the "searching out of things not known" (54–55). Although Asser is speaking specifically of the gathering of wisdom and the search for scholars, this inclusive movement may also be understood as embracing entrepreneurial sailors such as Ohthere and Wulfstan. Both of the interpolated narratives in the Old English Orosius serve to bring to the center of the Anglo-Saxon kingdom what was not found at home.

Ohthere's verbal map of the northern reaches and Wulfstan's itinerary localize Orosius's geography even as they extend it into as yet uncharted territory and unrecorded mores. The Anglo-Saxon interpolator also recasts the relationship between the text and its audience through distinct shifts in substance and voice, shifts which compromise and complicate the omniscience of the Latin history.

For the most part, the Old English version of the *Historia adversum paganos*, although it occasionally differs from its original in content, mimics the Latin in viewpoint and voice, presenting itself as a detached and omniscient authority which covers vast territories spatially and temporally. In contrast, the accounts of Ohthere and the Englishman Wulfstan speak locally and circumspectly. Each rests firmly on the credibility of a single witness who declines to tell of what he has not himself seen.

Anomalies in tone and perspective inevitably raise issues of textual integrity. One might be inclined to see these accounts as distinct texts, clumsily inserted. I would argue instead that, despite some anomalous qualities, the two narratives are in fact well integrated into the Old English version of the *Historia*. They begin in mid-folio (folio 8), with no break in the scribal hand. More importantly, lexical links are either forged or exploited to help the reader move from geography to voyage, from tribe to traveler, from general to particular. The last sentence of the tribal geography reads:

Sweon habbað be suþan him þone sæs earm Osti & be eastan him Sermende, & be norþan him ofer þa westenne is Cwenland, & be westannorþan him sindon Scridefinne & be westan Norþmenn. (13)

[The Swedes have to the south of them the Estonian arm of the sea and to the east of them the Sermende, and to the north of them, over the wastes is Cwenland, and to the northwest of them are the Scride-Finns and to the west Northmen.]

Then we hear: "Ohthere sæde his hlaforde, Ælfrede cyninge, þæt he ealre Norðmonna norþmest bude" (13) [Ohthere told his lord, King Alfred, that he lived northmost of all the Norsemen]. The transition seems oblique, but it is also lexically referential. The passage quoted above increasingly calls attention to the north and west. The heightened density of "be westannorþan . . . and be westan Norþmenne" and the playful recombining of west and north prepare us for Ohthere as our attention is drawn toward Halgoland. When we hear that Ohthere is "northmost of all Northmen," he is positioned lexically as well as geographically, recalling the pivoting and linking of the preceding political constellations.

Formal integration occurs in another way as well—and this third way has perhaps the most relevance for modern readers of such texts. While the end of the tribal geography prepares us for the voyage narrative, that account in its turn provides a startling new context for the geography. With the proper names, Ohthere and Alfred, and the simple preterite, "sæde," the text moves from general description to particular narrative. The introductory clause "Ohthere told his lord, Alfred" gives us, suddenly, a single teller and a unique occasion. Universal and impersonal geography is transformed into a tale with an individual speaker and a particular royal audience. In both voyage accounts—Wulfstan's and Ohthere's—the traveler is quoted as an authority on what he has seen and experienced. Ohthere in particular introduces an element of *reportage* through which the telling itself becomes an historical event. The larger, ostensibly neutral, disembodied text, the translation of Orosius's *Historia*, has been pegged to a time and a place by a contextualized narrative, that is, by an insert rather than by a frame. This localizing from within is so successful that modern scholars for years accepted William of Malmesbury's attribution of the Orosius translation to Alfred. In effect, they used the physical placement of the tale in Alfred's court to establish authorship, as if one could fix authorship through territory, as if the territory of the text and the territory of the court were both necessarily governed by the same individual.

The Territory of the Codex

In Cotton Tiberius Bi (although not in the tenth-century Lauderdale manuscript), the work of cultural definition continues well past the portion of the manuscript devoted to the translation of Orosius's *Historia*. The history is followed by the *Menologium* and *Maxims II*, perhaps of tenth-century origin, and version "C" of the *Anglo-Saxon Chronicle*, which can be placed in Abingdon from the year 977 on and which extends into the mid-eleventh century (Dobbie in *Anglo-Saxon Minor Poems*, lxv–lxvi). Although space permits only a brief look at these texts here, they can nevertheless be seen as continuing the complex and ambitious enterprise of geographical and historical self-definition begun in the Old English Orosius and its interpolations.

The *Menologium* reminds us that human events are enacted against a backdrop of recurrent sacred occasions. As a sacred calendar, it reasserts the Christian context established by Orosius, but with a distinctly local cast. Prominent mention is made of St. Augustine of Canterbury, and the months are named in Old English, not Latin, reminding readers of indigenous gods and pagan rituals. If Orosius's history places us in the sweep of world calamities, the *Menologium* orients us to recurring cycles of martyrdom and redemption, interspersed with seasonal reminders of equinoxes and the like. Dates are not unique, but perpetually repeated. The matrix of human territory and historical time that appears in the translation of Orosius is here deepened by the accrual of sacred time.

In addition, *Maxims II* and the *Chronicle* itself add two crucial dimensions to the *compilatio*. *Maxims II*, a collection of gnomes or wise sayings, may well be an attempt to preserve or resurrect the wisdom and cultural mores of Germanic ancestors. It records social and ethical norms, as well as putting dragons, demons, hawks, and wolves in their places. It maintains a self-consciously timeless, universal quality through a simple present tense sequence and a spare catalog of seemingly unconnected types.[14]

The *Chronicle* goes further yet. In it the emphasis shifts from Orosius in two directions, both of which are foreshadowed in Ohthere's account. Here, history is national, not global, and the eschatological thrust of the *Menologium* is further diffused as moral issues are placed in the context of a Germanic culture with a pagan past. The temporal sequence is made concrete with place names, battles, and royal genealogies. In style the *Chronicle* returns the Cotton manuscript to the narratives of Ohthere and Wulfstan in its particularity, parataxis, and emphasis on personal witness. It draws to a close shadowed by the knowledge that William of Normandy is soon to invade:

[Harold kynge] wæs to soðan gesæd þæt Willelm eorll fram Normandige, Eadwardes cingces mæg, wolde hider cuman & þis land gegan, eallswa hit syððan aeode. (Conner 36)

[(Harold of England) was truly told that William earl of Normandy, King Edward's kinsman, would come hither and subdue this land, even as it then came to pass.]

The last event recorded is the Battle at Stamford Bridge, won by Harold of England against Harold of Norway and the treacherous earl, Tostig. Here the circle closes. Ohthere the Norseman brought to Alfred images of open seas and deserted lands to the north. His countryman, Harold of Norway, some two centuries later, brings only death to Stamford Bridge.

In the Cotton codex, encounters with other peoples and other lands provide both preface and context, not for an investigation of foreign cultures or territories, but for the slow and piecemeal articulation of a national identity. The book, in all its patchiness and in the uneasy coexistence of its parts, reflects and shapes the history and the geography of its land of origin. Its makers claimed Brutus as their ancestor, forged their church in the image of Rome, and spoke in the accents of the pagan north. In adopting the Orosius translation as consort to the *Chronicle*, they place themselves within the history of Christian Europe. In their interpolations to book 1 of Orosius, they claim an affinity with the peoples of Germany, Scandinavia, and the Baltic. Through translation and ethnographic fragment the producers of Cotton Tiberius Bi begin the complex task of writing themselves.

Notes

Material from this essay was presented at the 1992 Medieval Academy meeting in Columbus and at the 1992 Fordham University conference on "The Expansion of Europe before Columbus, 1250–1492." I am grateful to the participants of both sessions, and, in particular, to Nicholas Howe and Robert Hanning for their responses to my essay. Many thanks also to the New York Meds, and especially to Sylvia Tomasch, always generous with her time and her encouragement.

1. "Imagining New Worlds: Factual and Figural Discovery during the Middle Ages," Lehman College, May 1989; "The Expansion of Europe: 1250–1492," Fordham University, March 1992.

2. For descriptions of the manuscript see: Bately, introduction and commentary to *The Old English Orosius*; Bosworth; Whitelock, ed., *The Anglo-Saxon Chronicle*; Elliott Van Kirk Dobbie, intro., *Anglo-Saxon Minor Poems*; Plummer; Sweet; and Conner.

3. The translation of Orosius, but missing the voyages, is also extant in *The Tollemache Orosius*.

4. For further discussions of translation in the Middle Ages, see Copeland, *Rhetoric, hermeneutics, and translation*; and Ellis.

5. For Orosius's Latin text, see *Pauli Orosii Historiarum adversum paganos*; translations are by Deferrari, *The Seven Books*.

6. The Old English Orosius 128.3–4 amplifies the Latin Orosius book 6.15, and 101.4–13 amplifies the Latin book 4.16. See also Bately, "Those Books," 58.

7. For further discussion of the role of geography in early English texts, see Otter; Howe, *Migration*; Stein in this volume.

8. Bately says "the additional material in the account of the geography of Europe relates to the situation before 889 (perhaps between 894–9)" (*Old English Orosius*, xc).

9. On authorship of the interpolations, see Bately, *Old English Orosius*, lxxix–lxxxi; and Liggins, 321–22.

10. Bately points out that the peoples referred to were often significant political entities rather than tribes (*Old English Orosius*, lxix n. 1).

11. Quotations from the Old English Orosius are from Bately's edition; all translations from Old English are mine.

12. See Bately, *Old English Orosius*, lxviii–lxix, for another description of the method here; also Malone, 67–78.

13. See Otter for the Anglo-Saxon definition of land as always to be cultivated (164).

14. On *Maxims II*, see Howe, *Catalogue Poems*; Hansen, 153–77. See also Conner for the relationship between the *Menologium*, *Maxims II*, and the *Chronicle* (xix).

5

Making History English

Cultural Identity and Historical Explanation in William of Malmesbury and Laȝamon's *Brut*

ROBERT M. STEIN

AFTER THE SURPRISINGLY QUICK and decisive victory of the Normans at Hastings, as William of Malmesbury narrates it, the Conqueror sends the body of the English King Harold to his mother for burial without ransom and proceeds victoriously to London, "ita Angli, qui, in unam coeuntes sententiam, potuissent patriae reformare ruinam, dum nullum ex suis volunt, alienum induxerunt" (3.247) [where the English who had they united . . . might have repaired the ruin of their country, introduced a stranger . . . to govern them (281)].[1] Resistance is afterward brief and unavailing. William violently subdues York, the center of opposition. And at Exeter he puts down what Malmesbury calls a rebellion with great ferocity "quia unus eorum, supra murum stans, nudato inguine auras sonitu inferioris partis turbaverat, pro contemptu videlicet Normannorum" (3.248) [because one of the citizens, standing upon the wall, had bared his posterior, and had broken wind, in contempt of the Normans (282)]. A part of the wall later falls down and makes an opening for the Normans to conquer "divino scilicet iutus auxilio" (3.248) [with God's help (282)].

In the writing of history in the twelfth century, the Norman conquest of the English marks a crisis of cultural identity, of the principles of legitimate sovereignty, and of historical explanation. As political and social experience become ever more complex, diverse, and compelling as objects of attention in their own right, the historian finds it less and less possible to explain the significance of experience by means of conventional historiographical categories. Early medieval history had been written to demonstrate a providential pattern in the world, however disordered the world seemed to be. Most frequently, methods of biblical typology provided the historian with a means of determining and organizing the historical event; thus Eusebius, to take one well-known example, sees Constantine as a new Moses and new David. Fulfilling in his imperial person the promise of redemption, Constantine is simultaneously *imperator* and *lux mundi* (412). The historical event is made by God *per signum*, and the historian's task is always to read the world as a book of signs asserting the continuance of the divine presence. In the twelfth century we find a great increase of historical writing, both in Latin and in the vernaculars. Yet the very thing that provokes historical writing at that time—the emergence of a complex secular world obedient to secular imperatives—-also disables its own most characteristic means of understanding. One result is that the historian is driven back on his material. I have written elsewhere about changes in the apprehension of the significant event, the new attention given to rhetoric, and the clash of categories of understanding in historical writing of the twelfth century ("Signs and Things"). Robert Hanning and Nancy Partner have demonstrated the emergence in Anglo-Norman texts of modes of judgment and evaluation drawn from classical historiography, modes of judgment that coexist uneasily (or not at all) with traditional methods, and to which the historian is drawn precisely to make sense of the defining event of the conquest.[2] William of Malmesbury, for example, tries to see the Normans as God's new Israel while seeing them simultaneously and unavoidably as imperial repressors of native English liberty.

What I want to draw attention to in this essay is a yet more radical consequence in the narratives of the twelfth-century historians. There is an attempt to find a new and absolutely unequivocal ground of certitude on which to anchor experience. In William of Malmesbury's *De gestis regum Anglorum* this attempt entails two imaginative simplifications. The first is a radical simplification of society. As political experience becomes more and more unthinkable (as I will argue in a moment, literally monstrous), William completes in imagination a process of social simplification only just begun as policy. For William, the conquest levels a diversity of peoples into a conqueror and a conquered, two *gentes* (peoples or nations or bloodlines) and two peoples only, each occupying the same space. The Celts, never treated seriously in William's narrative, disappear altogether. The Danes are described as merely temporary visitors even if they manage to install a king from time to time. The Mercians, Northumbrians, East Anglians, and the rest become by 1066 simply English.[3] The second is the simplification of the contested space itself. Geographical diversity is rewritten under the pressure of ideological purity, and in the course of William's narrative England becomes a totality imagined fully as sacred space, a material demonstration and guarantee of God's presence even though (or just because) it is "situated almost out of the world." The phrase is from the introduction to a long narrative demonstrating the sanctity of the English, which William inserts just before his description of the conquest, and it begins the process of transforming England from a space of contention and war into an unbroken material body, a part of Christendom that both signifies the salvation of the whole and guarantees it. William begins this narrative by noting the astonishing number of bodies found in England (five that he is sure of) "entire after death typifying the final state of incorruption," and he follows with the stories of sixteen saints, seven men and nine women (although he says that there are many more), all from the royal bloodline.[4] This has taken place "by God's agency," William writes:

quod ideo fieri credo caelitus, ut natio pene extra orbem posita, ex consideratione incorruptelae sanctorum, fidentius ad spem resurrectionis animaretur. Et sunt sane quinque omnino quos noverim, ceterum plures accolae praedicant sui: sancta Etheldritha et Wiburga virgines, rex Edmundus, achiepiscopus Elfegus, Cuthbertus antiquus pater, omnes inviolatis cute et carne, flexibilibus articulis, extremus vitali quodam tepore, speciem dormientium meditantes. (2.207)

[in order that a nation, situated, as it were, almost out of the world, should more confidently embrace the hope of a resurrection from the contemplation of the incorruption of the saints. There are, altogether, five which I have know of, though the residents in many places boast of more: Saint Etheldrida, and Werburga, virgins; king Edmund; archbishop Elphege; Cuthbert the ancient father: who with skin and flesh unwasted, and their joints flexile, appear to have a certain vital warmth about them and to be merely sleeping. (236)]

The sixteen stories are all variations of a single type of miracle story that will gain great currency in the later Middle Ages, a version of the passive romance. The female saint, a virgin in life, has an incorruptible body or body part, sometimes giving out sweet odors, after death. The male saint--often a child--is typically unremarkable in life. He is unjustly murdered, almost always for purely secular political reasons, but then the hidden body begins to perform miracles drawing attention to its location and revealing the crime. The miracles performed by the body both indicate and *are* the sanctity of the victim.[5]

William's narrative of the death of St. Edmund is paradigmatic in its concern for the saint's bodily integrity. The invading Danes torture and behead Edmund and then hide the head in the woods. Edmund's followers are called to the place by a voice, and they find the head being guarded by a wolf, "an animal," William writes "accustomed to prey on dead carcasses." The wolf tamely joins the procession to the tomb where the head is buried with the body and a small wooden chapel is erected. After a time the body begins to perform miracles, and the bishop of London decides to build a more splendid burial place. The body is discovered to be incorrupt, and the head reunited to it, showing only a small purple seam. Moreover, "hominis mortui crines et ungues sensim pullulare; quos Oswen quaedam sancta mulier quotannis hos tonderet, illos desecaret, sacra veneratione posteris futuros" (2.213) [the hair and nails of the dead man continue to grow: these Oswen, a holy woman, used yearly to clip and cut, that they might be objects of veneration to posterity (241)].

The story of the boy St. Kenelm follows this pattern very closely, but with variations that are decisive for our understanding of William's historical project. The body of Kenelm is recovered not by a miraculous voice but by a complex, mediated process of writing and translation—a metaphorical and literalized *translatio*. Kenelm, heir to the Mercian throne, is placed in the care of his sister who, having royal aspirations for herself, orders one of her servants to murder him while hunting in deep woods. But this crime "tam celate in Anglia commissa" (2.211) [which had been so secretly committed in England (238)] is revealed when a dove deposits a parchment roll containing an account of Kenelm's death on the altar of St. Peter's in Rome. The roll, however, is written in English, and no one can read it until finally an Englishman who happened to be in Rome "linguae involucrum Latialiter Quiritibus evolvens, effecit ut apostolici epistola regibus Anglis compatriotam martyrem indicaret" (2.211) [translated the writing to the Roman people, into Latin, and gave occasion to the pope to write a letter to the kings of England acquainting them with the martyrdom of their countryman (239)].

The selection of saints in William's narrative traverses England and constitutes its geography. Northumbria, Kent, Mercia, East Anglia—the space fills with miracle-working bodies and fragments of bodies in which the divine is experienced not as sign or as promise or as longing but as presence. Similarly, the bodies of the wicked are torn and destroyed. When Kenelm's sister hears the chanting of the crowd as they bring the recovered body to Winchcomb, she thrusts her head out of the window and reads the psalm *Deus laudem meam* backward, William says, in order to drown out the rejoicers.

Tum vero vi divina lumina veneficae, cavis orbibus evulsa, cruore versum polluerunt, "Hoc opus eorum qui detrahunt mihi apud Dominum, et qui loquuntur mala adversus animam meam." Cruoris signa exstant hodie. (2.211)

[At that moment, her eyes, torn by divine vengeance from their hollow sockets, scattered blood upon the verse which runs "This is the work of them who defame me to the Lord, and who speak evil against my soul." The marks of her blood are still extant. (239)]

Ultimately, the bodies of the wicked are rejected from "the bosom of the earth" and obliterated. A witch living in Berkeley, at the moment of her death, begs her children to try to rescue her body, even though they "cannot revoke the sentence already passed on [her] soul" (231) [et de anima quidem sententiam prolatam non revocabitis, corpus vero forsitan hoc modo servabitis (2.204)]. She tells them to sew up her corpse in the skin of a stag, lay it on its back in a stone coffin, fasten down the lid with lead and iron, place a large stone on top, and bind it with three iron chains of enormous weight. She asks for psalms to be sung for fifty nights and masses said for fifty days.

Ita, si tribus noctibus secure jacuero, quarta die infodite matrem vestram humo; quanquam verear ne fugiat terra sinibus me recipere et fovere suis, quae totiens gravata est malitiis meis. (2.204)

[If I lie thus secure for three nights, on the fourth day bury your mother in the ground; although I fear, lest the earth, which has been so often burdened with my crimes, should refuse to receive and cherish me in her bosom. (231)]

On the first two days devils break into the church and break the first two chains. On the third night a devil enters the monastery. He breaks the third chain, opens the coffin, bids the woman rise, takes her by the hand and out of the church in front of everyone.

ubi prae foribus equus, niger et superbus, hinniens videbatur, unci ferreis per totum tergum protuberantibus; super quos misera imposita, mox ab oculis intuentium, cum toto sodalitio disparuit. (2.204)

[At the doors appeared a black horse, proudly neighing, with iron hooks projecting over his whole back; on which the wretched creature was placed, and immediately with the whole party vanished from the eyes of the beholders. (231–32)]

Finally, in the prophetic dreams of King Edward, the conquest is foretold as England itself becomes a fragmented body whose viscera are eaten without end by strangers ("advenae quique divitias et viscera corrodunt Angliae, nec ulla spes est finiendae miseriae" [2.27]), and in a logic we know from dreams, it becomes simultaneously a whole and a part. The uniting of England with Normandy is imagined by William primarily as monstrosity:

Tunc quoque in confinio Britanniae et Normanniae portentum visum est: in una vel potius duabus mulieribus duo erant capita, quatuor brachia, et cetera gemina omnia usque ad umbilicum: inferius duo crura, duo pedes, et cetera omnia singula. Ridebat, comedebat, loquebatur una: flebat, esuriebat, tacebat altera. Ore gemino manducabatur, sed uno meatu digerebatur. Postremo una defuncta, supervixit altera: portavit pene triennio viva mortuam, donec et mole ponderis et nidore cadaveris ipsa quoque defecit. Putatum est a quibusdam, et litteris etiam traditum, quod hae mulieres Angliam et Normanniam significaverint. (2.207)

[At that time too, on the confines of Brittany and Normandy, a prodigy was seen in one, or more properly speaking, in two women: there were two heads, four arms, and every other part two-fold to the navel: beneath, were two legs, two feet, and all other parts single. While one was laughing, eating, or speaking, the other would cry, fast, or remain silent: though both mouths ate, yet the excrement was discharged by only one passage. At last, one dying, the other survived, and the living carried about the dead, for the space of three years, till she died also, through the fatigue of the weight, and the stench of the dead carcass. Many were of the opinion, and some even have written, that these women represented England and Normandy. (235)]

The uncorrupted body of the saint, or the fragment of the body that is paradoxically whole, stands over against this form of monstrous integration.

In William's narrative there is also another and alternative vision of social integrity, this time centered not on physical space nor on political unity but on the church of all true believers: the body of Christ visibly present in the Eucharist. Here the motifs of literal fragmentation are transformed into the efficacious sign of totality. At the moment of narrating the death of King William, a messy and confused affair because a lesser knight had, at the last minute, claimed the burial plot as his own and had to be paid off by William's son Henry to allow the funeral to continue, the chronicler quickly turns to the life of Berengar of Tours, who had at one time denied the real presence in the Eucharist. Berengar had argued, for example, that if the body and blood were present, little bits of Jesus' flesh would be chewed by the teeth of the communicants.[6] And to demonstrate the reality of the presence William narrates two eucharistic miracles. The stories are taken from *De corpore et sanguine domini* (89, 60), composed by Paschasius Radbertus about 831 in answer to some questions raised by newly converted Saxon churches. In the first one he tells that "presbyterum Plegildum visibiliter speciem pueri in altare contrectasse et, post libata oscula, in panis similitudinem conversum ecclesiastico more sumpsisse" (3.286) [the priest Plegild visibly touched the form of a boy upon the altar, and that after kissing him he partook of him, turned into the similitude of bread" (314)]. The other (quoted from Gregory of Tours, *Liber miraculorum*) concerns

Quale de pusione Judaico; quod, in ecclesiam cum aequaevo Christiano forte et ludibunde ingressus, vidit puerum in ara membratim discerpi, et viritim populo dividi. Id cum innocentia puerili parentibus pro vero assereret, in rogum detrusum ubi oc-

cluso ostio aestuabat incendium, multis post horis sine jactura corporis exuviarumque
et etiam crinium, a Christianis extractum; interrogatusque quomodo voraces ignium
globos evaserit, respondit, "Illa pulchra feomina quam vidi sedere in cathedra, cujus
filius populo dividebatur, semper mihi in camino ad dexteram astitit, flammeas minas
et fumea volumina peplo suo summovens." (3.286)

[The Jewish boy who by chance running playfully into a church, with a Christian
of the same age, saw a child torn to pieces on the altar, and severally divided to the
people; which when, with childish innocence, he related as truth to his parents, they
placed him in a furnace, where the fire was burning and the door closed: whence, after
many hours, he was snatched by the Christians, without injury to his person, clothes,
or hair; and being asked how he could escape the devouring flames, he replied "That
beautiful woman whom I saw sitting in the chair, whose son was divided among the
people always stood at my right hand in the furnace, keeping off the threatening flames
and fiery volumes with her garments." (313–15)]

In the particular genre of saint's life that William narrates, in his fascination with black magic, demonism, and witchcraft and in the emphasis on the reality of flesh and blood in the Eucharist we can see that complex of material having to do with the relation of parts to wholes so brilliantly recognized by Caroline Walker Bynum. In the introductory essay to *Fragmentation and Redemption*, "History in the Comic Mode," Bynum writes:

The twelfth and thirteenth centuries in western Europe saw renewed debate over
dozens of theological matters (such as the eucharist, the transmission of original sin,
the nature of the body-soul nexus) in which the relationship of part to whole is crucial,
and a new emphasis on miracles (such as stigmata, bleeding hosts, miraculous fasting,
incorrupt cadavers) in which bodies are the mediators between earth and heaven. It
was a period in which the overcoming of partition and putrefaction—either through
reunion of parts into a whole or through assertion of part *as part* to *be* the whole—
was the image of paradise. (13)

What interests me here is the emergence of this material in a monastic historical chronicle of the very early twelfth century particularly fascinated with secular processes and desperate to make sense of them. In one way, William's *De gestis* is an example of a much noted medieval social trajectory: intellectual and especially emotional tendencies having their origins in the monastic sphere become widespread in the secular world. William plays out in his history a set of concerns clustering around social and personal identity that will become a major part of lay spirituality in the next generations. Bynum argues, for example, that the priestly monopoly on the administration of the sacraments and on the interpretation of doctrine creates the body as a space of authority for lay and especially for women mystics ("Female Body"). William's sense of the monstrous social body, simultaneously English and Norman, is at the same time his deepest sense of himself, and it is this very sense that paradoxically authorizes his own writing of history:

De Willelmo rege scripserunt, diversis incitati causis, et Normanni et Angli: illi ad nimias efferati sunt laudes, bona malaque juxta in caelum praedicantes; isti, pro gentilibus inimicitiis, foedis dominum suum proscidere conviciis. Ego autem, quia utriusque gentis sanguinem traho, dicendi tale temperamentum servabo: bene gesta, quantum congnoscere potui, sine fuco palam efferam; perperam acta, quantum sufficiat scientiae, leviter et quasi transeunter attingam. (book 3, *Prologus*)

[Normans and English incited by different motives, have written of King William: the former have praised him to excess . . . while the latter, out of national hatred have laden their conqueror with reproach. For my part, as the blood of either people flows in my veins, I shall steer a middle course. (238)]

Writing under the patronage of Robert of Gloucester and holding the position of librarian at Malmesbury, William identifies himself culturally with the Norman ruling class, a cultural identification available by the time of the reign of Henry I to English elites (Barlow; also Turner). He would prefer to say nothing bad about them, to whom, he writes "tum pro genere tum pro beneficiis, fidem habeo" (2.228) [I am strongly bound both by my descent and for the privileges I enjoy (257)]. Yet he writes always from the position of the English, a conquered nation, and while identifying culturally with the Normans he simultaneously identifies himself with the contemptuous Englishman on the walls of Exeter, and with those heroic, resisting English warriors, few in number, who, "caritati corporum renuntiantes, pro patria animas posuere" (2.228) [renouncing every care for their bodies, put down their lives for their fatherland (257)], acts of defiance in which their bodies and their nation are obliterated. Writing the history is the necessary substitute for defiance, and it makes the body of the English nation whole and forever present. In the life of St. Kenelm as William tells it, the miraculous English roll was translated into Latin and Latin letters were taken back to England in order for the English to find both a present sign and a means of their own salvation: the body of the saint is simultaneously a sign of life, a vehicle of life, and life itself. In the same way, William looks to Rome and writes a Latin history of the English in order to make English history, which is also to say, to make history English.

* * *

In a recent article, Francis Ingledew has rightly recognized Geoffrey of Monmouth's fictional *Historia regum britanniae* as "in some sense *the* exemplary historiographical work of the Middle Ages" (669). Writing in the same patronage circle and intellectual milieu as William of Malmesbury, Geoffrey puts into play the new terms of Anglo-Norman historiography in his own work, precisely to make comprehensible, as Ingledew puts it, the "phenomenon of the Normans and the Anglo-Norman realm" (681). Ingledew points to Geoffrey's use of Virgilian schemes of historical understanding as an alternative to the history of salvation and signals genealogy, the emergent sense of nation as a self-conscious entity, secular prophecy, and eros as the constituent elements of the new historiography that Geoffrey constructs (680 and throughout).

As is well known, Geoffrey's *Historia* has a remarkably wide dissemination in Latin and in vernacular versions both in England and on the continent. There are several Latin recensions clearly rewritten at different times in the later twelfth century, and the text was translated by Geoffrey Gaimar (now lost), and soon afterward by Wace, whose *mise en roman* in octosyllabic couplets was later put into English alliterative verse by Laʒamon (Tatlock). These waves of Latin and vernacular dissemination, I want to suggest, continue the ideological work of the first phase of Anglo-Norman historiography into the conditions of Angevin state-making and in the process of recontextualization transform it. Just as the course of state formation in both the Angevin and Capetian realms on the one hand, and the continued working out of the political implications of the Gregorian reform long after the famous Concordat of Worms in 1122 radically destabilize the structure of political power, so also power and the necessity of its legitimation become an ever more pressing object of intellectual concern. This destabilization of power is therefore the moment when writing invades the political understanding both in the realm of political theory—a genre created essentially by the Gregorian reform—and in the emergence of the two new high medieval narrative genres, historiography and romance (Zink; Vance, 226).

For the remainder of this essay I want to look at what happens to genealogical narrative in the *Brut* in order to make some initial suggestions about the continuities and transformations in historical understanding during the Angevin period. Of Ingledew's constituent elements I choose genealogy because its illocutionary force lies precisely at the intersection of theory and practice: genealogical narrative both reflects political reality and intends to change it. As we shall see, the problematic that it especially engages grows out of a series of anxieties having to do with the instability of territorial occupation, ownership, and control. The composition of the *Brut* has been variously dated between 1185 and the mid-thirteenth century (Le Saux). Much as I would like to know that it was written during the reign of King John, and particularly after the cession of Normandy to France in 1204, my argument has to do with the continuous process of political change rather than any particular event.

Genealogy has been much studied, since Georges Duby's seminal work, as one of the more significant intellectual constructs of the twelfth century.[7] What I want to stress is its unrecognized participation in the important and widespread aspect of the high medieval *mentalité* that I discussed in connection with William of Malmesbury. In its way of creating a nexus of time, space, and land based on the continuity of blood, genealogy is one in a series of strictly speaking imaginary constructions that come into being at this time in both theological and secular realms of thought. Their common property is that they serve to provide a material embodiment for an ideal or symbolic entity. Like the body of the saint, which we saw in our discussion of William to be both the sign of redemption and its means, and the Eucharist, which is asserted in various ways to *be* the real presence as well as to signify it, so also the reality of a symbolic identity through time is in genealogy asserted as a physical and unbroken transference of bodily substance, a bodily permanence from generation to generation. Duby studied the reorganization of the family into a male bloodline and the corollary emergence of varieties of social coercion to guarantee the concentration and preservation of property along the lines of agnatic descent. The institution of primogeniture is one among many such coercive practices that both emerge from and validate the image of the generations, each following the other in unbroken succession (Duby, *Three Orders*, 164). Importantly for us, while they created or traced genealogies—often fictional as we know[8]—and concerned themselves in other ways with establishing their continuity with the past (the Normans in England were much involved with finding English ancestors for themselves [Ridyard; Townsend]), the Norman and Angevin ruling families did not follow the Carolingian model and adopted neither primogeniture nor agnatic descent as did their counterparts within the French regnum.[9] The family thus becomes over time an increasingly complex spatial network of alliances and land holdings. Land is continuously in the process of consolidation and division as it moves piecemeal both from generation to generation in time and from one alliance to another in space. Continuity of the family in time is in this situation not commensurate with the continuity of land in space. Far from being a mirror of social reality, genealogical narratives and origin stories are in this context strictly ideological entities: they represent the unsystematic fragmentations and reconsolidations of power and territory through the physical images of substantial identity, permanent presence, and linear succession.

The sense of historical narrative as linear succession from a single point of origin—the founding of Britain by the Trojan exiles—to a culmination in the present (generally given as a prophesied future) is the principal formal characteristic of Laȝamon's *Brut*, although not of Geoffrey's *Historia*. The formal transformation had been made for Laȝamon by Wace, who announces it unequivocally in his opening lines:

> Ki vult oïr e vult saveir
> De rei en rei e d'eir en eir
> Ki cil furent e dunt il vindrent
> Ki Engleterre primes tindrent,
> Quels reis i ad en ordre eü,
> Ki anceis e ki puis i fu,
> Maistre Wace l'ad translaté
> Ki en conte la verité.
> (1–8)

> [Who wants to hear and who wants to know
> From king to king and heir to heir
> Who they were and from where they came
> Who first held England—
> Which kings held it in order
> Who was first and who was after
> Master Wace has translated it
> Who tells the truth about it.] [10]

Laȝamon does not translate these lines, but the makers of the manuscript (Cotton Caligula A. ix.) find a kind of semantic equivalent to them in the *mise en page*. As part of the original design the names of the successive rulers are written in the margins in red ink at the points of their first appearance in the narrative (Le Saux 1). While these marginal glosses transform the text into a visual representation of unproblematic succession—each character has his assigned place in the text according to his place in the chain of generations—what the text actually narrates is the fact of genealogical disruption and discontinuity, the greatest of these being the coming of the English. Yet, there is an even greater discontinuity, never narrated, but haunting the narrative. The conquest of the Normans is inescapably implied by Laȝamon's presentation of the English.

Toward the end of the *Brut*, for example, there is a passage with no analogue in the sources. The English finally triumph over the British population, and Athelstan makes over the institutions of the country. In a gesture typical of his narrative practice, Laȝamon dramatizes the event. Rather than presenting it directly to the reader in the voice of the narrator, the event is given as news, "tidings" that have just come to Cadwathlader, the defeated and exiled British king. The reader sees the facts of conquest—the transformations of the land, of social institutions, and even of the language itself—through the eyes of the vanquished:

> þa tiden comen sone; to Cadwaðlader kinge
> into Brutaine; þer þar he wunede.
> mid Alaine kinge; þe wes of his cunne.
> me dude him to under-stonde; of al þisse londe.
> hu Aðelstan her com liðen; ut of Sex-londen.
> and hu he al Angle-londe; sette on his aȝere hond.
> and hu he sette moting; & hu he sette husting.
> and hu he sette sciren; and makede firð of deoren.
> & hu he sette halimot; & hu he sette hundred.
> and þa nomen of þan tunen; on Sexisce runen.
> & ȝilden he gon rere; mucle & swiðe mære.
> & þa chirchen he gon dihten; after Sexisce irihten.
> and Sexis he gan kennen; þa nomen of þan monnen.
> and al me him talde; þe tiden of þisse londe.
> (15965–78)

[These tidings came soon to Cadwallader the king,
Into Brittany where he was residing
With Alain the king, who came from the same clan:
He was given information about all of this nation:
How Athelstan had come traveling here out of Saxon lands
And how he had taken all Engle-land into his own hands,
And how he appointed the law courts, and how he appointed his parliament,
And how he established the shires, and created forests for deer,
And how he set up manor courts and how he divided counties in hundreds,
And the names of the villages in the Saxon language,
And how he was creating guilds, great ones and glorious,
And churches he was founding in the style of the Saxons,
And in Saxon he identified the names of the people;
And he was told about all the events of this land.][11]

While he never names them, the Normans are fully present in this passage, for the institutions listed here are in fact for the most part Norman rather than Saxon. The coming of the Saxons and their conquest by the Normans that it implies is not, however, in any way represented as an end or outcome of a historical progression, and the introduction of their institutions is not a dramatic culmination but part of a continual flux. The Normans and the changes they make are in fact overtly registered at several moments in the *Brut*, and always in the context of permanent change. They appear for example in the narrative of King Lud's fortification of Troynovant at a time when there were no castles in the land. The British King Lud creates the first of these quintessentially Norman structures, and calls the newly fortified town after himself in order to insure that posterity will correctly credit him. Posterity, however, is nothing but discontinuity and transformation; nothing remains identical to itself, and there is no historical memory:

Seoððen comen Normans; mid heore nið-craften.
and nemneden heo Lundres; þeos leodes heo amærden.
swa is al þis lond iuaren. for uncuðe leoden.
þeo þis londe hæbbeð bi-wunnen. and ef[t] beoð idriuen hennene.
And eft hit bi-ȝetten oðers; þe uncuðe weoren.
& falden þene ælden nomen;æfter heore wille.
of gode þe burȝen; & wenden heore nomen.
swa þat nis her burh nan; in þissere Bruttene.
þat habbe hire nome æld; þe me arst hire onstalde.
(3547–3555)

[Then came the Normans, with their nasty malice,
And named it as "Lundres" (those living here they harmed).
So has all this land fared, with aliens landing
Who have conquered this land and in their turn been driven away,
And others again would gain it, who were foreign people,
And would refashion the old names according to their whim
Of the good old boroughs, and change their names around,
So that there's not one borough, in this land of Britain,
Which still has the old name which it was first established with.]

The greatest of these discontinuities is, of course, the English takeover, a literally unimaginable occurrence that provokes a set of contradictions ranging from the desire to wish it away—in a much analyzed passage, Arthur is suddenly called "savior of the English," shifting the position of the English from unjust conquerors to victims of conquest (14297)—to the desire to assimilate it to business as usual. While preserving the form of narrative succession, Laȝamon converts succession narratives into stories of alliance. In so doing, the substantial identity of blood is preserved by being transferred from time to space in the identification of legitimate sovereignty with a racially pure territoriality. These narrative transferences from time to space can be found throughout the *Brut*, but they cluster especially densely around the Arthur section where they become combined with images of triumphant Christianity.

The first such transference is in the narrative of Arthur's ancestry, where alliance, racial purity, and religious war are combined with a repetition of the original founding story. The kingless Britons seek help from Brittany. They make an alliance with Constantine, the brother of the king of Brittany, who will ultimately become king of Britain and Uther Pendragon's father. The alliance is made to combat the invasions led by Melga and Wanis, two Northmen who have allied themselves with Picts, Scots, Irish, Saxons, and a host of others, all characterized as alien, heathen, and evil. Laȝamon gives Constantine a British ancestry and a British wife, using alliance to assert an identity between the British and the Breton ruling family, inserts a scene where the Britons do homage and fealty to Constantine and invest him with Britain, and above all depicts him as the savior of the faith against the enemy worshipers of Appollin, Mahound, and Tervagant. In the process he becomes simultaneously king, feudal overlord, religious champion, and a new founder. Britain is repopulated with Britons when upon the news of Constantine's arrival the inhabitants literally leap out of the trees in which they have been hiding like wild animals:

> Þet iherde Bruttes; þer heo wuneden in þan puttes.
> inne eorðen & inne stockes; heo hudden heom alse brockes.
> I wude I wilderne; inne hæðe & inne uærne.
> þat ne mihte wel neh na man nenne Brut iuinden.
> buten heo weoren in castle; oðer y burhȝe iclused uaste.
> Þa heo iherden of þissen worde; þat Costantin wes an ærde.
> þa comen ut of munten; moni Tusend monnen.
> heo leopen ut of þan wuden; swulc hit deor weoren.
> Liðen toward Lundenne; moni hundred þusend.
> bi straten & be walden; al hit forð hælden.
> & þa æhte wif-men; wæpmonnes claðes duden heom on.
> & heo forð wenden; tow|ward þere uerde.
>
> (6395–6406)

[This was heard by the British where they were living down in pits
In the earth, and in tree trunks they were hiding out like badgers,
In wood and in wilderness, in heathland and in ferns,
So that practically nobody could ever find a Briton,
Unless they were in a castle or in a town enclosed securely.
When they heard of this word that Constantine was in the land
There emerged from the mountains many thousand men;
They came springing out of woodlands as if they were wild beasts:
There went loping off to London many hundred thousand
On streets and through forests all men forwards went marching,
And the brave women dressed in weaponed men's clothing,
And off they all went towards the great army.]

This same motif is repeated from the other side in the narrative of the apostasy of Octa, Hengist's son. On his reconversion thousands of heathens emerge from the woods in a fearful multi-ethnic horde to form an alliance against Uther, who has tried systematically to eliminate them (9111–22).

The third instance is Colgrim's uprising immediately after Arthur is crowned. Colgrim is a Saxon with a following of "men of many nations." While Arthur, in direct discourse, defines this as a family vendetta, a fight against the men who betrayed and poisoned his father, the narrative continually characterizes the conflict as the struggle between Christian Britons against a gathering of heathen racial others:

Þer liðen to-somne; alle Scotleode.
Peohtes & Sæxes; siȝen heom to-gæderes
& moniennes cunnes men; uuleden Cogrimen.
(10003–5)

[To there proceeded in unity all the Scottish people:
Picts then and Saxons joined forces together,
And men of many origins accompanied Colgrim.]

Finally, the battle between the Roman emperor Lucius and Arthur is presented as a world-historical struggle between the Christian West and the pagan East. The text insists on the polyglot and multiracial composition of the Roman army while underplaying to the point of ignoring any difference within Arthur's forces. The Roman army is introduced in a long catalog of exotic names and places including one of the first occurrences in English of

"Africa,"[12] which here seems to mark a variety of otherness different in kind from the East:

> Þe æreste king þe þer com; he wes swiðe kene mon.
> Epistrod king of Grece; Eðion duc of Boece.
> þer com mid mucle wiȝe; Ittac king of Turckie.
> Pandras king of Egipte; of Crete the king Ipolitte.
> of Syrie þe king Euander; of Frigie þe duc Teucer.
> of Babilone Mæptisas; of Spaine the kaisere Meodras.
> of Medie þe king Boccus; of Libie þe king Sexstorius.
> of Bittunie Pollidices; of Iturie þe king Sexes.
> Ofustesar king of Aufrike; nes þer na king his ilike.
> mid him com moni Aufrikan; of Eðiope he brohte þa bleomen.
> (12657–66)

> [The first king who arrived there was a very courageous man,
> Epistrod, king of Greece; also Ethion, duke of Boeotia;
> With a great fighting force came Irtac, king of Turkey;
> Pandras, king of Egypt, from Crete King Hippolytus,
> From Syria, King Evander, from Phrygia Duke Teucer,
> Maeptis as from Babylon, from Spain the emperor Meodras,
> From Media King Bocus, from Lybia King Sextorius,
> From Bithynia Polydeuces, from Ituria King Sexes,
> Ofustesar, King of Africa—no king bore him resemblance—:
> With him came many an African, from Ethiopia he brought the
>   black men.]

The great violation of orderly succession that the text needs to assimilate and that these strategies are in fact designed to legitimate is the conquest of the Britons by the Saxons and the later coming of the Normans that this conquest invariably implies. What is most striking in this regard is Laȝamon's refusal to employ the English historiographical tradition that reinscribes the conquest back into salvation history by seeing the English as the bearers of a dynamic proselytizing Christianity.[13] For Laȝamon the English become simply the holders of the racially singular territory and the Britons are read out of history to live under their own laws in the Welsh borderlands while they wait for their transcendental home at the end of time. This, it seems to me, is the significance of the great transformation of Geoffrey that concludes Laȝamon's history. While Geoffrey includes a prophecy that the British shall occupy their lost kingdom again but only when all the relics of all the saints which once belonged to them and which "had been hidden away because of the pagan invasion" were on show (283), Laȝamon transforms this to a vision of salvation that is at once apocalyptic and singularly personal. The angelic voice speaks to Cadwathlader and instructs him to go to Rome,

> and þu scalt wurðe clene; al þurh mihte of ure Drihte.
> And seo[ð]ðen þu scalt i-witen; and faren to heofne-richen.
> for no most þu naueremære; Ængle-lond aȝe.
> ah Alemainisce men; Ænglen scullen aȝen.
> and næuermære Bruttisce men; bruken hit ne moten.
> ær cume þe time; þe iqueðen wes while.
> þat Merlin þe witeȝe; bodede mid worde.
> Þenne sculle Bruttes sone; buȝen to Rome;
> and draȝen ut þine banes alle; of þene marme stane.
> and mid blissen heom uerien; uorð mid heom seoluen.
> in seoluere and in golde; in-to Brutlonde.
> Þenne sculle Bruttes anan; balde iwurðen.
> al þat heo bi-ginneð to done; iwurðeð after heore wille.
> þenne scullen I Bruttene; blissen wurðen riue.
> wastmes and wederes sele; after heore i-wille.
> (16015–29)

[And you will become pure entirely by God's provision
From all your misdeeds, through the might of Our Lord,
And then you will depart and go to the heavenly kingdom,
For never more may you own the Angles' land
But instead the men of Almaigne will be owners of England,
And never more may British men be its possessors
Until the time arrives, which was announced long ago,
Which Merlin the prophet pronounced in his words.
then the British shall soon turn towards Rome
And draw out all your bones from their marble tomb
And carry them rejoicing away with them again,
Enshrined in silver and gold, into Britain's land.
Then at once the British will become emboldened:
Everything they begin to do will happen as they wish:
Then within Britain bliss will be abundant,
With fruits and fine weather, exactly as men want.]

Cadwathlader's personal salvation is doubly guaranteed—he will be home in *heofne-riche* and his body will be the efficacious sign of salvation for all. But the time of the British resurgence is a finality out of history. "Nevermore," doubly reiterated, is unconditional; the time to come is not like any other: golden age motifs cluster (fruits, fine weather, abundance, and the satisfaction of desire), and the body of Cadwathlader is translated from Rome into a redeemed "Brutlonde," that he himself redeems. Its effect is paradoxically to leave history for the English.

These narrative strategies of recuperation, organized as they are along the lines of private life, are, of course, prepolitical. But they are, more interestingly, also postpolitical: coincident with the emergence of the possibility and necessity of writing secular history there arises the simultaneous desire to escape once and for all from historicity. We have seen this desire in the effort to find a single, absolutely unequivocal constant in an experience that presents itself as otherwise permanent change, whether it is the longing for a transcendental home or the transformation in fantasy of diversity into an imaginary whole. And finally, these narrative strategies may themselves become precisely and dangerously political. For the narrative procedures we have been examining correspond to an ideological rethinking of social order that has its most important implication neither in historiography nor in fantasy but as practical social policy. As R. I. Moore has explained, this is the period when literate elites begin to conceive of secular society as homogenous and therefore to implement the process of systematic marginalization, persecution, expulsion, and ultimately extermination of groups imagined as alien in order to make society as they have conceived it naturally to be.

Notes

Early versions of parts of this essay were read at the 1992 MLA Convention in Toronto and at the 1994 MLA Convention in San Diego. I am grateful for the many comments that those readings elicited.

1. All quotations from William of Malmesbury are from Stubbs and will be identified by book and section number; translation based on Giles, identified by page number.

2. See also the essays in Breisach.

3. This ethnic simplification may well be the conclusion of a process set in motion at the time of King Alfred or before. The loose confederation of various Germanic tribes inhabiting England begins to assert its identity as a single *natio* (a people, race, tribe, or bloodline) by means of the historiographical fiction of the *adventus Saxonum*; see Howe, *Migration*.

4. The Anglo-Saxons compiled burial lists of saints on which this list may be

based. While there are memorial records from continental Europe, there are no other extant lists compiled on national principles. Cf. Rollason; Liebermann. Otter, *Inventiones*, suggests that the Anglo-Saxon lists may be influenced by Celtic memorial practices; see the Welsh "stanzas of the graves," a mnemonic listing of burial places of warrior heroes (Thomas Jones).

    5. On medieval hagiography, see Brown; Heffernan; Wilson, esp. the bibliography.

    6. On Berengar's eucharistic theology and the controversy with Lanfranc, see de Montclos. On the development of eucharistic theology and its relation to popular piety, see Miri Rubin; and esp. Beckwith. It is important to stress the early twelfth century date of *De gestis*. The social logic of William's narrative becomes a major constituent of lay piety some two hundred years later.

    7. See "Structure de parenté," "Remarques sur la litterature," and "Lignage, noblesse et chevalerie," all reprinted in *Hommes et structures du moyen age* and translated in *The Chivalrous Society*. The reorganization of the aristocratic family was first investigated by Schmid; since the 1970s, work on genealogy and genealogical narrative has burgeoned, including Spiegel, "Genealogy"; Bloch, *Etymologies and Genealogies*; and Barthélemy. For England, see esp. Dumville.

    8. On fictional and quasi-fictional genealogical accounts, see Spiegel, *Romancing the Past*.

    9. New work in local history will no doubt shed much light on the various ways that inheritances were complicated and property was transferred outside of the "normal" channels created by the reorganized family. One suspects fairly constant friction between the system, structurally considered, and the actual practical working of it. For developments in general, see esp. Brundage, 134–35; Herlihy, 79–111, esp. 95–98 on Norman and Angevin anomalies; Charles Donahue; also Searle. On the ruling family, see Poole, 320–31, 344–50; Baldwin, 80–101.

    10. Quotations from Wace are from Arnold; my translation.

    11. Quotations are from *Laȝamon*, ed. Brook and Leslie, citations identified by line numbers; *Lawman*, trans. Allen.

    12. The only earlier appearance to my knowledge is the use of "Afrisc" in the Old English *Exodus* (line 580), where the sense is very different. The Hebrew women, having been delivered from Egypt, are referred to as "African women adorned with gold." Modern editors have almost universally emended the expression.

    13. For the tradition, see Hanning. Daniel Donoghue has argued that this tradition can be found in Laȝamon, an argument that I do not find convincing.

6

Too Close for Comfort

Dis-Orienting Chivalry in the *Wars of Alexander*

CHRISTINE CHISM

THE *WARS OF ALEXANDER*, AN ALLITERATIVE North West Midlands poem, thought to date from the later fourteenth century, describes what is simultaneously a conqueror's dream and a xenophobe's nightmare.[1] While relating the exploits of Alexander the Great, a chivalric conqueror driven to separate himself from and place himself above all the kingdoms of the east, the poem incessantly embeds him in those worlds, disturbing his illusions of preeminence with the intimations of affinity. After describing its hero's Egyptian parentage and his effacement of this oriental origin, the poem is a mercilessly energetic description of his campaigns. Throughout the 5,800-line poem, Alexander drives onward, seeking new boundaries to obliterate, new kingdoms to encompass, in what becomes finally a need to escape the limits of history itself. As he ranges over the length and breadth of Asia, Alexander is impelled to transcend all chivalric expectations, to exceed every military precedent, and finally to set himself over every past, present, and future authority.

But Alexander is an iconoclast whose violence is painfully contained. As Alexander's campaigns incline farther and farther to the east, he is continually halted by the realization that his numerous adversaries know him, reflect back to him his own face, and adumbrate his own future. When this happens, he succumbs to an awful sympathy, arrested by the intensity of his emotions—a paralysis that ends only when he effaces the significance of the encounter and turns to meet the next enemy. His entire identity as a world conqueror and his chivalric enterprise are thus contingent upon his willful ignorance and rejection of his subversive resemblances to his enemies, of his oriental genealogy, and of his eventual fate—world conquest and sudden death.

Unlike the roughly contemporary alliterative poem the *Siege of Jerusalem*, where the struggle between West and East is driven primarily by religious, political, and economic imperatives, the conflicts of the *Wars of Alexander* are more pointedly generational—struggles that pit son against father, youth against maturity, inexperience and obscurity against historic fame, and finally chivalric iconoclasm against the delimiting structures of that iconoclasm's own origins and history. This generational conflict establishes indissoluble links between Alexander and his various adversaries—even as they succumb to him, they invoke his origin and mirror his future. In this way, the *Wars of Alexander* conflates genealogy and geography as contested territories, two linked fronts along which Alexander wages war, striving to efface the one and dominate the other. And while the poem shows his irresistible power to subdue the worlds of the east, it also insists on his complete temporal helplessness: his placement within a genealogy that links him to his enemies, his destined subjection to the same fate he imposes upon them.

Throughout the poem, then, Alexander is forced to face the idea that victory is not transcendence. He is repeatedly reminded of his own inscription within the processes of history and generation, and of his fundamental relationships to his oriental others. As the poem continues and Alexander runs the gamut of diverse adversaries from militant Persians, to ingenious Jews, to saintly Brahmans, to giant scorpions, his identity as a chivalric conqueror whose endeavor depends on singularity of will and solidarity of loyalty begins to break apart. His progress mobilizes an exploration of late medieval chivalric consciousness that is provocatively attentive both to its desire for labile, diversified, and polysemic others and to its need to ground its self-inventions upon their alienations.

The poem seems fascinated by moments in which the voices of Alexander's adversaries interrupt the strategic alienations that foreground his endeavor—moments in which his affiliations and likenesses to his enemies are revealed. Such moments are the militarily indomitable Alexander's only points of vulnerability, and the poem probes at them with sardonic persistence. In one confrontation of piercing clarity, as Alexander pauses on the banks of the impassable Ganges to question the Brahmans, the Indians convey to him their perception of his entire military enterprise: "It is ȝourselfe and noȝt oureself þat ai þe self hantis" (4794) [It is yourself and not us that you are forever pursuing]. As Alexander confronts different adversaries, his military victories are often prologue to such stunning epistemological ambushes. The idea that Alexander is chasing his own carefully exoticized shadows animates the poem in a multitude of different ways, transforming Alexander's conflicts of identity into familial, political and ideological ones. Alexander is a patricide and his murder of his Egyptian prophet-father, Anectanabus, becomes the model and the drive for his subsequent conquest of his other oriental predecessors, the great rulers Darius of Persia and Porrus of India.

Alexander's dilemma reimagines the political and ideological conflicts of a whole late-fourteenth–early-fifteenth-century generation of British nobility, haunted by the specter of their military ineptitude during recent crusades—and ferociously refusing that knowledge. The sense of futility that plagues Alexander—the recurrent apprehension that he is shadow-boxing his own "fonned fantasies" (5639) through Asia—reflects and reconfigures the misgivings of a late-fourteenth-century audience increasingly aware of the necessary connections and complex debts between themselves and their numerous eastern adversaries.

It is striking that a British poet of this period should have been energized to translate and amplify a poem of such length into careful and at times delightfully ironic alliterative verse.[2] I will argue that Alexander is a uniquely situated figure for the gentry of the North West Midlands who were this poem's probable audience. Themselves identified with and eager to appropriate the historical and ideological appurtenances of the English nobility, they would have been drawn to Alexander as a chivalric model, one of the Nine Worthies about whom a rich legendary history had accumulated. Throughout the Middle Ages, Alexander's ongoing appeal is attested by the five-century history of the Alexander romances which form a continuing genre, analogous in breadth and richness to the other notable Matters of British chivalric legend, Arthur and Charlemagne.[3] In the course of the *Wars of Alexander*, Alexander himself emerges as the preeminent chivalric hero, in contrast to his Egyptian father Anectanabus, to Darius of Persia, and to all the multifarious eastern rulers and warlords whose defeats the poem will relate. Despite his eastern and magical origins, Alexander becomes the founder of a chivalric empire and a worthy predecessor to fourteenth-century nobility who wished to look further back than Arthur or even Rome for desirable chivalric forefathers.

In addition, Alexander, as a successful world conqueror, would have had a particular charm to a late fourteenth-century audience of gentry who had been gradually but forcibly taught the futility of ambitions to conquer, regain, or convert the immense diversity of non-Christian lands to the east. In subduing those rich and exotic civilizations, Alexander single-handedly performs what two hundred years of historical crusading and all the efforts of a supposedly righteous, God-inspired cause could not accomplish.

As a chivalric model, then, Alexander is alluring because he provides a positive image of chivalric imperial aggression repeatedly and irresistibly subduing the incredible might and cultural power of the empires of Persia, India, and the lands beyond. Yet as a Greek ruler (and in the late fourteenth century the Greeks themselves were given the ambiguous status of schismatics), he himself hovers on the tenuous border between what the fourteenth century defined as East and West. As this poem makes clear, if Alexander is situated as an identification for Western chivalry, he is also its other—a figure whose contradictions and perplexities mirror its own. Thus the poem's interrogation of Alexander's conquest enables a potential self-analysis and critique for a culture still desperately invested in oriental conquest but gradually forced to realize the futility of its dreams.

Alexander's very genealogical ambiguity would have posed interesting and fertile problems for the poem's audience. His Egyptian ancestry, polytheism, and the mounting scope of his ambitions make him a figure just as easily appropriable by eastern conquerors as western ones. To cite one contemporary and very influential example, Froissart's chronicle describes the defeat of the European army at Nicopolis in terms that attribute Alexandrian ambitions to the Ottoman leader Bayezid (Lamorabaquy) as he rejoices in the captured tents of the Christian leaders:

Than Lamorabaquy . . . made as great myrthe as myght be, and sayd how he wolde shortely with great puyssaunce passe into the realme of Hungery, and conquere the countrey, and after other countreys upon the Crysten men, and to bringe them to his obeysaunce . . . he sayd he wolde reygne lyke Alysaunder of Masydone, who was twelve yere kynge of all the worlde, of whose lynage he sayde he was dyscended. (237)

Bayezid's ambition gathers even more menacing overtones when Froissart attributes to him a desire to become the new Alexander and attain the "signory" over Christendom. He can claim Alexander as a literal ancestor and chivalric model as easily as the alliterative poets of England can make Alexander one of the Nine Worthies, an example of illustrious leadership for the west.

It is my contention that Alexander is so successful and fascinating a chivalric hero for the late-fourteenth-century poet precisely because he is self-perplexed: traditionally, even his eyes were of different colors. He becomes a hybrid of eastern and western cultures who empowers himself as he attempts to obliterate his connections to his oriental origins, both ancestrally, by destroying his father and effacing his father's name, and politically, by trying to subdue to Greek rule all the kingdoms of the east. He represents western chivalry's admiration for and aversion to an oriental world it can never convert or conquer and from whose learning, science, and history Europeans had drawn a great part of their own.

Oriental Conjunctions

In the *Wars of Alexander*, the ancient eastern cultures, including that of Macedon itself, are exoticized, becoming redolent not of particular differentiable geographical, ethnic, or social practices but rather simply of foreignness. Mary Campbell notes that in the literary traditions upon which the poet drew "'the East' is a concept separable from any particular geographic area. It is essentially Elsewhere" (*Witness*, 48). The *Wars of Alexander* joins other late-fourteenth-century alliterative poems such as the *Siege of Jerusalem* and the *Morte Arthure* when it retrenches the boundaries between east and west in a way that refuses knowledge of the exotic except as that which is to be conquered, reduced, and assimilated. Before Alexander's fierce, mismatched gaze Egyptians, Jews, Persians, Indians, and monsters blur together into a brilliant but hazy mass. He sees not a collection of individually distinctive (or obnoxious) religions and societies, but simply a series of enemies. They are conquered not for their usury, or their past crimes, or their adherence to false philosophies, but because their deaths will give power and definition to the emerging world order the poem is written to explore.

Alexander's obsession with the violently charged boundaries between his chivalric authority and the empires of the east places the poem within a complicated history of medieval boundary policing. During the twelfth and thirteenth centuries, most of the historical sources describing the relations of Christians and non-Christians work from a model of two irreducibly adversarial worlds, drawn into uneasy mutual orbit. Twelfth-century chronicles and memoirs from all sides of the conflicts positively bristle with horrified cultural incomprehension. Usamah Ibn-Muqidh, a Syrian scholar and warrior, recounts one incident:

> One day I entered this mosque, repeated the first formula, "Allah is great," and stood up in the act of praying, upon which one of the Franks rushed on me, got hold of me and turned my face eastward saying, "This is the way thou shouldst pray!" The Templars . . . came in to him and expelled him. They apologized to me, saying, "This is a stranger who has only recently arrived from the land of the Franks and he has never seen anyone praying except eastward." . . . So I went out and have ever been surprised at the conduct of this devil of a man, at the change in the color of his face, his trembling and his sentiment at the sight of one praying towards the *qiblah*." (163–64)[4]

In Usamah's description, the violent exaggeration of the Frank's reaction forms a useful point of contrast to the diplomatic aplomb of the Templars. Throughout his memoirs, Usamah remains extremely wary of any European who has not been domesticated by at least some time in the Holy Land.

Where such accounts reinforce this aversion between east and west, the writings of many European church fathers and crusade-inspired clerics make it an ideological imperative. The twelfth-century abbot of Cluny, Peter the Venerable, was one of the first who fostered the model of east and west as two antagonistic worlds. Alarmed by the avidity with which well-to-do Christians all over Europe were embracing Islamic cultural products, philosophies, and rhetorical styles, he visited twelfth-century al-Andalus on a fact-finding mission to translate what he thought were the most crucial Islamic scriptures in order to reveal their erroneous deceptions and prevent bedazzled Christians from being seduced away from the glories of both their own tongues and their own faith. The works he translated as Islamic doctrine, however, included not only the Qur'an but four literary texts. Adapting his materials to a familiar medieval Christian schema, Peter offered his readers a vision of the Islamic heaven and hell. The results, as Maria Rosa Menocal understates it, were "a very imaginative vision of Islam" (42, 43). Peter's text represents the Islamic world as both threateningly foreign and degenerately enticing, a mixed message that persists in many subsequent representations, from such crusade chronicles as Odo of Deuil's to the *Wars of Alexander*.[5] This firm division of the world into east and west, then, was a very interested one, with advantages for those who deployed it. Even as it fostered persistent and often exploitable anxiety about the enemy without, it deemphasized the possibility of subversion from within. It posited essential differences between two monolithically defined cultures and faiths, differences that would, it was hoped, make cultural syncretism unthinkable. Throughout the period of greatest contact, this proposition was reassuring to conservative factions in Spain, southern France, and Italy, cultures that had been subject to thorough permeation by such threatening and enticing Arabic imports as the new Aristotelianism (Menocal, 27–70).

However, by the later fourteenth century, this conception of east and west as two worlds had undergone important challenges—challenges which the *Wars of Alexander* reflects. The first point of attack was the growing awareness of the sheer diversity and multiplicity of eastern lands. Different eastern cultures had been persistently orientalized for two centuries into sites for European projections; they served as literary landscapes for the fantasies of both chronicler and romance writer. European ignorance of the diversity and extent of its eastern neighbors was rapidly vanishing. There had been enough military trials of strength to prove that armed conquest or wholesale conversion was impossible. In addition, the countries of Europe had gradually realized how economically advantageous trade with eastern states could be, and had, in fact, come to rely heavily upon eastern luxuries, from spices to dyes to silks. As consciousness grew in Europe of the extent and richness of many eastern countries, and as merchant entrepreneurs sought ingress into an intricate and highly profitable system of trade that extended from Egypt and the Holy Land to China, there was a dizzying reversal in perspective. Perhaps Christian Europe and its desired crown, Jerusalem, rather than being the world's religious and cultural center and the heart of the *mappa mundi*, was to other navigators only a marginal sliver on the northwest edge of a world system more enormous and multifarious than the Roman Empire at its most extensive.

R. W. Southern describes the traumatic effect of this slow realization upon twelfth- and thirteenth-century Europeans who still cherished the beguiling dream of converting to Christianity the world of Islam, assimilating its knowledge and wealth, and uniting the world under the banner of a newly invigorated Christian world system.

There were ten, or possibly a hundred, unbelievers for every Christian. Nobody knew; and the estimate grew with each access of knowledge. One consequence of this was to make the Crusades seem either quite impossible, or in need of a drastic reassessment of its aims and methods. (*Western Views*, 43)

By the late fourteenth century, this need for reassessment was even more acute. In the first place, the loss of the last crusader stronghold at Acre to the Mamluks in 1291 had led to the cessation of the trade revenues that came from the control of the westernmost ports of Palestine. These trade revenues had helped finance and maintain the crusader kingdoms, which without them soon crumbled. With the kingdoms went the last real gains in a two-century bid to reestablish Christian European control of territory that was conceived both geographically and genealogically as the heart of the world and the cradle of Christianity.

In addition, Europeans could no longer easily participate in the elaborate system of trade and mercantile exchange, which had knit together countries from England to China from the twelfth century to the mid-fourteenth century. France, Italy, Flanders, and England had become dependent upon the silks, spices, and artifacts that flowed along these routes. That these mercantile linkages were extensive and intimate is attested by the grisly evidence that if there had not been such widespread and profitable traffic between the diverse countries, the bubonic plague certainly would not have spread from China to England with such devastating rapidity.[6]

By 1350, however, European countries had no direct access to either the northern or southern trade routes with the east and even their indirect access had become subject to strict and (they felt) humiliating regulation. The northern land routes over Asia had deteriorated with the fragmentation of the Mongol Empire (Abu-Lughod, 141). At the same time, the Mamluk sultanate in Egypt had consolidated its monopoly on the southern trade route through Egypt and the Red Sea. Venice successfully obtained a severely restricted access to trade through this route into the fifteenth century but only because it agreed to trade slaves to the Mamluks, slaves who were trained and employed to swell the ranks of the Mamluk military and thus strengthen them even further. The resentment caused by such mercantile regulation emerges very clearly in the accounts of the traders (European and otherwise) forced to undergo customs control at Alexandria.[7]

European responses to these altering circumstances bespoke both frustration and desperation. Possibilities of military conquest, always a favorite tactic, continued to entice despite repeated disasters. By the late fourteenth century, it had been over a century since a crusade had achieved notable success. The 1356 raid of Peter of Cyprus on Alexandria had won no permanent foothold and had led to no further campaigning. Yet the need for some response was felt to be acute, given the shifting power balances among Syria, Egypt, and Turkey. Most pressing to the English provincial gentry to whose interests the *Wars of Alexander* appeals was the newly emerging Ottoman Empire, whose armies in 1396 thoroughly trounced at Nicopolis an ill-judged crusade of knights from all over Europe, including sizable factions from the North-West Midlands reputedly led by the noblest families in England.[8]

However, alongside of this intensifying late-fourteenth-century defensiveness, there began to emerge for the first time in European and English writings an increasing sense of necessary connections between the countries of Europe and their easterly neighbors. The potential for connection had been there all along. Even geographically, it was difficult to maintain East-West distinctions in the face of many contested territories whose histories of occupation and repossession precluded clear categorization. For almost two centuries, Muslim-occupied Spain had formed the hybrid state of al-Andalus, a country where cultural interchange was so intense that for those two centuries it resisted geographical classification. Crusade narratives such as that of Odo of Deuil bespeak an intermittent but profound obsession not only with the Holy Land but also with the other "Eastern" center of Christianity, Byzantium, itself a challenge to clear lines of definition. In the second part of the fourteenth century, it seems to have become easier for European writers to acknowledge links to eastern cultures—not only geographically, but also in the most embattled territories of religion and theology.[9]

European and British writers and theologians began to propose relationships between Christianity and Islam that linked them by cause and effect, similarity, and fate. Southern discusses this convergence as a new development, discernible by 1350 and increasing into the fifteenth century (at the same time as the Ottoman conquests pressed Prussia and Hungary more and more closely).[10] At least one religious philosopher, the Benedictine monk Uthred of Boldon, who taught theology and promoted church reform at the University of Oxford in the mid-1360s, brought Christian, Jew, and Muslim together when he argued that salvation was offered to everyone, Christian, Jew, Saracen, or pagan, baptized or not, in a moment of intellectual illumination just before death. And Uthred was not the only writer to disregard two centuries of militant theological differentiation. In the fifteenth passus of the B-text of *Piers Plowman* (c. 1378), William Langland puts some startlingly evenhanded sentiments into the toothless, tongueless mouth of Anima, a figure whose whole dialogue strives to transcend the confining and equally problematic Christian polemics that Will interrogates throughout the poem. The passus ends by affirming the essential unity of Christianity, Judaism, and Islam as monotheistic religions rooted in the first line of the Christian Credo:

> Ac pharisees and sarsens, scribes and Jewes
> Arn folk of oon feith—the fader God thei honouren.
> And sithen that the Sarsens and also the Jewes
> Konne the first clause of oure bileve, *Credo in Deum patrem omnipotentem*.
>
> (15.603–6)

Here, the essential likeness of Judaism and Islam to Christianity is what enables their slow convergence. Building upon the monotheism they all hold alike, Anima imagines bringing them together to be as simple as conveying them "litlum and litlum" (608) through the Credo, just as one would teach it to a child. Anima's simplicity masks a surprising perception; merely by affirming the essential monotheism of Islam, Langland is going far beyond many of his contemporaries' more colorful representations of it as paganism or demonolatry.[11] Anima proposes a christianization that is not violent or adversarial, the education of a child rather than the conquest of an alien.

While Uthred and Langland envision possible intersections of Christianity and Islam as utopian and regenerative (giving the priority to Christianity, of course), three other fourteenth-century writers, John Mandeville, John Wycliffe, and Philippe de Mézières, deploy such resemblances to sharpen their calls for Christian reform. Langland himself, in tracing the origins of Islam to a Christian malcontent with corn in his ear (an astonishing view of Muhammad), makes the very existence of Islam a product of Christian chicanery—Christian corruption coming home to roost. Mandeville, Wycliffe, and Philippe castigate the divisions and problems of contemporary Christian Europe even more fiercely. In the work of all three writers, Islam reflects back to the works' Christian audiences their own negative images; Mandeville actually puts calls for Christian reform into the mouth of the sultan of Egypt. While each of these writers is heterodox and extraordinary in his thinking, it is significant that figures who move in such different social and political circles and write such different texts should construct and exploit similar connections between Christianity and Islam.[12]

Closest to the concerns of the *Alexander*-poet, Philippe de Mézières takes this same religious reflectivity a step further, using it as a call for crusade. After the defeat of the Christian armies at Nicopolis in 1396, Philip addressed a letter to King Philip of France, laying out the causes of the defeat— Christian division and decadence—and proposing reforms that would knit Christian knights into a militant order governed by the fourfold moral virtues of right rule (*règle*), discipline, obedience, and justice. Philippe in "L'épistre lamentable et consolatoire" places the same internal focus on the problems of Christianity as do Langland and Wycliffe and makes the same logical link between Christian reform and the dispelling of the Islamic threat. However, unlike his predecessors, Philippe's argument is driven by the need not only to mend Christian divisions but to avenge the defeat at Nicopolis and vindicate the honor of Christian Europe. He insists upon the intense shame of the 1396 defeat: "la grant vergoigne de la foy, la vergoigne de toy, de tous les roys crestiens et de la cretienté . . ." (458) [the great shame of the faith, your own shame, the shame of all Christian kings and of Christianity itself].[13]

This defeat is not just tactical. It strikes a mortal wound ("plaie") to the body of Christendom. This "plaie douloureuse" (458) can be cured, Philippe argues, by the nurturing of "une nouvelle génération de combattants qui possédera ces quatre vertus morales" (457) [A new generation of fighters who possess the four moral virtues]. In Philippe's argument, the internal reformation of Christian knighthood into a newly regulated and energized military order automatically gives rise to a number of consummations devoutly to be wished: the defeat of the Turkish enemies of the faith, vengeance for their shaming victory, and the restoration of Christian sovereignty as the highest exemplars of chivalry, monarchy, and virtue. One of the reasons Philippe tried to negotiate peace between France and England in the 1390s was to help heal the internal divisions between Christian monarchs in preparation for a newly animated and successful crusade, which would reverse not only the recent defeat of the crusaders at Nicopolis, but the accumulated defeats on military, economic, and religious fronts of nearly a century.

In both the letter and his enormous work *Le Songe du vieil pelerin*, Philippe de Mézières characterizes his work as a voice crying in the wilderness, the voice of a solitary old pilgrim whose prophecies are the more crucial for being in the large part ignored. But similar crusading sentiments, although they failed to spark a royal crusade, were by no means alien or uncelebrated among the nobility and gentry of the English provinces, the probable audience of the *Wars of Alexander*, whose livelihoods were augmented not only by campaigns in France but increasingly, as the fourteenth century neared its end, by itinerant crusades in Prussia and Hungary, including the siege of Nicopolis.

In sum, by the late fourteenth century, the pressures and demands exerted by the various eastern dynasties and sultanates were multiple and ranged across a whole spectrum of European interests: political, social, economic, and religious. The *Wars of Alexander* reflects and explores this multiplicity. Even as it depicts a hero frantically trying to reduce endless empires to a single rule, the poem is captivated by the sheer diversity of Alexander's enemies, and it expands upon its source's descriptions of them with considerable inventiveness. Alexander's adversaries range from his secret Egyptian father, to the Jews in Jerusalem, to the great emperors Darius of Persia and Porrus of India, to the Brahmans of the Ganges, to the mysterious Master of the Temple of the Sun, and to the unnervingly self-possessed queen of Prasiaca, Candace, with whom he has a very close encounter indeed. As the poem continues and Alexander passes into unmappable eastern desolations, gruesome monsters erupt from the very earth to harry and decimate his forces. There is a clear sense that resistance to his encroachments is worked into the very soil of the landscape which yields monsters and portents with inexhaustible variety and fecundity. Such an overriding sense of eastern multiplicity—the east as a range of kingdoms, some very similar to Alexander's Macedon, others nightmarishly alien—subverts the cognitive division of the world into two halves, East and West.

At the same time, the poem problematizes the possibility of any singular conquest, because the conqueror himself is shown to be self-divided and fragmented, a hybrid creature whose identity ultimately rests on the constant erasure of his genealogical and situational affiliations to those he destroys. Even as the poem relentlessly depicts an empire in the process of foundation, it subverts the whole concept of a successful and lasting empire. It intimates an unnerving but irrefutable sense of the essential reflectivity of both East and West, their mutual dependence upon each other, their mutual generation of each other. In the end the poem points to one of the most insidious anxieties of a European sensibility anxious to reduce relations between itself and its eastern neighbors to the simple, unidirectional relation of conqueror and victim. It perhaps hints that their own foundational texts and tenets, their science and learning, their cultural genealogies have been obsessively translated, adapted and appropriated from cultures and countries now distanced as Eastern and other, from the Jews, from the Greeks, and from the Arabs. The poem insists on the essential relatedness of geographically opposed cultures and constructs that relatedness in a particularly threatening way—a relationship of blood in the senses of both violence and generation. It is Alexander's horrified recognition of his oriental progenitor that foregrounds, drives, and is ineffectually effaced by his subsequent military conquests.

Breaking the Terrestrial Mirror

The first part of the *Wars of Alexander* is occupied with the story of Anectanabus, the Egyptian king turned itinerant sorcerer, Alexander's secret, oriental, and untrustworthy father. Anectanabus's arcane knowledge obviates the web of chivalric solidarities between leader and follower that will make his son, Alexander, the greatest ruler of the world. King Anectanabus deserts his people when he learns by augury that they are about to be overrun by the Persians. He doffs the chivalric regalia of rulership and assumes the guise of a wandering astrologer—an unchancy magician who can vanish at will, transform himself into a dragon, deliver a baby, stage earthquakes and portents, and usurp the prerogatives not only of kings but of divinities, with perfect equanimity and impunity. By giving Alexander's father such socially disruptive energy, the poem constructs for its hero, Alexander, an oriental ancestry that is covert, lawless, volatile, and extremely unchivalric.

However, the poem complicates and obscures this ancestry when it details the trickery/divine intervention that brings about Alexander's birth. After fleeing Egypt, Anectanabus seeks refuge at the court of Philip of Macedon. Immediately, he seduces Queen Olympados, by masquerading as the sun god Amon, and then convinces Philip that this is not just a visitation to be endured, a kind of divine *droit de seigneur*, but an actual honor. Anectanabus's stratagem meets with dazzling success, and Alexander is thus gifted with three fathers, one hidden, Anectanabus, and two publicly acknowledged, Philip of Macedon and Amon the sun god.

This overdetermined ancestry enables Alexander to recognize his two public fathers and displace the specter of Anectanabus. The two public (and false) fathers, Amon and Philip, render less problematic the complex of power and trickery that Anectanabus represents. Amon, the sun god of the Macedonians, provides a divinely purified non-Arabic source for Alexander's excessive energy, his military brilliance, and the supernatural invulnerability that guarantees his military successes. Philip of Macedon's chivalric finesse contrasts with Anectanabus's wanton disregard for the socially formative links of chivalric loyalty and service. Alexander internalizes the attributes of his two putative fathers as he is brought up in Philip's court, gaining an understanding of courtly virtue, both as a leader of knights and as a defender of noble women, so that several times he instructs Philip himself in loyalty to his queen. Even after he discovers his true father's identity, killing him in the process, Alexander declares his affiliation only to his two public fathers throughout the poem, virtually alternating them each time he announces his ancestry to some new soon-to-be-subject ruler. In other words (Alexander is nothing if not thorough), he follows his murder of Anectanabus's person with the obliteration of Anectanabus's name.

However, the poem's trajectory works insistently against Alexander's ancestral iconoclasm, translating, inverting, and bringing its objects back before Alexander's face each time he looks into a conquered enemy's eyes and sees an inscription of his own already determined destiny. This dialectic is set in motion in the actual scene of the patricide. Anectanabus takes Alexander up to a cliff above Philip's castle for some stargazing. He points out the fateful influences in the heaven that decree his own end at the hands of his son. Alexander, still ignorant of their relationship, is incensed at this resignation to fate and strikes Anectanabus on the back with such force that the astrologer "drives down to the depths of the dike bottom" (712). Anectanabus's astronomical (and hence Arab-originating) expertise is forcibly rejected, but it is clear that Alexander is not simply punishing fraudulence with death. He is also enacting an irrefutable proof that Anectanabus *is* fraudulent. Anectanabus must be killed by his own son; Alexander is not Anectanabus's son and Alexander has killed Anectanabus; therefore Anectanabus is a fraud. *Quod erat demonstrandum*. His severity is a nicely reasoned and deliberately iconoclastic attempt to break the prophecy by anticipating it.

But Anectanabus, uncharacteristically, is not willing to vanish. Even as he succumbs to his fate, he chillingly demonstrates his preemptive power:

> Þan Anectanabus, as him aȝt wele; augirly granys.
> Dryues vp a dede voyce and dymly he spekis,
> "Wele was þis case to me knawen and kyd many wyntir
> Þat I suld dee slike a dethe be dome of my werdis.
> Sayd I þe noȝt so myselfe here before
> I suld be slayn of my son as now sothe worthis?"
> "What? and am I," quod Alexander, "ane of þi childer?"
> "ȝha, son! Als glad I my god, I gat þe myseluen"
>
> (717–24)

[Then Anectanabus, as it was necessary for
him, groans greatly, drives up a dead voice
and speaks darkly: "That my fate has doomed
me to such a death is a thing I have known
very well for many winters. Did I not say
myself just now that I should be slain by my
son as has now come truly to pass?" "What?"
said Alexander, "and am I one of your
children?" "Yes, son! As it please my god,
I begot you myself."]

Here, Anectanabus becomes literally a voice from the grave animated only by words of his own deadly prophecy. And just as Alexander's blow was an attempt to enact a proof and destroy his father's authority, Anectanabus's revelation not only implicates Alexander in his death but finally and irresistibly reinstates Anectanabus's prophetic authority and, by extension, the validity of all the prophecies that will hound Alexander throughout the poem. The paradox of Alexander's position is underlined. By attempting to destroy Anectanabus's influence, Alexander has actually surrendered to it. His iconoclasm, however excessive and self-assured, is contained and rendered futile by his ignorance of his intimacy to that which he is destroying. The poet stresses the force of Alexander's horror by compressing it into direct dialogue. Alexander's aghast "What? Am I one of your children?" conveys the shock of the revelation and the way it reshapes his identity: from the son of a god and foster son of a king, to a king's bastard and parricide—a transformation that Anectanabus's vigorous "3ha! son" drives home.

This scene of patricide determines the shape of Alexander's subsequent conquests. It provides a paradigm of conquest that stresses the fall from a height of a kingly forebear whom Alexander replaces and also outlines a pattern of reaction for Alexander—paralyzing tears and determined evasions. The poem's subsequent narrative reiterates this paradigm with obsessive variation. Alexander will spend the rest of his career "driving into the deepest part of the dike bottom" all the tremendous oriental rulers and armies that oppose him. The poem, however, repeatedly underscores the tendency of such high/low binaries to invert themselves, given time. On numerous occasions, as the victorious Alexander stands over his fallen enemy, he receives the advice to regard the fall as the mirror of his own future and look to himself.

Darius of Persia's death is one of many that elaborates this somber injunction to self-examination:

> Þe same ensampill of myselfe [þou sees now betid].
> So gret I grew of my gods and gold in my cofirs,
> Þat kindly gods creatoure I kend noȝt myselfe,
> Bot for his feloȝe and his fere faithly me leued.
> Þus prosperite and pride so purely me blyndid,
> I couth noȝt se fra my sege to þe soil vndire;
> Þat at me failed þan to fynd fast at myn eȝen,
> Be þe myrrour no of meknes, I may a myle knawe . . .
> If all þe limpe as þe list, loke to þine ende,
> For die þe mose quen all is done, and ay þe day scortis.
>
> (3408–15, 3426–27)

> [The same example of myself you can see
> happening now before you. I grew so mighty
> of my gods and had so much gold in my
> coffers, that I did not know myself for one
> of god's natural creatures, but rather
> believed myself firmly to be his equal and
> companion. Thus prosperity and pride blinded
> me so completely, I could not see from my
> throne to the soil underneath. I failed to
> discern what was clearly before my eyes and
> now through the mirror of submission I can
> see it from a mile away. When everything
> seems to be going as you wish, I warn you,
> look to your end. For you must die when all
> is done, and your day already shortens.]

This foreboding passage transforms the dialectic of high and low from a synchronic structure to a diachronic cycle, making the gulf between dominance and submission less a function of position than of time which inevitably passes. The "myrrour . . . of meknes" into which Darius now gazes also presses home the affinities between the two players. The temptation, as Darius argues, is to be blinded by the moment of victory, the throne from which the underlying earth is hidden, even as it waits to engulf one.

Here Darius connects himself to a powerful trope in late medieval writing: it surfaces in the *memento mori* effigies upon the tombs of medieval nobility and is, in fact, particularly linked to members of the nobility and gentry who would have the most temptation to let their exalted social position obscure the fact of their mortality. This is not to say that it necessarily works to undermine social rank as such; on the contrary, it is constantly incorporated into the paradigm of the noble life cycle as a necessary stage: the voice of age admonishing the eager and ambitious youth, and the mature and prosperous man. In the *Parliament of Three Ages*, another North Midlands alliterative poem of the late fourteenth century, we find a passage that echoes Darius. Here Age addresses Maturity and Youth:

> I sett ensample bi myselfe and sekis it no forthire . . .
> I was als euerrous in armes as ouþer of ȝoureseluen . . .
> And as myche wirschip I wane, iwis, as ȝe bothe . . .
> Bot elde vnderȝode me are I laste wist,
> And alle disfegurede my face and fadide my hewe . . .
> Make ȝoure mirrours bi me, men, bi ȝoure trouth
> This schadowe in my schewere schunte ȝe no while.
> (269, 271, 276, 283–84, 290–91)

> [Seek no further for an example (proof); I
> give you myself. I was as eager in arms as
> either of you, and won as much worship as
> both of you. . . . But age crept under me
> before I knew it, and disfigured my
> face. . . . Make your mirror by me, by your
> faith. Avoid no more this shadow
> [reflection] in my mirror.] [14]

In this passage Age transforms himself, just as Darius does, into a mirror of the future of Youth, a dark reflection that should be faced straightly by those still "eager in arms." The *Parliament of Three Ages* insists upon the link between such spatial reflection and genealogy. The poem ends with Age declaring "I am thi sire and thou my sone, the sothe for to telle, / For Elde is sire of Midill Elde, and Midill Elde of ȝouthe" (646–47) [To tell the truth of it, I am your father and you are my son, for Age is father of Maturity, and Maturity of Youth].

The *Wars of Alexander* repeatedly traps its hero at this peculiar intersection. As Alexander subjugates all the rulers of the east, he repeats his initial parricide and expresses his need not just to avoid, but to deauthorize, break away from, and obliterate this "schadewe in [the] schewere" of his oriental enemies. And yet, with every king he drives down to the dust, the ground beneath his own throne becomes that much nearer. Genealogical conquests against his predecessors are reenacted as spatial and geographical ones, while genealogical affinities sharpen into actual reflections.

As Alexander presses ever further east, the text increasingly echoes with intimations of reverberation, reflection, projection, and equivalence between the conqueror and his enemies. Alexander encounters the Brahmans, who live a life without rank, culture, or luxury on the far side of the impassable Ganges. Alexander halts on the western bank and sends them letters asking to learn of their culture and society. They send him back a description that links them with the primal innocence of the golden age but also aligns them with a fourteenth-century Christian reformatory perspective. They live like a literalization of Christ's sermon about the lilies of the field: no cultivation, no building, no rulers or servants, no greed, no disease, and no excess. They believe in a single god and regard life as a brief pilgrimage to be used and not enjoyed. Alexander replies with an aristocratic sneer, condemning them for both pride and foolishness: they are blasphemously and foolishly trying to imitate the gods.[15] Their answer to him throws his accusation back in his teeth:

> Þe same ensampill, as me semes, into ȝoureself touches.
> For so þe qwele of qwistounes ȝoure qualite encreses
> Þat noþir gesse ȝe gouernour no god bot ȝourselfe!
> ȝe brixsill our benignite, our bonerte repreues,
> And beris apon vs blasfeme þat neuire bale thoȝt
> . . . .
> It is ȝourselfe and noȝt oureself þat ai þe self hantis.
> (4786–94)

> [The same proof, it seems to me, touches your
> own case, for as long as the wheel of fortune
> increases your quality, you believe in no
> governor or god but yourself. You upbraid
> our good will and reprove our gentleness, and
> attribute blasphemies to us who never
> intended evil. . . . It is yourself and not
> ourselves that you continually pursue!]

Until this episode, Alexander is able to evade the significance of such insights with relative impunity. Subsequent episodes, however, no longer simply foreshadow the futility of Alexander's conquest, they are actually deadly. Two hundred lines after the encounter with the Brahmans, Alexander and his armies are menaced in a narrow chasm by a basilisk that crouches on the brink and destroys vast companies simply by turning the glare of its eyes in their direction. Alexander climbs up to the beast and makes himself a shield as large as a barn door with a mirror on its outer surface: "Þe screwe in þe schewere his schadow behaldis, / And so þe sla3tir of his si3t into himselfe entris" (4981–82) [The wretch beholds his shadow in the mirror, and so the slaughter of his gaze enters into himself]. This lethal reflection is multivalent: the basilisk in its magical invulnerability and capacity to conquer lends itself to comparison with Alexander himself. Alexander's shield, which both hides himself and reflects his enemy, is a figure of his most crucial strategy, the willful nonrecognition upon which his conquest depends.

Alexander's closest encounter with a deadly reflection, however, marks his first direct venture into the realm of generation, genealogy, and by extension mortality. On his way back to Macedon, he pauses to subdue the nearby land of Prasiaca, called significantly by the poet Preciosa, which is ruled by the conqueror-queen Candace. Yet as the two conquerors face each other, battle seems less on Alexander's mind than the queen herself and the queen's family. Disguising himself as one of his own knights, he rescues the queen's daughter-in-law from a neighboring king and visits Candace at her court to receive her thanks, knowing that her sons would kill him if they recognized him but believing himself unidentified. But unbeknownst to him, Candace knows him; she had sent a portrait-maker into Alexander's camp to secure his likeness and has judged him a highly desirable figure. On the second day of his clandestine visit, she takes him by the hand without explanation and leads him into a private chamber whose gilded walls "stremed as þe son" (5412) [shone like the sun]. Although they are quite secluded, she leads him further into a "clochere with a kay" (5415) [an enclosed place locked with a key] which is devised to whirl rapidly by the power of twenty tame elephants. Once they are within, the room begins to revolve, and, as Alexander is wondering at it, the queen calls him by his name, "Alexsandire." At this he starts and pales, but the queen only laughs, takes his hand, and leads him even further into a "preue parlour" (5430). And it is here in this triply enclosed sanctum that the by now sinister queen takes out his portrait, saying, "Se þiselfe a sampill þat I þe sothe neuyn" (5432) [See for yourself a proof that I name you truly]. Alexander is terrified. It is clear that by capturing his portrait and luring him from familiar ground into her own exotically revolving sphere, the queen has conquered him. She mocks him, not too gently:

"Qui fadis so þi faire hew?" said the faire lady,
"Þe werreour of all þe werd and wastour of Ynde,

> Þou þat has brettend on the bent þe barbrins fokke,
> Þe pepill out of Panty, þe Persens and þe Medis,
> Loo, now, þe here withouten hiȝt into my handis sesed,
> Bot in woman's ward for all þi wale dedis!"
>
> (5435–40)

["Why does your beautiful color fade?" asked
the fair lady, "The warrior of all the world
and the waster of India, you who have broken
on the field all the barbarian folk, the
people out of Parthia, the Persians and the
Medes. Lo, now without warning you are taken
into my hands, into the power of a mere woman
for all your proud deeds."]

Alexander nearly explodes with rage, gnashing his teeth and shaking his head violently. When the queen teases him a little more, he declares:

> "I swete . . . þat I na swerd haue,
> For I na wapen haue, iwis my writh with to venge!"
> "Now, bald baratour on bent, if þou a brand hade,
> Quat prowis miȝt þi person apreue in þis stounde?"
> "For I vnwarly," quod þe [wee], "am to ȝoure will taken;
> I suld þe slaa þare þou sittis and þan myselfe eftir!"
>
> (5450–56)

["I sweat with rage that I have no sword,
because I have no weapon to avenge my wrath."
"Now, brave knight on the field! if you had a
blade, what prowess would your person prove
in this place?" "Because I unwarily," said
the man, "am taken within your power, I
should slay you where you sit, and then
myself after!"]

The violence of Alexander's reaction is a terrified response to the intimate control Candace has established over him by isolating him and then showing him his own face. As a figure who throughout the poem destroys any external authority whatsoever, Alexander finds this subjection to a woman absolutely unbearable. The queen is able to allay his anger only by assuring him that she does not desire dominion. This promise enables a brief affair between them which the poem emphatically downplays—within one hundred lines Alexander is on the road again looking for new enemies.

This pivotal scene touches the heart of Alexander's "haunting": the tantalizing fear that drives him to pursue the shadow in the mirror which betokens his enemies, his origins, and his mortality. Simultaneously the greatest warrior in history and history's greatest dupe, in his attempts to evade such a fragmenting self-recognition he finally becomes as restless, rootless, unchivalric, and volatile as his own fiercely effaced father. The self-conflicts that have been driving him onward finally begin to tear him apart. The last eight hundred lines of the poem confront him with increasingly fantastic and nightmarish enemies, while his ambitions grow wilder and wilder. Much of the time he is battling terrifying lethal beasts: giant lions and scorpions, who pick away at his army, destroy his provisions, and reduce his followers by huge numbers. More and more he is hounded by a sense of inevitable attrition. His ferocious man-eating horse, Bucephalon, which has been with him since his boyhood, dies of a lingering disease. At the same time, he grows tired of transgressing earth's boundaries and frantically attempts to transcend the boundaries of the earth itself. He rigs a flying machine by harnessing four winged griffins to a chariot and extending a great hook baited with raw flesh over their heads. The narrator's disengagement from his hero's increasingly desperate fantasy surfaces clearly:

> Þare was a miȝti montayne at to þe mone semed,
> He gessis it gaynir to god þan to þe grounde vndire,
> And slike a fonned fantasy þan fell in his hert
> How þat he liftid miȝt be fra þe lawe vnto þe liȝt sternes.
> (5637–40)

[There was a mighty mountain that seemed as
tall as the moon. He believes it to be
nearer god than to the ground underneath, and
a certain foolish fantasy then grew in his
heart: how he might be lifted from the ground
up to the bright stars.]

Alexander's attempt to stellify himself is as unsuccessful as are his other forays at historic transcendence. The griffins rise up until "midilerth bot as mylnestane na mare to him semed, / and all the water of þe werd bot as a wrethen neddire" (5651–52) [The earth seemed no more than a millstone, and all the water of the world only a coiled serpent]—a vision as dismissive of the significance of his travails as Troilus' own. But the Christian God prevents Alexander from reaching his goal and, cursing like Lucifer, he falls to the earth, frustrated but unhurt—a *deus ex machina* interference that encapsulates Alexander's distance from his late medieval Christian audience. Undeterred, Alexander then attempts to plumb the depths of the seas.

In these reckless excursions, the poet plays on the latitude allowed by his hero's hybrid identity both to validate Alexander's chivalric leadership and to alienate reassuringly the more transgressive (and baroque) excesses of his ambition from his fourteenth-century audience. If one recalls the ambiguous ancestry and legacy that make Alexander a model and ancestor appropriate by both European and oriental conquerors, the poem's evident relish in Alexander's imminent demise is spiced with a kind of vengeful fantasy. Alexander's ambition driven to these extremes is ultimately blasphemous because, as the Brahmans point out, it finally refuses to acknowledge any authority but its own self-generated one.

However, Alexander's less celestial ambitions would probably have awakened a certain sympathy among the British crusaders at Nicopolis at the end of the fourteenth century, who regarded war as their livelihood, the Turks as their enemies, and the signory of the world as their God-given right. Like them, Alexander finally desires a life of war that is perpetual, profitable, and undeterred by any entrapping sense of debt, cultural affinity, or even knowledge of his adversaries. He wishes for an identity as self-sufficient, volatile, and perpetual as that of the fiery phoenix which he glimpses wistfully when he visits the Temple of the Sun just before he hears the dismal prophecy that he has just two more years to live.

If, as I argue, Alexander embodies the ideology of the fourteenth-century British chivalry, his hybrid genealogy and his impossible ambitions expose the conflicts within that increasingly defensive audience. Other North West Midlands alliterative works express a similar interest in the quandaries of their chivalric heroes: *Sir Gawain and the Green Knight* delights in pinching its hero between the twin imperatives of courtesy and loyalty; the alliterative *Morte Arthure* describes an Arthur whose blend of ardent chivalry and excessive ambition echoes Alexander's own. What sets the *Wars of Alexander* apart from these works is its more exclusive focus on the interpenetrations of eastern and western cultures. Despite the difficulties of the poem's dating, it is arguable that the poem responds to the late-fourteenth-century dilemmas of a British warrior-class whose livelihood depended on war, but which was threatened by the late century reverses and negotiations for peace in the Hundred Years' War with France. In the last decade of the century particularly, both Charles VI of France and Richard II of England sought to redirect the energies of veterans disaffected with the prospect of treaty by actively promoting crusades against the Ottoman Turks encroaching upon Prussia and Hungary. In fact, the gentry and itinerant soldiery of Cheshire and the North West Midlands—the region from which the *Wars of Alexander* is believed to originate—were so horrified by rumors of this peace that in 1393 they led an armed rebellion. No less a personage than John of Gaunt suppressed them and, significantly, enlisted the bulk of them into his army, first to quell his Gascon subjects, but then to accompany him on the crusade against Nicopolis.[16] The highest nobility of England advocated the crusade against the Turks as a pursuit eminently possible, chivalrously and religiously admirable, and politically canny—an escape valve for provincial warriors so dependent upon constant military exercise that they tended to armed rebellion when deprived of it. When the Christian armies were decimated at Nicopolis, their defeat thus put an end to a century of disastrous military reverses, economic dependence upon oriental luxury goods, and, most troublingly, internal dissensions within and between European and Christian countries. To such recent developments, the traditional world-bifurcating strategy of crusade had proven a wholly inadequate response.

In the *Wars of Alexander*, Alexander's dilemma is similarly irresolvable; the poem proposes no way for him to escape it, no sense in which he can acknowledge the deadly reflexivities between himself and his enemies and still remain the great world conqueror he is driven to be. In that, the history of the poem's two manuscripts have done Alexander a service: they are fragments whose end is missing and therefore provide no account of his death. It is useless to speculate whether the poem was deliberately left unfinished, or whether the ending has been simply lost. The poem does, however, gesture at closure before breaking off: it ends with the list of Alexander's conquests that he inscribes upon the walls of his palace. Finally either the manuscript's history or the poem itself collaborates in the desires and aversions of its hero. The poem replaces Alexander's death with Alexander's monument, a gesture at immortality that even as it puts a final flourish to Alexander's conquests also redirects the reader's attention to his ambiguous and continuing legacy: a monument that is a wall—designed both to separate and commemorate—that refuses closure by echoing the interminable conquests of the poem itself. It is this ambivalent and reverberating legacy that ties the poem so closely to the late medieval audience, the gentry of the North West Midlands. It is precisely because Alexander is in such an impossible, uncomfortable, and familiar position that his character so vividly encompasses the self-contradictions, anxieties, and fatal self-evasions of late fourteenth-century provincial chivalry.

Notes

1. The *Wars of Alexander* survives in two fragmentary manuscript copies, Ashmole 44 in a mid-fifteenth-century hand and Dublin MS 213 in a late-fifteenth-century hand. Like most of the late-fourteenth-century alliterative poems, the author is unknown, though the poem's most recent editors speculate on the grounds of an unusual number of shared phrases and some intriguing descriptive echoes that the author may have originated in the North West Midlands and have influenced or been influenced by the *Gawain*-poet. The poem's dating is extremely tenuous—suggestions have ranged from 1361 to just before 1450. My argument does not presuppose a particular date, but I treat the poem mainly as dating from the late fourteenth century or early fifteenth century. I focus upon the broader historical developments of the fourteenth century, because that seems to have been the period when alliterative poetry had its greatest English vogue, and when the other alliterative poems to which it is compared are generally believed to have been written. See Duggan and Turville-Petre (intro. ix–li), the edition from which all citations are taken; unless otherwise indicated, translations of this and other works are my own.

2. The poem's main source is the I^3 version of the immensely popular late-twelfth-century *Historia de preliis Alexandri Magni*, of which forty-five manuscript copies survive. The *Wars* is a faithful translation, though the poet freely expands upon his source, introducing new episodes at several points, many of which are notable for their biting irony. The fact that it is a translation does not detract from its originality or from the significance attributable to the choice to translate it in the late fourteenth century. See Duggan and Turville-Petre, intro. xiii–xvii.

3. Thrupp offers a possible reason for this continuing attraction during earlier periods: that early medieval Christians may have been growing tired of perpetually measuring their civilization and their achievements against the splendor of the lingering monuments of Rome. Instead they reached back to a hero who "outclassed any Roman hero" and whose exploits predate the Roman world (273).

4. For a description of Arabic attitudes to European incursions during the crusades, see Maalouf.

5. Odo of Deuil's narrative is particularly interesting in the way it works to associate the Greek Byzantine Christians with the Islamic Turks, as cultures "arrogant in wealth, treacherous in customs, corrupt in faith" [superba divitiis, moribus subdola, fide corrupta], who are nonetheless cultured, sophisticated, and above all, rich (86–87).

6. In fact, by far the greatest time lag between first documented cases occurs in the interval when the plague traveled from inland China (1320) to the Chinese port of Zaytun (1345). After that interval, it swiftly struck Caffa on the Black Sea in 1346, Cairo and Damascus in 1347, Italy, France, and Britain in 1348, Germany and Scandanavia in 1349, and Moscow in 1351. See Abu-Lughod, 172–73.

7. A complaint from a group of merchants forced to remain in Alexandria until their goods spoiled has been included in Lopez and Raymond, 335–36; see Abu-Lughod, 236–41, for a fuller account of the Alexandrian customs regulations.

8. Atiya, the historian who focuses upon this crusade most fully, emphasizes the role of the English knightly contingent in this venture (44–45).

9. Gibb outlines the ways these cultures might have spoken to each other even

before the fourteenth century—their common respect for the heritage of the past, their need for continuity, and their balancing of faith and reason as ways to maintain it (160).

10. My argument here draws upon Southern's description of this convergence, augmenting the theologians he discusses with two other writers, William Langland and Philippe de Mézières. For Southern's discussion of fourteenth- and fifteenth-century developments, see *Western Views*, 67–107.

11. The civic cycle dramas of the late fourteenth and fifteenth centuries provide only one instance; in many Mahound is either an infernal demon or one of many deities.

12. Southern stresses the innovativeness of this reciprocity in Wycliffe's polemical writings (*Western Views*, 79–80).

13. Quoted from Thorlac Turville-Petre's edition; translations are mine throughout.

14. Quoted from Thorlac Turville-Petre's *Alliterative Poetry*; translations are my own.

15. I am not able here to explore how this exchange between Alexander and the Brahmans focuses fourteenth-century ecclesiastical and seigneurial anxieties about the social effects of a literal *imitatio Christi*, but such concerns clearly animate the episode.

16. Palmer comments on their eventual fate: "Although John of Gaunt himself eventually withdrew from this venture, there is good reason to believe that most of his Cheshire troops marched towards the Balkans under the leadership of his illegitimate son John Beaufort, and fought and died on the banks of the Danube" (184–85). See his excellent discussion of the complex negotiations between the various Christian monarchs and the papacy which lead to the crusading fervor at the end of the century.

III

GENDER, SEXUALITY, GEOGRAPHY

7
City Air Makes Men Free and Women Bound

JO ANN MCNAMARA

FREUD, WITH A FINE SCIENTIFIC DISREGARD for history, theorized that women are by nature hostile to the city and all its works (50–51). He viewed them as agents of disruption, distracting men from the duties and responsibilities of public life, that is, civilization. Aristotle, too, saw women as uncivilized or apolitical when he defined man as an animal that acts in a polis, consequently restricting women to the household. The readiness of women to convert to Christianity, compared to the reluctance of upper-class Roman men, is an indicator of their respective losses in relinquishing the rewards of pagan public life (Brown, *Religion*). Through grudging recognition of the virginity movement, the religion tolerated a limited autonomy for self-restrained women. But, as the church settled into the institutional framework of the Empire, consecrated women, even of the highest social class, often attracted scandal and even public abuse (McNamara, "Muffled Voices"). This is dramatically illustrated in the brief history of the foundation by Caesarius of Arles of a convent for his sister and her virgin companions. Originally, he had intended to domicile them in a relatively unbounded rural setting just outside the city but fear of invading Visigoths forced him to move the community within the protecting walls of the city. The consequent threat of city streets required a second set of walls enclosing the nuns permanently and irrevocably. Caesarius's rule for nuns, the only rule to prescribe strict enclosure in the early Middle Ages, remained popular throughout Gaul until urban life virtually disappeared (2.101–27).

Early medieval society was still inclined toward the classical equation of potency and manhood (Walters). On either end of the spectrum, gender tended to be subordinated to class interests in a society organized around kindred. It was not uncommon to find viragoes, manly women born into the potentate class, deployed as though they were men where necessary to serve family interests.[1] At the lower end, landlords' systematic demand for labor from women implicitly endowed them with extrafamilial status while unmanly servility pressed impotent men down toward the female, inferior, end of the scale. Monastic women and men met and mingled metaphorically and, in some cases, literally. Prudent fear of wolves, outlaws, and invaders did not prevent a certain freedom of movement among nuns living under the uncloistered and ungendered rules of Columbanus, Benedict, and Augustine. For centuries, syneisactic communities, where a majority of women ruled by powerful and learned abbesses were served by attendant monks and laborers, made up the porous center of the sexual continuum established by Aristotelian biology.

The return of "civilization," the urban life, changed all that. In perfect harmony with the ancient philosopher and the modern psychologist, medieval men made the city an instrument for the freedom of men and the containment of women. Where the antique pattern incorporated male slaves, children, and paupers into the unmanly portion of the population, medieval ideology imaged a broad womanless space wherein men became not only free but commensurable: equal to one another in their masculinity. The surge in population and material prosperity in the early twelfth century opened up a wide variety of practical choices for medieval men (Bynum, *Jesus as Mother*, 82–108). Women found that, as society became more institutionalized, their place within it became ever more confined and stereotyped. New professions generated by the church, secular government, and towns were not readily pinned to masculine warrior qualities. The new identities had to be gendered as well as classed, which meant that men had to prove women's incapacity to carry out public professional responsibilities by developing arcane skills that mysteriously qualified them to *man* the offices of the opening bureaucracy. The city drew much of its population from immigrants moving from rural areas where their labor had ceased to outweigh the costs of their livelihood to lord and family. We see young men of various social levels, a class seeking to make some fortune in the world which would lift them from prolonged adolescence to social maturity (Duby, "In Northwestern France"). Literary sources romanticized their entry into a world of male bonding and homosociability like King Arthur's Round Table. Religious sources enforced the exclusion of women by a virulent new flood of misogynistic rhetoric.[2]

Women were eliminated as participants in the definitive debates of the Investiture Conflict, and the triumph of the papal hierarchy extended the areas of their exclusion from the public life of the church (McNamara, "Canossa"). Ordination acted as a wedge between male and female monastics, incorporating monks into the clergy and virtually forcing nuns into the laity. Learning shifted from monasteries, where women had been educated in much the same manner as men, to episcopal schools intended to train a newly celibate clergy. With the imposition of celibacy on the clergy, ambitious men were drawn out of the kinship system and into the bosom of an anthropomorphized "mother church," whose child was the university. There, men could pose as ungendered representatives of the human whole, discoursing of love, sex, and the nature of the universe in the secret codes of Latin and scholastic dialectic.[3] In this comfortable situation, celibate men could denigrate the female body and tie the female soul ever more firmly to its fleshly prison. Women's capacity to comprehend what was happening and to validate their own experience was crippled by a "renaissance" which opened a vast armory of antique authority to men. So-called Humanists revived the study of the Christian fathers. Woman-hating based upon the concept of the natural evil of the female sex, the curse of Eve, was articulated freely in all sorts of public places.[4] Young scientists argued whether women were men inside out or, as Aristotle would have it, simply defective men. Aristotle won.

Universities were the frontier fortresses of the new gender system. They provided an ideology for male dominance and eventually a technical language for the creation of generic, ungendered men who occupied the whole category of "people," effectively obscuring women from view. The requirement of minor orders, which would not preclude a secular career and marriage for men who entered law, medicine, or other learned and administrative professions, effectively barred women from the whole range of anthropomorphized institutions that came to govern the high medieval world. In religion, women still had the monastic option, but the rising tide of misogyny drowned the hopes of women reformers in the apostolic movements of the late eleventh and early twelfth centuries (McNamara, "Herrenfrage"). Where women and men mixed together in lives of poverty and charity modeled on the New Testament, prelates saw nothing but cause for scandal. Under their assault, most male reformers responded by dismissing or cloistering their female companions. Whether they lived in the city or were confined to establishments outside the walls, Fontevrist, Gilbertine, and Norbertine nuns were subjected to rules of claustration fanatical in their attention to detail. All the new orders sooner or later determined that they were too rigorous and too pure to allow women to be admitted among them. Dominic provided an enclosed shelter for repentant female heretics to support but not to join his preachers. Even Francis of Assisi was unwilling to imitate Jesus in keeping company with women and severed himself and his brothers sharply from Clare and her sisters, whom he placed in a Benedictine cloister. Beguines were organized in semicloistered courts closed off from the common bustle of the city. Anchoresses were threatened with censure if they took too active a role in the networks of charity, work, credit, and education circulating in their towns. Gregory IX, in 1227, approved the order of the Magdalene for women who wanted to repent lives of sin or desperation. By the end of the thirteenth century, Pope Boniface VIII issued a bull that all religious women, regardless of the form of their vows or consecration, be strictly cloistered. Dependence, not complementarity, was their aim. No order could be formed solely of women, by women, and for women.

Driven behind walls, religious women were economically crippled by severe limitations on most enterprises and an inability to hustle for the larger donations that men could command. In the fourteenth century, escalating violence drove nuns from rural areas into the cities, putting their endowments at risk and increasing the burden of their care on their families, the clerical establishment, and employers who provided them with piecework. Even within the cloister, elements of the male structure interposed themselves between women. Men were required to act as advocates at law and business agents for women legally barred from acting for themselves. Finally, men monopolized the sacerdotal services that women required, a situation fraught with danger. Twelfth-century prelates violently criticized preachers who committed themselves too enthusiastically to the ministry to women, warning that the contact would pollute the purity of their thoughts if not of their bodies.[5] Visitation records as well as popular tales of nuns spontaneously aborted by miraculous means confirmed that confessors sometimes went so far as to seduce their penitents. Unwilling to countenance religious women who pursued their own spiritual development without male supervision, popes and bishops were repeatedly obliged to insist that male orders shoulder the obligations of the *cura mulierum* (de Fontette). At the same time, they sought to ensure that the bonds between religious women and their confessors did not reconstitute a syneisactic community. Fear itself became gendered. Men were threatened with loss of self-control and domination by the irrational powers of women. The myth of male nature governed by uncontrollable lust feeding women's uncontrollable urge to dominate man served a double purpose. It made men fear women and salved their consciences if they were swept away during the intimacies of their pastoral visitations.

Women internalized the threat. The influence of male confessors alienated them from their own experiences and drove them within themselves. They complemented male fear of pollution and the destructive powers of sexual attraction with their own fear of provoking male lust, which was powerfully manipulated to control women who went into the streets for charitable purposes or to support themselves by honest labor. Images of rape, pollution, mutilation, and loss of purity rage through the prescriptive literature offered to anchoresses and recluses. Cloistered nuns were not safe from the workmen, visitors, and confessors who invaded their precincts. The models of tormented martyrs, like Agnes, Catherine, and Ursula, overshadowed the powerful female saints of the early Middle Ages as models for religious women. A young royal bride was subliminally threatened by the marginal figures in her prayer book (Caviness). Hildegard of Bingen saw the church as a bride threatened with the corrupting and seductive powers of greedy prelates. Christine of Markyate had a vision of herself in a field where bulls threatened her with their horns, and she understood that if she stood perfectly still they could not touch her (*Life*, 33).

The isolation and consequent dependency of women religious provided a model for the secular world. Men and women performing the same work (and possibly competing for jobs) in a common workroom threatened the foundations of society. Marxist historians have proposed that the religious struggle against heresy masked a class struggle in cities all over Europe, based on the frequency with which artisans, especially weavers, confessed to heresy (Koch).[6] Married couples and celibates in the twelfth century were experimenting with a lifestyle which combined manual labor, charitable activity, and religious devotion. The negative reaction centered on gender: heresy was being defined as the association of men with women, and weaving was at the center of the conflict, because in the twelfth century it was a skill commanded by both women and men, though women were gradually being driven out of the better urban workshops. The underlying argument—that men could not consort innocently with women—was most succinctly stated by Bernard of Clairvaux, who said that it was easier to raise the dead than for men to resist women (Sermo 65, *Sermones super Cantica Canticarum* [PL 1088–93]). High-handedly dismissing the objection that women lived with Jesus and the apostles, Bernard concluded that men and women who lived and worked together, however chaste and blameless they might appear, were in truth heretics subverting the church through scandal. The Umiliati, who in 1238 set up a regular working community in Florence where they taught "families of workers" woolen manufacture and the gospel together, clung to the right side of orthodoxy by practicing chaste marriage (Elliott, 197–200). Others were not so lucky and were accused of Catharism or Waldensianism.

The association of women with heresy helped separate them out of crafts like weaving, where they had originally worked in large numbers, and in turn this promoted male bonding within the craft. Gradually, the honor of a trade came to depend on the fiction that women could not understand its mysteries. The more prestigious a trade was, the more masculine it was. Even activities that were commonly women's work in a rural setting, like baking and weaving, became men's crafts when transferred to an urban setting. Women's skills were considered incidental and peripheral, lacking the occult quality of guild training. "Women's work," like cloth finishing or spinning, was beneath a craftsman's attention and therefore consigned to lower status and lower pay. Their opportunities constrained at every level, devout secular women like the Beguines and, later, the Schwestren of the Common Life adopted a communal life supported by cheap hand labor which was not capital intensive. But their willingness to work cheaply, making a virtue of self-denial, became an offense against working men who resented the "unfair" competition. In the early fourteenth century, the claustration of Beguines and Tertiaries was enforced by mob violence, and in some cases they were burned at the stake.

But this could not be corrected. As is well known, women by tradition and sometimes by law were paid far less than men. Some oft-quoted statutes insist that women be paid less than men for the same work "because they eat less." Chrétien de Troyes makes the silk spinners sing: "We shall always work the silk but never get better clothing; we shall always be poor and naked; we shall always suffer thirst and hunger because they are stingy with our bread— a little in the morning and still less in the evening." In 1295, the Brussels Beguines petitioned the town council to allow them the same return for their labor as the members of the secular guilds (Mundy, *Europe*, 201). Their petition was, of course, denied. Other women were forced into an underground economy where they labored outside the cognizance of guilds and the law. In 1421, the spurriers of London lodged a complaint against smiths who supplied unlicensed competition with roughly forged iron for finishing: "chamberers, not householders, some of them women . . . [who] dwell in holks and hyrnes in hie sollers that they wardens may not see theym, and gothe oute of the Cittey to fayres and mayrketts and in to lords Innes and in to other privye places and sels such fals work in greate disceite hynderynge of all the comyn people and in greate dysclaunderynge of all the crafte" (Thrupp, "gilds," 255).

By the twelfth century, when towns became corporate persons, male burghers, upheld by oaths of mutual assistance, had developed a strong sense of mutual solidarity.[7] Guild members monopolized municipal offices on the somewhat specious excuse that they performed military service not possible for women.[8] This monopoly of public authority bolstered their control of trades. Municipal authorities excluded women from the governance assumed by the guilds, which, in turn, set apprentice and work rules incompatible with their household responsibilities, placing all men on a roughly equal base of superiority over all women. Women were often forbidden to enter a court of justice, and judges were warned not to give ear to their complaints. Lawsuits had to be brought for wives by their husbands, just as a male advocate had to represent nuns. A Florentine statute of 1294 gives the quaintly ambiguous caution: "Women are a sex to be locked up as dangerous in disturbing the course of justice" (Staley, 90).[9] City fathers in firm control of the courts took strong action against women caught stealing the raw silk put out to them for spinning. In Florence and Fiesole, the bishop periodically threatened to excommunicate spinners who wasted the wool entrusted to them (Renard).[10] In other cases, women were imprisoned for carelessness or theft.

The independent membership of women in guilds or guilds made up of women exclusively were, of course, not uncommon (Depping). But the conditions of this membership need a broad comparative examination. The linen manufacturers of Florence admitted women, but most of the female members lived in the countryside and paid a matriculation fee only half as large as those in the city. What looks at first glance like extraordinary privilege may be only an example of bringing cottage labor under guild regulation so as to eliminate independent competition (Staley, 353). Examination and apprenticeship fees for female linen weavers in Barcelona was similarly low in comparison to men, and other conditions suggest that the fee was only collected to bring them under guild control, not to enable them to rise to mastery and full participation. In Florence, workers in the wool trade were organized apart from the merchants. They could not visit guild offices or the establishments of those who gave them work but carried on all their dealings through a putting out system with guild representatives in country districts. In Venice, textile work was dominated by merchant employers, who bought wool or cotton and put it out to be spun in homes by women. Wage earners were barred from membership in the wool guild (Lane, 161). The *Livre des métiers* lists six female crafts in Paris, all on the putting out system. A comparison of the organization of trades reported by the provost of Paris and some subsequent tax roles suggests that the "trades" that seem to be solely female in membership may simply be taxable categories created by the royal bureaucracy, carrying no privileges for the workers. Even where women are organized into guilds of their own the initiative seems to come from public authorities. City ordinances often intervened in labor relations to the extent of obligating merchants to pay the workers for completed goods.[11] In the sense that it reaffirmed their superiority as a gender, male solidarity was even enhanced when one male authority undertook to protect women from another.

Working women had, therefore, virtually no adequate means of making a living. Unmarried women were excluded from most guilds to protect work for men (Kowaleski).[12] Women alone were usually reduced to low status and low-paid occupations, moving from one trade to another, which could not be relied on as full-time professions. Their status as perpetual "amateurs" prevented them from threatening male employment. In commerce, few women had a large enough trade to be classed as merchants. They usually sold produce, sausages, or other edibles which grain merchants or butchers scorned. Women are found to be in debt for smaller sums than men. As creditors, Jewish women and a few Christian women carried out the sorts of transactions which most citizens viewed with moral disapproval, small consumption loans and pawnbroking (Jordan, 19–23). They were rarely seen as merchants or producers in high-status work.

Unwanted children were abandoned in growing numbers, and the majority were girls. In 1435 a monk, Ambrogio Traversari, noted that in the Florentine foundling hospice "Boys are sent to learn their letters; girls learn womanly things. When they later become adults, the boys learn a trade which will support them; the girls are married with the institution providing a dowry" (Trexler, 261). This was little more than a pious fiction, however. In the late Middle Ages, men married late and demanded high dowries. Journeymen seeking advancement looked for wives among the widows and daughters of masters through whom they could inherit the mastership. Women who had neither advantage often learned crafts as servants but, being ineligible for guild membership, they remained vulnerable to the sorry fate of unmarried women. In addition, unmarried men (not to mention masters) relieved their sexual pressures by exploiting the servant population, which was notoriously vulnerable. One mother explained that she put her twelve-year-old girl into a foundling home rather than place her where she would be "harmed and become evil, as do the other servant girls" (Trexler, 268). Furthermore, in Italy, domestic slavery was almost entirely female. Male slaves were removed from the city to mines or galleys, and women were confined to households where they often participated in the "underground" economy of the household production unit and its equally illicit reproduction system (Stuard, 45).

The one trade that urbanization unquestionably opened to women was prostitution. Everywhere observers noted that a "surplus" of women seemed to be driving many into the streets. Modern historians have ascribed the overpopulation of women of every social degree to the imbalances created by clerical celibacy and a high male mortality rate. It is likely that former priests' wives, reclassified by papal fiat as concubines, were among the mysterious crowds of "repentant prostitutes" who threw themselves on the mercy of wandering preachers, who often urged men to marry them so as to reform them and take them out of the streets. In the early thirteenth century, Jacques de Vitry saw them soliciting students on their way to class. A consular order of 1201 claims that Toulouse had so many prostitutes that they had to be driven out of the city (Devic and Vaissette, 8.471, 633, 1351).

As time went by, the more common response was the tried and true solution of cloistering prostitutes in brothels run by city fathers, who regulated their behavior, kept them to their business, and paid for the effort out of the earnings of their charges.[13] Where, as in Paris, the city did not provide a public brothel, prostitutes worked out of bathhouses and were organized under the bath keepers' guilds or the barber's guild, which presumably acted to control work standards. At times, administrators had to appeal for charity for women who could not work because of illness, menstruation, or restrictions pertaining to holy feasts. More commonly, prostitutes became part of the much resented pool of cheap female labor which undercut male workers. Regulations for the Nuremberg brothels, around 1300, ordered that the women be supplied with looms so that they could work when otherwise unemployed.[14] In Augsburg they spent their days spinning.

Precautions were taken by prudent city fathers to ensure that "common women" in their *cura* could not exercise their fatal lures upon their customers. They were prevented from preferring particular patrons, from naming the father of their babies, and sometimes protected from rape (where presumably a woman was singularized by the man, who was thus impinging on public property) (Roper). Many cities were proud of the quality of their whores and celebrated public occasions and entertained visiting dignitaries with a visit to the municipal brothel. Thus women, by their absence from serious places where men pursued their professions and by their presence in confined spaces where men could control and use them to celebrate masculinity, helped to establish male commensurability. It also helped to secure masculinity from sliding down the one-sex continuum of Aristotelian biology into effeminacy. Christian horror of eunuchs and the classification of sodomites as mortal sinners grew steadily as women and men were physically separated and misogyny tainted heterosexual relationships.[15] Whether or not civic authorities consciously promoted brothels to avert the temptations of homosexuality, they clearly gave young men a chance to celebrate their manly virility without marrying and without compromising the young daughters of their masters who were kept virgin until marriage.[16] Journeymen who lacked the mastery of their craft also lacked the mastery of a wife, which marked the passage from bachelor boyhood to householding adulthood, and found solace in the municipal brothel that provided girls regularly inspected for health at a relatively low price. Finally, the fraternal setting of the experience, which systematically transformed women into objects for the use of men, was a useful contribution to their group socializing.

Needless to say, most city women were not confined to convents, sweatshops, or brothels. Gratian divided the social world into celibate clergy and married laymen. The social or political disabilities that hampered women from freely entering markets, law courts, and other public forums in pursuit of their own interests forced secular men to undertake their own *cura mulierum*. Despite the burdens upon individual men and the danger to the homosocial group, men had to be steered into marriage. There was no other way that they could be secure in undisturbed enjoyment of the city's freedoms. Increasingly, with the encouragement of canon law, the family centered on the married couple, which broke down the hold of kinship on individuals and facilitated a common definition of men as the controllers of women through their mastery of the household.[17]

In the industrial towns of the north, the craft family, dominated by the master, was often defined as the norm of civic order: a hierarchy with wife subordinate to husband, children to parents, servants to masters. In Augsburg, marriage was a necessary condition for voting and holding office since it showed the master's maturity and capacity for government. At one point in the fifteenth century, the council was even closed to widowers. Recognizing the inequality of husband and wife in the public world, a married couple approximated partnership within the domestic walls. Women participated energetically in the family production unit. A master's wife practiced the craft without the mastership, also supervising apprentices and children and even training maids to help out, also without the hope of mastership. Even in the fifteenth century, when guilds were tightening control, wives, children, and frequently maidservants were excepted from rules limiting the numbers of apprentices who could be trained in a craft or employed in a shop.[18] A wife might also keep books or run the sales end of the business in addition to ensuring the physical well-being of the entire household. But if she left, or the household broke up, her "membership" evaporated. In Genoa, where the patriarchal family dominated the aristocracy, the conjugal bond remained too strong among the working people for any other to be formed. Genoese artisans did not emulate the aristocrats in withdrawing marital support from their wives but continued to exchange a marriage gift for the dowry which almost equaled or even exceeded its value. Appreciation for women's contribution to the family economy was often expressed in wills where husbands made their wives their heirs, which would never happen among the aristocracy (Diane Hughes).[19] Nevertheless, it was an affection firmly based on a power structure enforced by gender-conscious men who were swift to discipline a husband who failed to keep his wife in order.

Even women who traded independently, registered as *feme sole*, were usually married and their industry tended to benefit their husbands more than themselves. In a few cases, wives imported raw materials needed in their husbands' industries (acting as their commercial agents) or they worked as part of an economic household unit (Howell, 20). Their husbands were protected from liability for their debts, consequently weakening the woman's position in the credit market. However, working women's independent participation in the market even by way of the household economy led to a relaxation of her tutelage, posing the threat that women might build on that economic position to weaken family commitments and to enter the male world of public prestige and authority. Married women who practiced an independent trade as a supplement to the family income undermined the general situation of men by underpricing them in the labor market, thus bringing cash into their own households at the expense of the whole institution of family authority. Gender solidarity eventually persuaded individual men to give up the marginal advantages of their wives' enterprises in exchange for an array of legal privileges that gave gender precedence over class.

The solidarity of husbands was disturbed only by competition among younger men for their daughters as wives to control. Escape from the socially demeaning laws that restricted serfs to marriage only with other serfs of the same master was a vital component of the "freedom" that men found on coming to the city. With a small stake to make their own way in a crowded world, young men of every degree were on the prowl for wives who could advance their hopes. Individual ambition had to accomplish what family strategy could no longer achieve.[20] They could try to attract an advantageous marriage through personal charm or flattery. They could look for a favored position as apprentice to an elderly master with a young wife or daughter or even attempt to take a bride by elopement or capture from her home or from a convent.[21]

Moreover, the well-known frailty of women and the reckless lusts of men seemed to gain countenance as the church reconstructed marriage as an indissoluble union based on conjugal love. The mutual consent of the two individuals, given sacramental status in the thirteenth century, advantaged the young contender over the prudent father. In such an atmosphere, women of good family had to be heavily protected not only from the consequences of male lust but even from the appeal of honorable love. The freedom of city men to marry whomever they could win by negotiation or seduction ran athwart their freedom to control the destinies of their own children. The insecurity of female virtue became a gnawing worry. Fathers were driven to ever more energetic devices to keep their daughters confined at home or marry them off before the fires of puberty scorched them with dishonorable liaisons (Klapisch-Zuber).[22]

The more elevated the family was in the urban social hierarchy, the more likely it was to guard its women as bankable wealth rather than to deploy them as working capital. Their vulnerability may explain the tendency of the urban patriciate to keep sons with their wives and children in their father's house.[23] Since wives gain influence through marital bonding, they tend to pry their husbands and children loose from the grasp of their in-laws. Thus the family "clan" acts as an index of women's low position in the household (Heers). In northern Italy, where patrician city men were freer than anywhere else in Europe, women were closely confined to their homes, particularly in the great republic of Florence. The chilly life of a Florentine wife, living on sufferance, cloistered tightly in her husband's house, often resulted from her dependence on her husband's family for society as well as sustenance. Even her costly clothes and jewels tended to be heirlooms that she never owned outright (Klapisch-Zuber, 213–46). Genoese aristocrats withdrew marital support from their wives in the twelfth century, leaving them to use their dowries. These tightly cloistered family enclaves are described with immense satisfaction in Alberti's depiction of his family "Paradise," where young brides were cut off from all roles but reproduction and then were distanced from their children, who belonged in the final analysis to their paternal kindred. The frustration of the women has been vividly recaptured in the lives of saints who suffered severe persecution in their effort to pursue an independent vocational goal.[24]

Even the power of widows to carry on a business was increasingly limited. Though a matriarch like Alessandra Strozzi, helped by extraordinary political circumstances, might actually be deeply involved in the work of a family firm, the corporate nature of the great merchant families increasingly ensured a plentiful supply of male relatives to take their place. Where great families dominated couples, few widows are found as heads of families.[25] They were integrated into their husband's family with their dowry administered by a father-in-law or brother-in-law or returned to their own, bringing their dowry money with them, and remarried. Everywhere a husband's family tried to keep the widow with her dowry and made it difficult to regain it without legal proceedings. Her own children ranged against her with their father's family. By the High Middle Ages, the development of the great merchant guilds tended to unite patrician men in an upper layer of exclusively male power and prestige which protected individuals from giving way to sentiment. Among the minor guilds, a similar supervisory layer of men alienated masters from the individual family production units grouped below them. They tended to protect a widow's right to continue the family business until the dead master's son came of age to inherit. But they restricted her ability to train apprentices and set up shop on a permanent basis. Sometimes continued business was conditional on marriage to a master of the same craft. Generally, if the widow married a man not of the same trade, she was excluded from the guild. The statutes of the poulterers of Paris, which enabled a widow to carry on the trade freely, was exceptional. Even so, if she wished to continue after marrying out of the trade, she had to buy the right. She would be equally obliged to buy the mystery if her new husband had not yet done so, "for the husband is not in the dominion of the wife but the wife is in the dominion of the husband."[26] Some guilds simply preferred to support her through a pension if she remained a widow rather than allow her to continue the business.

Widows who did not remarry were always a disturbing presence unless they retired out of sight to a convent. Young widows were very numerous, and the rich ones found it very difficult to achieve an autonomous establishment unless, like Elisabeth of Thuringia, they abandoned all their goods for bitter poverty. Their means were almost always limited to the dowry, and the in-laws and children were not required to supplement it to establish an independent home. A widow's last resort was the right to return to her natal family, who feared dishonor if a female relative was left unsupervised. If she were young, they often reclaimed her with her dowry to attempt a new alliance. This generally forced her to abandon her children to their father's family (Klapisch-Zuber, 117–31).

Women who embarrassed the family by their behavior could be relegated to a conventual prison. The Malmaritate in Florence became a model of quasi-nunneries for women who were not eligible or willing to become nuns, modeled on the Convertite for converted prostitutes. Unmatched girls without families were also confined, particularly girls abandoned to charity. At the foundling hospital of Florence, 61.2 percent of the children abandoned between 1404 and 1413 were girls. In the crisis of the 1430s the general rate went up, and the percentage of girls rose to 66 percent. By 1454, it was already apparent that the hospital had failed to provide husbands for many girls and that a place for unwanted adolescents had to be established. A pious sodality was formed to care for the young girls, provide them with dowries, and keep them until husbands could be found, which was often a very long time. Beyond these meager resources, the abandoned who survived could anticipate little but another round of the same sad cycle that had forced their mothers to give them up.

In summary, then, let us take another look at the walled city, where women were silenced and men bonded into commensurability. The clerical order was transformed into a womanless space by virtue of cloistering nuns and charging religious women who continued to pursue a public vocation in company with men with heresy. Clerical orders helped expand this womanless space into the learned professions, and the universities produced new generations of ungendered men who gained a monopoly of the legislating order. Correspondingly, women were cloistered in manless spaces, convents, brothels, and halfway houses for the anomalous unmarried or badly married. These spaces were so structured that they always required men to assume the *cura mulierum* and therefore could not be transformed into complementary spheres for women's autonomous activities. The only "norm" for women was, therefore, marriage and submission to the authority of a husband, a norm that was bolstered by economic and political privileges that made it virtually impossible for any woman to take an independent line. Married women were reconciled to this fate by certain privileges within the system: the right to carry on the trade if widowed (under supervision) or legal guarantees of support from her dowry, her family, or her husband's guild brothers. These privileges were also constraints in that she risked losing them and being confined to a convent, reformatory, or other institution if she did not behave according to the norm. Thus from the institution of the walled convent, a whole lineage of cloistered institutions for females (reformatories, schools, boardinghouses, dormitories, shelters) sprang. In these "total institutions" women were made "deviant" by the multiplication of norms controlling their behavior (Sherrill Cohen).

In the ancient city, men were defined as free citizens, and those individuals of the male sex who were subservient or passive, playing the woman's role in society and in sexual unions, were gendered as unmanly. In the early Middle Ages, before urbanization, powerful and active females were often gendered as manly, the sexually inactive monastic population was grouped in a porous middle, and weak and passive men were branded unmanly. But in the medieval city, the unwomanly female was cloistered out of sight, celibate men were enfolded into the institutionalized church, and secular men were coerced to play their proper roles of husband, father, and lord of the household. In return they held the freedom of the city, commensurate in gender to all other men, on a separate plane from all women, for whom the city meant not freedom but bondage.

Notes

1. Clover has laid this out from Nordic texts; the same thesis is advanced for Anglo-Saxon women by Hollis. I am presently preparing a paper on Gregory of Tours which will extend the same theory to the celibate.

2. Hartmann, 206–47, and Sedgwick, *Between Men*, have worked out various aspects of the importance of male bonding for the successful implementation of male dominance.

3. An analysis of the ability of men to have discourse with one another about women, long a difficulty for historians of women, has been extended by Noble into patristic thought, scholasticism, and ultimately the modern scientific establishment.

4. The creation of Eve sparked a debate over the likeness of women to the image of God. Abelard, Yvo of Chartres, and Ernaldus of Bonneval say that she is in the likeness of man who is in the likeness of God. Rupert of Deutz, Gilbert de la Porée, and the majority of theologians, including Hildegard of Bingen, say she is fully in the likeness of God. The argument is fully pursued in Newman.

5. For Marbod, Geoffrey, and Bernard, see von Walter.

6. The Council of Rheims, 1157, condemned weavers and women with them; see Mansi (21.843). Bernard of Clairvaux (*Patrologia Latina* 183.1092; hereafter cited as PL followed by volume and column numbers) also singles out male and female weavers.

7. This is also reflected in Judith Bennett's study of the ale wives of Brigstock, who did not enjoy rights commensurate with the ale husbands of other villages for whom it could be a major route to public power and activity.

8. Aside from the fact that most men preferred to let mercenaries do their fighting by the High Middle Ages, there is evidence that women did "man" the fortifications when an emergency required them to do so; see Mundy, *Men and Women at Toulouse*, 119.

9. No attempt is made by Staley to reconcile these legal disabilities with his presumption that women enjoyed full membership in guilds.

10. Martin Saint-Léon said that the reputation of the Paris silk workers was very bad (174). Etienne Garland complained that they stole the silk given them to spin and sold it to the Jews. An ordinance of 1275 threatened them with the pillory for such frauds; see Depping, 378.

11. An ordinance of 1387 of the Arte de Lana charged the consuls to be sure that the women spinners and carders were being paid for their work. This was repeated for the spinners in 1448.

12. Marriage alone gave women entry to the freedoms of Exeter through their husbands. Widows of prominent husbands were the only ones who could have access to a freedom.

13. Otis claims this for Toulouse.

14. Prostitutes could be sold to other brothels. It was also possible for a creditor to pawn a destitute woman to a brothel even if she had not been a common woman before then. Laws limited the power of fathers to sell daughters to brothels, but Sherrill Cohen cites a case of a husband pledging his wife to a Florentine brothel against money borrowed.

15. There is a strong element of encouraged brutality in many accounts of marriage: *Vita sanctae Godelevae*, in *Acta Sanctorum*, July 6, 405–11; *Life of Christine of Markyate*; Guibert of Nogent, *Autobiography*; even Abelard notes that Fulbert gave him authority to beat Heloise if she did not prove an eager pupil.

16. Sherrill Cohen cites at least one document that suggests that this was a real concern of the Florentine government (43).

17. Herlihy sees commensurability of families across social and geographical barriers as one of the foremost social achievements of the early Middle Ages. Some of the implications for the working families of the later medieval city are explored by Howell.

18. Toulmin Smith collected hundreds of late medieval statutes. Typical are the

leather sellers of London who decreed that "from henceforth no one shall set any man, child or woman to work in the same trade, if such person be not first bound apprentice and enrolled in the trade" (125). Wives and children only were excepted. The fullers in Lincoln, for example, ordered that a member was not to work in company with an ordinary woman while he may do so with a master's wife or handmaid. The same provisions seem to have been customary on the continent.

19. Howell has uncovered the same trend in her ongoing research in Douai, reported at the City University of New York Graduate Center Conference on "Women in the Medieval City," for which this essay was prepared.

20. Ennen thinks men brought their wives (91), but there is no evidence. I think it more likely that people of both sexes probably made the venture before being tied to marriage and children.

21. These hazards are vividly presented from Venetian police files by Ruggiero.

22. In Italy wives were more enclosed than anywhere else in Europe, which could conceivably relate to the greater freedom of Italian men in Italian cities. The fourteenth-century Paolo da Certaldo advised keeping them in the house (O'Faolain and Martines, 169), and Alberti repeated this advice. This was noted as a curiosity by a French traveler.

23. Diane Hughes notes that in the twelfth and thirteenth centuries, it was more common for several branches of the same family to occupy houses grouped around a square and protected by the same tower fortification. By the fourteenth, however, the houses of many of the aristocracy had grown many times larger and might be considered capable of comprehending these large families.

24. See particularly *Vita Sanctae Umilianae de Cerchi*, in *Acta Sanctorum*, May 21; and Aïtoff.

25. Heers (224) cites Josiah Cox Russell, who argues that the number is a good test of family solidarity through ability to restrain its members.

26. Lujo Brentano in his general introduction to Toulmin Smith's survey of guild records thought this one unique (cxxxii n. 2).

8

Land-Taking and Text-Making in Medieval Iceland

MARGARET CLUNIES ROSS

Settlement Ideology

One of the major and defining events of early Icelandic history was the emigration of the first settlers from their previous homes in Norway or the Norse and Celtic Atlantic colonies, their voyages to Iceland, and the process of establishing themselves on parcels of land in their new environment. These complex processes of settlement were referred to by medieval Icelanders as *landnám*, or land-taking, and, as might be expected from their momentous nature, they formed the subject of numerous written texts, both in *Landnámabók*, the Book of Settlements, and in the introductory chapters of most Íslendingasögur, or family sagas. And, as might also be expected, a number of ideological and structural patterns recur in these texts, so that they can be seen to form schemas that are mythic both in the sense of constructing stable cognitive models for making sense of human experience and in the sense of acknowledging the participation of supernatural powers in bringing the settlers to their new land and legitimizing their land-taking there.

The emigration of the first settlers to Iceland must have been a tremendous upheaval, not only in physical and geographical terms, but in conceptual terms, too. The immigrant society was obliged to "produce" its own social space in an entirely new environment and to justify that production, at least initially, in terms of the cultural paradigms that dominated the thinking of the groups from which they had come.[1] Two of those paradigms that concern me in this essay are, first, the normative distinction which established male space as the public, nondomestic, social and geographic domain in contrast to female space, which lay within the domestic environment, *innan stokks*, and, second, the common belief that there existed a supernatural space distinct from that of humans, the inhabitants of which interacted with and influenced the social practices of human society in a whole range of ways.

A major consequence of the first paradigm, in terms of the settlement of Iceland, was that *landnám* was, on the whole, conceived of as a male activity, and the symbolic representations of the production of social space in medieval Icelandic texts served to maintain the traditional Scandinavian distinction between male and female space and to make it seem natural and inevitable that the distinction should be so. Thus, as scholars such as Preben Meulengracht Sørensen have observed (*Unmanly Man*, 22), those few women who are represented as taking land in settlement Iceland are seen as exceptions, behaving like men because they had no men to act for them. Sørensen was writing of Unnr the deep-minded (or Auðr, as she is sometimes called), the best-known woman settler in Iceland. This view has been endorsed most recently by Carol Clover, when she writes that the literary representation of Unnr in *Laxdæla saga* shows her "in her role as the revered and authoritative head of the family, when in every respect she has taken over the conduct and social functions of the male householder and leader" (64). I do not dispute this view, but, as we shall see, the symbolic paradigms through which Unnr's land-taking is represented are distinctly different from those used to symbolize male land-taking and seem to be expressions of a felt difference between symbols appropriate to females and to males. In this respect, I find it difficult to discover in the mythic and symbolic representations of social order that "one-sex" model of sexual difference that Clover has argued for in Old Norse thought.

The second cultural paradigm of spatial representation that concerns me in this essay is that of the interaction between the divine and the human. As we shall see, the medieval Icelandic texts insist on the importance of supernatural forces in directing the first settlers to their parcels of land and determining their location and extent, whether those supernatural forces are pagan deities, the Christian God, or ancestral spirits. Material presented here will tend to dispute the often-asserted claim that the first settlers in Iceland felt themselves to be largely autonomous and free of the cultural pressures of their homelands. Peter Foote has recently expressed this view thus: "They had no heavy burden to bear of ancestral custom and local tabu and no immemorial theophanic landscape to move in" (Preface, ix; also Byock, 52). I do not suggest that the Icelanders did not modify their inherited cultural paradigms as time went on, for they patently did so, but I do contend that they applied quite conventional ideological processes to the new environment and the problem of land division in a place where there had been virtually no human habitation before.

In his seminal study of medieval Icelandic rituals associated with the primary settlement of the new land, Dag Strömbäck observed that the first Scandinavian immigrants did not come with empty heads; rather, they brought with them ideas and customs from their predominantly Norwegian homeland (198–99). It is reasonable to suppose that these preconceptions led them to act in certain ways in their new geographical surroundings. The dual subjects of how the first settlers established their claims to the new land and the legitimating signs of supernaturally acclaimed ownership were important ones in medieval Icelandic literature. The late twelfth, thirteenth, and early fourteenth centuries were the great ages of literary production in Iceland, and written texts were undoubtedly created for an audience of the dominant families of that time. Not only did the long genealogies that appear in several indigenous genres have an important relationship to actual or potential land claims (Meulengracht Sørensen, *Saga and Society*, 19–27; Clunies Ross, "Old Norse Textual Worlds"), but accounts of how ancestors laid claim to territory with divine backing must have had an important legitimating function for those who claimed descent from them. In addition, as many of these accounts also represent the ancestral male land-taker as engaged in a conquest of the land that succeeded by means that involved the symbolic or ritual expression of masculine power, their production as texts must have reinforced the very patriarchy that doubtless both produced and consumed them.

It has been argued that the Book of Settlements, *Landnámabók*, was composed with a retrospective eye, not to detail the events and land-takings of the settlement period but to record the title of twelfth-century families to the estates they owned then and to secure their claims to them. This is probably an overstatement of a twelfth-century bias,[2] for there is much in *Landnámabók* that is not explicable in these terms, yet we cannot escape the hermeneutic circle in which early settlers are represented by their descendants as invoking supernatural revelations of an authority that was significant, as invested in the pioneers, to the extent that their descendants were successful in the colony. Again, we must moderate this position somewhat, for not everyone mentioned in *Landnámabók* was the ancestor of a powerful Icelandic family. There is good reason to believe, too, that the initial gathering of material for the compilation of *Landnámabók* took place at about the same time as the initial writing down of the Icelandic law code, over the winter of 1117 to 1118, so that both can be seen as manifestations of community members' desire to give written record to their history and customs.

It is possible to deduce the basic premises that their descendants represented as influencing the first settlers' behavior in a new territory from a study of the medieval settlement texts. The social and cultural significance of the customs they describe is likely to have been still accessible to medieval Christian Icelanders even though they no longer believed in the religious foundations of these practices.[3] The most important of them is the way in which the texts represent the very process of settling an uninhabited territory. The Icelandic settlers inherited a world-view that at least partly animated the earth as a female being (a common enough idea in many cultures) and represented the process of settling and defining individuals' territory upon it in terms of a sexual encounter between a man and a woman through which the male dominates the female and in the process legitimates his possession of her.[4] Following this line of thought, unoccupied land equated in human terms with a woman who was not yet possessed by a man, a state of affairs that must have been considered unnatural (paradoxically) in early Norse society, where all women, married or unmarried, were legally under the guardianship and protection of a man. Although I know of no overt expression of this idea, one might say that, theoretically at least, an unoccupied land represented a natural anomaly that needed no justification to remedy, while its "taking" (in Icelandic, *landnám*) required an exertion of the masculine will. The idiom of settlement, then, fell in line with a dominant societal view of male-female relations in early medieval Scandinavia.[5] Hence it comes as no surprise that the settlement of Iceland is largely represented in medieval texts as a male activity, in which land-taking males (*landnámsmenn*) lay claim to territory for themselves and their households and stave off rival claimants. The texts I examine here reveal this masculinist ideology, particularly in their representation of rituals accompanying the settlement, which are often strikingly phallic. The acts of the few female land-takers (*landnámskonur*) who are mentioned in the Icelandic texts are described in significantly different terms from those of the men, a difference that presumably reflects a subconscious awareness of the inappropriateness of the male paradigm to women settlers.

The second major premise of the first settlers in Iceland concerns the existence of spirit beings who lived in the land and protected its well-being. The medieval texts reveal a conviction that Iceland had not previously been settled by human inhabitants (it was said to be *óbyggð*), yet there was a belief that it was not empty of anthropomorphic beings but inhabited by groups of creatures called *landvættir*, literally "land-beings," who were normally invisible. The imagined gender of the *landvættir* is unclear, but I incline to think they were regarded as male, given the nature of the activities attributed to them. Though they were different from humans and different also from the pantheon of Scandinavian deities like Óðinn, Freyr, and Þórr, the *landvættir* were thought to be able to influence human affairs in certain ways in their role as guardians of the land. In particular, they could protect it from hostile external influences and cause harm to its enemies. In this respect, if the land itself was feminized, the *landvættir*'s protective role was a masculine one, and this gender assignment probably explains the close association in several texts between the use of incantations arousing the *landvættir* to defend the land and the sexually expressed idiom of humiliation, called *níð*, applied to their victims. *Níð* frequently took the form of poetry in which an aggressor threatened his enemy either with actual homosexual rape or with the allegation of having been subjected to it, feminized, and so dishonored (Almqvist; Meulengracht Sørensen, *Unmanly Man*). The application of this commonly articulated Old Norse equation between passive homosexuality and moral degradation and dishonor is explicable in the context of territorial threat if enemies of the land and, after settlement, of the society domiciled in the land were imagined as intruding male violators of her honor who had to be humiliated just as a man would who threatened to have sexual relations with another man's wife.

The third major premise affecting Icelanders' representation of the settlement was the belief that when the early settlers approached the island for the first time, the place where they landed and/or (more commonly) later established their farms was not determined by chance but was influenced by supernatural forces, specifically, by those gods who had power to determine events and human behavior, according to the established cosmic view of the emigrant society. These supernatural beings were not the *landvættir* but the major gods of the Old Norse pantheon, whose cults were well established in mainland Scandinavia. It appears likely from the medieval texts that the first settlers did not imagine that these deities were initially present in the new land; rather, they had to be introduced by means of some vector that could transport their supernatural power from the homeland to the new colony. There is thus a clear difference in the Icelanders' view of the two major kinds of supernatural beings who influenced the settlement. The *landvættir*, the land's guardian spirits, had always been in Iceland and, as we shall see, had to be approached with caution during the settlement period, because for them the settlers were themselves intruders, at least to begin with. The major Norse gods, on the other hand, had to have icons imbued with their power taken to the new land by the settlers themselves. In parallel fashion, there is evidence for the belief that the mana-imbued icons of Christianity had to be physically transported to Iceland by early Christian settlers or later evangelists in order for the new religion to take root on the island.

There were thus several culturally specific imperatives that predisposed the early settlers' environmental interactions. The force of these imperatives can be most clearly detected in certain rituals that people are said to have performed to help them legitimate their land claims where there was no obvious preexisting title to any particular piece of land.[6] In this respect the new situation differed markedly from rules governing land-ownership and the inheritance of family lands in Norway that were controlled by *óðal* law.[7]

In what follows I shall examine the evidence for the ways in which the early settlers went about making sense of their new environment by the process they called land-taking (*landnám*). The texts represent the land-taking process as the settlers' primary means of familiarizing themselves with the new territory. The first action was to lay claim to those parts of the new land that could form the working estates for groups of individuals, some of them kinsfolk, others not, who were under the guardianship of a single individual, usually a man (*landnámsmaðr*), though sometimes a woman (*landnámskona*). Meulengracht Sørensen has characterised these combinations of kin and nonkin that were centered on farms or estates as "gårdfællesskabet" (*Saga og samfund*, 37–43) [the farmstead community (*Saga and Society*, 27–33)], and argued that they were the basis of the emergent Icelandic body politic. These collections of individuals had almost certainly come together in Norway or in other Norwegian colonies and had consolidated their status as solidary groups on the boats that made the voyage out. In the medieval texts the processes of finding suitable land and then settling on it are represented as the major means by which settlers engage with their physical environment. That is to say, land-taking as an activity is privileged above all other means of relating to the new place, and this is undoubtedly a consequence of the fact that early Scandinavian society in the homeland, as in Iceland, had an agricultural and pastoral economic base. The whole rationale of a text such as *Landnámabók* reflects this mind-set. It is reflected also in the way *Landnámabók* is structured on a broad geographical basis, moving clockwise round the island, quarter by quarter, beginning with the west and finishing with the south.[8] Within the quarters, primary land claims are recorded with details of the names, geographical antecedents, and genealogies of the first settlers, followed by a listing of the areas of land they claimed and, in many cases, remarks on the natural features, especially rivers and headlands, that marked the boundaries of the estate. This is frequently followed by an account of those later settlers or family members to whom the *landnámsmaðr* granted land within his claim and a list of the first settler's descendants.

It is probably the case in all colonial societies that the single most important means of discovering the nature of a new territory is the process of exploration for the purpose of finding the best land for settlement and farming for a quickly increasing immigrant population, and Iceland is no exception to this rule. According to Ari Þorgilsson in *Íslendingabók* (1.9), all the habitable land was taken up within sixty years of the beginning of the settlement.[9] There is no evidence of exploration for purposes of what one might call scientific discovery or pure curiosity in the Icelandic texts, though here and there they reveal an appreciation of natural features of the landscape and a felt affinity between individuals and the environment. This sense of identity with place is always mediated by the sense of satisfaction in land-ownership, as the following verse quoted in *Landnámabók* (2.272; S238, H203) makes very clear:

Thengil the Fast-Sailing went from Halogaland to Iceland, and with Helgi's approval [i.e., Helgi the Lean, first settler in this area] took possession of land from Fnjosk River north to Grenivik, making his home at Hofdi [= "headland"]. His sons were Vemund, father of Asolf of Hofdi, and Hallstein who made this verse as he was sailing in to land and heard of his father's death:

> Hofdi's drooping,
> Thengil's dead;
> the hillsides smile
> at Hallstein.[10]

Here the land is represented as mourning the death of the father while smiling its approval to the son who is to inherit it. In composing this verse, Hallsteinn thus ratifies and celebrates his own inheritance of his father's land claim.

The Voyage Out: Gaping Heads and the *Landvættir*

It is hardly surprising that an enterprise as risky as a journey undertaken by small groups of people in open boats from a known land to an almost completely unknown one should be accompanied by rituals designed to safeguard the voyagers and to direct them safely to their new homes. We know from poems like the eddic *Sigrdrífumál*, stanza 10, that apotropaic measures using runes carved on the stem and blade of the steering oar and burnt into the oars could be invoked to protect ships at sea from the fury of the waves:

> Brimrúnar scaltu gera,   ef þú vilt borgit hafa
>   á sundi seglmǫrum;
> á stafni scal rísta   oc á stiórnar blaði
>   oc leggia eld í ár;
> era svá brattr breki   né svá blár unnir,
>   þó kømztu heill af hafi.[11]
>   (Neckel and Kuhn, 191)

[You must prepare surf-runes, if you want to
protect a sail-steed at sea; you should carve
them on the stem and on the blade of the
steering oar and burn them into the oar; then
you will come safely from the ocean, however
steep the breaker or however dark the waves.]

The sea was often imagined as a hostile and rapacious woman, named Rán in Old Norse poetry, who delighted in destroying ships and tearing at men in cannibal fashion. One of the most evocative skaldic representations of a storm at sea on the voyage from Norway to Iceland is attributed to the Viking Age poet Egill Skalla-Grímsson:

Þel høggr stórt fyr státi
stafnkvígs á veg jafnan
út með éla meitli
andærr jǫtunn vandar,
en svalbúinn selju
sverfr eirar vanr þeiri
Gestils ǫlpt með gustum
gandr of stál fyr brandi.

[The furious troll of the tree (the storm)
mightily beats out a file on the smooth path
of the prow-bull with the chisel of storms;
while the coldclad enemy of the willow
mercilessly grinds with it (i.e., the file)
the swan of Gestill (name of a sea-king) with
gusts over the prow.][12]

This and numerous other skaldic representations of ships portray the dangers of sea travel in northern waters in terms of a struggle between the stormy sea itself, imagined as a troll or ravenous sea goddess, and its prey, the ship, represented as an animal, whether a horse, ox, stag, or other beast (Meissner, 208; Hallberg, 54). A powerful and even shocking half-stanza attributed to the eleventh-century Icelandic skald Hofgarða-Refr indicates that the ship's sides could be painted red. In a storm it looked as though the rough, feminized waves were tearing at the "animal's" flank, causing it to bleed:

En sægnípu Sleipnir
slítr vindriðinn hvítrar
Ránar rauðum steini
runnit brjóst ór munni.

[The Sleipnir [horse] of the sea-peak,
wind-ridden, tears his breast spread with red
stain out of the mouth of the white
sea-goddess.] [13]

It was presumably to protect the "surf-beast" (*brimdýr*, *Helgakviða Hundingsbana*, I, verse 50, line 7; Neckel and Kuhn, 138) and those it carried from destruction both by the sea and by other malevolent forces that Viking Age ships bore prows that had attached to them carved and sometimes gilded animal heads. Poetic evidence, such as that from the poem *Haraldskvæði*, composed in honor of King Haraldr Finehair of Norway about 900, indicates that the animal heads were often represented with gaping mouths, something we also find in several surviving carved heads on Viking Age objects, including a bed. The ninth-century Norwegian Oseberg and Gokstad ship finds both contained several animal head posts with gaping mouths (Roesdahl et al., 271–72). The skaldic evidence suggests that the animal heads were detachable and were often secured to the ship's prow when people wanted to bear down on opponents with hostile intent, as in a naval battle. This was the case in the verses from *Haraldskvæði* which celebrate a famous naval battle at a place called Hafrsfjǫrðr. Haraldr Finehair's opponents came from the east,

kapps um lystir,
með gínǫndum hǫfðum
ok grǫfnum tinglum

[keen for a fight, with gaping heads and
carved prow ornaments.] [14]

It seems likely that the function of the gaping heads was protective of those on the ship and of its cargo and threatening to the seafarers' enemies, whether these were human aggressors or spirit beings that controlled natural forces.

A revealing comment in *Landnámabók* indicates that it was often the practice of those who made the voyage to Iceland to travel in ships whose prows also bore carved animal heads with gaping mouths. Chapter 268 of the *Hauksbók* text contains a statement apparently based on an otherwise lost version of the first Icelandic law code, Úlfljótslǫg, to the following effect:

Þat var upphaf hinna heiðnu laga, at menn skyldu eigi hafa hǫ fuðskip í haf, en ef þeir hefði, þá skyldi þeir af taka hǫfuð, áðr þeir kœmi í landsýn, ok sigla eigi at landi með gapandi hǫfðum eða gíndani trjónum, svá at landvættir fælisk við. (*Landnámabók*, 2.313)[15]

[It was the beginning of the heathen law that people should not have ships with (carved) heads at sea, but, if they had, they should remove the heads before they came within sight of land, and not sail toward land with gaping heads or yawning snouts, lest the land spirits be frightened at them.]

This passage, which is usually regarded as an authentic part of the first Icelandic law code, gives us a number of clues to the earliest settlers' state of mind when they approached Iceland for the first time. First, it confirms the information we gain from skaldic poetry that the animal heads were removable and supports the notion, canvassed above, that the heads were placed on ships' prows on special occasions to intimidate enemies, especially in time of war. The passage quoted here seems to indicate that people might resort to using the heads in stressful times when external threats could be expected, such as on the voyage to an unknown land, and that it was difficult if not impossible to prevent individuals from using them. The stipulation that the heads should be removed before people came within sight of the land of Iceland and the reasons given for this directive confirm that gaping heads were considered to have a frightening, if not a threatening, effect on those they were directed against.

In this case, the fragment of Úlfljótr's law also reveals the settlers' belief that Iceland was inhabited by *landvættir* who might be frightened by the gaping heads, which, it is implied, would not be a desirable outcome. The new settlers needed the spirits of the land to see them as allies and not enemies. There is considerable evidence that people in Viking Age Scandinavia believed that *landvættir* could be disturbed by a gaping animal head mounted on a pole or other erect object like a ship's prow. Bo Almqvist adduces a good deal of varied evidence from Iceland and Norway through to thirteenth-century England from what was the old Danelaw to show that the erection of a head (often a horse's head) on a pole, with its mouth gaping toward the perpetrator's enemy, was an acknowledged means of insulting and defaming him (1.89–118). This was a form of *tréníð* or carved calumny which functioned just like the poetic *níð* mentioned earlier, and it conveyed similar messages, of phallic aggression. Apparently such a device could cause local spirit beings to run amok and attack territorial and societal enemies. The trick was to harness their powers in one's own favor and against outsiders. In a well-known passage of *Egils saga* (chap. 57, 71–72), Egill uses such a *níðstǫng* or pole of calumny to arouse the Norwegian *landvættir* and cause them to expel his enemy, King Eiríkr Bloodaxe, from Norway. The *Landnámabók* passage under examination here clearly shows the fear that the gaping heads on the prows of the early settlers' ships, doubtless placed there to protect them from evil influences on the voyage out, might disturb the spirit beings inhabiting the new land and turn them against the settlers at a time when, as newcomers to Iceland, they needed to propitiate rather than offend them.

There are two other places in *Landnámabók* where these spirits are referred to (S329, H28 [2.329–32]; S330, H289–90 [2.332–33]), and these, together with their mention in a few other sources, lead Almqvist to the conclusion that the *landvættir* were conceptualized as

> the supernatural rulers of the country and nature. They were thought to dwell in cliffs and mountains and they were offered sacrifices, because they were thought to be able to bring luck in husbandry, hunting or fishing. Furthermore they were feared, since they were apt to run amok if aroused and they would then cause disaster to people and drive them away from their homesteads. Under normal conditions they were invisible, but persons with second sight could perceive them, and all indications point towards the assumption that they were regarded as having human shape, just like the elves (*álfar*, *huldafólk*) in later Icelandic folk-belief. (1.148–50, 222–28)

Later I shall investigate further the semiotic of the gaping head on a pole, along with other apotropaic objects mentioned in accounts of the early settlement in Iceland, because these are by no means isolated examples of the use of poles or staves to threaten others. I shall also address the question of whether the *landvættir* were considered by the early settlers as the actual rulers of the land of Iceland, as Almqvist and Strömbäck argued. All the evidence concerning the settlers' animal-headed ships confirms that these functioned to protect them from the dangers of the voyage out and any unknown, hostile forces they might encounter, just as dragon, horse, or other heads on poles were thought to carry the message of aggression and dominance to the opponents of Norwegian kings and other high-ranking men in the home society. Faced with the *landvættir* of an unknown land, however, the prospective settlers seem to have been caught between the desire to protect themselves and assert their authority while not wishing to antagonize those supernatural beings whose support people needed in a new country. Hence we find the suggestion in the fragment from Úlfljótr's law that, although it was thought inadvisable, people could not be stopped from traveling to Iceland in ships with carved heads.

Carrying Sacred Power to the New Land

Many individuals who traveled to Iceland resorted to some form of sacrifice or divination in order to discover what the future had in store for them and where in the unknown land the spirits wanted them to settle. A case in point is the story of Ingólfr Arnarson, said to have been the first settler to actually take up a land claim in Iceland. Meulengracht Sørensen has shown how the story of Ingólfr and his foster brother Hjǫrleifr functions in the *Sturlubók* version of *Landnámabók* as an exemplum of good and bad fortune, which are both implicated in the settlement of Iceland ("Sagan um Ingólf"). It is significant that the story attributes Ingólfr's good fortune to his willingness to sacrifice and resort to auguries before undertaking the voyage to Iceland, even though these practices are not Christian:

Þenna vetr fekk Ingólfr at blóti miklu ok leitaði sér heilla um forlǫg sín, en Hjǫrleifr vildi aldri blóta. Fréttin vísaði Ingólfi til Íslands. (*Landnámabók*, 1.42; SH7)

[That winter Ingólfr held a great sacrifice with the intention of seeking a good omen concerning his future, but Hjǫrleifr was never willing to sacrifice. The revelation directed Ingólfr to Iceland.]

This passage suggests that the spirits needed to be involved in the act of breaking ties with the homeland and transferring a man's individual luck (*heill*) from the old country to the new. Hjǫrleifr, who refuses to sacrifice, is unlucky and runs into misfortune after misfortune en route to Iceland and in the brief period he is on the island before he dies, murdered by Irish slaves. Ingólfr's slaves discover his body as they are searching the countryside for their master's high-seat pillars (searching therefore for his luck), and Ingólfr himself later reflects upon the misfortune that comes to a man who is unwilling to hold sacrifices. In a later chapter of *Landnámabók* (2.332–33; S330, H289–90), the place where Hjǫrleifr was murdered is explicitly said to have been declared by the *landvættir* off-limits for human settlement. There is a clear sense here that Hjǫrleifr's bad luck transferred from Norway to Iceland, just as his foster brother's good luck did. The story leaves it open to the audience to conclude, as Ingólfr did, that Hjǫrleifr's bad luck resulted from his unwillingness to sacrifice and so involve supernatural beings in his plans. As a text composed for a Christian audience, the existing narrative does nothing to specify the nature of the auguries nor the identity of the beings who caused them to take effect, but it does nothing either to denigrate such activities. In fact, the later mention of the Icelandic *landvættir*'s endorsement of Hjǫrleifr's death spot as a place where humans should not settle shows that the spirit beings of the Icelandic countryside operated with the same ideas of good and ill fortune as did those of Norway.

In the context of this apparent Christian acceptance of the importance of certain kinds of auguries, it is worth quoting Ælfric's *De auguriis* to throw light on what seems to have been an important distinction Christians felt able to make between auguries carried out with and without the influence of sorcery and demons. I think this distinction may explain what may otherwise appear to be an amazing tolerance of paganism in the medieval Icelandic texts. In lines 80–87, Ælfric distinguishes between Christians, who, like pagans, cast lots concerning themselves "by means of the devil's power" [mid ðæs deofles cræfte] and people who cast lots "in worldly things without witchcraft" (*Ælfric's Lives of the Saints*) [on worold-ðingum butan wicce-cræfte]. The former practice he calls sorcery (*wiglung*), while he terms the latter *wissung*, or direction. He gives a most illuminating example to show what he means by *wissung*, for it would include what the Icelanders called *landnám*, or the allocation of land to oneself: "that he may allot himself pastures, if men wish to divide anything."[16] It seems to me, then, that *Landnámabók*'s approval of the early Icelandic settlers' use of auguries to assure that their luck, social status, and authority were tranferred from their old land to the new could be seen as *wissung*, without the necessary involvement of devils or pagan gods. Of course, some early settlers who had a reputation for the worship of particular deities like Þórr and Freyr may have attributed the transfer of their luck to these gods, as we shall see shortly, and *Landnámabók* records that belief without obvious disapprobation. However, those like Ingólfr, whose settlement is represented as paradigmatic for the new Icelandic society—a society that was shortly to embrace Christianity—are shown to have transmitted their luck from the old land to the new and to be successful in their *landnám* by virtue of their consultation of auguries, but these rituals are never linked to specific pagan gods. This allows those who created these textual paradigms of settlement to endorse the ritual shorn of its pagan associations with specific heathen gods.

Several practices mentioned in family sagas or in *Landnámabók* can be understood as rites of passage, intended to ensure an individual's separation from his or her home society, a safe transition from Norway (or another place, such as the Faroes or the British Isles) to Iceland, and a reincorporation into the new environment of the unknown land. I think we can see that the practices mentioned in Icelandic texts conform to Arnold van Gennep's tripartite structure for rites of passage, with the marginal or liminal period between separation and reincorporation being occupied by the sea voyage. The transition is thus from land to land over water, and it involves for the individual not only his or her bodily transport, together with kin, chattels, and animals, but the successful transfer of the social status the person enjoyed in the old country to the new society as well as the transfer of his personal luck, both of which required supernatural assistance.

Medieval Icelandic writers attributed to their ancestors the desire to ratify their actions in claiming land by reference to the perceptible signs of divine guidance and supernatural authority. They also record some cases of early settlers bringing mana-imbued objects with them to Iceland. From this one can infer that the gods as well as their protégés needed to be installed in the new land, that the travelers required divine guidance to bring them to their new homes, and that human authority over land and property needed to be backed up by tangible signs of divine approval. It is in this context that we can understand the well-known practice, frequently described in *Landnámabók* and in family sagas, whereby individual settlers detached and brought with them to Iceland the pillars of the high-seats from their Norwegian homes (*ǫndvegissúlur*), which they proceeded to throw overboard when they came within sight of land. The paradigmatic example of the *landnámsmaðr*, Ingólfr, who, as we saw earlier, had conducted a sacrifice the winter before he sailed for Iceland, gives all the characteristics of this rite:

Þá er Ingólfr sá Ísland, skaut hann fyrir borðǫndugissúlum sínum til heilla; hann mælti svá fyrir, at hann skyldi þar byggja, er súlurnar kœmi á land. . . . [Three years pass and then] . . . Þau missari fundu þeir Vífill ok Karli [two slaves] ǫndvegissúlur hans við Arnarhvál fyrir neðan heiði.

Ingólfr fór um várit ofan um heiði; hann tók sér bústað þar sem ǫndvegissúlur hans hǫfðu á land komit; hann bjó í Reykjavík; þar eru enn ǫndugissúlur þær í eldhúsi. En Ingólfr nam land milli Ǫlfusár ok Hvalfjarðar fyrir útan Brynjudalsá, milli ok Øxarár, ok ǫll nes út. (*Landnámabók*, 1.42–45; SH8–9)

[When Ingólfr caught sight of Iceland, he threw his high-seat pillars overboard, hoping for an omen of good fortune; he said he would settle where the pillars came ashore. . . . (three years pass and then) In that year Vífill and Karli (two slaves) found his high-seat pillars at Arnarhvál, below the heath. In the spring Ingólfr traveled across the heath; he established his home where his high-seat pillars had come ashore. He lived at Reykjavík, where the high-seat pillars can still be seen in the hall. And Ingólfr claimed possession of land between Ǫlfus River and Hvalfjord beyond Brynjudale River, between it and the Øxar River, including all the headlands.]

No mention is made here of the deity to whom the preliminary sacrifice was made, nor of the spiritual force that directed the high-seat pillars once Ingólfr had thrown them overboard. It is simply said that he did this *til heilla* (for good fortune). However, similar narratives associate the act with the god Þórr, and it is reasonable to assume that this association was conventional. Þórólfr Mostrarskegg, for example, was said to be a great sacrificer who believed in Þórr. He threw his high-seat pillars overboard when he came to Breiðafjǫrðr in the west of Iceland:

... þar var skorinn á Þórr. Hann mælti svá fyrir, at Þórr skyldi þar á land koma, sem hann vildi, at Þórólfr byggði; hét hann því at helga Þór allt landnám sitt ok kenna við hann. (*Landnámabók*, 1.124 and nn. 3-4; S85, H73)[17]

[Þórr was carved on them. He declared that Þórr would come ashore where he wanted Þórólfr to settle. He promised to dedicate his whole land claim to Þórr and name it after him.]

What is consistent in both these accounts, and in numerous others, is the fact that a numinous object, identified with a god and signifying the power and authority of a household head, is let to fall into the sea by the owner himself, who thus surrenders the symbol of his authority completely to the supernatural power that supports it and allows that power to direct its embodiment to the place in the new land where it has determined the settler will live. The settler's liminal situation exists during the period of his sea voyage and until he finds his high-seat pillars and knows where to establish his permanent dwelling. In most narratives of this type there is an interval of a few years before the pillars are found, and during this time the *landnámsmaðr* often occupies a series of temporary dwellings. It is significant that it is only after he has regained the insignia of his authority that he is said to take (*nema*) to himself areas of land as his land claim. Hence settlement narratives like that of Ingólfr and many others indicate that, whatever the reality of the early settlement of Iceland in terms of people's freedoms from the constraints of Norwegian society, the settlers are guided and authorized by supernatural authority in their taking of land. In the Ingólfr narrative, the narrator involves his audience in the continuing recognition of both the means of authorization and its connection with Ingólfr's family by the observation that "the high-seat pillars can still be seen in the hall there [at Reykjavík]."

The semiotic significance of high-seat pillars and other symbols of supernaturally sanctioned authority is made even clearer by two other exempla in *Landnámabók* which follow a pattern similar to that of the Ingjáldr story. They show that the supernaturally sanctioned transfer of authority from one country to another by means of a numinous object was of predominant importance in the settlement story. They represent both Christian and non-Christian settlers as following similar procedures. Both examples show that personal luck involved the whole family as well as the individual family member and that it was thought of as being transmitted along patrilineal lines. The first example is of the settler Ørlygr Hrappsson, who had been fostered by Bishop Patrekr in the Hebrides and who was, therefore, at least a nominal Christian. The bishop guided his protégé to Iceland and foresaw exactly where Ørlygr's landtaking would be: "at a place where from the sea he could keep two mountains in view, each with its valley, and he was to settle beneath the southern mountain. He was to establish his farm there and have a church built, dedicated to St. Columba."[18] Here, in accordance with the Christian ideal of celibacy, the bishop is related to Ørlygr by the fictive kinship tie of fosterage rather than by blood, and St. Columba replaces Þórr. Bishop Patrekr had also given Ørlygr mana-filled objects for the church: timber, an iron bell, a plenarium, and consecrated earth, which he was to place under the corner posts of the church. This story shows the same ideological framework as that of the many accounts in *Landnámabók* where a settler is established on an estate with the support of a non-Christian supernatural being and where the transfer of power is effected through the settler's carrying with him an object transmitted patrilineally and filled with spiritual power emanating from his supernatural patron.[19]

In this context, we should perhaps look again at Ari Þorgilsson's well-known statement in the first chapter of *Íslendingabók* that the Irish hermits who were in Iceland when the first Scandinavian settlers arrived abandoned the land, leaving behind them Irish books, bells, and crosiers. From this, Ari says, one could tell that they were Irish (*Landnámabók*, 1.5). We might add that one could also tell that they were Christian. These religious objects were probably also thought of as imbued with spiritual force, so that, although Iceland did not become Christian again for over one hundred years, the land remained subject to their powers, and there was a sense in which the territory of Iceland itself remained Christian, even though its human inhabitants for the most part did not. This may have been the underlying reason why Ari gave this statement such prominence in his first chapter, given his obvious desire in *Íslendingabók* to promote the Christian character of medieval Icelandic society. It is tempting also to wonder whether his observation that at the time of the settlement Iceland was covered with trees between mountains and seashore is meant to convey something of a sense that this was an almost paradisal land when it was first discovered by Scandinavians, fertile, wooded, inhabited by holy men, and, above all, already Christian.

The second example is told of the family of the famous poet and Viking

Egill Skalla-Grímsson, whose paternal grandfather, Kveld-Úlfr, died on the voyage out, shortly before the family reached Iceland. Kveld-Úlfr instructed his son Skalla-Grímr to make him a coffin and build his home in Iceland where the coffin came ashore. It was thrown overboard and came ashore in an inlet; it was there that the family farm of Borg was built, after which the whole fjord, Borgarfjǫrðr, is said to have taken its name (*Landnámabók*, 1.68, 70–71; S29; also *Egils saga*, chap. 27). Úlfr's body here functions as a family talisman, whereby the family luck, which had been much tried by the royal house in Norway, was transmitted safely to Icelandic soil. The patriarchal body in the coffin parallels the floating high-seat pillars both in shape and in function. Missing is the association with Þórr, but we know from *Egils saga* and the poetry attributed there to Egill himself that this family saw its fate as connected with the patronage of Óðinn.

The idea underlying this episode is not essentially different from those associated in the early Middle Ages with the fertility of kings' corpses or the powers of saints' relics. In all these cases, the sanctity of the supernatural being has to be physically present in order to effect change, and in the case of newly settled Iceland this necessitated the physical transportation of a mana-filled icon or symbol of the being's power. The same idea is to be found in Christian writers' presentations of pre-Christian Scandinavian cults associated with the supernatural powers of kings and their ability to ensure good crops. The best-known example comes from Snorri Sturluson's account in *Hálfdanar saga svarta*, chapter 9, of how the pagan Norwegians divided King Hálfdan's body into four parts and buried each in a different part of the country to ensure good crops (Lönnroth). Comparable ideas of the transfer of prosperity associated with family lands appear in Icelandic sagas like *Vatnsdœla saga* and *Víga-Glúms saga*. They indicate that the land-taking of particular families was linked with the favor of specific deities and that these gods were thought by the early settlers to ensure the fertility of their domains (Holtsmark; Gabriel Turville-Petre).

It is instructive to contrast these various examples of the land-taking of male settlers with that of the *landnámskona* Auðr (or Unnr) Ketilsdóttir, called *djúpúðga* (the deep-minded). Although in many respects Auðr performs what is usually a male role in her settlement story, in that she successfully leads members of her family to Iceland from the mixed Scandinavian and Celtic society of the Western Isles, there are some significant differences between the male paradigm of settlement examined above and Auðr's land-taking. First, although she brings family members to Iceland, it is her son's children who accompany her. That is to say, she looks after and arranges the marriages of the son and daughters of the patriline she married into, not the one she was born into. Auðr's role is important, therefore, but it is different from that of a male settler. She establishes landowning groups for her affinal descendants through marriages and alliances, not by a personal assertion of divinely sanctioned authority.

Another significant variation from the male norm in Auðr's settlement story is that she is not the first member of her family of birth to arrive in Iceland, so she is not in a position to act as an agent of transfer of the agnatic family luck, even if her gender allowed her to fulfill this role, which we may doubt. In *Landnámabók* (1.139; S97, H84) we are told that she made land at Vikrarskeið, where her ship was wrecked. No auspicious signs accompany her setting foot on Icelandic soil, even though Ari Þorgilsson (who claimed descent from her through her grandson Óláfr feilan) wrote in *Íslendingabók* that she was the most important settler in the western fjords. It is surely significant that her first act upon arriving is to visit two of her brothers who are already in residence in the area. One, Helgi bjólan, is mean to her while the other, Bjǫrn austrœni, shows her hospitality. The following spring Auðr sets out on her own to look for land and eventually "took possession of the entire Dales district at the head of the fjord [viz. Breiðafjǫrðr]." As with the contrasting stories of Ingjáldr and his brother Hjǫrleifr, we are surely meant to understand this narrative of the mean and generous brothers as an exemplum of the way in which siblings should behave toward one another. Auðr's well-being and dignity is retrospectively important to the twelfth- and thirteenth-century creators of Icelandic history, who included descendants of both her affinal and her consanguineous kin.

All these narrated events underline the difference between a female and a male settlement paradigm. Although Auðr is said to lay claim to a large tract of land, neither rituals nor supernaturally sanctioned symbols of her authority are mentioned. This may be in part because *Landnámabók* is at pains to indicate that Auðr was a Christian, though we have seen above that the attribution of Christianity to a male settler was no bar to using the standard male settlement paradigm. Again, no supernatural events are recorded in connection with her land-taking activities. Instead, the place-names that celebrate various of her acts as she moves about exploring the territory are mundane, domestic, or personal in their scope. One place is said to have been named Dǫgurðarnes ("Breakfast Point") because that is where she and her companions ate their first breakfast while looking for land. Another headland is alleged to have taken the name of Kambsnes because Auðr lost her comb there.[20] The place-name Krosshóll, "Cross Heights," is said to have been named for her habit of saying her prayers at a spot where she had had Christian crosses erected. Meulengracht Sørensen points to the *Landnámabók* author's grasping at these "unhistorical fabrications" (*Saga and Society*, 5) as evidence that many twelfth-century reconstructions of the past were not securely based on traditional report. This is likely to be true, but in the case of Auðr's settlement, there is possibly an additional reason for the text's resort to etiological stories that fail to convince modern etymologists. There were cultural constraints on the role a woman could play in these narratives which would have made the attribution to her of the dominant male settlement paradigm impossible. On the other hand, as a woman, she can be represented as an archetypal marriage-broker and land-taker for the good of her affinal family.

A large number of land-taking stories from both *Landnámabók* and family sagas indicate that those settlers who took large tracts of land for themselves in the first sixty years or so of the Icelandic *landnám* did so (as the texts represent it) with the manifest approval of supernatural forces, whose support was expressed through visible tokens and symbols of the authority vested in the settlers. Secure in the power that derived from this authority, they were then able to share their lands with family members and grant it or sell it to others in exchange for various ties of dependence. The act of claiming land for oneself while declaring that one had some form of supernatural backing for it was expressed in Icelandic by the idiom *at helga sér land*, to sanctify land for oneself, that is, to appropriate land for oneself by resort to supernatural authority. Those settlers who are represented as believing in pagan gods are said to have dedicated their lands to a specific deity. One example of several in *Landnámabók* concerns Ásbjǫrn Reyrketilsson, who "dedicated his land claim to Þórr and called it Þórsmǫrk" [Ásbjǫrn helgaði landnám sitt Þór ok kallaði Þórsmǫrk (*Landnámabók*, 2.346; M8)].

When he examined these and other practices of the early settlers in his 1928 article "Att helga land," Dag Strömbäck was inclined to represent the transfer of good fortune (*heill*), which they undoubtedly involved, as a means to the end of making the *landvættir*, as the ruling spirits of the land, well disposed to the human intruders in their domain, to pacify them before depriving them of their territory and their authority. His interpretation depends on the assumption that the *landvættir* were owners as well as guardians of Iceland, that they were "nature beings" (*naturväsende*) who were the land's rulers and first owners (206).[21] It is not clear from the medieval Icelandic texts themselves that the *landvættir* were actually thought to own the land in the sense that a human could lay claim to an estate, nor that they were disturbed at the thought of dispossession, nor that the *landvættir* were the real object of a number of the practices that Strömbäck refers to in his article. Their role as bringers and confirmers of human luck, whether good or bad, is certainly supported by the texts, and the passage from Úlfljótr's law, examined earlier, confirms the medieval belief that the early settlers thought it inadvisable to disturb the *landvættir* for fear that they might turn against them and possibly drive them from the island (Almqvist).

In my opinion a number of the land-claiming rituals described in sagas and in *Landnámabók* were directed not at the *landvættir* as the first owners of the land but at other humans. In the foregoing discussion I concentrated on the settlers' use of supernaturally sanctioned authority to justify their land claims. One must not, however, ignore the frequent competitiveness of the land-taking situation in Iceland and the fact that might was undoubtedly sometimes right. It seems to me that the main purpose of a number of the rituals described in the texts was to assert the dominance of one individual over other possible human claimants to a piece of land, thus securing the territory by the symbolical means of showing one's dominance over other men rather than through actual physical aggression.

Typically, the measures relate to areas of land that did not yet have an owner, and, as such, they are seen to be comparable to practices attested from mainland Scandinavia, as Strömbäck has shown, where claims to particular geographical areas might be disputed or not yet established. They include various uses of fire to mark out one's land claim (S346 [M10]), a custom possibly reminiscent of the activities of a community that once practiced swidden agriculture,[22] the erection of wooden poles to stake one's claim (*Landnámabók*, 2.230–31; S194, H161), shooting an arrow (burning or otherwise) over territory one wishes to secure,[23] and so forth. It is highly probable that these rituals were at least residually associated with various of the Norse gods: Óðinn is often represented as dedicating enemy armies to himself by shooting an arrow over them (*Vǫluspá*, in Neckel and Kuhn, 24.1–4), while Þórr is associated with the protection of the household and family property through high-seat pillars and other stave-like objects in various Old Norse myths and sagas. In each case, marking out something as one's own with a stave-like symbol of one's power serves either to appropriate the object for oneself or to ward off aggressors, either potential or real.

The hypothesis that the customs of erecting poles, carrying fire, and so forth were directed at human rivals rather than the *landvættir*, though they may have been thought of as authorized by the gods, is also supported by a passage in the *Hauksbók* version of *Landnámabók*, which claims that people who arrived later in the settlement period accused those who got there earlier of taking too much land. The later arrivals asked King Haraldr Finehair to establish some sort of reasonable measure of what constituted a sufficiency of land, and he did so with reference to the custom of carrying fire over an area of land, urging that "no man should take possession of a larger area than what he could carry fire over in a day with his crew" (*Landnámabók*, 2.337; H294).[24] Directions then followed on how this was to be done. It involved setting up smoky fires at intervals over the area so that one could be seen from the next and so on. Clearly the procedure was designed to allow eyewitnesses to the land claim to verify the extent of the land taken and does not seem to have been directed at the *landvættir* as owners of the original title to the land. The whole point of the procedure was to establish a fair standard claim of land in the eyes of other settlers and to set some limits to the geographical extent of any individual's claim. Other descriptions of the use of fire to secure a land claim support this interpretation. Helgi the Lean is said to have "built a great fire at every estuary and thus dedicated to himself the whole district" [gerði eld mikinn við hvern vatsós ok helgaði sér svá allt herað (S218)]. Here Helgi places his fires right by the natural boundary markers of his estate to make its extent doubly clear.[25]

Another passage of the *Hauksbók* version of *Landnámabók* makes it clear that claim procedures deemed appropriate for women were very different from those specified for men and did not involve the use of staves or fire. Chapter 276 of the *Hauksbók* text of *Landnámabók* specifies that a woman settler could take as much land as she could walk around from dawn to sunset on a spring day, while leading a half-grown heifer in good condition. Here the symbolic emphasis is on the demarcation of territory appropriate for female and domestic activities; the woman must lead a young female cow, who, like herself, provides food in the form of milk.[26] The differentiation between what was permitted to men and to women may indicate that it was not thought proper for women to use fire to mark out territory. If this practice was considered to have been originally authorized by Óðinn and passed on to his male favorites, there may have been a taboo on women using it. Thus, the way women were allowed to claim land would have given them a considerably smaller area than men, who were able to involve their crews in carrying fire over the territory.

The Symbolic Meaning of Rituals Involved in the Settlement of Iceland

I proposed earlier that the gaping animal heads that ornamented the prows of the settlers' ships, together with similar figures to be found on Norwegian archaeological remains of the Viking Age, functioned as symbols of threat and dominance directed at alien and possibly hostile groups or individuals, human or supernatural. On the voyage out to Iceland, the gaping heads were probably directed at human enemies the settlers thought they might encounter on the way and at the anthropomorphic spirits of the ocean that were considered to be hostile to ships and sailors. These gaping heads perform a function analogous to the well-attested Viking Age Norwegian and Icelandic practice of erecting a *níðstǫng* or pole of calumny often topped by a gaping animal head to slander one's enemies and create supernatural disturbances to bring them distress or sometimes drive them away from their home territory. In the latter case, the *landvættir* might be involved in the act of expulsion. The gaping heads on the ships' prows seem to have been expected to have had the same kind of effect on the Icelandic *landvættir*, and that presumably was why Úlfljótr's law advised settlers to remove the heads from their ships' prows when they came within sight of the new land. They wanted to keep the land spirits of the new country both in place and well disposed to them because they needed their support to prosper in Iceland.

Several studies, among them those of Almqvist and Meulengracht Sørensen, have concluded that the *níð*-pole and the animal head atop it (often that of a mare) connoted the act of *ergi* or sexual denigration of one man by another through the suggestion that the aggressor had been able to use his rival sexually. The female animal head thus denoted the victim, while the erect wooden pole had a phallic connotation and stood for the aggressor. From a functional point of view, the *níð*-pole conveyed contempt for the victim, and its purpose was to expel him from the social community as unworthy. It seems to me likely that animal heads on prows and on bed boards (as in the Gokstad example) would have had a similar meaning, though here the objective might well have been to declare any aggressor at sea or intruder into a matrimonial bed as the potential victim of an assault if they dared to attack or intrude. All these icons thus ritualized the act of aggression and sexually expressed subjection.[27]

Most of the objects we read of in early Icelandic texts as involved in landtaking rituals have comparable shape and significance to the *níð*-poles and animal-headed ornaments on ships, beds, and other domestic objects. The high-seat pillars that are so often mentioned in these texts are also, of course, domestic objects and appear to have symbolized the authority of the master of the house. They may also have been considered to ward off intruders by virtue of their transferred power. They are associated with the god Þórr in some cases, doubtless in his capacity as the god who protects the world of gods and men from the incursions of giants and other hostile groups. In that role, as I have recently argued, Þórr is closely associated with the protection of the honor of the male head of a household through securing his women from the sexual attentions of other males, a function that is linked in Old Norse myths with the god's hammer, Mjǫllnir, to which Viking Age craftsmen gave a clearly phallic shape ("Þórr's Honour"). By casting one's high-seat pillars into the sea and allowing them to drift ashore, one allows the god most closely associated with protecting the home to effect one's transition from one land to another, as we have seen. This process also transfers one's domestic authority overseas and so allows one to take land for a new home secure in the support of supernatural authority, expressed through the god's icons, the high-seat pillars. In the texts the conjunction of legitimation and the opportunity to appropriate land is referred to as one's *heill* or luck while the act of legitimized appropriation itself is *at helga sér land*.

Objects like the Icelandic settlers' high-seat pillars functioned both as talismans and as symbols of power and authority. In an Icelandic context, authority over others was frequently expressed in a sexual idiom, and involved male-to-male dominance expressed through the threat of homosexual rape. It seems to me that the settlers' high-seat pillars and other objects such as staves, poles, and arrows used to mark out land utilize this same sexual idiom and employ a phallic display, initially directed at the feminized land itself and then at other settlers, which is intended to reinforce their dominance over their neighbors and mark out the extent of their territory. Some of these phallic markers are presented as overtly endorsed by supernatural authority, but it seems likely that, even where they are not, there may have been an understood connection with the Norse gods, particularly Þórr and Óðinn.

These Icelandic examples of what I think were phallic guardians and symbols of the settlers' territorial authority are by no means unique in the repertoire of the human expression of one's relationship to territory on the one hand and to other conspecifics on the other. In many human societies fetishes or icons with erect penes or other indications of phallic power function to ward off spirits or as property or boundary markers. The herms of ancient Athens are a case in point (Wickler; Wrede, 39–42). These squared pillars with a human head and erect penis but no other body parts may be compared with Icelandic high-seat pillars or the *tjǫsnur* or phallic pegs that marked the dueling field. According to ethologists, such icons can be seen as the human semiotic equivalents of penile displays in certain kinds of monkeys which reinforce their dominance over neighboring groups and mark out their territory (Eibl-Eibesfeldt, 485–88). They consider that such conduct may be the ritualized expression of aggressive male mounting behavior that is designed to show dominance over other male individuals. If so, the medieval Scandinavian examples I have considered here convey a remarkably similar message, and we are fortunate to be in possession of a group of Old Icelandic texts that so clearly delineate the means individuals used to make sense of their new territory and impress their claims to land upon others.

Notes

1. On the concept of social space, see Lefebvre; I am indebted to Andrew McRae for this reference.
2. Rafnsson has argued the case for twelfth-century shaping of the evidence, while Benediktsson has urged a note of caution in "Markmið Landnámabókar" and "Some Problems in the History of the Settlement of Iceland."
3. See Meulengracht Sørensen, "Freyr in den Isländersagas," on representations of the cult of Freyr in Icelandic sagas and *Landnámabók*. For the contrary position, that the sagas are unreliable as evidence for the pre-Christian religion, see Baetke; and Olsen, based on archaeological evidence (or the lack of it).
4. In Old Norse myth the earth is personified as a female supernatural being, Iǫrð, mother of the god Þórr, defender of the territory of gods and humans. In skaldic poetry, many kennings for the earth conceptualize it as an animate female being (Clunies Ross, "Hildr's ring"). Frank (63–65) has shown that early Norwegian skalds represented the ruler's domination of his kingdom in terms of male sexual conquest.
5. The settling of new territory—actually unpopulated or perceived as such by the settlers' own kind (as in Australia and North America)—is frequently represented in terms of male subjection of a female. Territorial conquest is often accompanied by phallic displays, as we find in the Icelandic material. In many postmedieval European settlement texts, the land is represented as a virgin and conquest involves deflowering her (Kolodny, *The Lay of the Land*, and *The Land before Her*), but I do not see this specific emphasis in the Icelandic material.
6. There is good evidence (Strömbäck) that these land-taking rituals were known in Norway and other parts of Scandinavia, but the Icelandic situation may well have made them more important in the legitimating process.
7. *Óðal* land was not the property of any individual but belonged to the *ætt* or lineage as a family heritage. Nevertheless, such land was at any given time in the individual ownership of a family member, and when that owner needed to dispose of it (for example, at the point of death), it had to be offered first to members of the family to which it belonged and within which the land descended. Male agnates took precedence over other kinds of kinsmen in respect of rights in *óðal* land. On *óðal* law, see Magerøy, 24–48; Hastrup, 190–92; for the procedures in mainland Scandinavia, see Strömbäck, 210–20.
8. On the traditional basis for such spatial arrangements, see Lindow.
9. Except where noted, all citations from *Íslendingabók* and *Landnámabók* are from Benediktsson's edition. In citations, S = Sturlubók, H = Hauksbók, and M = Melabók; the number refers to the relevant page. Translations throughout are my own.
10. "Þengill mjǫksiglandi fór af Hálogalandi til Íslands; hann nam land at ráði Helga út frá Hnjóská til Grenivíkr; hann bjó í Hǫfða. Hans synir váru þeir Vémundr faðir Ásólfs í Hǫfða ok Hallsteinn, er þetta kvað, þá er hann sigldi af hafi ok frá andlát fǫður síns:

>Drúpir Hǫfði,
>dauðr es Þengill,
>hlæja hlíðir
>við Hallsteini."

Trans. Pálsson and Edwards (103).

11. All poetry of the Elder Edda, including *Vǫluspá* below, is from the Neckel and Kuhn edition; my translations.

12. Text from Nordal's edition (172); trans. E. O. G. Turville-Petre, 23.

13. Text from Finnur Jónsson's edition, vol. 1A, 321 (verse 3) and 1B, 296; trans. Foote, "Wrecks and Rhymes," 66, with some minor alterations. Sleipnir is the name of Óðinn's eight-legged horse.

14. *Haraldskvæði* is sometimes called *Hrafnsmál*. I cite verse 7 from Helgason's edition (17).

15. This chapter of *Landnámabók* details a grant that was said to have been based on law codes of western Norway; see Benediktsson, *Landnámabók*, 1.xcvi–ci; and Jóhannesson, 160–62. See also *Landnámabók*, 2.370; S379, H325, regarding a settler whose ship's prow had a bull's head (*ok hafði þjórshofuð á stafni*).

16.

Hleotan man mot mid geleafan swa þeah
on worold-ðingum butan wicce-cræfte
þæt him deme seota gif hi hwæt dælan willað
þis nis nan wiglung ac bið wissung foroft.
   (*Ælfric's Lives of the Saints*, 84–87)

[Nevertheless a man may cast lots in faith in
worldly things, without witchcraft, that he
may allot himself pastures, if men wish to
divide any thing (i.e., any land); this is no
sorcery, but is very often a direction]. (Skeat's translation)

17. We are also told that Þórr (presumably the pillar with the Þórr image) was washed ashore on a headland, later called Þórsness, and that Þórólfr built a farm and temple nearby. The mountain on the headland was regarded as sacred. For a slightly different account, see *Eyrbyggja saga*, chap. 4 (Sveinsson and Þorðarson, 7–10).

18. "Byskup bað hann þar land nema, er hann sæi fjǫll tvau af hafi, ok byggja undir enu syðra fjallinu, ok skyldi dalr í hvárutveggja fjallinu; hann skyldi þar taka sér bústað ok láta þar kirkju gera ok eigna enum helga Kolumba" (*Landnámabók*, 1.52; S15).

19. *Landnámabók*, 2.307–8; S297, H258, tells how Þorhaddr the old, temple priest from Mærir, took both earth and pillars from the temple to Iceland, landing at Stǫðvarfjǫrðr, where he "laid the Mærir sanctity over the whole fjord" [lagði Mærina-helgi á allan fjǫrðinn].

20. On Viking Age combs, see Jesch 14; also Ambrosiani.

21. The hypothesis is based on postmedieval folkloric concepts of supernatural beings, usually located in specific places, who have been thought of as having the power to lead people and animals astray. These beings, often referred to by the Swedish word *rå*, are frequently represented by folklorists and historians of religion as the supernatural owners of nature; see Hultkrantz.

22. Place-names in *-torp* and *-röd* (*-ryd*, *-red*, *-rud*) from Viking Age Scandinavia provide evidence of increased clearing of woodland for settlement and agriculture.

23. Strömbäck (203–10) argues that the function of shooting a burning arrow over territory was to fix the land in place by magical means, by analogy with practices recorded particularly in *Guta saga*, where the the first man to encounter the island of Gotland stabilized it by carrying fire over the island (Pipping 62); similarly, Lid, cols. 579–81. Parallels to this notion occur quite widely in folklore; see Mitchell, 152–53 and n. 7.

24. "Þeim mǫnnum, er síðar kómu út, þóttu hinir numit hafa of víða land, er fyrri kómu, en á þat sætti Haraldr konungr þá hinn hárfagri, at engi skyldi víðara nema en hann mætti eldi yfir fara á degi meðskipverjum sínum." Note the involvement of the crew in the process, emphasizing the continued role of the solidary unit formed to undertake the voyage to Iceland in the act of settlement and land-taking.

25. It is possible that he intended the bounds of his estate to be thus ratified by supernatural beings. Water courses and other landscape features were associated with the *landvættir* or other deities; see Meulengracht Sørensen, "Freyr in den Isländersagas," 733 n. 3, apropos S355, H313, in which a certain Þorsteinn Rednose is said to have made sacrifices to a waterfall and had food-scraps thrown into it.

26. On the mythic parallels for women's settlement of new territory provided by the Gefjon myth, see my "Myth of Gefjon."

27. On *nið*-poles as the preliminary to duels, see Meulengracht Sørensen, *Unmanly Man*, 30–32; in my "Þórr's Honour," 48–76, I argue that the phallic pegs used to stake out the dueling ground may have had a similar symbolic value to the *nið*-pole itself; representing phallic power and aggression, they are possibly associated with Þórr's hammer.

9

Courted in the Country

Woman's Precarious Place in the Troubadours' Lyric Landscape

GALE SIGAL

A Shadow Falls Outside Court Walls

In the troubadours' imaginary landscape, the rural setting of the *pastourelle* is reserved for the unregimented gender relations that occur "naturally" in the countryside. The courtly realm fashioned by the same poets for their *canso*, in which etiquette between male and female is firmly regulated, refined and polite, makes a vivid and telling foil against which the action of the *pastourelle* can be refigured.[1] The field frequented by the lyric shepherdess provides a setting where the knight encounters a female accessible in all the ways that the courtly lady is not. The countryside appears idyllic in the pastorals of another time, but in the topography shaped by the troubadours, its isolation—its removal from the public sphere (that is, the court)—renders its female populace vulnerable to the predatory knight's trespass. A mapping of the *pastourelle* shepherdess's relation to the court, an institution that purports to protect the lady, reveals not only the country girl's vulnerability but the precarious place reserved for all women in the troubadours' lyric landscape.

The poetic landscape cultivated by the troubadours left little growing room for their most celebrated flower, the courtly lady. Since this revered *domna*, "always isolated in splendor" (Goldin, *Mirror*, 35) is already perfect, she needs no space to grow. Her sublimity can only be diminished by movement or change (Goldin, *Mirror*, 75–77). Such a constricted and rarified greenhouse atmosphere allows for no contact between the enthroned lady and her "audience": she is adored and worshipped from afar.

If the feminine ideal promoted by the troubadours in their veneration of the *canso domna* is perfectly inaccessible and immobile, the imperfect but impassioned shepherdess created for the *pastourelle* is all too human. The articulate and colorful *pastourelle* country girl can never enter courtly society, but the *canso* lady can never escape it. When Virginia Woolf muses in *A Room of One's Own*, "I thought how unpleasant it is to be locked out; and I thought how it is worse perhaps to be locked in," she contemplates a dilemma whose outlines are reflected in the problematic dichotomization of the female image in medieval lyric (Burns, esp. 254). Given such conditions, the *pastora* has the advantage of her freedom (relatively speaking). Unconstrained by the expectations of an elitist world or its dictates of fashion, she is allowed speech and mobility. But, although granted this flexibility, the vivacious speaking female in medieval verse has little legitimate, safe space. The *pastourelle* poet may allow female self-expression in the lyric countryside, but that freedom is invariably accompanied by the threat of physical harm.

The *pastora* braves the open air, coping with inclement weather and rough terrain, but the most menacing elemental force with which she contends is the aggression of her would-be lover-knight, an intrusion as "natural" (hence, inevitable and ubiquitous) as the pasture in which they meet. Outside the protective courtly edifice that shelters the lady, gender relations are reduced to their "natural" state, devolving into a hunting scenario in which, however virtuous or refined the shepherdess, she nonetheless becomes the knight's prey. Beyond the commanding ethic of the court, when "no one" (except, of course, the shepherdess and us) is looking, the wandering knight-narrator sheds his courtly armor, and the churl he is within emerges in full glory. Courtliness, as the poet presents it even to his aristocratic audience, far from being a dignified code of conduct reflecting an enduring set of values, is instead portrayed as a set of rhetorical and physical gestures to be assumed or discarded at the user's convenience.

The troubadour Marcabru's agile manipulation of horizontal and vertical images in the well-known and possibly first *pastourelle*, "L'autrier jost'una sebissa," offers a compelling critique of knightly courting in the country.[2] Marcabru's masterful handling of topographical imagery reveals a conception of place that works simultaneously on geographical and sociological planes. Furthermore, the images of elevation, leveling, and degradation that pervade the lyric lend themselves to a revealing analysis of social and sexual dominance.

When the knight-narrator of this lyric encounters the shepherdess on the rural "planissa" [plain], the poet is conspicuously setting the pastoral scene; but he is also representing topographically the different planes on which aristocratic knight and rustic field girl exist. In crossing the "plain" to greet her— "Ves lieis vinc per la planissa" (8) [I came to her across the plain]—the knight reveals his intention to level, both literally and figuratively, the difference in social status that separates the shepherdess from him. The knight takes a transgressive detour in order to greet the solitary shepherdess: "Destors me sui de la via / Per far a vos compagnia" (16) [I have turned from my way / To keep you company]. Marcabru's knight admits his trespass when later in the lyric he says:

Ben conosc al trespassatge
Qu'ab aital toza vilana
Pot hom far rich compaignatge.
(59)

[I know well from passing by
that with such a young peasant girl
a man can strike up rich companionship.]

His abrupt salutation when he first addresses her—"*toza*" [young girl]—reveals her status as one who can never "earn" the treatment accorded to a lady.[3] The horse-mounted rider towering over the pedestrian girl of the field is a metaphorical reflection of the hierarchical relationship between *cavaliers* and *vilana*.

Although the *pastora* of Marcabru's "L'autrier jost'una sebissa" is warmly clothed, the knight introduces himself with the pretext that he is concerned for her comfort in the cold: "Dol ai car lo freitz vos fissa" (10) [I am pained because the cold pierces you]. Since the knight's initial description of her attire reveals a girl fully wrapped in warm, sensible garb, his concern is unconvincing. Indeed, rejecting the knight's (feigned) pity, she proclaims her vigor: "Pauc m'o pretz si·l vens m'erissa, / Qu'alegreta sui e sana" (13) [Little do I care if the wind ruffles my hair, / For I am cheerful and healthy].

The *vilana* is completely covered—comically—from head to toe; she sports a cape, coat, and fur, shirt, shoes, and woolen socks:

L'autrier jost'una sebissa
Trobei pastora mestissa,
De joi e de sen massissa,
Si cum filla de vilana,
Cap' e gonel' e pelissa
Vest e camiza treslissa
Sotlars e caussas de lana.
(1–7)

[The other day, beside a hedge
I found a lowly shepherdess
Full of joy and common sense
Just like the daughter of a peasant woman
A cape, a coat and fur,
She wore, and a coarse shirt,
Shoes, and woolen stockings.]

In contrast to the conventional blazon, no mention is made of the beauties of her complexion, tresses, or body, perhaps impossible to make out beneath such cumbersome cloaks. Parodying the courtly portrait, these lines betray the girl's class and her divergence from the "classic" lyric lady simultaneously.

This contrast serves as a convenient metaphor for the divergent prosodic clothings of *canso* and *pastourelle*. The distinguishing garb enclosing the female indicates different generic as well as social codes. Whereas the unattainable *canso domna* is described in terms of her physical attractions rather than her garments—her hair, cheeks, nose, lips, and skin, for example, come under direct scrutiny[4]—the more accessible *pastora* is described in terms of the immediate physical barrier between her and the knight, her clothes, while her physical and facial features go unnoted. Ironically, the court setting provides enough distance to allow the exalted *domna* to be portrayed in more fleshly terms, even while the singer may gallantly renounce her carnal allure.

The central line, "si cum filla de vilana," is pivotal, functioning with both halves of the strophe: the knight sees a shepherdess who, in her joy and good sense, behaves "just like the daughter of a peasant woman" and who is also dressed "just like the daughter of a peasant woman." Her peasant status, lineage, attire, and behavior are not only fully established, but reiterated.[5] Furthermore, since she is called a *vilana* in the middle of every strophe (five of these twelve lines are identical), the word *vilana*—the marker of her class—becomes a key word of the lyric.

In spite of the knight's initial emphasis on her earthy demeanor, several strophes later he tries to flatter the shepherdess by proposing that her mother "was a courtly peasant girl":

Toza de gentil afaire,
Cavaliers fon vostre paire
Que·us engenret en la maire,
Car fon corteza vilana
(29–32)

[Young girl of noble condition,
Your father was a knight
Who got your mother with you
For she was a courtly peasant girl]

But the knight's humor at the *pastora*'s expense is obvious to the audience to whom he regales his adventure in light of his opening description of her, which portrayed a *toza* who was, in every way, a peasant, descended from a peasant woman. How, then, does the paradigmatic *vilana* of strophe 1 assume a "noble condition" [toza de gentil afaire] by strophe 5? The knight mythologizes her birth, transforming her mother into an oxymoronic "courtly peasant" [corteza vilana] and her father into a "cavaliers." If her father were a *cavaliers*, the shepherdess would be a half-breed, illegitimate but noble. The knight is insinuating that her mother acquiesced to the same arrangement with the *toza*'s (purportedly knightly) father that he proposes to her, a union between upper and lower class that could have produced mixed offspring. William D. Paden's translation of line 2 of the poem, "I found a half-breed shepherdess" [Trobei pastora mestissa], captures the knight's later implication that she has mixed blood (*Medieval Pastourelle*).[6]

The knight furthermore formulates a rationale for his pursuit of her: this kind of relationship already runs in the family. Since he had first described her as looking "just like the daughter of a peasant woman," her sudden courtliness (like her illegitimacy), must spring from her paternal line. The *pastora*'s mother's putative union with a knight makes the daughter semi-courtly, a hybrid; it makes her father anonymous and aristocratic simultaneously. This adjustment of her paternal lineage suits the knight's purposes brilliantly: it "elevates" the *pastora* from her peasant (but legitimate) roots, giving her the noble blood she could never otherwise possess; it also uproots her from her peasant paternity and the land that gives her self-definition and dignity. To the knight, the earth that grounds the shepherdess has no value; the pasture, which she may use but does not own, bestows no status. Consequently, her position, as far as the knight is concerned, is fluid; he can lift her to a higher position on the social ladder as easily as he can move her from the open field to more private cover (75–77, cited below), or reinvent her paternity.

After exhausting more flattering and tactful approaches, the frustrated knight invites the *pastora* to "form a couple":

... Pareillar pareilladura
Devem, ieu e vos, vilana.

A l'abric lonc la pastura,
Car plus n'estaretz segura
Per far la cauza doussana.
                (73–77)

[Let us prepare to pair off
You and I, peasant girl,
Under cover, beside the pasture
For you will feel safer there
To do the sweet thing.]

The shepherd girl has consistently refused the knight's offers of companionship, but he persists, suggesting that physical union will bring about equality in their social positions. The knight's "paired" words "pareillar pareilladura / devem" (73–74) [let us prepare to pair off] imitate the desired pairing and paralleling (lying side by side). The double meanings in this witty line are difficult to convey in English through a single translation. I have emphasized the knight's desired coupling, as does Margaret Switten, "we should prepare to form a couple" (53), and Leslie Topsfield, "You and I, my peasant love, / should make a pair by pairing" (90). In contrast, Frederick Goldin's translation, "let us become a couple of equals" (*Troubadours*, 75) and Rouben Cholakian's similar "you and I should form a well-matched couple, peasant girl" (70) stress the knight's desire to level out class differences. In the Old Occitan, the narrator encompasses all these meanings simultaneously, implying that their pairing off will make them social peers, as if physical paralleling, that is, lying side by side, will engender social parity.

The invitation to pair off echoes the knight's earlier suggestion that their coupling would "double" the *vilana*'s beauty:

E seria·us ben doblada,
Si·m vezi'una vegada,
Sobira e vos sotrana.
                (47–49)

[And it (your beauty) would be doubled
If I saw myself just once
Above and you below.]

With these lines, the knight's offers of equality are exposed for what they really are: they are aimed not at lifting the girl up to a more exalted rank but at lowering both aristocrat and peasant to the ground, the natural plane/plain. Further, the knight's discourse reveals that, although he is more than willing to lower himself to her plane, he nevertheless intends to remain, in every sense, "on top." The doubling of the *pastora*'s worth, that is, her beauty, is predicated not upon equality (lying side by side), but upon her lowering herself literally beneath the knight: he means to put her in her proper (lower) place.

If, as Marcabru's knight declares to the shepherdess, every creature "reverts to its nature" [Toza, tota creatura / Revertis a sa natura (71–72)], the social hierarchy is rendered irrelevant. Whether the *pastora* is viewed from the perspective of her assigned place in the social order or in the natural world, she is to be dominated: socially, her peasant status humbles her; in the natural realm, her inferior strength makes her vulnerable to any man.

The vulgarity with which the *pastora* is approached, and the ease with which she becomes a target, can amuse and flatter the listeners in the audience—male and female—as long as they identify with the aggressive knight or the untouchable lady, both safely removed from such assaults. But the underlying message of female vulnerability is otherwise quite threatening to women. Sometimes, as in Marcabru's "L'autrier jost'una sebissa," the shepherdess outwits her seducer and impresses us. But when unsuccessful, as in many an Old French version, she may pay a high price for her failure.

Although from the start, the *vilana* is unreceptive to his suit, Marcabru's knight grows increasingly bolder as the song progresses. His method of persuasion, however, remains verbal. In contrast, the knight of many an Old French *pastourelle* grows so intent on conquest that he disregards the *bergière*'s resistance completely, resorting to physical force.[7] More significantly, perhaps, "[e]ven when *pastourelles* do not actually depict rape, they consistently celebrate its threat" (Gravdal, "Camouflaging Rape," 361–62; *Ravishing Maidens*, 166 n. 4). Where some critics see the male threat in the *pastourelle* as ineffectual and comic, Kathryn Gravdal reads it as real and realized, adducing the rape scenes scattered throughout the Old French *pastourelle* corpus as evidence.[8]

Such brutality against the field girl reveals that the female encountered beyond the court's surveillance is not entitled to any of the prerogatives designed for the "courted" lady. A shepherdess, having no place at court, is disqualified from receiving the ordinary courtesies required there. Apparently, it is *only* at court that courtly virtues apply. The threat underlying the *pastourelle*, however, extends well beyond female peasants. The imperious lady can turn into the vulnerable shepherdess should she be found alone outside territory demarcated for her as safe. Should she wander beyond court bounds, she cannot, by definition, be a lady. In the troubadour's lyric landscape, the court defines and circumscribes the lady; beyond its purview, the lady has no meaning.

Outside castle walls, the lady is nowhere to be found; the only women scattered about the lyric countryside are working girls. Or, as Paden proposes, invoking the historical context, they may be prostitutes ("Rape," 336). Thirteenth-century Occitanian law permitted prostitution as long as it was outside city walls: the French ordinance of 1256 expelled prostitutes from the center of towns; they "were to be 'put outside the walls'" (Otis, 15–24, esp. 19–20). Thus, for Paden, "an encounter of a man with a shepherdess in the fields outside a city could immediately raise the possibility of prostitution, a possibility which would be realized only if the man proposed it and the woman accepted" ("Rape," 336). In addition, the knight's proffered gifts and other material enticements lead Paden to counter Gravdal's interpretation that the *pastourelle* is a celebration of rape with his view that "the theme of sexual license in a country setting carries overtones of prostitution" rather than rape.[9]

But whether viewed as a "celebration" of prostitution or the threat of rape, the sexual license implicit in either interpretation of the genre furthers the argument that there was no legitimate, safe space for women. If the court provides a haven only for the lady, every other woman can be had for a price. If prostitutes as well as "innocent" working girls haunt the outskirts of town or the countryside meadow, how can the wandering knight tell one from the other? Consequently, any woman found outside the court is fair game because she might be persuaded to offer what the knight seeks. The only women exempt from propositions of this nature keep themselves literally off limits— within bounds of court walls—where such approaches are considered unacceptable. The virtuous peasant girl (or the errant lady) can find as little shelter from the predations of the wandering knight as the prostitute. In a masculinist culture, all women out in the open are there for the taking.

In fact, Marcabru's knight makes a veiled suggestion that union with him can enrich the *toza*: he offers her "ric compaignatge / Ab amistat de coratge" (61–62), which can be translated as "a fine cash companionship / with real affection" (Goldin, *Troubadours*, 75), or more ambiguously as "noble company / with heartfelt friendship" (Switten, 52). But the tone of both the Old Occitan and the Old French *pastourelle* is often more seductive or predatory than businesslike, as though the knight seeks something for nothing, even while he may gesture toward a payment or bribe. Nevertheless, as Paden points out, this offer is occasionally accepted by the "shepherd girl," and a bargain is struck ("Rape").

Marcabru's *pastora* knows that union with the knight would bring her down literally and figuratively, for submitting to him would automatically place her on the lowest rung of the social ladder (and one that has no corollary for men), that of whore:

> Mas ieu, per un pauc d'intratge,
> Non vuoil ges mon piucellatge
> Camjar per nom de putana.
> (68–70)

[But I, for a cheap entrance fee,
Do not want to exchange my virginity
For the name of whore.]

In the final analysis, the attitude toward women that makes the *pastourelle* a celebration of the threat of rape is similar to one that views the interchange between prostitute and client as a harmless, delightful, or comic scene. In a patriarchal society, only a thin line can be drawn between rape and prostitution: "rape and prostitution can be seen as two sides of a coin, conjoined through the glorification of virginity and chastity" (Fisher, 350). And prostitutes, then as now, have little protection against rape. The knight's offer of "ric compaignatge / Ab amistat de coratge" may be his most material attempt at persuasion, but the offer of enrichment fails because the shepherdess foresees a place lower on the social scale than her own. Should she allow the knight's transgression, should she sell herself, Marcabru's *pastora* knows she would become worthless.

The Singing Shepherdess

Despite his blandishments over her gentility, Marcabru's knight continually reiterates the field girl's true social position by addressing her throughout the lyric as *toza* or *vilana*. Hence, when he tells us, "trobei pastora mestissa" (2) [I found a half-breed shepherdess], Marcabru is referring simultaneously to the discovery by the knight-narrator of the shepherdess and to his own authorial invention ["trobei"] of a mixed creature, a courtly peasant hybrid. Such an anomaly—a lowly shepherdess who can rhetorically hold her own with a knight and retain her virtue and dignity in the process—is truly a literary creation of which to boast!

The "corteza vilana" of the lyric is an oxymoron because courtly ideology prohibits a *vilana* from becoming a *domna* no matter how refined the young girl's manners, beliefs, or suitors may be.[10] And regardless of the register in which she expresses herself or the emotional and intellectual range of her responses—she can be dull, witty, vivacious, aggressive, passive—the singing shepherdess makes no claim to courtly stature. Her commonness is grounded in her forthright and transparent speech, especially in contrast to the knight's courtly double-talk. From the knight's viewpoint, the "best" she can be is "mestissa" [mixed]; she may be a "corteza vilana" [a courtly peasant girl] if she turns out to be, as he hopes, illegitimate. But in a metaliterary sense, this pastora is a *corteza vilana* because her honest eloquence, wit, and grace would befit a courtly lady, if only such ladies could speak.

Whether or not illegitimate "half-breeds" everywhere roamed the actual medieval countryside, Marcabru's shepherdess flatly denies the suggestion that she is one, by invoking her ancient familial connection to the land:

> Don, tot mon ling e mon aire
> Vei revertir e retraire
> Al vezoig et a l'araire . . .
> (36–38)

> [Sir, all my lineage and my family
> I see returning and going back
> To sickle and plow . . .]

In responding that she descends from a long line of field workers, the *pastora* sets her birthright and legitimacy straight. She is also boasting a stable and ancient heritage, as though that, in itself, has value. Her connection to the land, like the integrity of her physical being, has its ancient dignity, a dignity that transcends the more recent idea of "courtliness." Her connectedness to the land manifests itself in the proverbial and long-lived wisdom she confidently espouses. It is this dignity—and the territory in which it is rooted—that the knight means to invade in his promotion of the false hope of equality through sexual union.

The shepherdess's pride in her ancestry (while the knight reveals nothing of his) contrasts with the knight's patronizing assumption that she feels inferior. He regards the peasant girl as inferior and insignificant because her ancestral line is purely peasant. The peasant girl, in Marcabru's shaping hands, takes the view that her lineage is as pure and, therefore, as dignified as any. That no trace of aristocratic blood can be detected in her peasant line indicates that her line is unmixed, pure, wholly legitimate. One wonders whether Marcabru is implying, as Paden suggests, that the knight can make no such boast of his own lineage ("Reading Pastourelles," 5–6). Not feeling demeaned by her pure peasant status, the *pastora* finds little favor with the knight's offer to change it. The knight may devalue her; he may try to undermine her dignity and persuade her of her inferiority, and he may believe his offer of equality quite tempting, but the shepherdess easily rejects it, not merely because she knows it is empty, but because she does not feel inferior to begin with. Neither cowed nor overwhelmed by the knight, she proudly holds her own ground.

An ironic reversal has occurred in which a dignified and eloquent *vilana* is pitted against a *vilan* in knight's armor. As soon as he breaches the gates of the court, this knight becomes a churl, as the *pastora* is well aware:

> Mas tals se fai cavalgaire
> C'atrestal deuria faire
> Los seis jorns de la setmana.
> (40–42)

[But some pass themselves off as knights
Who should be doing likewise (i.e., working the land)
Six days of the week.]

The shepherdess exposes a rupture in the natural order when knights behave like churls. In the social world Marcabru critiques in this lyric, place rather than class defines behavior. The comportment of a knight should remain the same whether he is at court or in the country, whether he addresses a lady or a field girl. But in this poem, as in most *pastourelles*, the gates of the court function to demarcate high from low class, appropriate from inappropriate behaviors, civilized from beastly existence. Again and again in the lyrics, place, not propriety or breeding, determines behavior.

Since the knight has a stake in devaluing the shepherdess's lineage, he proposes to rearrange it to suit himself; in doing so, he bestows a false and ig/noble value upon her.[11] Yet in crossing the plain/plane that separates them, the knight has already sunk, metaphorically, to her level. In this sense, he has already leveled the playing field. But contrary to his promise to level out hierarchical difference, the knight actually sinks to a level beneath the peasant, for when knights behave like churls, the hierarchy should be inverted. Ironically, therefore, although a *vilana* can never be elevated to the status of a *domna*, in the eyes of Marcabru's audience, the *vilana*'s wit and dignity make her appear far above the knight who intends to outwit her.

If Marcabru's knight signals his instantaneous awareness that the creature he meets is very different from the courtly *domna* by portraying her in a parodic version of the courtly blazon, the girl, when she speaks, is so witty, rational, and refined that she does not suit our expectations of a peasant at all. The *pastourelle* shepherdess's language is sometimes so logical and polished that Joan Ferrante views her as "a figure for the courtly lady" (70). And if, according to Gravdal, the shepherdess "is the courtly lady, dressed in a shepherdess costume" ("Camouflaging Rape," 37; *Ravishing Maidens*, 118–20, 169 n. 33), evidently it is only via the privileges granted aristocratic women within the refuge of the court that a woman can hope to be treated like a lady. But if the *canso* lady never speaks, how can we know how she sounds? What Ferrante and Gravdal imply is that, given the opportunity to speak out, the *domna* would sound as logical, intelligent, and clever as the *pastora*. Hence, the knight's characterization of the peasant girl as a *gentil toza* or *corteza vilana* is corroborated: she is a peasant whose bearing is courtly. Rather than being a courtly lady in shepherdess's costume, perhaps we should see the lady as the *pastora*, dressed up and shut up.

Marcabru creates a peasant girl who acts like a lady; what distinguishes one from the other is not her lineage but her location; where she is "found" (that is, invented, rooted)—in the country or the court—determines all. In the country, the female speaks and is open to victimization; in the court, she is silent but venerated. In terms of pure invention, however, Marcabru's lady and his *pastora* have identical lineages, as they share the same artistic sire.

Whereas the *canso domna* is mystified, her responses indecipherable, the *pastora* expresses herself fluently. She reacts; she retorts. A fathomable woman, robbed of her mystery, the meager *matière* she provides for song resides primarily in her vulnerability. Nevertheless she sometimes serves her poet's ends as a disguised mouthpiece. Through her, opinions can be expressed with impunity since they belong to an insignificant outsider. And cries for change erupting from "the voice of the 'other'" lack potency (Earnshaw, 121). Unthreatening, pathetic, and vulnerable, the speaking female may vent dissatisfaction, but she helplessly accepts the status quo: "A non-person in legal codes, the ward or charge of men, she has a freedom of dissent like the fool, and can give voice to the frustrations felt by the whole population" (Earnshaw, 126). Her poet, like the later Chaucer, can disclaim the views of such disempowered characters. In deprecating knights who act like churls, Marcabru's *pastora* registers her discomfort and disorientation at the knight's trespass into her territory. Aristocratic men who desire peasant women behave inappropriately, below their birth. The *pastora* finds the ideas that knights should seek out peasant girls, that the classes should mix, or that aristocrat and peasant should be equal unnatural.

For Marcabru's *vilana*, what is natural is the pairing of social equals:

Don, oc; mas segon dreitura
Cerca fols sa follatura,
Cortes cortez' aventura,
E·il vilans ab la vilana;
En tal loc fai sens fraitura
On hom non garda mezura,
So ditz la gens anciana.
           (78–84)

[Sir, yes; but according to what is right
The fool seeks his folly,
The courtly, courtly adventures
And the peasant boy, the peasant girl;
Wisdom is fractured in such a place
Where a man does not observe moderation,
So say the ancients.]

Since Marcabru's *pastora* recites the misdeeds of the aristocracy, it is not surprising that she rejects the knight's offer to be "raised up" to it. Her continual address to him as "Don" or "Senher" [Lord] manifests her wish to retain, even emphasize, class distinctions. She desires to preserve the socially prescribed distance between peasant and courtier. Ironically, she has become the spokeswoman for the courtly value of *mezura*, a value that maintains what she considers the "natural" boundaries of class difference. The lowly shepherdess, through her "common" sense, bears the courtly moral home.

Although she lacks status both in the real medieval world and as a poetic figure, the *vilana* speaks for values that maintain the status quo. Paradoxically, Marcabru creates a champion for his idealized version of courtly life—in which knights do act like gentlemen—out of a peasant girl who can never enter into it. The knight's desire to raze class barriers is seen by the peasant girl not as a means of elevation but of depredation. She prefers class barriers in place. If, through her wit and common sense, the *pastora* outmaneuvers her opponent, his parries come to appear vulgar and clumsy. Consequently, how can most listeners ultimately fail to be brought around to the shepherdess's conclusion that social division is good, even for the peasant?

No social revolution is brewing here, for it is not the downtrodden peasant, but the errant knight, who pleads for the fluidity of class distinctions, and he does so, not because he is a social reformer, but because he is a deceitful and voracious opportunist. Whatever he tells the *pastora* to the contrary, he surely knows that class distinctions are not swept away by passion. Predatory or churlish as he is, the knight is not automatically demoted from the ranks of chivalry, nor does the encounter between himself and the *pastora* elevate the peasant girl or transform her into a lady. Born a peasant, a peasant she is destined to remain.

The *pastourelle* knight's duplicity hinges not on an attempt to conceal the woman's identity or his love from her—major preoccupations of the *canso* lover—but rather on his effort to represent his intentions as sincere, honorable or beneficial to her. The *pastourelle* knight's cleverness is proven by his success in fooling the girl (while the audience looks on in amused admiration). Courtliness, in its artifice, has a duplicitous potential, one that the *pastourelle* knight is fully adept at manipulating.[12] The *toza*'s directness, on the other hand, manifests her lack of aesthetic sensibility and sophistication. In her ignorance or rejection of artifice, she simultaneously reveals her uncourtliness and "simple-minded" inability to deceive. Although the shepherdess's lack of courtly sophistication is often satirized as gullibility or stupidity, the biting humor of the *pastourelle* may just as frequently arise from our surprised expectations, as the country girl battles for respect and dignity amid the onslaughts and clever ruses of the seducer knight.

Marcabru brilliantly fashions a debate in which the boastful protagonist fails to win over his female object, and in lowering himself to her level, loses the audience's respect without disparaging those of his kind who take their courtliness with them outside the court. True gentlemen, the *pastora* implies, never cross the plain that brings them face to face with a shepherdess. On the other hand, when Marcabru's peasant girl upholds hierarchical courtly values, she is transformed into a witty, fashionable, and forceful character.

Marcabru enters virgin territory to make a space for his marvelous, articulate *pastora*. She becomes his most persuasive advocate for courtly hegemony, precisely because she is exiled from it. But the empowerment she gains from speaking is tainted: it resides in her promotion of a system that locks her out and keeps her down. And while choosing to be locked out rather than locked in (or up) may be a logical preference, as Woolf mused hundreds of years later, Marcabru has his shepherdess cling to the system as though it were benevolent, natural, and inevitable rather than a painful and problematic choice.

The Courtly Mystique

Since the lyric countryside is portrayed as a place where gender relations are naturally predatory, the court, with its refinements and formalities, appears as an appealing alternative. The court is typically imaged as a bastion of polite and respectful treatment for women, where they not only have a central position but where male aggression is transformed, ritualized into distanced awe and worship, into *court*ship. Bounded by the rustic and wild, the court is idealized as a civilizing site, a refuge where natural impulse is subjugated to rules of comportment and etiquette. Although women are ostensibly better off when such courtly prerogatives are bestowed upon them, these benefits, when closely scrutinized, are double-edged, for they justify not only the brutalized treatment of women outside the court's purview but also promote the strict regulation of feminine behavior within its domain.

The lady is as carefully crafted and artificial a construct as the court that (safe?)guards her. At the same time that they promote the court as a haven for women, the troubadours are reserving it for an imaginary female called the *domna*. Modern critics have seen this lady as almost everything but a woman; she has been considered a male fantasy (Goldin, *Mirror*, 70–77; Ferrante, 70), a "myth of female sexual identity, a misreading of the feminine in terms of the masculine" (Burns, 263), a poetic device that "still sells everything from cars to cigarettes . . . an empty signifier in opposition to which masculinity can be defined" (Burgwinkle, "Ethics," 78, 85), an essentially virginal and therefore virtually neutered love-object (Bloch, *Misogyny*, 147, 155), and an androgyne (Kay).

This lady, however construed, usurps female public space. Unladylike women are exiled, in effect, from this refuge. The woman who desires protection against masculine predation must transform herself into the desired, silenced lady. Highly "regarded" by many, such a *domna* is also guarded, watched, spied upon: "La dompna es agradans e plazens, / per sa beutat la gardon mantas gens . . ." (Anon., "En un vergier sotz fuella d'albespi"; Appel, 90) [The lady is pleasant and pleasing, / because of her beauty many regard her . . .]. The lady is universally admired, but no matter how intently she is scrutinized, she cannot be known. Whether she might reciprocate his love no one, not even the suitor, seems to know. Her impenetrability serves a convenient literary purpose: it sets the lovelorn "sufferer" free to conjure any number of imagined scenarios and responses.

The lover of Bernart de Ventadorn's *canso* "Era·m cosselhatz senhor" (Goldin, *Troubadours*, 140–45), for example, remarks on his lady's mysterious sign:

Manhtas vetz m'es pois membrat
de so que·m fetz al comjat:

que·lh vi cobrir sa faisso,
c'anc no·m poc dir oc ni no.
                    (53–56)

[Many times it reminds me afterwards
of what she did when we parted:
I saw her cover her face,
so that she could not tell me yes or no.]

An indecipherable sign such as this allows the lover room for rumination; the mystery breeds song as well as sorrow. Only the absence of the lady as poetic subject threatens to make song impossible:

E s'aissi pert s'amistat,
be·m tenh per dezeretat
d'amor, e ja Deus no·m do
mais faire vers ni chanso.
                    (21–24)

[But, on the other hand, if I lose her friendship,
I hold myself disowned
by love, and then God never let me
write a *vers* or *canson* again.]

To lose the power to create song is a far more grievous threat than to lose a lady the singer doesn't know he's ever had, and whom he can revere just as eloquently from afar.

Although the singer may dream (and compose songs) about his lady, her "actions" consist primarily of gazing and smiling. But even these gestures cause trouble if they are indiscriminate: should she gaze or smile promiscuously, she courts disfavor. Thus, Bernart's narrator pleads that his lady's "traitor eyes," which once smiled on him, refrain from straying elsewhere:

Li seu belh olh traïdor,
que m'esgardavon tan gen,
s'atressi gardon alhor,
mout i fan gran flahimen
                    (41–44)

[Her beautiful traitor eyes
that once looked on me with much gentleness,
if they look like that elsewhere
they do wrong, great wrong]

The lady's mystery and magnificence are there to be admired; they work the magic of ennobling the lover. The more mysterious she is, the more miraculous and magical the lover's suit can be. Success is determined not by the lady's response to her wooer (since she shows none), but rather by the singer's ability—something akin to the literary critic's—to interpret the enigmatic, to make meaning out of nothing. While her worshiper strives to read her indecipherable gestures, she remains unmoved and unknown. His interpretations can therefore be illimitable.

Such open-endedness leads variously to confusion, suffering, joy—a panoply of passions, all fertile ground for song. Bernart's lover's tears unleash a flood of written words:

> De l'aiga que dels olhs plor,
> escriu salutz mais de cen,
> que tramet a la gensor
> et a la plus avinen
> (49–52)

[With the water I weep from my eyes
I write more than a hundred greetings
and send to the most beautiful,
the courtliest.]

The lover's plaint spells out some further effects of lyric love-longing in Cercamon's "Quant l'aura doussa s'amarzis" (Goldin, *Troubadours*, 98–99), including the Lady's power to raise or lower the supplicant:

> Ni muer ni viu ni no guaris,
> ni mal no·m sent e si l'ai gran,
> quar de s'amor no suy devis,
> non sai si ja l'aurai ni quan,
> qu'en lieys es tota le merces
> que·m pot sorzer o descazer.
> (31–36)

[I neither die, nor live, nor get well,
I do not feel my suffering, and yet it is great,
because I cannot tell the future of her love,
whether I shall have it, or when,
for in her is all the pity,
that can raise me up, or make me fall.]

In the territory of the court, the silencing of the lady renders the lyric self-reflexive. Because what makes her dignified, respected and adored are qualities "found" (invented) by the worshiping singer rather than intrinsic to her, the lady can be stripped of them at will.[13] The courtly ethic maintains the illusion that the *domna* is prized for her inherent goodness. In Bernart's *canso* "Lancan vei la folha" (Goldin, *Troubadours*, 148–55), the narrator invokes the mirror image as a reflection of his lady's worth:

Be deuri' aucire
que anc fetz mirador!
Can be m'o cossire,
no·n ai guerrer peyor.
Ja·l jorn qu'ela·s mire
ni pens de sa valor,
no serai jauzire
de leis ni de s'amor.
        (41–48)

[I would have gladly murdered
the man who first made the mirror.
When I think about it,
I don't have a worse enemy.
The second she looks at herself
and realizes how much she's worth,
it won't be me who enjoys
her or her love.]

The singer disclaims credit for crafting the mirror (that is, his song) that reflects his lady's beauty; he further declares the mirror-maker—who is, in actuality, himself—his greatest enemy. From lyrics like these, we come to understand that the lady's glorious virtue—which made the singer feel unworthy of her—is really his own invention. The singer's recognition and praise actually determine the lady's value. The more Bernart's singer declines to call attention to his part in building up the beloved's worth, the more aware we become of the rhetorical game he is playing.

In flaunting his indifference to the lady's response, the lover of another of Bernart's *cansos* ("Be m'an perdut lai enves Ventadorn" [Goldin, *Troubadours*, 134–37]) betrays how irrelevant her role in the love relationship really is: "no sai domna volgues o no volgues, / si·m volia c'amar no la pogues" (26–27) [I don't know one woman that I could not love, / if I wanted to, whether she wanted it or not]. Such nonreciprocal "love" bestows dignity on the lover, not the beloved. The kinds of miracles Bernart and other troubadours attribute to the divine lady are, therefore, very much *man*-made.[14]

The lady's qualities, as limned by the poet, are so conventional that to all eyes but her lover's she is interchangeable with any other *domna*. Courtliness assures that the personality of the *canso domna* always remains a cipher. Responsiveness would make her human rather than transcendent; her mystique usurps the place of personality. In contrast, we can come to know the articulate *pastora*, but her personality is rendered meaningless to her errant pursuer for a different reason: her personal qualities are irrelevant; her sexuality, her vulnerability define her. No matter how elegant her comportment, she receives the treatment accorded to any *vilana*. The awe reserved for the lady, on the other hand, enlarges her importance. The lady's value is not centered solely on sexual or biological attributes; but she has become so vacuous she is no longer fully human. She is a literary icon shaped for courtly poets to worship and real women to emulate.

Cornered in the Court

If women are sheltered from male depredation only at court, apparently this refuge is provided at some cost. Inside castle walls, ladies don't talk back. Set amid a thriving social sphere, but silenced into iconic perfection, the lady is squarely in the public eye without an audible voice, to be seen and not heard. A prisoner of the pedestal, she has no voice and no choice. Any fresh, outspoken, aggressive—in short, "unfeminine"—behavior is unacceptable.

The passive, silent, emotionless, but intensely desirable and ennobling lady imagined by the troubadours is undoubtedly still a paragon for many. Even if the troubadours were reflecting an ideology they perceived already in place rather than actually initiating it, their lyric construction of gender relations may have instilled in the female audience such a fear of the unruly male, the outside, and the natural as to convince women that courtly confinement and its concomitant strictures on their behavior were instituted for their own good.

Jane Schulenburg documents a similar movement in the church's treatment of nuns at this time. Nuns were "forcibly enclosed" (avowedly for their own protection) when their freedom of movement became inconvenient to the upper hierarchy of the church. The claustration instituted at the council of Wocandus involved not only restrictions on the nuns' freedom to act, but also on their freedom of speech and thought. Enjoined to take vows of obedience and chastity, those abbesses who refused were deposed, and secular princes put in their place. Once enclosure was achieved, the physical violation of a cloistered nun was considered much more grievous (and the punishment more severe and costly) than the violation of her sister outside the cloister.[15] Similarly, as the Church underwent a process of feminization, and as it became the "Bride of Christ," according to Jo Ann McNamara, it crowded women out, simultaneously controlling and devaluing them.[16] During the twelfth century, when women were losing many of their former rights and their political power was vastly diminished, the "male-centered institutions of the aristocracy and the Church developed elaborate myths featuring women" (Burns, 260)—and lyric poetry reiterates this dynamic in its creation of the courtly lady. If the feminization of the Church went hand in hand with the diminished power and participation of women in it, it was paralleled by the glorified vision of the perfect and beloved lady whose invention likewise facilitated the subordination or exclusion of real women in courtly society.

Since the *canso*'s idealized *domna* promotes the silence and paralysis of women in the public realm, the only literary terrain vaguely hospitable to women as individuals with thoughts, feelings, and the language to express them is the unregulated countryside of the *pastourelle*. The court as the troubadours fashion it provides the cocoon-cell within which a woman can be transformed into a lady, admired by men and immune to their predation—if only she surrenders her speech and freedom, her self-determination and identity. Speech, in the mouth of a woman, is considered so powerful that it is eradicated from her idealized image. Once she surrenders herself, she becomes venerable and twice as beautiful, like Marcabru's *pastora*, whose beauty "would be doubled" if only she would submit to the knight. The freedom to speak in the female voice exists outside the court, but when the poet gives women that freedom, it is in the disempowered context of the field and peasantry. On the margin, female freedom is inevitably accompanied by the threat of rape. In dichotomizing the female population into the mute, revered lady and the low but lively shepherdess, the troubadours marginalize all women.[17]

If, in the *pastourelle*, the speaking woman incurs the threat of violence, her proficiency with words can also deflate it. While not adept at duplicitous speech, the shepherdess's straightforwardness, logic, and cleverness in responding to the knight's pretensions would seem vastly beyond a common peasant's purview. The *pastora*'s verbal dexterity is her only weapon against the warrior-knight, presumably a stronger fighter than thinker (and whose dull-wittedness is sometimes satirized). In contrast to the inert, exalted, and remote *domna*, whose function prohibits all movement either physical or emotional, the *pastora* must marshal all her physical strength, mental agility, and verbal dexterity in self-defense—in order merely to maintain her same (lowly) place. In the countryside, the woman's need for a clear and direct voice is conspicuous: it is a vehicle not solely of self-expression but also of resistance, of protest, and, if need be, a means by which to shout a cry of alarm or shriek in pain. Such are the dangers of being "courted" in the country.

Notes

I gratefully acknowledge the support of Wake Forest University and those who commented on versions of this essay, including Jane Schulenburg, Dick Olsen, Gillian Overing, Julie Edelson, Sylvia Tomasch, and Sealy Gilles. Sarah Watts, Claudia Thomas, Nell Gifford-Martin, and David Weinstein inspired me to broaden my interdisciplinary thinking. My debt to Frederick Goldin goes far beyond this essay.

1. Ferrante stresses that "in the *canso*, the form in which most Provençal love poetry was written, the woman never appears or speaks for herself, and is rarely even described—the poet is entirely taken up with his own fantasies" (70). The Occitan *pastorela* (Old French *pastourelle*) recounts a knight's random encounter with a shepherdess and his attempt to seduce her. Old Provençal has about 30 examples, and Old French, over 150 (Paden, *Medieval Pastourelle*, iv; Earnshaw, 90–94). Throughout this essay, unattributed translations are my own.

2. Citations from "L'autrier jost'una sebissa" (P.C. 293.30) are from Dejeanne; translations are from Switten, 51–53, with slight alterations of my own.

3. Earnshaw notes: "[t]he epithet *toza* marks her as a lower class woman (der. *tonsa*, girl) in contrast to the word *donsela* or *donzelha* (der. *dominicella*, maiden, young lady)" (125). See also Paden, "Troubadour's Lady," 33. The word *toza* may also mean prostitute; *Petit Dictionnaire Provençal-Francais*, s.v. "toza"; and Paden, "Rape."

4. The *domna* of Bernart de Ventadorn's *canso* "Ab joi mou lo verse e·l comens," for example, is evoked by specified attributes of form, glances, face, charming ways, and so on (Nichols, 42–43).

5. Earnshaw suggests that this line functions as a refrain that "establishes a mock inequality between the speakers, because she is patently his intellectual superior" (125).

6. Others have translated "mestissa" as "of lowly birth" (Goldin, *Troubadours*, 71) or "humble" (Switten, 51), an indication of her lowly—rather than mixed—blood.

7. In "Camouflaging Rape," Gravdal cites twelve *pastourelles* in which brutal rape is depicted (364–65 and n. 15); in *Ravishing Maidens*, she likewise notes that rape occurs in "approximately 18 percent of the extant Old French pastourelles" (38 of 160 texts) (105 and n. 4). Rape occurs in only one Old Occitan text.

8. In the late nineteenth century, Hueffer assumed that the blatant sexuality of the encounter was "toned down" to suit "the fastidious taste of a courtly audience" (78). Jones, writing in the 1930s, saw the *pastourelle*'s boastful narrator as a figure for the poet himself; the knight's designs on the peasant girl were best understood as memorable autobiographical scenes (5). Recently, Earnshaw has stated that the *pastourelle* allowed men to "empathize with a knight trying ... to get past the women's armor of wit" while women "could see themselves as ... carriers of the highly valued quality of *mezura*" (90–91).

9. Gravdal counts twenty-six Old French *pastourelles* in which the knight attempts to bribe the *pastora* (*Ravishing Maidens*, 169 n. 25).

10. Although a *pastora* can never be elevated into a *domna*, a *vilan* can be made courtly or a courtly man can become a churl through the *domna*'s response, as in Guillaume IX's *canso*, "Mout jauzens me prenc en amar" (Goldin, *Troubadours*, 42–45). Apparently, the status of men in both genres is more fluid than that of women, especially those of the lower class. Judith Bennett notes that the consistent thread in women's history is that they remain in the subordinate position no matter how their condition may improve ("'How's That Any Different from Today?': Continuity and Change in Women's History," lecture at Wake Forest University, Fall 1994). Marcabru's knight promises to raise the *pastora* up to his level—as long as he continues to remain above her.

11. He deflates her status as easily as he inflates it, as though social rank can be adjusted merely through language. Once he realizes that his attempt at seduction is futile, he pointedly addresses her as "toza vilana" (60) [young peasant girl] in contrast to his earlier "toza de gentil afaire" (29).

12. That courtly artifice can disguise predatory motives is a leitmotif of troubadour poetry. But polished manners can also buffer the lady from direct assault. See, for example, Bernart de Ventadorn's "Non es meravelha s'eu chan," in which the lover worries that if false and true lovers use the same language the lady will not be able to discern his sincerity (Goldin, *Troubadours*, 126–28).

13. As Burns aptly notes, the lady "can play the role of 'lord' only as long as [her lover] is willing to relinquish it to her" (266).

14. The *minnesinger* Walther von der Vogelweide (1170–1230) was the first to articulate overtly the poet's implicit power over the lady, exposing the poetic cliché that the lady merits praise independently of the lover's song; see his "Saget mir ieman, waz ist minne?" and "Lange swîgen des hât ich gedâht" (Goldin, *German and Italian Lyrics*, 97, 114–19).

15. Jane Schulenburg, "A Historian's Response," paper presented at the 28th International Congress on Medieval Studies, Kalamazoo, May 1993; published in *Forgetful of Their Sex*.

16. Jo Ann McNamara, "Clerical Celibacy and the Ungendering of Institutional Man," paper presented at the Twenty-eighth International Congress on Medieval Studies, Kalamazoo, May 1993.

17. The *alba* lady in some respects bridges the gap between the *canso*'s iconic female and the voluble *pastora*, but in putting her status and safety at risk, she too becomes a marginal figure; see my *Erotic Dawn-Songs of the Middle Ages*.

10

Assault from Behind

Sodomy, Foreign Invasion, and Masculine Identity in the *Roman d'Enéas*

VINCENT A. LANKEWISH

The *Roman d'Enéas* and the State of Sodomy

The elaborate description of the tomb of the Amazon warrior Camille featured in the *Roman d'Enéas* might lend itself more readily to a discussion of architectural ingenuity than of the representation of sodomy in this twelfth-century text, and yet this description brings into relief related anxieties about foreign invasion and masculinity that reverberate throughout the romance and that are thoroughly imbricated in the queen of Latium's conception of Enéas, the Trojan with whom her daughter Lavine is in love, as a "sodomite wretch." Revered by the romancer as the greatest of the world's hundred marvels, Camille's mausoleum immortalizes the cross-dressed queen of Vulcane who comes to Latium to help the Latins defend themselves against the impending Trojan takeover of their land, but is killed when Arranz, a Trojan soldier, follows her from behind and, in a surprise attack, hurls a dart that impales her in the chest. After Camille's corpse is brought back home, her compatriots construct a spectacular sepulchre, the details of which occupy nearly two hundred lines in the text. Rising well over a hundred feet in the air, the tomb comprises a three-story building roughly in the shape of an inverted pyramid and mounted on a pillar that is itself set atop two intersecting arches. Camille's casket is placed on the third level of this building. Over the peak of its pitched roof a mirror is set

> iluec poënt tres bien veor,
> quant l'an les vendra aseor,

ou fust par mer ou fust par terre;
ja ne fussent conquis par guerre;
bien veoit an el mireor
qui ert asis desus la tor
lor enemis vers aus venir,
donc se pooient bien garnir,
aparoillier aus deffandre;
n'erent legier pas a sorprendre.
    (7605–14)

[in which they could see very well when
someone was coming to attack them, whether by
sea or by land. They would never be
conquered in war; whoever was seated at the
foot of the tower could see in the mirror
their enemies coming toward them. Thus they
could supply themselves well and prepare
themselves for defense; they would not be
easy to surprise. (204–5)][1]

 The tomb, thus, has a dual purpose: to commemorate Camille's chivalry and to ensure that her former subjects never need subjugate themselves to foreign rulers. Magically, the mirror gives those who gaze at it access to hitherto secret military information, rendering foreign enemies' efforts to take the country by surprise ineffectual by giving its inhabitants time to prepare for attack.[2] Although Camille's countrymen may turn their backs temporarily while they peer into the mirror and penetrate its surface, in so doing they come face to face with their enemies—or, at least, the phantasmatic image of their enemies—and, in turn, may pivot and prepare for a frontal assault. Although possessing clairvoyant powers, this pier glass also may serve a more immediate function by enabling a native visiting the tomb to see the "real" reflection of anyone, especially an enemy, approaching from behind and thereby turn to meet her or him head-on. In short, the looking glass aims to protect Camille's people from being caught off guard and suffering a humiliating defeat, such as that which Camille experienced at the hands of Arranz, by encouraging them to assume an active role in their country's defense rather than remain vulnerable to foreign forces. This mirror reflects deep anxieties about unexpected attacks by "aliens"—anxieties that inform the queen of Latium's animosity toward Enéas and that, at the same time, encode an antipathy to male "passivity."

Shortly after Camille's burial, the queen of Latium discovers, much to her dismay, that Lavine has fallen hopelessly in love with Enéas. She reacts with a horror that is not altogether inexplicable, for the Trojan warrior has come at the command of the gods to conquer and reclaim the kingdom of Latium, which belonged to Enéas's ancestor, Dardanus, before he settled the region that would become Troy. After Lavine fearfully reveals to her mother the identity of the man responsible for her lovesickness, the queen explodes into a wild diatribe against the Trojan:

> Que as tu dit, fole desvee?
> Sez tu vers cui tu t'es donee?
> Cil cuiverz est de tel nature
> qu'il n'a gaires de femmes cure;
> il prise plus lo ploin mestier;
> il ne velt pas biset mangier
> molt par aimme char de maslon;
> il priseroit mialz un garçon
> que toi ne altre acoler;
> o feme ne set il joër,
> ne parlerast pas a guichet;
> molt aime fraise de vallet;
> an ce sont Troïen norri.
> Molt par as foiblemant choisi.
> N'as tu oï comfaitemant
> il mena Dido malement?
> Unques feme n'ot bien de lui,
> n'en avras tu, si com ge cui,
> d'un traïtor, d'un sodomite.
> Toz tens te clamera il quite;
> se il avoit alcun godel,
> ce il seroit et bon et bel
> quel laissasses a ses druz faire;
> s'il lo pooit par toi atraire,
> nel troveroit ja si estrange
> qu'il ne feïst asez tel change,
> que il feïst son bon de toi
> por ce qu'il lo sofrist de soi;
> bien lo lairoit sor toi monter,
> s'il repueit sor lui troter;
> il n'aime pas poil de conin.
>
> (8565–95)

> [What have you said, foolish madwoman? Do
> you know to whom you have given yourself?
> This wretch is of the sort who have hardly
> any interest in women. He prefers the
> opposite trade: he will not eat hens, but he
> loves very much the flesh of a cock. He
> would prefer to embrace a boy rather than you
> or any other woman. He does not know how to
> play with women, and would not parley at the
> wicket-gate; but he loves very much the
> breech of a young man. The Trojans are
> raised on this. You have chosen very poorly.
> Have you not heard how he mistreated Dido?
> Never did a woman have any good from him, nor
> do I think you will have, from a traitor and
> a sodomite. He will always be ready to
> abandon you. If he finds any sweet boy, it
> will seem fair and good to him that you let
> him pursue his love. And if he can attract
> the boy by means of you, he will not find it
> too outrageous to make an exchange, so that
> the boy will have his pleasure from you,
> while in turn sufficing for him. He will
> gladly let the boy mount you, if he in turn
> can ride him: he does not love coney fur. (226–27)][3]

After this graphic depiction of the life that Lavine can expect to lead as Enéas's wife, the queen explains that sodomy is a threat against nature and easily could result in depopulation. She concludes: "[C]este amistié voil que tu les, / del sodomite, del coart" (8610–11) [I wish you to give up the love of this sodomite wretch (227)]. She then urges Lavine to marry Turnus, the native to whom she has been affianced for seven years.

How are we to account for this outburst that assigns a fairly specific meaning to the often indeterminate term "sodomy" by identifying it with anal intercourse between males?[4] My possibly unexpected answer to this question lies in the primacy of "territory" in this text and in the important role that territory played not only in medieval marriage practices but also, relatedly, in medieval constructions of gender and sexuality. In his recent work on gender and genre, Simon Gaunt points to the fruitfulness of examining romance within the contexts of early-twelfth-century conflicts between the Church and secular authorities over the right to regulate matrimony and of the emergence of the *iuvenes*, young landless knights attempting to find their fortunes by marrying heiresses. In the light of studies by Georges Duby, Erich Köhler, and Jean-Charles Huchet, Gaunt illuminates the extent to which romance maps not only the Church's attempts to "[break] up secular power bases" by favoring exogamy over endogamy, but also the phenomenon of the *iuvenes*, men "d'estrange terre" [from a foreign land] seeking wealth outside their own kinship systems (Gaunt, "Epic to Romance," 14–15, and *Gender and Genre*).[5] Although he acknowledges the importance of such historicized accounts of romance, Gaunt foregrounds the not unrelated concerns about gender that inform the genre, noting that the *Enéas* distinguishes itself from the *chansons de geste* by displacing male-male bonds with heterosexual love and thereby constructing masculinity *in relation to* femininity (Gaunt, "Epic to Romance," 14, 25–26). I want to argue, however, that if the desire to acquire territory is at least partly responsible for this generic transformation, then the *Enéas* also encodes its own resistances to being read as an unequivocal endorsement of compulsory heterosexuality, for territory in this text becomes not only a means of reinscribing male homosocial bonds, but also of imagining erotic relations between men that threaten the very heterosexual identity that the text invites us to embrace.[6]

Until recently, critical analyses of the queen's accusations have far from satisfactorily examined their relation to the *Enéas*'s overarching concerns with gender and sexuality, much less the links between these concerns and the text's focus on the acquisition of land. Edmond Faral, for example, argues that the queen's monologue mirrors medieval preoccupations with sodomitical practices and that the queen, along with the poet, must have been relying on the myth of Ganymede, recounted by Ovid in the *Metamorphoses*, in establishing connections between sodomy and the Trojans (*Recherches*, 131–33). Faral further attempts to establish these connections in his discussion of Mempricius and Malgo, two kings indicted as sodomites in Geoffrey of Monmouth's *Historia regum Britanniae*, citing the *Enéas* to prove his case (*La Legende arthuriene*, 2.100, 311–12). Yet J. S. P. Tatlock disputes Faral's contentions. Although he allows for the possibility of a link between sodomy and the Trojans, he considers Faral's appropriation of the *Enéas* as evidence of this reputation questionable (352–56). Noting that neither Dares Phrygius (in *De excidio Troiae historia*) nor Guido de Columnis (in *Historia destructiones Troiae*) makes any mention of Trojan sodomy, Tatlock asserts: "Remembering that tradition may be added to at any moment, and that any transmitter felt at liberty to add color and explanation, one is justified in believing the passages in *Enéas* as more likely to be due to the morals of the twelfth-century than to anything else" (354).

In his monumental study of the *Enéas*, Raymond J. Cormier agrees with Tatlock that Dares does not refer to the Trojans as sodomites, yet he calls attention to Dares's revelation that Aeneas and Antenor "betrayed" the Trojans. Cormier notes: "*Recreant*, 'cowardly, renegade, surrendering' in any dictionary, is the Old French word for weakling; it requires little imagination to understand how peace-lovers and traitors (especially in a recently post-Heroic society) might be associated with 'outlaws,' whether queer or heretics" (222). Cormier also notes references to Ganymede and to Trojan "effeminacy and faithlessness" that appear in Virgil's *Aeneid* as possible explanations for the queen's accusations. Yet he attempts to offer a more illuminating gloss on the passage by considering it in relation to the "problem" of homosexuality that emerged in the Church, particularly after the mid-eleventh century, and to Christian arguments against such behavior that condemned men who "behave like cloacal women," that asserted the importance of propagating humankind, or that attacked "sexual aberrations" on moral grounds (Cormier, 222).[7]

In this essay, I offer another interpretation of the queen's accusations against Enéas that situates these charges more fully within the context of romance's concomitant interests in territory, marriage, and foreign "invasion" and the profound relation of these interests to male-male desire. In so doing, I align myself not only with Gaunt, but also with William Burgwinkle ("Knighting") and Susan Crane (39–54), both of whose work points to the importance of examining the tensions between compulsory heterosexuality and male homoeroticism that inhere in the *Enéas* and, specifically, in the queen's assertions.[8] I begin by briefly considering the queen's attack as a by-product of a gender battle staged in this romance between men like Latinus, the king of Latium, who embrace the Trojan cause and its perpetuation of patriarchal power and women like the queen who resist that power. By referring to Enéas as a sodomite, the queen may be calling attention to her anxiety about relations among Trojan men that may not be literally "sodomitical" but that exclude women and, again, threaten their authority and identity.

Despite the appeal of these explanations for the queen's outburst, the sodomy charges need to be examined more closely in relation to the territorial conflict precipitated by the Trojan invasion of Latium, a conflict that further fuels the queen's argument with her husband. In the light of Jonathan Goldberg's recent theorizations of "sodomy" as a word "capable of being mobilized in more than one direction," the term in this text may figure an invasion in which the Trojans repeatedly "come up from behind" the Latins and take them by surprise (*Sodometries*, xv). At the same time, "sodomy" is not merely a metaphor for an invasion or surprise attack. Although "sodomy" may figure invasion, "invasion" also may figure "sodomy." Indeed, invasion is represented through highly charged, often erotic, language as an act of anal penetration that may be construed as either a humiliating sexual violation or, conversely, as a source of pleasure for the "sodomizer" and the "sodomized," as an act worthy of retribution or of respect, depending upon one's position. The work of Guy Hocquenghem, who has demonstrated the extent to which Oedipal culture has associated anal desire and passivity with the loss of identity, is especially useful in illuminating the ways in which the *Enéas* destabilizes the active/passive dichotomy inscribed within "sodomitical" relations. Although the romance's valorization of the active, penetrating partner ultimately is inescapable, the *Enéas* nonetheless invites us to question the meanings of masculinity and constructs a space in which anal desire is at least imaginable and passivity's "passivity" is not presumed. Finally, drawing on Crane's argument, I suggest that Enéas's newly acquired landholdings, although the outcome of heterosexual courtship, actually reinforce bonds among Trojan males and cast a pall over the emergent heterosexual love in the romance, a love whose "failure," I argue, via the work of Judith Butler, the romance repeatedly dramatizes.

"She Shook and Trembled with Anger": Medieval Sexual Politics

When Enéas first arrives in Latium, Latinus wholeheartedly welcomes him and offers no resistance to the Trojan's claims to his land or to Lavine, the means by which Enéas will gain the territory. Although his wife wishes the prince, Turnus, to have Lavine, as well as the government of the kingdom, Latinus wants to submit to divine will. He maintains:

> [M]ais sorti est et destiné
> et tuit li deu ont creanté
> que uns estranges hom l'avra,
> de cui real ligniee istra
> (3239–42)

> [But it is fated and destined, and
> all the gods have decreed, that a foreign
> man shall have her, and from them a royal
> line will issue. (120)]

In relating his beliefs to Enéas's messenger, Latinus does not simply reveal his willingness to accept the gods' will; he also exposes an underlying conflict between himself and his wife. She is responsible for the betrothal of Lavine to Turnus. Latinus states:

> Ge l'ai promise estre mon gré
> et ancontre ma volanté
> a un prince de cest païs
>
> (3233–35)

> [Without wishing it, indeed against
> my will, I have promised her to a prince
> of this country. (120)]

Although Latinus has consented to the marriage, he has done so reluctantly. His wife has succeeded in overpowering him and advancing an agenda that may be both personal (i.e., maintaining authority over her husband and men in general) and political (i.e., enabling herself and Turnus to maintain control over their kingdom). In the light of the queen's personal motivations, Latinus's swift agreement to Enéas's demands may be a means by which he, an aging king, wrests lost power back from his wife and, at the same time, shows his respect for divine authority. The enmity between husband and wife revealed in this dialogue between Latinus and Enéas's messenger also may be emblematic of tensions between men and women, perhaps even implicitly of those between Enéas's parents, that ultimately translate into conflicts between the Trojans and the Latins, respectively.

This enmity only increases when the queen learns of Latinus's intention to forsake his agreement with Turnus. Although Latinus "desirrot an son corage / del Troïen lo mariage" (3279–80) [in his heart . . . greatly desired the marriage with the Trojan (121)], the queen "l'a dessentu, / dolante et correçose an fu" (3281–82) [disapproved of it, and was sorrowful and angry over it (121)]. She subtly ridicules the king:

> "Rois," fait ele, "molt me mervoil
> ou tu as pris icest consoil
> que nostre fille vels doner
> al Troïen . . ."
>
> (3285–88)

["King," she said, "I wonder greatly
where you have gotten this idea, that
you wish to give our daughter to the
Trojan." (121)]

Then, further attempting to control her husband's behavior, she orders him: "Ne tel penser!" (3288) [Do not think of it (121)]. She then states her reasons for objecting to this union. As she presents her case, she makes no mention of Enéas's sodomitical practices, basing her argument instead on her belief that the Trojans, whose country has been brought to ruin by Paris's abduction of Helen, are neither an honorable nor a law-abiding people. In the course of this diatribe the queen displays her contempt for Enéas by referring to him simply as "li Troïen" [the Trojan]. Refusing to dignify him with a name, she identifies Enéas as the representative of a people not worthy of respect. Conflicts between queen and king, thus, point to animosities between the invaded and the invaders, and, later, when the queen accuses Enéas of sodomy, she even will remark that this sexual practice is part of the Trojans' upbringing.

At this point, however, she focuses on a single Trojan, Turnus's rival, and maintains that after a long journey "[c]il a mestier grant de sejor" (3299) [this man is in great need of repose (121)]. She tells Latinus that once Enéas has exploited and "dishonored" their daughter, "il la vos avra guerpie" (3305) [he will abandon her to you (121)]. In making this argument, the queen either has ignored or overlooked the fact that Enéas has come to restore Trojan control of Latium and that he has no intention of leaving. Yet as proof of Enéas's fickleness in romantic affairs, the queen also reminds Latinus of Enéas's well-known abandonment of Dido, the queen of Carthage, with whom he did "sa volenté" [his will], but whom he then deserted.[9] Finally, the queen asserts that Enéas has no capital assets to offer Lavine. He is an opportunist. She observes sarcastically:

[I]l li donra molt grant doaire:
tote la mer qu'il a siglee
puis qu'il torna de sa contree;
n'a autre terre n'autre feu
        (3320–23)

[He will bring her a very handsome dowry:
all the sea on which he has been sailing
since he left his country. He has no other
land or fief. (122)]

Despite the queen's protestations, Latinus does not reverse his decision: "Ne la donrai pas a celui, / li deu l'otroient a cestui" (3345–46) [I will not give her to the one when the gods have granted her to the other (122)]. The queen's response to her husband's obstinacy is indicative of the extent to which Latinus, Enéas, and, perhaps, the gods themselves represent a challenge to her own power and to her vision of her kingdom's future. The romancer remarks:

> Quant voit que nel puet trestorner,
> plorant et o molt laide chiere
> en sa chanbre revint ariere;
> de mautalant fremist et trenble,
> andous ses paumes fiert ansanble
> (3354–58)

[When she saw that she could not sway him,
she retired to her chamber, weeping, and
in a very ugly mood. She shook and trembled
with anger, and beat her palms together. (122)]

This anger, however, is quickly turned into action:

> "Lasse," fait el, "malaüree,
> que ma fille sera donee
> a un homme d'estrange terre,
> . . . .
> Ge li ferai öir novelles,
> bien tost li cuit movoir tel guerre,
> qu'il nos an guerpira la terre
> ou il an perdra tost la vie.
> De ma fille n'avra il mie,
> se il molt chier ne la conpere;
> ja ne la fille ne la mere
> n'avront par lui maintenement. . . ."
> (3361–63, 3372–79)

["Alas," she said, "unhappy woman, that my
daughter will be given to a man from a
foreign land. . . . But I will have news for

him. I think that very soon I will stir up
such a war against him that he will abandon
the land to us or quickly lose his life in
it. He shall have none of my daughter unless
he pays very dearly for her. Neither
daughter nor mother will ever fall under his
protection." (122–23)]

These lines are significant for several reasons. First, they point to the queen's exclusion of her husband from any part of her plan and to the power with which she invests herself. Next, they reveal her commitment to maintaining Latin control of the kingdom. Preventing the loss of her land may be more important than preventing the loss of her daughter. If the king will not ensure the safety of Latium, then she must see to it herself. This is not to say, however, that Lavine is unimportant to her mother. In stating that neither she nor her daughter "will ever fall under [Enéas's] protection," she not only establishes a bond with Lavine, but includes her daughter in her vision of power for women, although she undoubtedly threatens Lavine with the loss of her mother's love if she will not "let this traitor be." Finally, these lines establish the queen as the catalyst of the ensuing war between the Latins and the Trojans. Very soon thereafter, she sends a messenger to Turnus "manda li celeement" (3391) [to warn him secretly (123)] of the king's breech of promise. Enéas clearly poses a threat to the world that she has created for herself, a world that she will go to great lengths to protect.

That the Trojans are avatars of a patriarchal tradition that threatens to wipe out women like the queen is evident throughout the romance. The tie between Enéas and his father, Anchisés, exemplifies the masculine power that the queen attempts to challenge. When father and son meet face to face in the Underworld,

Ensi li demostrez toz
et fiz et peres et nevoz,
si com doivent de lui issir
et l'un avant l'autre venir
(2969–72)

[Anchises showed him all—fathers and sons
and nephews—as they would issue from him
and come one after another. (115)]

Still, the Trojans are not simply proponents of patriarchal tradition, for they also privilege erotically charged warrior friendships over heterosexuality. The queen's charges of Trojan "sodomy" may be grounded at least partly in her apprehension of the primacy of male-male bonds among men like Nisus and Euryalus, about whom the romancer remarks:

[A]moient soi de tele amor
qu'il ne pooient de greignor:
unques plus voire amor ne fu
que d'aus, tant com il ont vescu
(4913–16)

[They loved one another with such a love
that they could have none greater. There
was never a truer love than that between them,
as long as they lived. (152–53)]

It is against both the patriarchal traditions reflected by Enéas's interactions with his father and the male bonds reflected by Nisus and Euryalus that the queen fights. Yet the queen is not alone in her resistance to such male power structures. Dido, for example, no doubt, has assumed "masculine" power by founding and ruling the city of Carthage. Although she ultimately becomes one of patriarchy's finest victims, choosing to kill herself after Enéas abandons her, rather than risk living with her reputation for chastity ruined, she is bold enough to question the "commandment" of the gods that Enéas leave her, arguing that the gods have given little indication that they are greatly concerned about him (*Enéas*, 1831–40; Yunck, 93). If anything, they have "afflicted" and "harried" him on a daily basis. Dido implicitly questions the ways in which the will of the gods becomes an excuse for male power—for the gods, be they male or female, clearly have endorsed an invasion that will perpetuate and strengthen patriarchy and male-male relations. Pallas's mother, who sides with the Trojans before her son's death at the hands of Turnus, also doubts the power of the gods, perhaps wondering whether the war with Latium really is divinely ordained. Camille challenges female stereotypes even more dramatically. When the Trojan Tarcon ridicules her for eschewing her proper role as a woman, she replies defiantly: "[M]ialz sai abatre un chevalier / que acoler ne dosnoier" (7123–24) [I know better how to strike down a knight than to embrace him or make love to him (195)]. Camille disrupts gender norms by occupying the cherished male territory of the battlefield. Significantly, she gains the respect of Latins such as Turnus, who deeply mourns her death at the hands of the Trojans. By fighting on the side of the Latins, she implicitly may be carving out a new place for women.

Despite such instances of flagrant resistance to male power, we must consider several questions that point to the need for a more satisfying explanation of the queen's sodomy charges. To what extent are these women, particularly those aligned with the Latin cause, truly challenging patriarchy? In the event of a Latin victory, Turnus will assume control of the kingdom, not the queen, not Camille, nor even Lavine. Male rule will be perpetuated. If the queen's attack on Enéas is motivated by a desire to protect women's power, why does the queen not simply call Enéas a misogynist? Perhaps such accusations would not serve sufficiently to express her rage. Referring to him as a sodomite and thereby implying that he is "unnatural" or somehow less than masculine may be a more satisfying way of expressing hostility toward the man whose presence signals her own demise. But, if this is the case, why does the queen depict Enéas as the "active" and, therefore, supposedly more powerful participant in the sexual act—the sodomizer—rather than as the "passive" and supposedly weak, effeminate, and, in some way, demoralized one—the sodomized? In the light of these questions, I want to offer an interpretation that does not dismiss the struggle between men and women as a motivation for the queen's outburst, but that situates this disruption of gender norms within the context of the text's related concerns with territory and male-male desire.[10]

"That Utterly Confused Category": The Polyvalence of Sodomy

In *Sodometries*, his study of Renaissance texts, Goldberg invokes Michel Foucault's description of sodomy in the first volume of *The History of Sexuality* as "that utterly confused category" and examines the "bankruptcy" of this term, as well as the uses that have been made of it precisely because of its indeterminate meaning (18–20). Goldberg shows, for instance, that European invaders who legitimized their slaughtering and conquest of New World natives by accusing them of engaging in acts of sodomy were not so much identifying specific sexual practices as marking cultural differences that threatened European power. He notes: "[T]hese acts—or accusations of their performance—become visible only when those who are said to have done them also can be called traitors, heretics, or the like, at the very least, disturbers of the social order that alliance—marriage arrangements—maintained" (19). Goldberg initiates his analysis of the polyvalence of sodomy with a discussion of pro-American paraphernalia produced during the Persian Gulf War that illuminates my own yoking together of "sodomy" and foreign invasion. During the war, an advertisement appeared for a T-shirt on which the face of Saddam Hussein was superimposed over the anus of a camel facing away from the viewer. The T-shirt bore the message: "America will not be Saddamized." Goldberg notes: "The statement equates Saddam Hussein's invasion of Kuwait with rape, and implies that all forced entries are acts of sodomy" (1). And, indeed, the Iraqi leader is represented in the ad as the homosexual, foreign villain, guilty of "sodomizing" Kuwait and, implicitly, America. Yet as Goldberg astutely points out, this statement ironically serves to incite a role reversal in which America asserts its masculinity, resists passivity, and becomes the sodomizer—albeit the "heterosexual sodomizer" who strongly values male homosocial bonds, but nonetheless is homophobic. In fact, Goldberg points out, this role was constructed and legally protected by the 1986 U.S. Supreme Court decision in *Bowers v. Hardwick*, which "tacitly upheld the right of heterosexuals to perform sodomitical sex and denied that right to homosexuals" (8).

Goldberg makes a connection between representations of sodomy and foreign invasion that may serve as a useful lens through which to examine the *Enéas*. On the one hand, Enéas himself is the foreign, "homosexual" sodomizer who is to be retaliated against by the Latins for his invasion of Latium. On the other hand, he may be the native, heterosexual sodomizer—native because the Trojans' ancestors originally inhabited Latium and heterosexual because, despite his strong male ties, Enéas marries Lavine at the romance's end. As native, he is authorized to attack the Latins. As heterosexual male, he not only restores patriarchal power, but also promotes homosocial bonds, while, at the same time, perpetuating homophobia. In its own way, then, the romance, like *Bowers v. Hardwick*, forbids acts of "homosexual" sodomy, while sanctioning their heterosexual counterparts, and, through its construction of the eponymous hero as the active partner in anal intercourse, produces a model of masculine identity that glorifies the heterosexual, phallic penetrator. And yet, as I hope to demonstrate, the romance also imagines the pleasures and powers of passivity, even if those pleasures and powers ultimately are exposed as ignoble.

In this light, I want to argue that the queen's depiction of Enéas as "homosexual" sodomizer is indicative of Latin perceptions of him as an invader who has triumphed by taking the Latins "from behind," inserting himself into their land, and transforming them into passive recipients of a phallus motivated by a desire for territory. Imagining the invasion in these terms simultaneously serves to construct anal intercourse between men as an "assault from behind." As such, this sexual practice becomes dishonorable for the active male, who unfairly pins his partner in a vulnerable position, and especially for his passive counterpart, who surrenders himself to another man and is "feminized" in the process. Nonetheless, the queen's portrayal of Enéas as active only reinforces her recognition of his power. By assuming this role, he is able to display his military prowess, retain his "dignity" as a man, and, in turn, fully embrace the role of romance hero, in contrast with Latinus, whose passivity, even if it is self-selected, points to his political ineptitude and his emasculation.

This privileging of active over passive role-playing has a long history that David M. Halperin has traced back to ancient Greece where "the relation between the 'active' and the 'passive' sexual partner is thought of as the same kind of relation as that obtaining between social superior and social inferior" (30). James A. Brundage indicates that this principle held true in Roman society, as well. In fact, Roman laws dealing with adult male homosexuality focused on the passive partner in this sexual act and "reflected a feeling that a man who submitted passively to sexual relations with another man betrayed the masculine virtues proper to free male citizens" (49). Although John Boswell does not examine explicitly attitudes toward active and passive roles in twelfth-century France, he has shown that some medieval societies tolerant of homosexuality also considered the passive role in male anal intercourse dishonorable.[11] Historically, then, the stigma attached to passivity has been significant. To what extent does the *Enéas* simply reproduce such sexual hierarchies? In what ways does this romance attempt to dismantle them?

Although a central goal of Hocquenghem's *Homosexual Desire* is to expose capitalism's dependency upon and psychoanalytic theory's complicity in the suppression of Freud's polymorphous perverse—the "constitutional bisexuality of men and women"—Hocquenghem's study also lays bare the social mechanisms by which the active partner in anal intercourse between men, although himself constituted as "homosexual" in this act, might escape some of the censure to which the passive partner is subjected and actually promote "the rule of the phallus" (75). According to Hocquenghem, the "rule of the phallus" maintains that, in order for a man to establish and retain his identity within an Oedipal society, he must sublimate his anal desire and, like all "healthy" men, vie for and define himself through the phallus (95–106). This policing of anal erotism leads to a "paranoiac fear of seeing [homosexuality] appear around him"; yet "[t]o reject the conversion of anal libidinal energy into the paranoia mechanism would mean to risk loss of identity, and to discard the perverse re-territorialisation which has been forced upon homosexuality" (599, 100).

Within this context, Hocquenghem examines the now classic separation made by Sandor Ferenczi of male homosexuals into "object-homo-erotics and subject-homo-erotics," that is, respectively, active and passive, masculine and feminine. According to Ferenczi, the masculine, active homosexual "feels himself a man in every respect, is as a rule very energetic and active, and there is nothing effeminate to be discovered in his bodily or mental organisation," while the passive homosexual "feels himself to be a woman, and this is not only in genital intercourse, but in all relations in life" (299–300; quoted from Hocquenghem, 123). While Ferenzci does not fail to pathologize the active partner, his analysis nonetheless gives that partner at least a slight edge over his passive counterpart—perhaps because the active partner still somehow perpetuates phallic power. The passive partner is particularly stigmatized for failing to privilege the genital over the anal. In fact, Hocquenghem maintains that psychoanalysis "inevitably strikes down all manifestations of anal erotism with constitutional guilt," for the sodomized, according to Jean-Paul Sartre, at least, knows that "there is no orgasm but the genital one: only shame and pain are anal" (Hocquenghem 128). To be a passive sodomite, then, is to risk losing one's masculine identity and to subject one's self to an ongoing sense of humiliation and guilt—presumptions that, Hocquenghem believes, are part of the Oedipal "plot." Against this backdrop, I want to turn now to the figurations in the *Enéas* of foreign-invasion-as-sodomy and sodomy-as-foreign-invasion and explore the ways in which this text, through its celebration of the Trojan victory over the Latins, invites us to accept and yet at times incites us to resist the active/passive, genital/anal, heterosexual/"homosexual" hierarchies inherent in these figurations.

"Putting Themselves Entirely Inside": Sodomy and Foreign Bodies

The *Enéas* figures the Trojan invasion of Latium as an act in which Enéas "enters" another man, Latinus, who willingly permits, if not welcomes, that entry, even as Turnus, his once-future son-in-law, refuses and attempts to resist this penetration. From Enéas's perspective, that invasion ought to be enjoyable for the Latin population as a whole, which should welcome his divinely ordained rule. For the queen, however, this invasion of her land might be construed as a sexual assault perpetrated by one man against another since both she, through her assumption of masculine power, and Latinus are "men" being violated against their will. Moreover, despite the fact that the land that she wishes to protect is allegorized as a feminine body, "la terre," it is still part of a nation, "le païs," whose identity is profoundly masculine.[12] The queen's accusations against the leader of foreign forces, therefore, may reflect her own, as well as other citizens', perceptions of the invasion as a humiliating sexual violation of the very worst kind. At the same time, the queen senses that Enéas's invasion is pleasurable not only for Enéas, but for Latinus as well—a perception paralleled in the queen's and her daughter's representation of sodomy as satisfying to both active and passive partners. In their respective speeches on sodomy, the queen and Lavine imagine the sodomizer's pleasure in anal intercourse but also imply that the sodomized is neither resistant to nor a victim of Enéas's desire. He may even be a willing participant himself. Granted, the boys and the young men that Enéas supposedly sodomizes do not necessarily enjoy this activity. In fact, the queen tells Lavine that Enéas might even use his wife as a means of attracting boys with whom he wants to have sex and suggests that Enéas will permit them to have intercourse with Lavine if subsequently he may sodomize them. Yet both the queen's and Lavine's anxieties suggest that they believe that sodomy involves a contractual agreement between males. Lavine's belief that Enéas "a asez garçons o soi, / lo peor aime mialz de moi" (9159–60) [has plenty of boys with him, and loves the worst of them better than me (238)] points to a fear of a community of males who engage in sexual activity and exclude women. In this context, I want to examine further the ways that the text constructs Enéas as an invader who forces himself upon the Latins, but whose penetration of their land provides him and at least one of the invaded with pleasure.

In their vigorous attempts to affirm Enéas's heterosexual identity, many critics have stressed his growing love for Lavine and overlooked the importance to him of the land that he will acquire through his marriage to her. That land represents a military and a cultural victory, but also becomes a signifier of the priority of male-male bonds over heterosexuality, even if the former are "products" of the latter. Significantly, the *Enéas* commences and concludes not with images of love, but of Trojan land that has been lost and gained. As the romance begins, we witness the destruction of Troy by Menelaus, who "gasta la terre et tot lo regne" (3) [laid waste the land and all the kingdom (55)] and "destruist les murs" (7) [destroyed the walls (55)]. Upon observing this destruction, Enéas is commanded by the gods to reclaim his ancestors' country; they never mention, nor do they make any promises of, love. Although in Hades Anchisés explains that Enéas eventually will win the land and the hand of Latinus's daughter, the marriage appears to serve a purely political function. The loss of Troy, thus, is countered at the end of the romance when Enéas

> ot le mialz d'Itaire,
> une cité comence a faire,
> bons murs i fist et fort donjon
> (10131–33)

> [had the best part of Italy, and began
> to build a city. He made good walls there,
> and a strong fortress. (257)]

Although the marriage of Enéas and Lavine is briefly described, the text concludes with the fulfillment of Anchisés's prophecy as the romancer describes Enéas's newly acquired landholdings, their governance by his descendants, and, ultimately, the foundation of Rome.[13] It is to Enéas's arrival and settlement in Latium, however, that I would like to turn next in order to consider more fully the implications of the queen's accusations of sodomy.

Upon landing in Lombardy, Enéas speaks to his fellow Trojans at length about their accomplishments:

> "Seigneur," fait il, "c'est le contree
> que nous avons tant desirree,
> c'est Lombardie li païs
> que tant nous ont li dieu pramis;
> ci sont nostre travail finé,
> ici sera nostre herité,
> li dieu nous ont mis a cest port."
> (3069–75)

> ["My lords," he said, "this is the country
> which we have so desired, this is the land of
> Lombardy, which the gods have promised us.
> Here our hardships are ended, here will be
> our domain. The gods have brought us to this
> port." (117)]

To say that the possession of this territory is important to Enéas undoubtedly is to understate its value to him, for the language clearly reveals that Enéas's desire centers on the geographic: "country," "land," "Lombardy," "domain," "port." It is ruling the new nation, regardless of the wishes of its inhabitants, that matters to Enéas, who is ready to begin "la grant guerre / al regne et al païs conquerre" (3115–16) [the great war to conquer the realm and the country (118)] and take these people against their will.

That there might be some doubt in his own mind as to the propriety of such actions, that Enéas might construe his own invasion as a violation, is suggested when Enéas sends his messengers to Latinus. Bearing gifts, these men are to inform the king that they are seeking "pais et concorde et amor querre" (3130-31) [peace and concord and love (118)] and to request that Enéas "segurs fust en sa terre" (3132) [be safe in the land (118)]. The latter request may even pun on Enéas's truest wish: that he be "secure" in his inheritance of Latium. The messenger Ilioneus explains that Enéas

> ça nos an a a toi tramis,
> quel consentes en ton païs
> et que l'acoilles en ta terre
> (3197-99)

> [has sent us here to you, that you
> might admit him to your country and
> receive him in your land. (119)]

He then tells a half-truth when he informs Latinus that the Trojans simply desire safe haven in Latium rather than possession of the king's land:

> An ta terre volons remaindre,
> ne te porras ja de nos plaindre
> que te forfaçons de noiant;
> nos ne somes mie tel gent
> qui ta terre voillons gaster,
> ne sor toi prendre ne rober;
> de cele part ou nos seron
> avra molt grant destrucion,
> par nos n'abaisseras tu pas.
> (3207-15)

> [In your land we wish to remain. You will
> never have cause to complain of us that we
> have betrayed you in anything; we are not the
> sort of people who would want to lay waste
> your land, or to plunder or rob you. Though
> you may have great trouble in your land, it
> will never happen through our action. (120)]

He concludes his plea by stating that Enéas and his men "servirons toi a ton plaisir" (3222) [will serve you at your pleasure (120)]. Latinus, well aware of the prophecy about Latium's future, immediately foresees that that prophecy is about to come true and readily chooses to submit. He tells the messengers:

> An cest païs est bien venu
> vostre sire, si com je pens;
> il lo verra a po de tens:
> gel maintendrai a mon pooir
> (3225–29)

> [For my part, your lord is welcome
> in this country, as he will see in a
> very short time. I will sustain him as
> best I can. (120)]

Yet Latinus's willingness to receive Enéas and the Trojans does not diminish the fact that Enéas and his followers are prepared to use deceitful means to attain their end. Although the romance endorses acts of invasion and, perhaps, in turn, acts of sodomy, it also questions these acts. The gods may have revealed to Enéas his fate as the founder of a long line of kings, but Enéas still must play the invader and will not hesitate to use force in overthrowing Latin rule to achieve that end. In this light, the figuration of Enéas as sodomitical *assailant* gains currency, as Enéas reveals his intention to sneak up on the Latins and impose his government upon them. At the same time, this figuration perpetuates views of anal intercourse between males as an assault by one man upon another.

Within this context, the queen's reaction to Latinus's quick surrender becomes highly intelligible. Although she ostensibly challenges her husband because she wants to protect her daughter, it immediately becomes apparent that she wishes to protect her country and its cultural superiority. She states:

> Li Troïen n'ont giens de foi,
> ne il ne tienent nule loi
> . . . .
> Ge ne crerrai ja lor ligniee
> (3289–90, 3298)

> [The Trojans have no honor at all, nor do
> they hold to any law. . . . I will never
> believe in their lineage. (121)]

Lavine also becomes an emblem of these concerns:

> "Lasse," fait el, "malaüree,
> que ma fille sera donee
> a un homme d'estrange terre,
> qui toz est essilliez par guerre"
> (3361–64)

> ["Alas," she said, "unhappy woman, that
> my daughter will be given to a man from a
> foreign land which is wholly ruined by war." (122)]

Preventing this intruder from attaining power becomes a means of preserving Latium's identity. Furthermore, as the queen's messenger tells Turnus:

> Ce senblera molt grant desroi,
> s'estranges hom s'anbat sor toi;
> s'il conquiert ce dont es saisiz,
> donc seras tu an fin honiz
> (3453–56)

> [It will be accounted a very great
> catastrophe if a foreign man falls
> upon you and conquers your possessions. (124)]

In the light of the correlation that Hocquenghem believes psychoanalysis has established between passive anal intercourse and the loss of identity, might a vigorous defense against foreign invasion facilitate an endogamous marriage, thereby preserving the political status quo, as well as Turnus's masculinity?

Undoubtedly, Turnus has much to gain by defeating the Trojans. He tells Latinus: "[D]e ta terre m'as erité, / o ta fille m'as tot doné" (3849–50) [You have endowed me with your land: you have given me all of it, together with your daughter (132)]. Later, he requests the help of the barons and explains:

> [S]i con fui primes eritez
> et de la terre sui saisiz;
> et quant li rois m'en est failliz

> et nos a mis el convenir,
> mon droit m'aidiez a maintenir
> (4160–64)

[Since I was the first heir and am
possessed of the land . . . I beg that
you help me to maintain my right. (138)]

Although the queen emphasizes to Lavine that Turnus loves her, whereas Enéas simply wants the land, Turnus is preoccupied equally with inheriting Latium. Despite his personal stake in these matters, he also plays a pivotal role in the larger political and cultural battle that begins officially when Enéas's son, Ascanius, shoots a deer belonging to an aristocratic Latin girl.

Thereafter, Enéas's efforts to penetrate the country only intensify, as do Latin perceptions of him as an intruder. The Latins do not use the word "sodomitical" to describe Enéas's attack. Yet the images that they invoke in their discussion of his invasion and Latinus's receptiveness to it suggest anal intercourse or, at least, the active/passive roles typically associated with this sexual act. As Turnus points out, Latinus readily has permitted the Trojan forces to penetrate Latin land. When the queen's messenger comes to inform Turnus that Latinus has broken his promise to give Lavine and the land to him, the messenger calls attention to Latinus's passivity, as he observes:

> [L]i rois est vials, tot a guerpi;
> qui que face desmesurance,
> n'an baillera escu ne lance
> (3446–48)

[The king is old, and has abandoned
everything. Though he may make a show
of arrogance, he will not take up shield
or lance. (124)]

Later, the Latins remark "que bien malvés atrait / li rois Latins a en aus fait" (3789–90) [that King Latinus had done very badly in receiving them (130)]. Perhaps the most significant image of Latinus's apparent passivity occurs in the language that Turnus uses in response to Latinus's submission to Trojan authority. The romancer remarks that Turnus heard

ce que li rois lor respondoit
que as Troïens se pandoit
et molt les voloit retenir
et an sa terre consantir
(3817–20)

[what the king answered to them: that
he inclined towards the Trojans and
greatly wished to keep them and admit
them to his land. (131)]

Latinus not only complies with the Trojans' wishes, but actively expresses his enthusiasm for their presence in Latium, suggesting that "passivity" in politics and, by analogy, in acts of anal intercourse between men is not necessarily passive. Turnus thereafter reveals his contempt for Latinus's behavior:

"Sire," fait il, "molt me mervoil
ou tu as pri icel consoil
que Troïens vels retinir.
Il ne sorent onques partir;
ne vollent estre meteier,
nen ont cure de parçonier,
ainçois vollent le tot avoir.
Ce saches tu an fin de voir,
Troïen sont de tel maniere
que, qui saquialt an l'achaintriere,
que tot de fors lo chanp lo getent,
de tot an tot dedenz se metent;
se les aquiauz an ton païs,
atant t'an es de tot forsmis."
(3823–36)

["Sire," he said, "I wonder greatly how you
can have conceived this desire to keep the
Trojans. They do not know how to share; they
have no wish to become owners of half;
rather, they want the whole. Know that this
is always true: the Trojans are of such a
nature that whoever receives them within his

walls will be thrown outside in the fields
by them; they will put themselves entirely
inside. If you receive them in your country,
you will soon be thrust forth from all you
own." (131)]

While castigating Latinus for desiring invasion by the men from Troy, a desire that Hocquenghem might consider "anal," Turnus simultaneously berates the Trojans for their avarice. Indeed, the Trojans are of a particular "nature." If they happen upon a man who will permit them within "his walls," they will insert themselves so completely and with such force that this man will lose everything in his possession, for they will break down the walls that hitherto have protected his territory. Turnus remarks further:

[S]e il lor loist longues errer,
tot te voldront deseriter.
Mes ce vials tu, ce m'est avis;
tu as atrait an cest païs,
tu ne vels pas o als partir,
ainçois lor vels le tot guerpir.
                (3841–46)

[If they are permitted to go so far
they will wish to dispossess you completely.
But I think that this is what you wish.
You have brought them to this country. You do
not wish to share it with them, but rather to
abandon everything to them. (132)]

Turnus, no doubt, participates in discourses that, Hocquenghem has shown, stigmatize the desire to be "passive." At the same time, he attributes to Latinus an active longing for and enjoyment of invasion that may be a means of expressing male desire for penetration of the anal walls. Throughout this discussion, Turnus's language constructs Latium as the humiliated, passive male body, taking within its walls the whole of the Trojan phallus. That Latinus might take pleasure in this act or ought to be commended for his shrewdness in respecting the will of the gods by warmly receiving a foreign ruler—a reception, perhaps, to be emulated by new subjects of Norman-Angevin power—is, of course, inconceivable to the queen, Turnus, and the Latins. From the

Latin perspective, permitting such a "violation" only can result in an embarrassing loss of their country's identity. The Latins will "be thrust forth" from their land. Turnus, thus, seeks to protect Latium against this violation, while, at the same time, ensuring that he is not passive. Turnus maintains: "[S]e par lui per plain pié de terre, / mal porrai donc autre conquerre" (3489–90) [If I should lose a single foot of land through him, I would not well be able to conquer another (125)].

The initial battles between the Trojans and the Latins only exacerbate Turnus's anxieties about losing his land and his masculinity. While Enéas goes to Palantee to enlist the help of Evander in his fight, for example, Turnus attempts to take by surprise the castle that Enéas has built in Latium, at which time the Trojans immediately raise the drawbridge, close the gate, and retreat inside. Enéas's walls are not to be penetrated. Turnus circles the castle "por agaitier / par ou an porra domagier" (4859–60) [to discover in what way it could be damaged (151)]. Yet

> [d]olanz et angoissos estoit
> que forstraire nes an pooit;
> il ne lo tenoit mie a geu
> qu'il n'i trove nul foible leu
> ou il lor poisse asalt faire
> (4861–65)

> [he was in sorrow and anguish that he
> could find no weak place where he might
> make an assault against them. (151–52)]

Even after Nisus and Euryalus slaughter the Trojans in a surprise attack in which they, too, come up from behind their enemies, Turnus seeks revenge, but is unsuccessful. After ordering a withdrawal,

> [t]ot anviron vet agaitant
> et lo chastel tot porvoiant,
> la ou plus foible lo verroit
> (5367–69)

> [he goes all about, studying and
> examining the whole castle, in order
> that he might see where it is the weakest. (161)]

Turnus evidently is bemused by this phallic wonder, whose power and purpose he does not really recognize. Although he longs to transform the castle from penetrator to penetrated, he cannot enter:

> [S]es enemis devant soi voit,
> si ne lor puet noiant forfere;
> il font a lui lancier et traire;
> s'en pais ne laisse lo chastel,
> il i laira bien tost la pel
> (5386–90)

> [He sees his enemies before him, but
> cannot harm them at all. They have him
> thrust at and shot at. If he does not
> leave the castle in peace, he will very
> soon lose his skin there. (162)]

Although Turnus and the Latins eventually gain entry to the castle, Turnus's plan backfires due to Trojan ingenuity. Once he and his troops are within, the Trojans lock the castle gate, thereby imprisoning their Latin enemies. The Trojans turn the tables on Turnus's attempt to "sodomize" them:

> Or est Turnus molt entrepris,
> anclos avoc ses enemis,
> mestier li est molt grant d'aïe:
> de çaus defors ne l'avra mie
> (5547–50)

> [Now Turnus is much taken by surprise,
> shut up with his enemies and in very great
> need of help: he will have none from those
> outside. (165)]

When Turnus kills two Trojans, Enéas's men become afraid, but no sooner has Ilioneus reprimanded them for their cowardice, than they charge ahead "qu'il vont ariere reculant" (5572) [until the enemy was withdrawing backward (165)]. Turnus only narrowly escapes when a Trojan opens the castle gate to exit and rescue those Trojans who previously had been left outside.

Consequently, Turnus "molt en est liez, quant il fu fors" (5584) [was very glad of it when he was outside (166)] and orders his army to withdraw from the Trojan fortress. Turnus's success as a "sodomizer" is short-lived indeed. He can take no pleasure in assuming the active role because there is no place for him to insert himself. That role has been reserved by the gods for Enéas and his men. Yet Turnus cannot permit himself to play the passive part and even fears accusations of cowardice when he accidentally gets stranded at sea in the height of battle (*Enéas*, 5803–46; Yunck, 170–71). Later, he seeks to exonerate himself with a second attempt at assuming the active role. He tells Camille:

> El bois m'en irai anbuschier
> desus por lo chemin gaitier
> . . . .
> Se iluec lo puis antreprendre,
> molt par li quit dur estor randre
> (6957–58, 6965–66)

[I will go into ambush in the woods above,
to lie in wait along the road. . . . If I
can surprise him there, I think I will give
him an extremely hard battle. (192)]

After learning of Camille's death at the hands of Arranz, however, Turnus comes out of ambush, failing yet again to come up behind his enemy.

The Trojan attack on Camille, however, seems to challenge the legitimacy of assaults from behind and of the active partner's power. When Arranz spies Camille seizing a beautiful helmet from the body of a dead Trojan soldier, he follows her from the back and, subsequently, kills her with his dart. In a rare instance, the romancer implies that there is something less than chivalrous about Arranz's behavior:

> Ne se fioit pas tant an soi
> que il osast o li joster,
> ne sol de devant li aler,
> mais desriere la parsivoit
> a chascun tor qu'ele faisoit
> (7144–48)

[He did not have so much faith in
himself that he dared joust with her
or face her alone, but he followed her
from behind at each turn she made. (195)]

Nonetheless, the romancer shortly thereafter celebrates the Trojan capacity for deception as he describes a tent with a trompe l'oeil effect that the Trojans set up near Laurente: "De loing sanbloit ce fust chastiaus, / et a mervoille par ert biaus" (7301–2) [From a distance it seemed as if it were a castle, and it was marvelously beautiful (198)]. Enéas's tent is especially striking: "[D]esus toz les autres paroit, / donjon sanbloit, car grant estoit" (7319–20) [It rose above all the others, and seemed like a fortress, for it was large (199)]. The tent produces the desired effect, for the Latins believe that the castle is real and, thus, fear the Trojans' strength. Yet Turnus scorns such tricks as he evaluates Arranz's assault on Camille:

Ja li cuiverz qui vos a morte
ne vos osast sol esgarder,
s'il vos veïst vers lui aler;
il vos feri an dessotant,
il ne vos vint pas al devant
(7412–16)

[The coward who killed you would
never have dared even to look at you,
if he had seen you coming toward him.
He struck you by surprise, he did not
come at you from the front. (201)]

If the romancer critiques this taking of enemies from behind, through his own words and those of Turnus, he undercuts his own critique not only by celebrating the Trojan victory, but also by attributing to Turnus in the castle and the ambush episodes the desire to assume the active role and to engage in a similar assault. In the end, however, Turnus recognizes the importance of embracing passivity, for Enéas finally succeeds in breaking down what little remains of Turnus's and the Latins' power. Thus, while the *Enéas* might, on Hocquenghem's terms, assert the "rule of the phallus" over "anal desire," the text also seems to resist psychoanalysis's assumptions about passivity by suggesting that invasion and anal erotism can be enjoyed without guilt and without the loss of identity if one *chooses* to submit. If the Latins simply would welcome the Trojan takeover, Enéas might argue, they, like Latinus himself, actually might enjoy being "sodomized," rather than feel that they are being assaulted by a man.

Still, in the climactic battle, the Latins refuse to surrender willingly.

> [C]orut sont as portes fermer
> et vont desor lo mur monter,
> nes voltrent pas dedanz coillir
> (9625–27)

> [They ran to shut the gates, and climbed
> up on the walls, not wishing to admit
> the Trojans inside. (247)]

Yet Enéas attacks the city and finally confronts Turnus, who initially flees from his enemy. When Enéas observes Turnus's departure,

> a dos lo vait sivant desriere,
> puis li a dit an tel meniere:
> "Ne veintroiz mie par foïr,
> mais par combatre et par ferir.
> Retorne toi, si vien avante"
> (9749–53)

> [he followed him at his back and
> addressed him in this manner: "You
> will never conquer by fleeing, but by
> giving combat and striking blows. Turn
> around and come forward." (249)]

Although the romance suggests elsewhere that there is nothing wrong with taking an enemy from behind, here Enéas incites Turnus to face his opponent, thereby enabling Enéas to prove himself twice the man by taking his enemy head-on. Undoubtedly, the romancer also implies here that assuming the passive role *is* less than masculine; consequently, Turnus faces his foe. Yet Enéas triumphs by splitting Turnus's shield and piercing him in the thigh, "que il chaï a genoillons, / voiant sa gent et ses barons" (9771–72) [so that he fell to his knees in the sight of his followers and barons (250)]. Turnus may not be sodomized in any literal sense, but he subjugates himself in a moment that, from Enéas's perspective, perhaps ought to be pleasurable, but, for Turnus, represents a humiliating defeat. Yet he decides to give in:

> "Sire," fait il, "a toi me rant
> . . . .
> Nule deffanse n'ai vers toi,
> Lavine est toe, ge l'otroi,
> o li te les tote la terre"
> (9781, 9785–87)
>
> ["Sire," he said, "I surrender myself
> to you. . . . I have no defense against
> you. Lavine is yours: I grant her to you,
> and with her I give up all the land." (250)]

Although Enéas seems content with Turnus's submission to his will, when Enéas sees him wearing a ring that he had taken from Pallas after killing him, he becomes incensed and, in order to avenge Pallas's death, beheads him. Choosing to submit, it seems, is still not sufficient. Turnus's earlier attempts to be assertive and "play the invader" must be fully checked. While the *Enéas* partially destigmatizes passivity, in the end, the romance ridicules this behavior; yet it also punishes any Latin attempts to overcome it and challenge the Trojan phallic power that has been ordained by the gods.

"Never a Truer Love": Lavine's Land as a Site of Sodomitical Desire

While the *Enéas* as a whole may confirm the queen's vision of her enemy as active sodomite through its representation of Enéas as triumphant invader, the marriage with which the romance concludes no doubt challenges her and Lavine's construction of him as "homosexual." I want to end, however, with a brief examination of the heterosexual closure with which we are presented in this romance. Although the *Enéas* ultimately constructs the relationship between its heroine and hero as *the* paradigm of love, the romance simultaneously destabilizes that construction through its representation of relationships between men as primary; through its exposure of ambivalences within the heroine's and hero's expressions of affection for one another; and, finally, through its revelation of the political profit that Enéas stands to make by "loving" Lavine, for their wedding will guarantee Enéas the land through which Trojan heritage may be preserved and perpetuated. Thus, I want to consider the means by which the romance questions its heterosexual/heterosexualizing impulses even as it attempts to institutionalize them. In the light of the primacy of male-male bonds in this romance, I want to join Crane in her assertion that love between men and women "is a secondary formation that clarifies and develops masculine relations."[14] That is, I want to adapt Crane's thesis and show that not only the courtship and marriage of Lavine and Enéas but also the landholdings that this marriage brings to Enéas serve as sites for the elaboration of male-male desire, even if that desire is mediated by male-female relations.

As I have shown, the queen's concerns about the privileging of male bonds among the Trojans may not be altogether unfounded. Yet she is clearly reluctant to have her daughter remedy this situation through a marriage to Enéas. Rather, she prefers to see heterosexuality asserted through Lavine's espousal to a native. Critics have been eager to prove that the *Enéas* attempts to limit male bonds and valorizes relations between men and women, as Lavine and Enéas fall in love near the romance's conclusion. At the same time, however, their "romance" may serve as a vehicle for the reinstatement of the very bonds that it seeks to displace. Gaunt points out that Enéas and Lavine's father are themselves joined together through their transactions around the possession of Lavine's "body" and the land that it signifies ("From Epic to Romance"). Likewise, Enéas and his father are bound to each other after Enéas promises his father to comply with the gods' wish that Enéas reestablish Trojan control of Latium—a wish fulfilled by Enéas's victory over Turnus.[15] I want to add that the "love" between Lavine and Enéas also serves to establish the priority of male bonds by virtue of its contrast with the love between male pairs such as Nisus and Euryalus, Enéas and Pallas, and even Enéas and Latinus—love which reveals that between the hero and heroine as its hollow copy. Although critics such as Cormier have argued just the reverse—that male-male relations are revealed as hollow copies of heterosexuality—the text also encodes its own interrogation of such interpretations.

In order to advance this argument, I want to draw upon "Imitation and Gender Insubordination," in which Butler attempts to reveal heterosexuality's claims to precedence over homosexuality as specious. In her analysis, Butler challenges beliefs that homosexuality is a "bad copy" or a pathetic parody of heterosexuality on the grounds that heterosexuality itself is an imitation of a sexual identity for which there is no original model. That is, heterosexuality is a construct with no legitimate claims of priority. In fact, Butler suggests that heterosexuality presupposes homosexuality, albeit always already *as* a copy. Yet she argues, "if the homosexual *as* copy *precedes* the heterosexual as *origin*, then it seems only fair to concede that the copy comes before the origin, and that homosexuality is the origin, and heterosexuality the copy" ("Imitation," 22). Despite the logic of this position, Butler recognizes the problem here, noting that "it is only *as* a copy that homosexuality can be argued to *precede* heterosexuality as the origin" ("Imitation," 22).

In the case of the *Enéas*, however, we witness male-male relations *as* "origins"—not simply as "copies-as-origins"—and heterosexuality as a copy that seems to "fail" in the light of the masculine bonds celebrated by this romance. In addition, heterosexuality is constructed as an identity whose genesis, for Enéas, at least, may have little to do with love. Yet Michael Warner has argued that heterosexuality—bound to "fail" repeatedly, according to Butler—has "been failing for centuries with great success" (18–19). And we cannot overlook the fact that at the romance's end, Nisus, Euryalus, and Pallas are dead, while Lavine and Enéas are not. Nonetheless, the specters of these Trojans, who have been powerful participants in the invasion and the intense male-bonding that it signifies, may have loomed large enough to prompt at least one fourteenth-century poet to expand significantly the conclusion's treatment of love between the hero and the heroine—an expansion that Eve Kosofsky Sedgwick might argue, constitutes an attempt to recover from "homosexual panic," from the fear, that is, that Enéas's heterosexual desire is not pronounced enough to offset the male bonds that dominate the romance.[16] Even without models of loving relationships between men, however, the romance dramatizes the "failure" of the love between Lavine and Enéas.

Before the queen discovers that her daughter has fallen in love with Enéas and charges him with sodomy, she remarks to Lavine that Enéas's interest in her is secondary to his interest in acquiring Latium. His desire to win the battle is

> plus por la terre
> que il ne fait por toe amor;
> ja mais ne t'amera nul jor,
> se puis savoir an nul androit
> que de t'amor noiant li soit
> (7866–70)

[more for the land than for love of you.
He will never love you at all, and you
can know that love of you will never in
any way be important to him. (210)]

After she has been struck by Cupid's dart and become enamored of Enéas, Lavine recalls her mother's remarks:

[L]i Troïens ne s'en sent mie,
ne li est gaires de ma vie.
. . . .
Lasse, comant porrai amer,
se ge ne truis d'amor mon per?
. . . .
il an estuet dous en un cople
et chascuns soit vers l'autre sople
et face li ses volantez
    (8165–66, 8171–72, 8175–77)

[The Trojan does not feel love at all; my
life is hardly anything to him. . . . Alas,
how can I love if I do not find my partner
in love? . . . it takes two to make a pair,
and each should be submissive to the other,
and do his will. (217)]

If Lavine recognizes her beloved's distance from her and the legitimacy of her mother's claims about his real interests—male-male relations and land—she also expresses some ambivalences of her own and wonders on two occasions if she should love both Enéas and Turnus equally until the outcome of their battle is known, in order to assure her safety, regardless of the winner—a position that she ultimately renounces in favor of loving Enéas alone. Yet when Enéas fails to visit his army near Lavine's castle and thereby avail himself of the opportunity to gaze on his bride-to-be, she echoes her mother's perceptions about the real objects of his affection.

"Ce est," fait ele, "verité,
que ma mere m'a de lui dit;

de feme lui est molt petit,
il voldroit deduit de garçon,
n'aime se males putains non."
                    (9130–34)

["What my mother told me is the truth,"
she said: "Women mean very little to him.
He would like his pleasure from a boy, and
will have no one except male whores." (237)]

Although Enéas proclaims his love for Lavine after receiving a letter from her, attached to an arrow and shot out to him from her window, he is ambivalent about this emotion. In one of the romance's famous interior monologues, Enéas's voice of reason points out that this arrow—unlike the one with which Cupid impaled Lavine—has not struck the hero. After Enéas claims that he has been pierced by love's dart, he tells himself: "Tu manz, molt cheï loing de toi" (8967) [You lie; it fell very far from you (234)]. He then adds:

[P]anse de ta bataille.
Ne sai que ceste amor te vaille,
car se tu voinz, ce puez savoir
que donc la t'estuet il avoir
                    (8983–86)

[Think instead about your battle.
I do not know what this love avails you,
for if you win, you know that then you
will surely have her. (234)]

Love itself is not a requirement for having Lavine. Success in combat is emphasized, since it will guarantee Lavine and, in turn, the land linked to her. As anticipated, Enéas wins the battle. Thereafter, he confers with Lavine's father and plans to return to marry her in eight days.

According to the romancer, Lavine witnesses Enéas's victory and then observes his departure: "Quide qu'il ne l'ait gaires chiere, / quant il ne vait a li parler" (9842–43) [She thought that he hardly held her dear, since he did not go to talk with her (251)]. Lavine then states:

Molt par li est de moi petit,
de fol plait me sui antremise,

n'a soing de moi an nule guise;
or avra par unbre de moi
la terre et lo regne de roi;
se il an a tote l'enor,
molt li sera po de m'amor;
s'il est seisez de l'erité,
asez me manra puis fierté,
tornera moi el val desoz,
il an avra les chastiaus toz.
(9846-56)

[I mean very little to him indeed; I am
entangled in a mad affair, for he has no care
for me in any way. Now, through the pretext
of winning me, he will have the king's land
and realm. If he has all the rule, my love
will mean very little to him; if he is
possessed of all the heritage, then he will
treat me with much cruelty and will hold me
unworthy of him, for he will have all the
castles. (251)]

Lavine thereafter takes note of the fact that Enéas has not come to her castle, nor even looked up at her:

Or li est vis, quant a vencu,
que il ait tot escombatu,
et bien quide avoir sanz moi
l'enor; il s'an velt faire roi
(9893-96)

[Now it seems to him, since he has won,
that he has gained everything through
the battle, and indeed he thinks that
he will have dominion without me. He will
make himself king. (252)]

Although Lavine may be off the mark in her assumption that Enéas will dispense with her so easily—for such a move, no doubt, would invite only further Latin contempt for their new leader—she may not be off base in acknowledging just how peripheral her love, as opposed to her political value, really is, for as Huchet has observed: "The nuptial focus of the romances of antiquity had strong implications. . . . The genre shared the preoccupations of the chivalric class in its frantic quest for heiresses who would provide land and assure the continuance of a lineage" ("Romances," 40–41).[17]

Clearly, Lavine's body in this romance becomes a means of carrying out property transactions, rather than an exclusive object of desire. Although Lavine's love seems to have motivated Enéas to fight even more aggressively, that fight is still rooted in a desire for political conquest. True, Lavine makes Latium even more attractive, yet the text still suggests that the land and the male-male relations that it signifies have priority. If the queen's accusations of sodomy, then, are an expression of resistance to Enéas's impulses to invade and "sodomize" the Latins and their land, they are not to be taken lightly. The acquisition of the land brings to a close a series of transactions between men—between Enéas and his father, Nisus and Euryalus, Enéas and Pallas, Enéas and Latinus, even Enéas and Turnus—and privileges male-male relations even as their place ostensibly is usurped by heterosexuality. "Eneas ot le mialz d'Itaire, / une cité commence a faire" (10131–32) [Enéas had the best part of Italy, and began to build a city (257)], which his descendants continued to rule. This foregrounding of land over love perhaps signals that, in fact, there never has been a truer love than that between Enéas, his newly acquired land, and the male-male desire that that land comes to represent.[18]

Notes

1. All citations in Old French are from the Salverda de Grave edition, *Enéas: Roman du XIIe Siècle*, and are quoted by line number in the text. Translations are from Yunck and are quoted by page number in the text.

2. On the tomb and its magical mirror, see Faral, *Recherches*, 81–82, 161–67.

3. For a more graphic translation of this passage, see Gaunt, *Gender and Genre*, 77.

4. Brundage notes that the medieval term "sodomy" "included all kinds of deviant sexual practices, but . . . was also used in a more specific sense to mean anal sex" (213). Nonetheless, the word's meaning is often ambiguous; the *OED* defines "sodomite" simply as "one who practices sodomy," while "sodomy" itself is described as "an unnatural form of sexual intercourse, esp. that of one male with another." This is not to say that "sodomy" is by any means an empty signifier. Bray, for example, has traced Renaissance associations between sodomy and heresy back to the twelfth century (19). See also Boswell; Goodich; and Bullough.

5. On endogamy and exogamy, see Duby, *Medieval Marriage*; Huchet, *Le Ro-*

man médiéval, 36–38; and Brundage, 182–84, 192–94. On the *iuvenes*, see Duby, "Dans la France"; Köhler, *L'Aventure chevaleresque*, and "Sens et fonction du terme 'jeunesse' "; and Huchet, *Le Roman médiéval*, 37.

6. I adopt Crane's use of the term "heterosexual" to describe "the identity-generating complex of meanings that surround male-female courtship in the late Middle Ages" (41). Among those critics who see the *Enéas* as an endorsement of heterosexuality are Adler; Grillo; Laurie; and Margolis.

7. Of course, Cormier's use of the term "homosexuality" is subject to question in the light of ongoing debates about the emergence of homosexual "identity" and the applicability of the term "homosexual" to individuals prior to its coinage in the late nineteenth century. On this debate, see Boswell; Halperin; and Gaunt, "Gay Studies." In this essay, I place the term "homosexual" in quotation marks to signal the problematic use of the word in discussions of medieval texts and use it primarily to designate male-male sexual relations that may be, but are not necessarily, indicative of a homosexual identity.

8. For the foundational considerations of the tensions between compulsory heterosexuality and male homoeroticism, see, of course, Gayle Rubin; Sedgwick, *Between Men*; and, relatedly, Rich.

9. That this observation conflicts with her later charges of Enéas's sodomy is apparent. Although the queen begins her monologue by stating that Enéas is "de tel nature / qu'il n'a gaires de femmes cure" [of the sort who have hardly any interest in women], thereby suggesting that he has only a "preference" for men, by the end of the monologue, the attack becomes so extreme as to render the earlier qualification almost meaningless. Although in her first conversation with Latinus the queen discusses Dido and calls attention to the fact that Enéas "fist de li sa volenté" (3311) [did his will with her (122)] and then deserted her, in her speech to Lavine, she largely overlooks this fact and focuses almost exclusively on his abandonment of Dido and Dido's subsequent suicide. When the threat of Enéas's union with her daughter is more imminent, the queen is more willing to dismiss information that she previously had found useful to her case.

10. On "gender trouble," see Butler, "Imitation."

11. Boswell notes that among Germanic tribes in the early Middle Ages "[n]o man could be sexually passive with another and retain the respect accorded to a fighting adult male." Scholars agree that "the derogatory import of the accusation of *nið* or *ergi* derived from the suggestion not of same-gender sexuality but of passivity; active homosexuality was not reprehensible." Scandinavian literature of the High Middle Ages suggests a similar attitude toward passivity (183–84, 234).

12. I am grateful to Susan Crane for calling this distinction to my attention.

13. A fully historicized reading of this romance, no doubt, would enhance the analysis that follows. Numerous critics have drawn parallels between the Trojans and the Norman-Angevins, Enéas and Henry II, and the love triangles of Enéas, Lavine, and Turnus and Henry II, Eleanor of Aquitaine, and Louis VII. Significantly, the *Enéas* was written circa 1154–56, just two to four years after Henry II married Eleanor, and not long after he ascended to the throne of England and reflects the expansionist designs of the Norman-Angevin dynasty. Thus, Burgwinkle ("Knighting") argues that the *Enéas* attempts to vindicate the *Normans* of charges of sodomy by associating them with a "higher" love between men—for, as Cormier has observed, the Nor-

mans, reputedly descendants of the Trojans, were themselves deemed responsible for bringing sodomitical practices to England (Cormier, 223). According to Birns, however, Norman claims of Trojan ancestry also represented a "secular paradigm which strengthened current political authority" (49). On the relationship between the *Enéas* and mid-twelfth-century France, see Angeli, 100; Cormier, 222; Yunck, 39; Poirion, 213–29, esp. 213–16; Blumenfeld-Kosinski, 143–59, esp. 157–58; Huchet, *Le Roman médiéval*, 12–14; Patterson, 179–80; Gaunt, "Epic to Romance," 7–9; and Burgwinkle, "Knighting," 10–11. For discussions of Norman-Angevin claims of Trojan ancestry, see Bezzola, 2.2, 531, and 3.1, 126; Blumenfeld-Kosinski, 158; Birns, esp. 49; and Tanner.

14. Crane cogently argues that "courtship appears a development from chivalric relations, an overt sexualizing and regendering of chivalry's combative and fraternal components" (48). See also Marchello-Nizia.

15. For consideration of the ways in which male-male desire is transacted over women's bodies, see Gayle Rubin; and Sedgwick, *Between Man*, intro. and chap. 1.

16. For a discussion of this conclusion, see Yunck, 259–60. For discussions of "homosexual panic," see Sedgwick, *Between Men*, 82–96, and *Epistemology of the Closet*, 19–21.

17. For further discussion of the importance of the land, see Yunck, 26; Poirion, 213–16; Rousse, 149–67, esp. 164–65; and Burgwinkle, "Knighting," 30.

18. I wish to thank Susan Crane for her incisive readings of many versions of this argument and for sharing the manuscript of her recent book, *Gender and Romance in Chaucer's Canterbury Tales*, while I was in the early stages of formulating my argument. Segments of this essay were presented as conference papers at the Twenty-seventh and Twenty-eighth International Congresses on Medieval Studies, Kalamazoo, May 1992 and May 1993. I am grateful to those present on both occasions for useful insights and suggestions. I also wish to thank Simon Gaunt and Laura Kendrick for many helpful observations.

IV
THE TERRITORY OF TEXTS

11

Judecca, Dante's Satan, and the *Dis*-placed Jew

SYLVIA TOMASCH

> How could a poet effectively represent absence without having established some presence to play against it?
> —Teodolinda Barolini, *The Undivine Comedy*

FROM THE OPENING OF THE *Commedia* in a *selva oscura* to the *altre stelle* at the end of *Paradiso*, Dante's self-assigned task is not just to confront the darkness of woods and soul but by means of poetry to illuminate the shadows, to banish the hidden and the obscure. The task of illumination is so fundamental to the experience of the pilgrim, of the poet, and of the readers of the poem that it has convinced audiences of the appropriateness of the strategy as well as of the correctness of the content: conversion is a turning to the light. In the words of one recent critic, "The *Commedia* makes narrative believers of us all" (Barolini, 16). It comes as a surprise, then, when repeatedly the poem seems to refuse illumination, preferring to let darkness reign; where wholeness is anticipated, we sometimes discern only want. Two notable instances of foiled expectations include "the virtual absence of the figure of Augustine" (Hawkins, 471) and the lack of explicit "symbolical representation of the consecrated host" (Sinclair, 415). Such omissions have been explained as examples of hidden presence: the saint and the eucharist emerge in other forms, as Augustine's texts substitute for the saint and Beatrice stands in for the host. In these and other instances, nondenoting is precisely what calls attention to the thing itself so that, despite poetic omissions and denials, absence makes its presence known.

In this essay, I intend to explore a different kind of absence, one whose unacknowledged presence not only occurs within the *Divine Comedy* but has remained, unrecognized, through almost seven centuries of readings of the poem. This absence is located in the name of the singular geographic site, the "Judecca" [giudecca (*Inf.* 34.117)].[1] In the *Comedy*, Judecca encompasses many meanings: it is the bottommost pit of hell, it is the circle named after the archtraitor Judas, and it is the place where Satan finds his eternal unrest. Yet the primary denotation, the one upon which these others depend, has been almost completely forgotten: first and foremost, "Judecca" is the medieval Italian name for the Jewish ghetto.[2] In Dante's re-etymologizing of the name, he does more than merely expand its semantic field. He blanches the Judecca of its original referent, then reinscribes it with definitions that more comfortably fit the christianist ideology of his poem. In the language of twentieth-century state terrorism, the ghetto and its inhabitants have been "disappeared."

In the course of the poem, Judecca as "home to the Jews" is the sense never expressed. Indeed, the re-etymologizing that Dante performs depends upon the erasure of the original inhabitants: not only is the ghetto elided, but Jews themselves never appear *as Jews* anywhere in the *Divine Comedy*.[3] Although Dante's encyclopedic cosmology is replete with non-Christian figures, including some located in unlikely places (such as the pagan Cato in Purgatorio and the Muslim Saladin in Limbo), the whole of the *Commedia* does not include even one postbiblical Jew. Hebrews, of course, are numbered among the heavenly host (as precursors of Christians they have a sort of associational presence), but the Jews of Dante's Florence are profoundly absent.

What I intend to argue in this essay is that Dante's re-etymologizing of the Judecca entails a relentless repression of Jewish referentiality that nonetheless returns in distorted form. Although it has often been noted that Satan's cannibalistic consumptions parody the Eucharist and that his physical form entails a sacrilegious re-embodiment of the Christian savior, it has never been recognized that Satan's actions, location, and form are all diabolic reflections of Dante's incompletely repressed vision of the Jew. Within the medieval mythology out of which Dante drew his poetic figures, it is finally not surprising that the silenced demon be entombed within the Judecca and that the dephallicized devil be aligned with the grotesque and circumcised Jew. The erasure of the people and the substitution of the place is completed by the transmutation of persons: Jews are disappeared from the Judecca and Satan appears in their place. Despite their literal absence, in the horrible ingestive activities and the incomplete and monstrous body of the devil, Jews are repeatedly made metonymically present.

How is it that no one has discussed the appearance/nonappearance/disappearance of Jews in the *Divine Comedy*?[4] I believe the answer lies in the conversional nature of Dante's narrative strategy, the paradoxical character of which reflects the fundamental dilemma of Dante's Christian culture. Despite its Jewish foundations, Christianity has repeatedly endeavored to indulge in the fantasy of an unblemished beginning. But the name of Dante's Judecca shows not only that an immaculate origin is necessarily phantasmatic but that there is no uncontaminated place, not even the paradoxically purified pit of hell. It is precisely this alternation of dis/associations—dreams of purity versus nightmares of purification—that produces the *Dis*-placement of Dante's Jews.

The overwhelming silence regarding the place of the Jews within the *Divine Comedy* reveals how thoroughly subsequent readers have acceded to Dante's authoritative maneuvers. It is therefore of compelling importance to understand the powerful christianist hermeneutics that not only informs the *Commedia* but has also informed successive readings of it.[5] Despite the extraordinary variety of interpretations, critics—willing narrative believers all—have not, in this context, been resisting readers. Participating in the christianist ethic of medieval studies in general, Dante scholars have not managed to construct a hermeneutics liberated from the constraints of the Jewish-Christian problematic with which Dante himself struggled. That the poet fabricated his cosmology according to medieval Christian premises goes without saying. That later readers have so thoroughly granted the premises of Dante's construction—the naming of Judecca, the absenting of Jews, and the judaizing of Satan—suggests that we, as medievalists, are implicated in an ongoing, unacknowledged christianism as well.

Hebrei dicunt . . . Iudei fabulant

Fundamental to christianist thinking is the typological, supercessionist distinction between Christians and Jews,[6] an important element of which is the discrimination between good Hebrews and bad Jews employed so effectively by Dante in his poem. Augustine expresses this discrimination clearly when he writes:

> both expressions, although contrary to one another—that is, "enemies" and "beloved"—are appropriate, though not to the same men, yet to the same Jewish people, and to the same carnal seed of Israel, of whom some belonged to the falling away, and some to the blessing of Israel himself. ("Predestination," *Basic Writings*, 1.808)

The pervasiveness of such dualistic rationales would lead us to expect to encounter in the *Comedy* both the positive and the negative incarnations of the

Israelite seed.[7] Moreover, our understanding of Dantean poetic symmetry would lead us to anticipate the duplication of the heavenly Hebrews *in malo* as infernal Jews. However, while there are numerous medieval precedents for inclusion of Jews in hell, in the *Comedy* the negative niche remains unfilled.[8]

The Hebrews of *Paradiso* are of course not Jews but rather proto- or pre-Christians released from the netherworld during Christ's harrowing of hell (*Inf.* 4.55–61). Dante specifically names Rachel, Sarah, Rebecca, and Judith in describing the celestial rose (*Par.* 32.8–10), but such positive Hebrew figures must be contrasted with the negative Jews cited in Beatrice's discourse to the pilgrim:

> "non siate come penna ad ogne vento,
>   e non crediate ch'ogne acqua vi lavi.
> Avete il novo e 'l vecchio Testamento,
>   e 'l pastor de la Chiesa che vi guida;
>   questo vi basti a vostro salvamento.
> Se mala cupidigia altro vi grida,
>   uomini siate, e non pecore matte,
>   sì che 'l Giudeo di voi tra voi non rida!"
> (*Par.* 5.74–81)

["Be not like a feather to every wind, and
think not that every water may cleanse you.
You have the New Testament and the Old, and
the Shepherd of the Church, to guide you; let
this suffice for your salvation. If evil
greed cry aught else to you, be you men, and
not silly sheep, so that the Jew among you
may not laugh at you."]

According to Beatrice, Christians, unlike those who laugh in ignorance and scorn, have a proud foundation for their superiority. By virtue of the completeness of their scripture as well as their relationship to Christ, Christians surpass their Hebrew forebears as well as their Jewish neighbors. It is not simply that "Hebrews speak [while] Jews tell tales," but that the revelation accorded Christians allows them to speak truly, while other (specifically Jewish) discursive modes are necessarily revealed (and revalued) as fabulations.

What is most interesting about Dante's deployment of the traditional dichotomy, however, is that it does not work. Beatrice's discourse suggests three distinct terms for consideration: Christians (New Testament believers and followers of Christ), Hebrews (Old Testament believers but not followers of Christ), and Jews (contemporary nonbelievers). From these three terms, two sets of contrastive pairs follow: Christians versus Hebrews/Jews and Hebrews versus Jews. Within each set, the members do not stand in a simple oppositional relation; rather, they are simultaneously linked to and dissevered from each other. Christians are enjoined to imitate Hebrews in their testamentary belief but also to distinguish themselves through the fulfillment of the earlier book. Similarly, Hebrews are valued over (and Christians must guard against emulating) their descendants, the evil, greedy, sniggering Jews. But the possibility always remains: if Christians are like and unlike Hebrews, are they not also like and unlike Jews? In Beatrice's own words, "Giudeo di voi tra voi," may mean not only "the Jew among you" but also "the Jew within you." Beatrice's admonishment, meant to clarify distinctions, thus reveals the prevailing Christian anxiety as to the difficulty of ultimate severance.

To avoid the chance of confusion between "water [that] may cleanse" and that which stains, a more ruthless alternative offers itself, one that Dante in fact exercises in the *Divine Comedy*: the extirpation from the poem of any contemporary Jew. Dante's excision of Jews *as Jews* is unexpected yet fitting within the terms of the anamnesis with which Christianity is plagued.[9] Jews and the Jewish beginnings of the Christian faith are remembered, but only selectively; in the *Comedy*, they are represented, but only metonymically. Although medieval Jews are absent from hell, Judecca is nonetheless the place of Judas, proleptically one of their number, and of Satan, their demonic counterpart. And both of these are located in that section of the infernal city that corresponds to the Italian ghetto. By means of such substitutions, Dante makes the Jews in the *Divine Comedy* both absent and present.

The Localization of Jews

Jewish (non)representation in the *Comedy* clearly reflects the historical instability of the place (in both senses) of Jews within medieval Christian society. Michael Camille has drawn attention to a troubling representation of Jewish location that occurs at the head of a 1233 Norwich tallage roll (Figure 11.1). In this cartoon, Jewish townspeople, accompanied by devils, stand along turreted city walls. These battlements, Camille suggests, not only "represent the city of Hell, but they may also be the walls of the ghetto, which in most towns and cities in Europe isolated the Jews from the rest of the inhabitants, the barrier between 'us' and 'them' that allows for objectification in repre-

Figure 11.1. City walls, with devils and Jews, tricephalous Isaac above. London, Public Record Office, E 401/1565. Head of a roll of the Issues of the Exchequer for 1233. By permission of the Public Record Office.

sentation" (184).[10] Although Camille generalizes about the isolation of Jews "in most towns and cities in Europe," it is not at all clear what conditions of segregation applied specifically to the Jews of Dante's Italy. In fact, although different practices occurred in different locations as populations and politics shifted, separation was more likely to have been the usual practice. The northward movement of Italian Jews in the thirteenth and fourteenth centuries corresponded with the expansion of their prosperity; at the same time, the consolidation of their role as moneylenders coincided with increasing official hostility.[11] Even at the height of their Italian prosperity, "ghettoization" (in the sense of forced separation and marked distinctions) was an increasing fact of life for Jews during Dante's lifetime, although permanent compulsory confinement within the walls of a separate quarter was not established anywhere in Europe before the sixteenth century.[12] What Dante does therefore in his construction of the city of Dis is to anticipate in his poetry the stratagems later implemented in western societies. In a move of poetic prescience, in naming the infernal center "Judecca," Dante sets into play an imaginative program of segregation before that program was actualized in public policy.

In the *Commedia*, "Judecca" signifies not only the place, the Jewry, but also the collective body of Jews, which was, during this period, increasingly seen as a canker on the body of Christian society. Each individual Jew was understood to exemplify every Jew so that all Jews could, and would, be blamed for the actions (or fictive actions) of any individual, at any time, in any place.[13] Dante's acceptance of this prevalent attitude is clear from his restatement of the deicide charge: "Però d'un atto uscir cose diverse: / ch'a Dio e a' Giudei piacque una morte" [Therefore from one act issued things diverse, for one same death was pleasing to God and to the Jews] (*Par.* 7.46–47). In naming the center of hell "Judecca," he thereby generalizes Judas's betrayal onto all Jews; in erecting his ghetto, he "localizes" their consequent social subjugation.

Localization involves the profaning of sacred space, here, the absent synagogue. Like the Jews who worship in it, the synagogue as the heart of the Jewry exists only metonymically in Dante's Judecca, but it can do so because Christian scripture establishes a fundamental connection between the devil and the Jewish temple: "I know the blasphemy of them which say they are Jews, and are not, but are the synagogue of Satan" (Rev. 2.9). As the center of the Jewish quarter, the synagogue building, like the ghetto itself, was a contested site, sometimes protected by secular rulers, sometimes burned, sometimes repaired, sometimes allowed to go to ruin (Grayzel, 61). Numerous medieval illustrations presume complicity between Jews and the devil when they depict the iconographical figure, Synagoga, with her crown askew, banner broken, blindfolded (or blinded) by a demon, with a hellmouth nearby. Personified as the drooping, rejected widow, Synagoga is most often presented in typological relation to Ecclesia, the virgin bride.[14] Although Dante does not explicitly name the synagogue, I would argue that within the system of metonymy he so effectively deploys it needs no explicit naming in order for its presence to be felt.

The prevalence of the medieval image of Synagoga might lead readers to expect direct reference to it or to the synagogue, but instead of the iconographic figure or the Jewish temple there is "only" the mosque. While still outside the walls of Dis, the pilgrim discerns the mosques ("meschite" [*Inf.* 8.70]) within, burning red with the flames of heretical unbelief (*Inf.* 8.73–75). Inside the city, he later meets two schismatics, Mohammed and Ali (*Inf.* 28.31–36), who in life worshiped in the alien temples. In the course of the poem, both Jews and Muslims are thus put in their proper places: Muslims occupy mosques, while Jews abide in the "cerchio di Giuda" (*Inf.* 9.27), the Judas-circle. Even so, this residential difference is subordinate to the profound connection implied between both peoples: both sets of habitations exist within the encircling walls of Dis; both sets of beliefs lead down to " 'l più basso loco e 'l più oscuro, / e 'l più lontan dal ciel che tutto gira" [the lowest place, and the darkest, and farthest from the heaven that encircles all] (*Inf.* 9.28–29). Within the context of inclusive heresy established within the city of Dis, Dante's process of territorial representation works to elide the historical particularity of Christianity's two great religious foes. Inside the walls, the enemy is exposed as multiple yet unitary, distinctive yet undifferentiated. Although heretics appear in various guises, at bottom, it is implied, they are all the same.[15] In this way, the profane temple of the Jews is suggested, repressed, and superseded by the appearance of the mosques. The external enemy substitutes for the internal, and Jews are further encouraged to disappear.

But this process of erasure is necessarily unsuccessful, for, in terms of the Christian universe that Dante's poem imitates, the cosmic center is always already impure. If, in the *Commedia*'s inclusive and concentric system, the circuit of Judas is farthest from heaven, it is also at the center of the cosmos. If Judecca is the antitype of the ultimate Christian city, it is also the contaminating seed at the core of Christian society. And if Christians conceive of their sacred history as being founded in the "old" testament texts, then not only are Jews at the origin but they *are* the origin of that history. In Dante's poem, geography recapitulates theology: at the core of his Christian universe, at the center of his concentric spheres, is the absent and unnamed Jew. In this context of sacred impurity it is therefore significant that the gates of Dis gape open (*Inf.* 8.125–26), for the breach signals the fluidity between the inside and the outside of the segregated quarter. The untotal incarceration of the Jews within the body of the Christian city reveals the internalization of the other and signifies the impossibility of true separation, the originary loss of the pure. The opening in the walls serves not only as a sign of Christ's prior arrival but also as an emblem of the insecurity of identity that is fundamental to the Jewish-Christian problematic. And this incomplete elimination of the polluting element is itself the flawed center of Dante's metonymic method, for reinscription of the absent term inevitably occurs.

By recalling the absent Jews of the *Inferno* prior to the present Hebrews of the *Paradiso*, Dante reverses the historical chronology of the Jewish people; in doing so, he reminds readers of the degeneration of Judaism while at the same time preserving the progressive typology of Christianity. In his construction of the city of Dis, Dante attempts to confine that degeneration first by building his ghetto and then by peopling it with the most demonic incarnation of Jewish error, Satan himself. Similarly, in their gradual confinement of Jews to historical ghettos, European Christians of the Middle Ages attempted to resolve their own Jewish problem. Enforcing dress codes, expelling and recalling Jews as financial needs dictated, prohibiting free commerce and social intercourse, all of these enacted what Gavin Langmuir calls a self-fulfilling prophecy of denigration and disaster (*Toward a Definition*, 342). But just as the growing volume of statutes reinforcing physical and political separation could not begin to resolve the problem of final distinctions between Christians and Jews (or between Christianity and its others, or between true Christians and false), so too in the *Comedy* anxiety about such unresolvability leads not only to the fearful multiplication of others but also to horror at the inevitable openness and impurity of Self—horror that is evaded through the absence of the grotesque Jew but embodied in the monstrosity of Satan. As we shall see, the imperfect elision of the Jews is carnalized in the incompleteness of the very body of the devil as well as manifested in Dante-pilgrim's journey out of Judecca via Satan's trunk. That journey, retold as a movement toward transcendence and perfection, in fact reveals the eternal return of the always deficient enemy, the ever-partially repressed Jew.

Satan's Defective Body

In line with orthodox Platonic/Christian doctrine that considered the devil to be the essence of materiality, in *Inferno* 34 Dante stresses Satan's bestial physicality. Huge bat wings, tricolored faces, weeping eyes, chins dripping blood and tears, shaggy flanks with matted hair, all reveal the devil's essential contrast to God's purity and rationality. Simultaneously in this tradition, however, the devil is understood to constitute the essence of nonbeing and nothingness:

Each circle of hell as we descend is narrower and darker. There is nothing in that direction, literally nothing: silence, lack, privation, emptiness. God is expansion, being, light; Satan, drawn in upon himself, is nothingness, hatred, darkness, and despair. His isolation stands in utter contrast with the community of love in which God joins our minds with the first star (Parad. 2.29–30). (Jeffrey Burton Russell, 217)

Materiality and nothingness, logically in absolute contrast, are in the figure of Satan improbably but necessarily conjoined. The devil is not merely lack, he is lack materialized; he is not only nothingness, he is nothingness manifested in physical form. To the list of privation and emptiness, however, we must add a corporeal absence that has heretofore been entirely overlooked; at the very center of null corporeality stands Satan — a Satan without genitals.

In choosing to depict a genital-less devil, Dante appropriates the dominant tradition of medieval demonic imagery (Figure 11.2).[16] During the traverse of Satan's body by Virgil and his piggybacked pilgrim, Dante might have emphasized Satan's utter carnality by stressing the grossness of the demon's nether parts (Singleton, n. to *Inf*. 34.76–77). He might have named that which on male figures is usually found "là dove la coscia / si volge, a punto in sul grosso de l'anche" [where the thigh turns just on the thick of the haunch (*Inf*. 34.76–77)]. But he does not. By means of this circumlocution, Dante deflects his readers' attention so successfully that these lines are consistently interpreted as referring to the "hip" alone (Singleton, n. to *Inf*. 34.76–77). He thus leaves the place undenominated and the point (the "punto") unnoted.

That Dante chooses the option of nonexplicitness makes sense in terms

Figure 11.2. Genital-less demon ingesting and defecating sinners. Taddeo di Bartolo, Hell fresco, Collegiate Church of San Gimignano, circa 1320. By permission of the Archivi Alinari/Art Resource.

of the Augustinian notion of evil as nothing in itself but the privation of good ("Enchiridion," *Basic Writings*, 1.662). How to stage such negativity is Dante's great problem in the portrayal of Satan: how can one be true to absence, when it is presence that poetry calls into existence? Dante's resolution of this dilemma is to have it both ways. Satan is most certainly present: he looms large (even phallic-like), pretending to possess real power while revealed to be ultimately powerless. At the same time, he incarnates absence: he illustrates in his own body his truly impotent state. Dante demonstrates

Satan's paradoxical position by excluding that which traditionally represents masculine, generative power. Just as, according to Léon Poliakov, the Jews' special clothing was the "visible sign" that they were "corporeally different" (67), so too Satan's missing genitalia signify his manifest corporeality and the eternal impossibility of infernal satisfaction. Like those of the grotesque, grimacing Jews of medieval illustration, Satan's deficient body is the mirror of his essentially defective being.

In an act of "infernal cannibalism" (Freccero, "Bestial Sign," 161) that is a further perversion of Ugolino's devouring of his children, Satan eats his own progeny; imperfect even in his own impotence, he symbolically castrates himself. Nonetheless, although unable to sire offspring directly, he is simultaneously understood to be the progenitor of the Jews. Around the pronouncement of John 8.44 — "Ye are of your father the devil, and the lusts of your father ye will do" — coalesced the Christian tradition of Jewish demonic filiation.[17] Thus, Satan's (self-)castration not only is the ultimate materialization of the metaphysical argument concerning evil as lack, even more compellingly, it reveals the utter incompleteness and insufficiency of the Jews. For beyond the idea of demonic castration lies the physical image of Jewish circumcision. If Satan is father to the Jews, then their circumcision is his as well, magnified to suit the paternal form.

Following Paul, Augustine argues that the need for bodily circumcision was superseded in favor of "circumcision of the heart" ("On the Spirit," *Basic Writings*, 1.470).[18] The physical fact of Jewish circumcision was therefore taken as evidence that Jews were essentially carnal and irredeemably literal. Seeing only the sign of the covenant rather than its signification, Jews reject the divine pact, despise the Messiah, and lose the chance of salvation. Their blindness matching that of their progenitor, they are also segregated, silenced, and damned in Dante's hell. Metaphorically imprisoned within the walls of the poetic Judecca, they are "cut off" from human (that is, Christian) civilization.

That this further connection between Satan and the Jews comes in the last canto of *Inferno* is no accident. It is here that Dante-pilgrim turns away from the sight of sin, directing his steps upward and outward to the possibility of purgation and ultimately to the vision of salvation. This is the pilgrim's last look at Lucifer:

Io levai li occhi e credetti vedere
    Lucifero com'io l'avea lasciato,
    e vidili le gambe in sù tenere;

> e s'io divenni allora travagliato,
>   la gente grossa il pensi, che non vede
>   qual e quel punto ch'io avea passato.
>   (*Inf.* 34.88–93)

[I raised my eyes and thought to see Lucifer
as I had left him, and saw him with his legs
held upwards—and if I became perplexed then,
let the dull crowd judge who do not see what
is the point that I had passed.]

This is the second time that Dante calls specific attention to the unnamed point of absent presence. Again he speaks cryptically of the "punto" noted before: the turning point that was left unnamed, the unmarked genitals of Satan. Although Virgil tells the pilgrim a bit earlier in the canto that "oramai / è da partir, che tutto avem veduto" [we must depart, for we have seen the whole] (*Inf.* 34.68–69), I would contend instead that their departure from hell is contingent upon the recognition not of wholeness but of lack. Virgil, the non-Christian who gazed with incomprehension at the supine body of Caiaphas (*Inf.* 23.123), is not equipped to recognize the essential lack of what they have not seen.[19] Dante, in contrast, invites his readers to see what *must* be seen: omission and privation, the evil which is Satan. What Dante does not do, however, is name the thing itself: he cannot say if the devil's genitals are present or if they are not. For naming bestows completion, and this the poet cannot do.

What Dante does instead is delineate the partially depicted demon and the absent present Jew. Throughout the first *cantica*, by means of the strategies of metonymy, Jews are variously represented: in the Judecca, in the mosques, and in the figure of Satan himself. In *Inferno* 34, at the cold and silent center of Dante's cosmos emerges what is perhaps the strongest indication of the systematic repression at work throughout the poem: the devil's dephallicized body evokes the circumcised penis, a synechdochal symbol of the Jews. Yet such castration ironically bespeaks the power of the Jews, for, although the *Commedia* does its best to purge and transcend the Jewish center, in trying to recapitulate only Christian wholeness it repeatedly manifests what it seeks to avoid. Dante's metonymic gestures are attempts at deliverance, but they nonetheless return readers to their beginnings—to the already polluted, the already fallen, the already profaned, the already judaized core.

Dis-located Digestion

Dante's attempts at purified transcendence inevitably fail not only because Jewish presence shows forth at the central location but also because Jewish narrative provides the allegorical foundations of the text itself. If (as the *Letter to Can Grande* informs us), Dante's journey should properly be read as a christianizing revision of the Hebrew exodus, so too the Satanic feast observed by the pilgrim needs to be understood as an infernal reversal of the Jewish seder, commemorating not the archetypal journey to deliverance but the eternal imprisonment of its misguided celebrants. The critical tradition has consistently marked Satan's consumption of the traitors as a eucharistic parody, as Dino Cervigni writes:

> Lucifer's cannibalism reifies the metaphor of food, as both spiritual and intellectual nourishment. The Dantean text, therefore, constitutes a parodic rewriting of a fundamental Johannine text (John 6), where Christ, the Word made flesh, confounds his listeners by inviting them to eat his body and drink his blood. The Dantean Lucifer perverts Christ's offer of himself to his disciples, for Lucifer feeds himself on his followers. (46)

What is missing from such accounts of Satan's cannibalism, however, is a recognition of the mimetic connection between the demonic meal and the Jewish feast. In his redefinition of the Eucharist, Satan does indeed eat his progeny, but in doing so he once again imitates his progeny: the all-devouring appetite of Satan is also the misdirected hunger of the Jews. It is not just that the devil's ingestive activities invert the actions of God; they also displace and pervert those of the Jews. While they parody the Eucharist, they also evoke the Passover.

The demonic eating reflects the literality of Jews themselves, who, according to medieval Christian opinion, completely misunderstand the nature of the Eucharist.[20] To them the host is only bread, not a sacred object, and most emphatically not the body of Christ, which the members of the church share and which they themselves become. Rather, Jews remain linked to the body of the devil, who in his isolated and empty eating enacts a failed imitation of the eating of God. As Virgil instructs the pilgrim,

> onde nel cerchio minore, ov' è 'l punto
> de l'universo in su che Dite siede,
> qualunque trade in etterno è consunto
> (*Inf.* 11.64–66)

[in the smallest circle, at the center of the
universe and the seat of Dis, every traitor
is consumed eternally]

The selfsame "punto" thus appears for a third time at the cosmic center: here at the core of the universe, consumption is eternal but also eternally flawed. Satan's cannibalism is a further form of self-castration, which is itself an aspect of incorrect consumption, appetite turned upon itself. Self-devouring repetition necessarily leads back to the lack that can never be satisfied; incompletion is the hallmark of evil and of its exemplars, the Jews.

Because of the centrality of sacred eating within the Christian system, Jewish denial of the real presence of the host was felt to be particularly threatening during the later Middle Ages when there occurred a generalized crisis in eucharistic belief. The Church tried to address such concerns by declaring the doctrine of transubstantiation (1215) and the feast of Corpus Christi (1264), but the widespread accounts of heresy, along with such ecclesiastical declarations, provide evidence for growing collective doubt, doubt that manifested itself in anxiety, and anxiety that revealed itself in, among other symptoms, hostility toward Jews.[21] That doubts about the eucharist and libelous accusations against the Jews—desecrations of the host and murders of Christian children for use of their blood to make Passover matzohs[22]—arose simultaneously should not be surprising, given that it was from Jews that Christians originally learned about the efficacy of ritual eating (Feeley-Harnik). The need of the primitive church to use the sacred meal to differentiate itself from its Jewish source is similarly seen in texts like the *Divine Comedy* that work to reimagine the universe in explicitly Christian terms. But substituting the Christian meal for the Jewish one paradoxically maintains the same relation between them that the redefinition was meant to bring about. Rather than eliminating either, both occasions, the seder and the Last Supper, are still extant in the *Commedia*, first, through Satan's infernal inversion of the meal, and, second, in the person of Judas.

Through the eating of Judas—a celebrant of Passover, a participant at the Last Supper, as well as, here in the poem, a portion of Satan's own meal—the Jewish feast and its celebrants are reinvoked. During the Last Supper, Judas was the sole participant who stayed within the old definition of the feast, the Jew who, remaining Jewish, condemned himself by "eating and drinking 'damnation'" (Schiller, 2.35) instead of the body and blood of Christ.[23] Rather than sacred bread and wine, Judas presumably ate merely the bitter herbs enjoined by the Passover ritual. The crime for which he is punished thus consists not only of betrayal of his avowed lord but also of improper consumption.[24] In his description of the three traitors, Dante emphasizes the special nature of Judas's crime and punishment: of the three traitors, only Judas's head lies within the red demonic jaws, only his face cannot be seen, only his mouth—the organ of incorrect ingestion—is crushed in Satan's own maw (*Inf.* 34.58–63).[25] In the *Comedy*, divine retribution thus feeds Judas properly: he is the one who deserves, first and foremost, to be eaten by Satan. His position reinforces his error, and, in the mode of *contrapasso*, his punishment suits his crime: mistaken eating transforms him into the devil's meat. In his own ingestion, Satan thereby compounds the error of Judas and his other Jewish offspring: consuming only humans, he neglects to eat God, either as word or as flesh. He is as willfully blind as his progeny, or, to put it another way, his progeny follow their father, and they follow him down to the infernal table where there is only the eating of bitterness forever.

Consistent with an Augustinian metaphysics, the consequence of incorrect eating is emptiness and lack. Unlike Christ, Satan cannot incorporate sinners into his body, not even by swallowing the traitors he is chewing. He lacks the satisfaction of complete digestion—a process endlessly repeated, to be sure, but presumably able to provide a kind of selfish pleasure that is at the same time the more horrible for the sinners undergoing passage through the demonic alimentary canal. Defecation, the process antithetical to ingestion, was often prominently featured in depictions of archdemons (see Figure 11.2); it was also used to characterize medieval Jews, who were thought to be closely linked to impurity and filth.[26] In Dante's hell, however, there is no such, even temporary, satisfaction. Although Robert Durling claims that "Hell is the belly that produces shit; Purgatory, the belly that produces new life" (84), the bodily functions of Dante's demon show only an incomplete imitation of the digestive process. As countless texts and illustrations inform us, all who are sinful enter hellmouth but none comes out again—except Dante. Ingested then excreted, a wandering exile seeking his true progenitor, he alone returns to tell his tale.

That tale is fundamentally the story of escape from bondage. The pilgrim's release from the infernal center recalls the Jews' own celebration of freedom in the feast of Passover—but with the important substitution of the knowing Christian for ignorant Jews. Because Jews failed to properly effect their own holiday, Dante himself takes on the role of *verus Israel*. Like good Christians before and since, Dante tries to leave the Jewish past behind and below him in the bowels of hell. In detailing the demonic feast, Dante does indeed provide a parody of the Eucharist; in doing so, however, he also parallels the process of the earlier Christian rewriting of the original Jewish holiday.

Recognizing that an elided Passover exists in the absent communion reminds us that modern interpretations of the *Divine Comedy* also stress the occasion of Easter without attending to the Jewish feast that lies beyond it. When Dante, the tale-bearer, is finally released from hell, his evacuation serves to further his journey to union, purity, and perfection. It also serves as a sign of the incapacity of Christianity to completely digest the Jews.

Christianism, Medievalism, and the *Dis*-placed Jew

What has consistently marked the tradition of reading the *Divine Comedy* is the inability of commentators to recognize the Jewish presence at its center. Such christianist blindness underlies the collective shortsightedness of much medievalist scholarship and is an attribute of even some of the most perceptive readings of Dante's text. For instance, about the endings of the first and third *cantiche* Kathleen Verduin writes that

> the two culminating visions toward which the Pilgrim is led and by which he is momentarily absorbed, that of Satan the Destroyer and of God the Creator, loom before the Pilgrim and reader as the ultimate polarities of the universe; they guide us to perceive that in Dante's eyes the distinction between Heaven and Hell is as fundamental as the difference between life and death, between being and non-being, between existence and nothingness. (213–14)

What is omitted in such readings of the polarities of Dante's universe is the the profound and irresolvable distinction between Christians and Jews. Yet even this binary, expected and repressed in the *Divine Comedy* as well as in subsequent readings of it, is of course finally unstable. As often as the Jews are made to disappear just so often do they reappear, precisely because Christian identity is founded upon counterdefining the Jew. It is in the necessarily incomplete oscillation of identity between the Christian whole and the Jewish part that Satan and the Judecca come to exist. *This* is the tale that Dante—and *dantisti* along with him—cannot tell.

The issue of voice—of the strategies of narration, of control of the text, and of the right to speak—is crucial to any understanding of the *Comedy*. The silencing of Satan (his mouths stuffed with sinners, Satan cannot speak) is the lingual counterpart to his emasculation; his lack of words provides further proof of his impotence. Such punishment similarly suits his idolatrous seed, who correspondingly lack the Word. In the *Commedia*, Jews do not speak; they do not even tell their own tales. At the end of *Inferno*, as Dante is struggling out of the bottommost circle of hell, his is the only voice we hear. He speaks in place of Satan and in the stead of those embodied in the demon. The question then becomes, shall he also speak for modern readers?

After a last look back at Lucifer, Dante escapes from the dark and bitter realm of the "old" testament, turning his face to the sun of the new. It is strongly suggested that readers do the same.

> Lo duca e io per quel cammino ascoso
> > intrammo a ritornar nel chiaro mondo;
> > e sanza cura aver d'alcun riposo,
> salimmo sù, el primo e io secondo,
> > tanto ch'i' vidi de le cose belle
> > che porta 'l ciel, per un pertugio tondo.
> E quindi uscimmo a riveder le stelle.
> > > > (*Inf.* 34.133–39)

[My leader and I entered on that hidden road
to return into the bright world; and caring
not for any rest, we climbed up, he first and
I second, so far that through a round opening
I saw some of the beautiful things that
Heaven bears; and thence we issued forth to
see again the stars.]

When Dante so gratefully departs out of hell, that salvific moment occludes the prior event of historical release—the Jewish escape from Egyptian slavery—on which his own journey is patterned. Localized in the place from which he flees is the damned, demonic remnant, left behind in the Christian march towards wholeness, salvation, and light. The invitation to join him in his stellarward movement is very powerful indeed. But if readers too readily accept that invitation, we are in danger of forgetting that the void at the center is called "Judecca." So appropriate has Jewish absence seemed to the binarism of the Christian scheme that critics have anticipated that absence in their readings of the *Comedy*'s poetics; in fact, they have surpassed Dante in their desire to fulfill that scheme, for he at least did choose to name the center "Judecca." Instead of recognizing the oscillation of identity between Christian and Jew that creates meaning at the infernal centerpoint, readers have too often reduced such complexity to a conversional poetics to which they themselves can aspire.

Situating her reading within the *Comedy*'s reception history, Teodolinda

Barolini argues that critics have habitually accepted Dante's ideology of form. She proposes that critical distance is necessary in order for us to "fully grasp the genius of his poetry" (20), for how can we see his narrative completely if we continue to interact with it only within the terms that it itself sets up? "Standing resolutely outside of the fiction's mirror games," she suggests, "we can begin to examine the formal structures that manipulate the reader so successfully that even now we are blinded, prevented by the text's fulfillment of its self-imposed goals from fully appreciating its achievements as artifact" (16). Although I doubt that standing entirely outside is possible, I do agree with the imperative for greater distance than has generally prevailed. Medievalists need to develop a stance that will allow us to attend to Dante's narrative strategies as well as to ponder the repercussions of our blinkered praise.

By acceding so entirely to the power of this text, we lose more than critical distance. We lose the opportunity, and forget our obligation, to gather even the smallest traces of the dispossessed. While it is significant, to be sure, that a fictional demon has no genitals, eats his children, and cannot speak, what surely matters more are the consequences of such castration, exclusion, and silencing not only for Dante's absent contemporaries and their descendants but also for the generations of the readers that have followed. Throughout his great poem, Dante skillfully works to convince us of the rightness of his vision of the universe; however, even as we struggle to understand it, we need not accept its legacy whole. We can begin to attend to what Dante leaves out of his poem as well as to what he puts in. With great effort and careful attention, we can learn to hear those who have no certain place within this universal program. I do not suggest that we speak *for* them—that would be an appropriation of a kind that Dante has already made familiar. I suggest instead that we need to note, and even better, to *listen* to the silence of those who, having been displaced, have no voice, and cannot speak.

Notes

In the long course of writing this essay I have incurred many debts, which I gratefully acknowledge: to the participants of the 1988 Stanford Dante Institute, especially Rachel Jacoff, Jeffrey Schnapp, and William Stephany for their comments on early versions; to my Carleton College students, for their skepticism; to Brian Sostek and Susan Christie for their research assistance; to Chiara Briganti for help with translations; to the International Congress on Medieval Studies, Wake Forest University, and the University of North Carolina at Chapel Hill for lecturing opportunities; to the National Endowment for the Humanities and the Research Triangle Foundation of the National Humanities Center for fellowship time and space; to Larry Silver, David

Smith, and Leslie Moore for their helpful readings; to the members of the New York Meds, particularly Sealy Gilles and Robert Stein, for their thoughtful suggestions; and above all to Peter Travis for his consistent encouragement and remarkable insights.

1. Kleiner has recently examined the geography of Inferno, without, however, noting the peculiarities of Judecca that I address here. All quotations and translations of the *Comedy* are from Singleton.

2. Singleton notes that "la Giudecca" is the common name for the ghetto, but he stresses that Dante's primary derivation for the term is from "Judas" (n. to *Inf.* 34.117); similarly, *Enciclopedia Dantesca*, s.v. "Giudecca."

3. While Caiaphas (*Inf.* 23.109–26) is unquestionably and originally Jewish, he is not presented as "a Jew." He lacks every distinctive attribute—a pointed or knobbed hat, a round, yellow badge, a long, pointed nose, a grotesque face, a grimacing expression—that was typically used to overdetermine the portrayal of Jews in medieval art. On such depictions, see Blumenkranz, *Le Juif médiévale*.

4. To my knowledge, only Seiferth (149) mentions the utter absence of Jews (*as Jews*) from the poem.

5. I understand christianism to be a larger category than anti-Semitism but one that includes the latter as a subset. Christianism is not confined to opinions about Jews nor is it even necessarily negative in its views of its others. One need not profess Christianity to see the world through a christianist lens; in fact, our training as medievalists encourages us all to do so. On the historiographical distortions caused by the absence of attention to Jewish history and Jews in history, see Langmuir, *Toward a Definition* chaps. 1 and 2. On the omission of Christian in lists of norms, see Jonathan Boyarin, 101–3; also Shapiro.

6. On typology, see Paxson, who does not, however, interrogate the political consequences of such binarisms.

7. On the pervasiveness of this dualistic argument in the later Middle Ages, see Jeremy Cohen.

8. The existence of postbiblical Jews is alluded to in *Inferno* 27.87 and *Paradiso* 29.102, but none figures as a character in the poem.

9. On European anamnesis, see Lyotard.

10. Camille does not specify dates for such enclosures, but Grayzel, citing the "Juzataria" mentioned in the 1243 constitution of the Republic of Avignon, suggests that separation but not segregation was the rule throughout the twelfth and thirteenth centuries (60 n. 96).

11. Overall, Jews were trapped between two conflicting attitudes: protection, as exemplified by the twelfth-century bull, *Sicut Judaeis*, of Calixtus II, which forbade assaults or forced conversions, and antagonism, as seen in the regulations of the Third (1179) and Fourth (1215) Lateran Councils that restricted the legal rights of Jews and other outgroups and promoted segregating fashions, such as the wearing of distinguishing badges (*Encyclopedia Judaica*, s.v. "Badge, Jewish"; "Italy"). In Italy, partly because Jewish settlement was much older and more continuous, Jews were more fully integrated into all levels of Italian society. Nonetheless, during Dante's lifetime anti-Jewish activities occurred throughout Italy. For instance, the mendicant orders instigated mass, forced conversions in the last decade of the thirteenth century (Starr). And on November 9, 1304 (two years after Dante's exile), Giordano da Rivalto preached in Florence against alleged Jewish sacrifices of Christian children (David Abulafia, "Mon-

archs and Minorities in the Christian Western Mediterranean around 1300: Lucera and Its Analogues" [paper presented at the conference "Christendom and Its Discontents," UCLA, Los Angeles, January 1991], 39).

12. The Venetian ghetto, established in 1516, was the first permanently segregated quarter in Italy. Pope Paul IV ordered the compulsory segregation of Jews in Rome in 1555, and by the end of the century such practices were widespread throughout Europe (*Encyclopedia Judaica*, s.v. "Italy"; "Jewish Quarter").

13. As Poliakov states: "What is new about the incident [the 1298 Rottingen massacre] is that for the first time *all* the Jews of the country were held responsible for a crime imputed to one or at most several Jews" (1.100, original emphasis). This ease of substitution is one important component in the late medieval shift from anti-Judaism to anti-Semitism, according to Langmuir (*Toward a Definition*, chap. 4), who argues that after the feast of Corpus Christi was made official in 1264, unresolved Christian doubts led to the increase in anti-Judaic and then anti-Semitic activity (chap. 13). For another explanation for the changes in late medieval Christian attitudes, see Moore. During the period immediately preceding the writing of the *Comedy*, treatises *contra judaeos* proliferated. Particularly after the Fourth Lateran Council, repressive laws were enacted, most Jewish economic activities were proscribed, and mass burnings of the Talmud occurred (Jeremy Cohen, 63). Separate Jewish districts were established in Sicily, Speyer and Worms, Strassburg, Paris, Rome, Avignon, Aragon, and Marseilles (Grayzel, 59–60). Massacres of thousands occurred throughout the Rhineland in 1096 in the wake of Urban II's preaching of the first crusade and thereafter sporadically but steadily during the twelfth and thirteenth centuries (Poliakov, chap. 4; also Langmuir, "The Tortures of the Body of Christ" [paper presented at the conference "Christendom and Its Discontents," UCLA, Los Angeles, January, 1991]) 16–18). These massacres were in part a consequence of the spread of the two "chimerical" fantasies, accusations of ritual murder and of desecrations of the host (Langmuir, *Toward a Definition*, chap. 13). Expulsions from the countries of western Europe followed: Anjou and Maine, 1289; England 1290; France, 1306; Spain, 1491; Portugal, 1497.

14. On medieval representations of Ecclesia and Synagoga, see Seiferth. On Synagoga, also see Blumenkranz, "Synagoga méconnue." For depictions linking devils and Synagoga, see Blumenkranz, *Le Juif médiévale*, 53–54; Camille, 175–80.

15. Seiferth reproduces a striking example (his figure 60) of the congruence of Jewish and Muslim representation: the frontispiece of a 1508 Latin *disputatio*, in which "the pointed hat of the Jews is found on the banner of Saracena, while on Sinogoga's banner the name Machotemus appears" (148).

16. In making this determination, I surveyed demonic images in the Princeton Index of Christian Art as well as in such texts as Robert Hughes; and Schiller, esp. plates 389–404.

17. On the perceived relationship between the devil and Jews, see Trachtenberg.

18. Although Jesus' own circumcision was attested by Luke (2.21), as far as possible it was dissociated from the still circumcised/circumcising Jews (Blumenkranz, *Le Juif médiévale*, 80–82).

19. Cervigni takes Virgil's statement at face value, stressing that "the Pilgrim *has seen* everything" (62, his emphasis). However, the fact that Virgil thinks he has seen it all does not mean that the pilgrim has done so, nor does it mean that readers should observe only what is explicitly put before them.

20. On the medieval Eucharist, see Miri Rubin; also Beckwith.

21. On the crisis of eucharistic belief, see Bynum, *Holy Feast* esp. 48–69. On the resulting hostility toward Jews, see Moore; also Langmuir, "Tortures."

22. Langmuir notes that the first accusation of ritual cannibalism occurred at Fulda in 1235 at Christmas (rather than at Easter) (*Toward a Definition*, 268).

23. The characteristics ascribed to Judas (his relation to the devil [John 6.70] and the impropriety of his eating [John 13.18]) were also attributed to medieval Jews. On Judas's actions and appearance during the paschal feast, see Schiller, 2.32–38 and plate 73ff.

24. On proper and improper eating in Dante's writings, see Kilgour, chap. 2.

25. The devil's red face would seem to be linked to the iconographic tradition that made ruddiness a Jewish characteristic; on Judas's coloring, see Mellinkoff. (This essay was completed before the publication of Gow.) Satan's three faces also recall other elements in the medieval iconography of Jews; on the Norwich cartoon's three-faced "Isaac, Jew of Norwich," see Camille, 183. On Satan's three faces, see Freccero, "The Sign of Satan," 167–79; and John Block Friedman, "Medieval Cartography."

26. An exemplary story appears in *Matthew Paris* (Vaughan, 142–43). See also Moore, 38.

12

The ABC of Ptolemy

Mapping the World with the Alphabet

KATHLEEN BIDDICK

> It is the sorting out that makes the times, not the times that make the sorting.
> —Bruno Latour, *We Have Never Been Modern*

IN A COGENT ESSAY CRITICAL OF THE WAYS in which "rationality" has become a mantra for dividing the premodern from the modern, Brian Stock has shown how the desire to push the boundaries of modernity either back to the Middle Ages, a modernizing tendency, or forward to later times, a medievalizing tendency, leaves untouched the multiple and syncopated linkages between rationality and its technologies—scientific instrumentation, textuality, and subjectivity (120). Bruno Latour takes Stock's critique even further, claiming that periodization itself is the problem of the modern. Using Boyle's vacuum pump as an example, Latour shows how this "invention" can be considered as modern and revolutionary only if one starts periodizing—for example, by including certain events on a time line and excluding others (such as magic and religion) that would derail the invention's teleology (72). Thus does Latour conclude that "time is not a general framework but a provisional result of the connection among entities" (75).

In effect, Stock and Latour both work to derationalize rationality, thereby opening up possibilities for cultural studies of its technologies and drawing our attention not to the question of power and rationality, but to the political power *of* rationality (Asad). How does "rationality" intervene to redraw, to "re-cognize," what counts as knowledge? Stock's and Latour's work is especially useful for interrogating medieval knowledges and has inspired my own interest in the tension between so-called traditional practices of medieval cartography—specifically, *mappae mundi*, the ubiquitous cartographic representation from the twelfth to the fifteenth centuries—and purportedly rational and "modern" Ptolemaic cartographic practices, which became dominant in western Europe in the fifteenth century and were notable for locating and representing objects in gridded space. The current textbook narrative of medieval cartography typifies this tension. Although such narratives are quite sophisticated and in fact eschew any notion of linear progression in medieval mapping, they nevertheless keep separate medieval *mappae mundi* from Ptolemaic maps: "[W]hereas the didactic and symbolic *mappaemundi* served to present the faithful with moralized versions of Christian history from the Creation to the Last Judgment, Claudius Ptolemy's instructions on how to compile a map of the known world were strictly practical" (Woodward, 504). Typically, the literature on medieval maps regards *mappae mundi* as encyclopedic, "unscientific," whereas Ptolemaic cartography is considered a first step toward a "modern" practice. *Mappae mundi* get sorted out as "traditional" and Ptolemaic maps as "rational."

This essay tells a different story by superimposing the "messy," monster-infested, encyclopedic medieval *mappae mundi* on the gridded Ptolemaic maps rather than sorting them out. Indeed, as I show, the overlaps and misalignments of these two cartographic practices trace out technologies of temporality that need to be better understood in medieval cartography in particular and medieval studies in general.[1] To explain what is at stake in viewing the relationship between these cartographic practices as I do, I want to turn briefly to the work of anthropologist Johannes Fabian, who has studied early modern ethnography (a mapping practice in its own right) and its constructions of time and the other. Fabian claims that early modern ethnography came to deny what he calls the "coevalness," or contemporaneity, of its encounter with the other. According to Fabian, such denial occurs when there is a "persistent and systematic tendency to place the referent(s) of anthropology in a Time other than the present of the producer of anthropological discourse" (31). In other words, rather than seeing itself as coeval with its referent, or part of the same time, anthropology tends instead to deny this coevalness and imagine itself as part of an allegedly more modern and rational time and its referent as part of a more primitive, irrational time. I argue here that it is medieval Christians who denied coevalness to Jews just as social scientists rendered primitive their anthropological "referents." To rephrase Fabian, there is a "persistent and systematic tendency" to place Jews in a time other than the present of Christendom.

What follows is an attempt to delineate some of the ways in which medieval Christians used technology to translate the corporeal co-presence of Jews among whom they lived into a temporal absence. I call the translation from coevalness to ontological absence "detemporalization," because it is essentially a process by which in this case Jews were taken out of time. Medieval maps provided one important discursive site for detemporalizing Jews. Such a site was neither neutral nor insignificant, for, as we shall see, translating Jews from time into space was a way in which medieval Christians could colonize—by imagining that they exercised dominion albeit in an phantasmatic space.[2]

Although one of the goals of this chapter is to bring the temporal ideology of medieval mapping practices into view, medieval maps cannot be thought about in isolation, since the very notion of a map as an isolated, stand-alone object is an effect of modernist cartographic space. Both *mappae mundi* and Ptolemaic maps need to be studied as links in a chain of graphic translations that dispossessed medieval Jews in different ways. This chapter, therefore, reads maps within a *network* of translations in order to discern their interacting detemporalizations. The network includes diverse but relevant textual material, such as twelfth-century anti-Jewish polemic, fourteenth-century travel literature, and fifteenth-century Christian-Hebrew studies, as well as the technological media of translation, namely, astrolabes and alphabets.[3]

The "Mother" of the Astrolabe: Dispossessing the Jew's Body

I start with the dispossession that takes place in the most widely disseminated of medieval anti-Jewish polemics, Petrus Alfonsi's *Dialogue against the Jews* (1108–10). In this *Dialogue*, Petrus Alfonsi, himself a converted Jew, educated in Arabic, learned in biblical Hebrew, an ambassador of Arabic science to France and England, disputes with his former Jewish self, which he enfolds in the persona of Moses. He uses his *Dialogue* like a knife to excise this former self.[4] His polemic is distinctive for deploying not only scientific arguments, but also, for the first time in this genre, scientific diagrams. He uses these tactics to discredit talmudic knowledge for its irrationality.[5] In the *Dialogue*'s longest scientific excursus, Alfonsi attacks the talmudic exegesis of Nehemiah 9.6, "the hosts of heaven shall worship thee," which locates the dwelling of God in the west. Only rabbinical ignorance of the concepts of time and longitude, according to Alfonsi, could allow such error to persist. After unveiling Moses' ignorance, he then proceeds to teach him an astronomy lesson wherein he asserts the relativity of east and west, of dawn and sunset. Alfonsi's lesson teaches the concept of longitude whereby the contingent position of the observer using an astrolabe to take measurements determines relative timing and spacing. By marking such a difference between talmudic interpretation and the instrumentality of astronomy, Alfonsi implicitly constructs that observer as a Christian (male) and excludes Jews from this privileged site, the site of the one who knows. Alfonsi thus uses the "reason" of science in this excursus to deny his coevalness with Moses and to relegate him to a time other than the present of his scientific discourse.

The astronomy lesson of the *Dialogue* was grounded in the use of an astrolabe. Astronomy texts and astrolabes dating from the eleventh and twelfth centuries document Jewish and Arabic use of the astrolabe in Andalusian Spain.[6] Of the six Andalusian astrolabes surviving from the eleventh century, one of the oldest, dated to 1029–30 from its inscription, has scratched on its surface the Hebrew equivalents for certain engraved Arabic starnames (Figures 12.1a, 12.1b). This graffiti attests to the cross-cultural use of this instrument. Scientific texts also indicate active Jewish participation in astronomical and astrological studies at Andalusian courts in the early twelfth century. A Toledan Jew, Abraham ibn Ezra, wrote eight noted treatises in astrology, among which numbers his treatise on the astrolabe (1146–48). The earliest set of astronomical tables in Hebrew, drawn up by Abraham Bar Hiyya in 1104, just predates the conversion of Petrus Alfonsi. The *Dialogue* thus misrepresents the actual technological expertise of the Jews and in so doing dispossesses them of their own astrolabes as well as their scientific texts.[7]

This evidence for such close intertwining of Arabic and Jewish astronomical studies and their shared use of astrolabes makes Alfonsi's dispossession of Jews from astronomical discourse all the more stunning. Alfonsi strips Jews of their coeval contribution to Andalusian astronomy and then infantilizes and feminizes their talmudic learning as the "verba jocantium in scholis puerorum, vel nentium in plateis mulierum" (PL 157.567) [joking words of schoolboys and the gossip of women in the streets (my translation)]. Alfonsi could imagine the "universal" rational principles of the astrolabe as a means to purify him of his "pre-conversion" self, of the talmudic Jew, whom he abjects in the *Dialogue*. Since the astrolabe relativizes time by linking it to the circuits of the sun and stars, Petrus Alfonsi, with astrolabe in hand, need no longer remain incarnated temporally, ontologically, in that abject place from which Moses is said to come in the *Dialogue*. Alfonsi literally writes for himself a new place in the sun. The astrolabe thus becomes the instrumental means by which Alfonsi can both dispossess himself of his former Jewish self and through its possession ward off the shattering aspects of the dispossession he effects; in a word, the astrolabe is, for Alfonsi, a fetish.[8]

This uncanny dispossession of identity accomplished by Alfonsi in his polemical astronomy lesson can be read as a powerful moment of "internal colonization" of the Jews in medieval Christendom. He uses science and logic

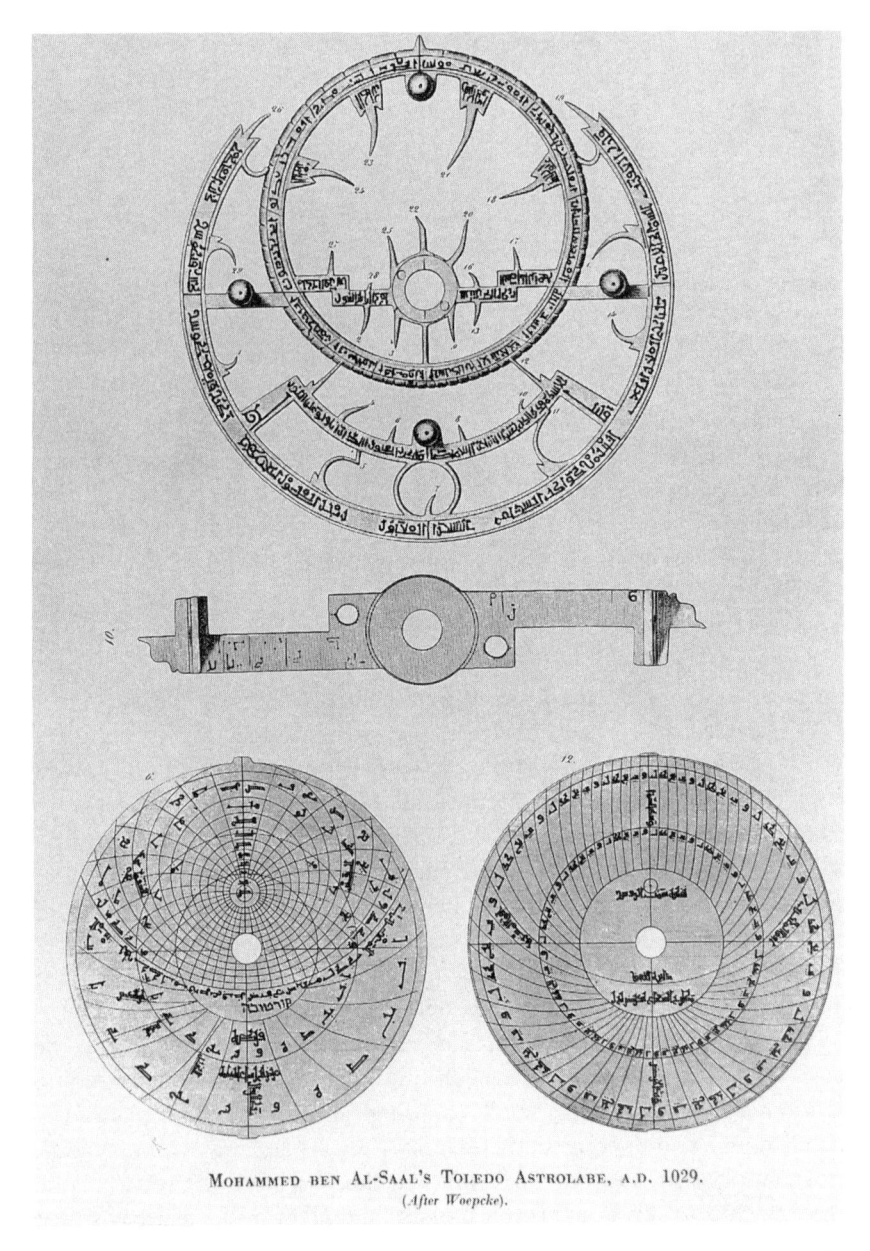

Figure 12.1a. Andalusian astrolabe by Mohammed ben Al-Saal, 1029. From Robert William T. Gunther, *The Eastern Astrolabes*, vol. 1 of *The Astrolabes of the World* (London: Holland Press, 1972), no. 116.

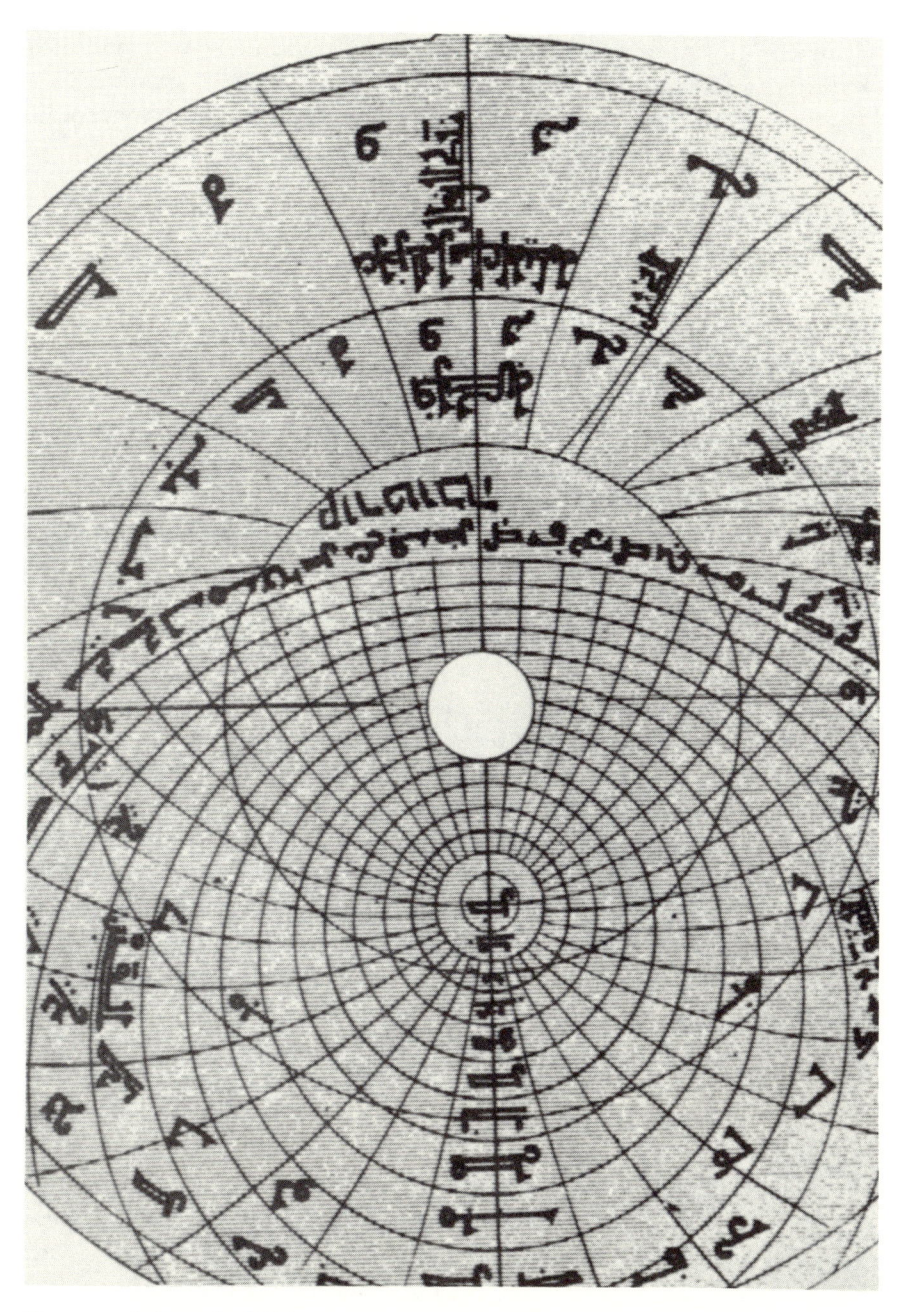

Figure 12.1b. Detail of Hebrew equivalents of engraved Arabic star names on astrolabe by Mohammed ben Al-Saal, 1029. From Robert William T. Gunther, *The Eastern Astrolabes*, vol. 1 of *The Astrolabes of the World* (London: Holland Press, 1972), no. 116.

first to stratify knowledge into talmudic and Christian categories and then to hierarchize these categories as abject and rational. Thus, Petrus Alfonsi is able to deny the construction of coevalness with the rabbi even as they speak. Such detemporalization is a key symptom of colonial encounter.

Theological Telephones

At the very time Alfonsi was writing his anti-Jewish polemic, Christian biblical scholars of the Victorine school in Paris engaged local Jewish intellectuals in ways that Beryl Smalley and her students have thought of as cooperative, respectful, curious. These same Victorines were also very interested in Alfonsi's *Dialogue*. Victorine texts are to be found bound in eight of the sixty-eight manuscripts in which the *Dialogue* traveled with other texts. Two volumes of the Alfonsi text were also in their Paris library. Did Victorine interaction with local Jewish intellectuals construct a coevalness that might be said to counteract Alfonsi's radical detemporalization of his Jewish interlocutor, or did encounter and detemporalization intersect in Victorine work as it had for Alfonsi?

Let me begin to answer that question by considering an important text, contemporary with Alfonsi's *Dialogue*, that precipitated renewed interest in maps. In 1110, just over a decade after the crusader siege of Jerusalem, Honorius Augustodunensis wrote his *Imago mundi*, a cosmography that dealt with celestial and terrestrial geography, the measurement of time, and the six ages of universal history.[9] Largely conservative and deeply derivative, its simplicity and clarity nevertheless guaranteed its wide circulation and broad influence. During the twelfth century Honorius's text can be found traveling bound with Hugh of St. Victor's *De arca Noe* (1128–29) as well as with Petrus Alfonsi's *Dialogue against the Jews*. The library of St. Victor possessed two copies of this *Imago mundi*, and when Hugh of St. Victor wrote his *Descriptio mappe mundi* in 1128 or 1129, he drew upon Honorius's treatise.

The early twelfth century marks a turning point for the production of *mappae mundi*. Knowledge of biblical place-names and locations was crucial to Victorine innovations in biblical studies. Both cartographic texts and the maps themselves were produced for their schoolroom and served as inspiration for meditations on temporality and history. Hugh of St. Victor viewed history as a narrative sequence, a *series narrationis*: "if we investigate things carefully according to the sequence of time, the succession of generations and the arrangement of truths taught, we can claim confidently to have reached all leaves of divine scripture" (Deferrari, *Hugh*, 27). He also desired that this temporal "sorting out" be drawn (*depingere*) because things cannot show themselves without such aids ("res ipsas non possunt presentare") (Dalché, 133). His insistence on representing the "visibility" of *series narrationis* through the media of *mappae mundi* thus marks a new direction in that mapping tradition. What once functioned heuristically in Carolingian biblical pedagogy came to be joined among the Victorines to theological notions of the visible and sacramental—that is, *mappae mundi* could now be deployed as a technology of the visible, not unlike the sacraments themselves, especially the Eucharist.[10]

To refine their literal studies of the Bible, Hugh of St. Victor and his students consulted with Jewish rabbis about the Hebrew text of the Old Testament as well as rabbinical interpretation. The requirement that Jews serve as intimate artifacts of the Old Testament vexed the coevalness of such encounters—in Beryl Smalley's compelling words: "the Jew appealed to him [student of the Bible] as a kind of telephone to the Old Testament" (362). This theological telephone served as yet another technological device, like the astrolabe, that could drain Jews of their coevalness in the early twelfth century.

The danger this detemporalization posed to Jews is most starkly seen in Victorine mapping of Jews in their apocalyptic thought. The Victorine literal readings of the Bible not only inspired their interest in history, geography, and maps but also prompted apocalyptic speculations. The apocalyptic mapping of Gog and Magog can help to track this detemporalization of Jews in *mappae mundi* described in such pedagogical works as Hugh's *Descriptio*.[11] The significance of this place and the identity of the people of Gog and Magog became a topic of early patristic speculation as well as Qur'anic commentary. Not mapped as a locus on late Roman maps from which prototypes of the *mappae mundi* borrowed, nor for that matter, depicted on the early *mappae mundi* of the Beatus Apocalypse group, the appearance of Gog and Magog on twelfth-century maps under the influence of Victorine biblical studies is therefore noteworthy.

What interests me in the textual and pictorial tradition of *mappae mundi* in the twelfth century is precisely the growing tendency to link the Jews with stories of the enclosed peoples of Gog and Magog, who, according to apocalyptic tradition, would erupt in the last days. As early as Orosius in the fifth century, links in this chain of associations begin to be forged. He attached to the story of the birth of Alexander the Great, builder of Alexander's Gate to enclose Gog and Magog, a tale of the deportation of Jews to the area of the gate from which they will eventually erupt in the last days (Andrew Runni Anderson, 63). Importantly, in his *Descriptio*, Hugh of St. Victor textually maps Gog and Magog with the apocalyptic tradition: "contra has regiones, in occeano septentrionali, sunt insule in quibus habitant gentes ille

Gog et Magog, de quibus in Apocalipsi legitur" (Dalché, 145) [abutting this region, in the western ocean are islands in which live that people, Gog and Magog, about which it is written in the Apocalypse]. In his widely disseminated canonical encyclopedia of biblical history, *Historia Scholastica* (1173), Peter Comestor, a member of the Victorine circle who retired to St. Victor in his last years, further forged the links in the chain between apocalypse, Gog and Magog, and Jews by specifically identifying the ten lost tribes of Israel as the peoples enclosed behind Alexander's Gate (Andrew Runni Anderson, 65). Victorines thus inscribed Jews on *mappae mundi* when they marked the site of Gog Magog. What kind of temporality did this inscription map back onto Jews? The apocalyptic telos marks the end of time as it becomes radical space. The combination of long-distance telephone calls to the Old Testament made by Victorines via Parisian Jews in tandem with their locating Jews as the enclosed peoples of the apocalyptic Gog and Magog thus had the effect of a double detemporalization. It robbed them of a *past* in the present by dispossessing them of their coeval engagement with science and hermeneutics in the medieval world. Moreover this apocalyptic scripting deprived them of a *future* in the present, that is, an open-ended, contingent, "history that will be."[12] To understand the deepening process of dispossession, I now turn to the problem of inscription itself.

Graphic Dispossession: "For I Had Lettres"

The astrolabe, Gog and Magog, and Jews come together in the *Travels of Mandeville*, the popular travel book of the later fourteenth century, only to be further overlaid with alphabetic maps of difference in which the Hebrew alphabet is marked as a tool of threat and conspiracy against Christians.[13] The *Travels*, like the work of the Victorine school, has, nevertheless, been praised for its tolerance by scholars such as Mary Campbell (*Witness*) and Stephen Greenblatt. Yet the Jews, Greenblatt notes, were the "most significant exception to tolerance" (50). The force of their exclusion strikes even more when the *Travels'* model of human diversity is taken into account.

The *Travels* draws on notions prevalent in late medieval astrology regarding the influence of the movement of the stars and planets on human nature to account for human diversity. It was not "who" you were, but "where" you were that produced difference. The reliance on contingency of place instead of some fixed notion of human essence did foster tolerance, but, at the same time, this astrological model of human diversity intersected with an apocalyptic tradition of "astrological" theology. It is to that tradition that I now turn briefly, since an understanding of its influence on Mandeville can help to delineate how a profound dispossession of Jews rests at the heart of this so-called tolerant astrological model of human diversity.

Throughout the fourteenth century, medieval scholars increasingly sought to "rationalize" the "time-line" of biblical history, especially the Book of Revelation, by joining work in astronomy and astrology with biblical chronology.[14] Valerie Flint has observed that early on in the *Imago mundi*, Honorius consistently interpolated information on astrology and magic into his revisions of his world history ("World History"). Pierre d'Ailly (1350–1420), whose *Imago mundi* (1410) Christopher Columbus read and annotated, attempted to align the relative chronologies found in world histories (drawn from such diverse sources as biblical history, Greek and Roman history, papal lists, and the events of "modern" history) onto an "independent" time line dated by astrological conjunctions. In particular, students of conjunctions had studied the "historical" paths of Saturn and Jupiter through the zodiac and observed their relations to each other in order to map astrological conjunctions. Using these conjunctions as chronological points, d'Ailly then constructed his astrological time line, which provided for a serial transition from past to future, from history to prophecy.

This star-map of history, a "scientific" approach to temporality, depended on successful prognostication to authorize itself. Prognostication verified the directionality of the time line. The ensuing pressure to predict events contributed to overdetermining the search for signs of the last days: "l'astrologie devient une herméneutique de l'apocalypse chrétienne" (T. Gregory, 566; also 560). The apocalyptic strains of this astrological theology, its anxiety over precisely determining the coming of Antichrist, joined it with popular strands of anti-Semitism prevalent in dramatic and visual traditions in which the predicted eruption of the ten enclosed tribes from Gog and Magog were read as a sign of Antichrist.[15] The temporal project of astrological theology inadvertently linked popular anti-Semitism associated with the lore of the last days to astrologically influenced models of "human diversity."

In spite of the tolerance fostered by this astrological model, the *Travels* uses the medium of the alphabet to exclude Jews from its model of human diversity. What the astrology relativizes, the alphabet reinstalls as a hard line between West and East. The *Travels* uses a geography of the alphabet as one of its chief ploys to exclude Jews.[16] It traces the forms and names of the letters of an alphabet when it finally comes to the borders of a region. Such topographical edges and their alphabets occur along Mandeville's route in the following order: Greek, Egyptian, Hebrew, Saracen, Persian, and Chaldean.

This alphabetic mapping exercise ends as the traveler comes to the islands of India, the moment at which the narrative turns from a traceable land route to a route marked by the interruptions of the many islands of an archipelago.

As the *Travels* encounters Indians it waxes "rational," just as Alfonsi did when he encountered talmudic interpretation in his *Dialogue*. As readers cross to the Indian archipelago they leave behind alphabets to enter a world governed by stars. The astral geography of the archipelago receives its longest treatment on the Indian isle of Lamary where, in a state of nature, the Lamarians go naked and hold sexual partners and property in common. The conceit of the family "tree" is undone by the Lamarians, for children can be parceled out to any sexual partner. Not surprisingly, the Lamarians are the first cannibals to be encountered in the *Travels*: they literally undo familial genealogy by eating children.

The account of Lamarian cannibalism in the *Travels* would undoubtedly resonate with Christian readers who were familiar with exempla and ritual murder stories that portrayed Jews as the local cannibals of Christendom (Hsia, *Myth*; Langmuir, *Toward a Definition*, 263–82).[17] At this moment, in which the Christian reader might think of Jews along with Lamarians, the travel-writer introduces the astrolabe.[18] It is in this famous section that the *Mandeville*-author insists on the roundness of the earth and its circumnavigability by means of yet another lecture on longitude:

The whiche thing I prove thus, after that i have seyn. For I have ben toward the partes of Braban and beholden in the Astrolabre that the steere that is clept the transmontayne is liiii. degrees high, And more forthere in Almayne and Bewme it hath lviii. degrees, and more forth toward the parties Septemtrioneles it is lxii. degrees of heghte and certeyn mynutes, for I self have mesured it be the Astrolabe. (120)

After this technological interlude, the *Travels* then leaves behind the cannabalistic Lamarians in order to pass on to the lands of Prester John. The site of Gog and Magog, however, stands directly in the way. Once again Jews interrupt the intinerary, but this time not evocatively, as in the case of the Lamarians, but overtly, as the *Travels* describes the ten lost tribes enclosed in Gog and Magog. According to the *Travels* Jews cannot escape their enclosure in Gog and Magog because the only language they know is Hebrew, a language unknown to local communities outside the enclosure:

and also thei conen no langage but only hire owne that noman knoweth but thei, and therfore mowe thei not gon out. And also thee schull understonde that the Iewes han no propre lond of hire owne for to dwellen inne in all the world, but only that lond betwene the mountaynes. (177)

The *Travels* also insists here that the Jews have persisted in this seemingly counterproductive behavior of only learning Hebrew in order to be able to recognize each other as fellow conspirators in the last days:

And thit natheless men seyn thei schull gon out in the tyme of Antecrist and that thei schull maken gret slaughter of cristene men, and therfore all the Iewes that dwellen in all londes lernen all weys to speken Ebrew, in hope that whan the other Iewes schull gone out, that thei may understonden hire speche and to leden hem in to cristendom for to destroye the cristene peple. For the Iewes seyn that thei knowen wel be hire prophecyes that thei of Caspye schull gon out and spreden thorgh out all the world. And that the cristene men schull ben under hire subieccioun als longe as thei han ben in subieccioun of hem. (178)

So far I have been reading the *Travels* for the ways in which it uses alphabets to guarantee "Western" civilization and the stars to explain "natural" (Eastern) diversity; but, in this context, one language, Hebrew, and its alphabet occupy a highly ambivalent status in this reading. The Hebrew alphabet is mapped in the *Travels* at a border in the west while the Hebrew language is located in the space of the apocalypse. Thus, the narrator casts Hebrew as a language of conspiracy, a technology of Antichrist. Hebrew is the the language of a people doomed to be a "who you are," a people excluded from the *Travels*' tolerant diversity of "where you are." Jews interrupt the so-called "rational" tolerance of the text. If, according to Greenblatt, the narrator "takes possession of nothing" (27), it does not mean that he refrains from dispossession. Secure in his rationalism, in the "lettres" that guarantee him access to forbidden places (53), the narrator can continue the medieval Christian rational project of dispossessing the Jews, this time layering the astrolabe with the Hebrew alphabet.

The *Travels* is certainly not the first medieval text to play with alphabets; significantly, however, it produces its practices of inclusion and exclusion through alphabets. It uncouples the alphabet from its acoustical/graphic modalities in order to map letters as territory itself. The letter thus becomes a cartographic code.[19] The *Travels* uses the alphabet to represent the space of territory and not the *time* of reading and writing. I now want to argue that the astrolabe, which features in the *Travels*, also produces alphabets as cartographic codes.

More astrolabes are preserved from the later medieval period than from Andalusian Spain and we know that they were used to tell time, as Figure 12.2, a reproduction of a diagram from Geoffrey Chaucer's essay on the astrolabe, illustrates. Readers of the *Travels* who wished to tell time with the astrolabe would find themselves using the alphabet as a code. Telling time with this in-

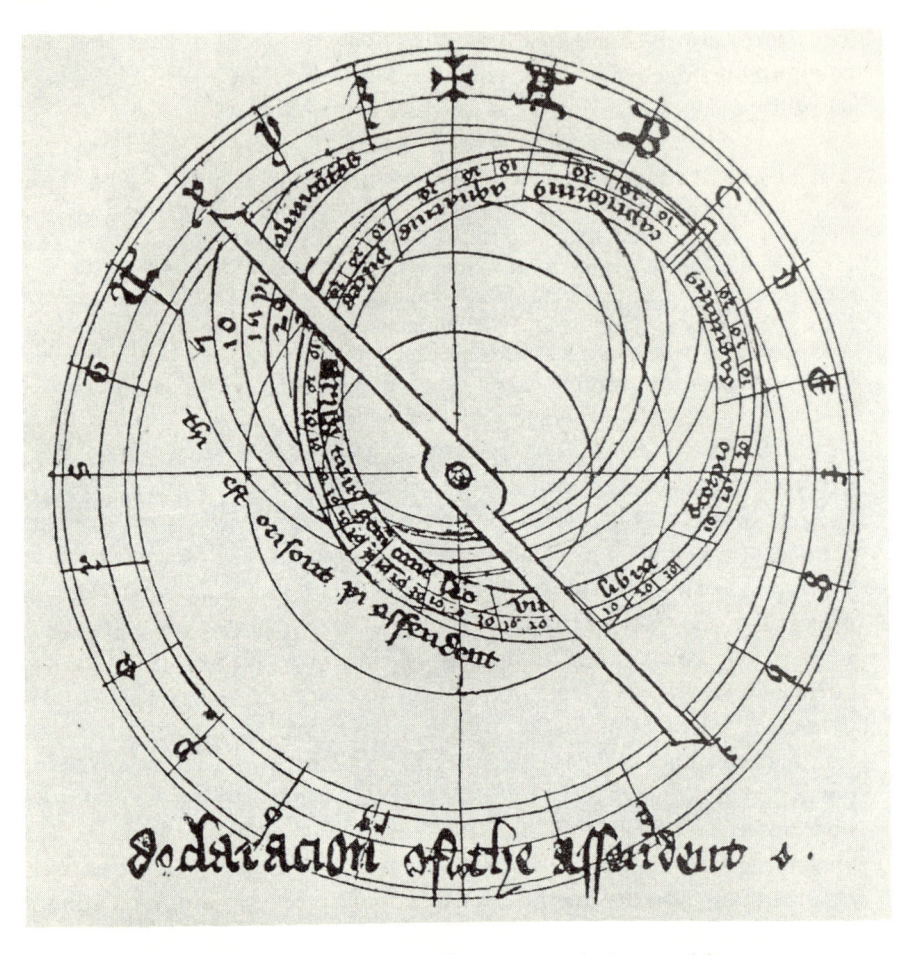

Figure 12.2. From Chaucer's lesson on telling time with the astrolabe; anonymous. Cambridge, MS Cambridge Dd.3.53. From Robert William T. Gunther, ed., *Chaucer and Messahalla on the Astrolabe*, vol. 5 of *Early Science in Oxford* (Oxford: Oxford University Press, 1929).

strument involved the cross-correlation of the altitude of the sun read from the rule on the backside of the astrolabe with the positioning of the rete to correspond to the date of the reading on its frontside. As Figure 12.2 illustrates, the pointer on the label would then fall on one of twenty-three capital letters of the alphabet, or a cross, which marked respectively fifteen-degree increments of the twenty-four-hour day on the outer border of the astrolabe. The user would then count off the positions of the letters to arrive at the hour of the day. The alphabet thus serving as a code on the astrolabe is significant for the following reasons: (1) the use of the alphabet as a code occurs on a portable object with movable parts; (2) the reading of the code is repeatable; and (3) the alphabet as spatial demarcations encodes time. In sum, the *Travels* mobilizes this rational instrumentality to code alphabets as territory with implicit reference to a master alphabet, namely Latin, and to fix Hebrew as an apocalyptic language of conspiracy.[20]

So far I have suggested that the strategic invocation of scientific rationalism in the form of astronomical discourse on longitude and latitude, grounded in the use of the astrolabe, emerges at critical moments of encounter with Jews in the work of Petrus Alphonsi and *Mandeville's Travels*. The *Travels* not only uses that strand of rationalism but also incorporates the apocalyptic cartography of the Victorines, who in spite of their purported tolerance linked Jews with the peoples of Gog and Magog and the fantasized annihilation of Christians at the hands of the Jews in the last days. The *Travels* then takes one step further. Not only does Mandeville measure with the astrolabe, he also mimics the use of the alphabet as it is used in reading time off the astrolabe. Like the alphabetical code on the astrolabe, alphabets in the *Travels* are cartographical codes that excise the alphabet from the temporality of reading words. This detemporalizing of the alphabet is used to detemporalize Jews.

These different "rational" moments attest to the violence that can lurk in between time and space in medieval mapping practices. I now wish to consider, at last, the printed editions of Ptolemy's *Geography* along with Christian-Hebrew studies that developed just as the *Geography* came to press. What might seem separate endeavors, cartography and humanist philology, I argue are intimately intertwined in intensifying detemporalization of the Jew. Put another way, it is not surprising to see Christian intellectuals, such as Pico della Mirandola, deeply involved in Jewish Kabbala and Ptolemaic geography. What Michael Taussig has described for a New World colonial context as the "search for the White Indian," I appropriate here as the "search for the old Talmudic Jew" in the fifteenth century among Christians who install that fully disappeared, dispossessed, finally expulsed Jewish body into mechanical reproduction, that is, into printing itself.[21]

The ABC of Ptolemy: The Alphabet as Territory

An understanding of the changing epistemological conditions of the alphabet is important to an understanding of the reception of Ptolemy's *Geography* in the fifteenth century; it is therefore worth pausing here to note further aspects

Figure 12.3. Letter "M" from Marie de Bourgogne's alphabet, Codex Bruxellensis II 845. From Pierre Dumon, *L'Alphabet Gothique dit de Marie de Bourgogne: Reproduction du codex Bruxellensis II 845* (Antwerp: De Nederlandsche Boekhandel, 1973).

Figure 12.4. Letter "A" from the Damiano da Moille alphabet, Parma. From Stanley Morison, ed., *The Moyllus Alphabet: A Newly Discovered Treatise on Classic Letter Design Printed at Parma c. 1480* (New York: Pegasus, 1927).

of alphabetic transformation. The effects of this process can be noted most starkly by comparing two exemplary alphabets that date to a time of growing interest in the *Geography*: the 1460 alphabet of Marie de Bourgogne and the 1480 alphabet of Damiano da Moille (Figures 12.3 and 12.4).[22] Damaino da Moille's alphabet is the first printed version of the roman alphabet, although a manuscript treatise on the roman alphabet by Felice Feliciano (1460–63), which did not make its way into print, was being written at the same moment as the execution of Marie de Bourgogne's alphabet.

The differences between the Gothic and Roman alphabets are starkly drawn. The Gothic letter "M" of the Marie de Bourgogne alphabet, illustrated in Figure 12.3, seems to pun acoustically on "M" for "mâchoire" or jaw. The jaw is drawn in the resemblance of the clitoris, the orifices burst out of the elaborated, fragmented frame of the Gothic letter, as if genitals gird the dissolving ductus of this letter. The roman letters of the Damiano da Moille alphabet, in contrast, are "constructed" from the principles of geometry, as the illustration of "A" in Figure 12.4 shows. The Damiano da Moille letters feature none of the punning acoustical or corporeal aspects of the Marie de Bourgogne letters. The letters of the roman alphabet materialize within their own self-sufficient geometric grid. So constructed, roman type effaces its own historicity to produce a timeless, monumental space, cleansed of the corporeal excess of the Marie de Bourgogne letter. Historians of roman letters trace their development to the Este court in Ferrara and the Gonzaga court in Mantua. It is also at the Este court where astrologers approved Nicolaus Germanus's manuscript edition of Ptolemy, which served as the exemplar for the 1482 and 1486 Ulm editions. It is in the constructed "roman" alphabet of Damiano da Moille and not in the florid Gothic alphabet of Marie de Bourgogne that printers set editions of Ptolemy's *Geography* in the fifteenth century. This choice of typeface, I want to argue, is more than just a "style." Rather, the choice to print with roman typeface further unhinged cartographic space from temporality. Let me turn to a discussion of a printed edition of the *Geography* to expand on this claim.

First translated from Greek into Latin in 1405–9, Ptolemy's *Geography* presented its Christian students with a practical guide to constructing maps on a grid of longitude and latitude and offered a list of these coordinates for over eight thousand place-names grouped by the imperial regions current in the late antique world.[23] A work much published among Italian and German printers, an edition of a *Geography* staked a claim for the publisher's city in a trans-European humanist culture. Each edition of the *Geography* became what Lisa Jardine has termed "the basis for further collaborative attention, repersonalising and revivifying the 'dead letter' of the printed page" (24).[24]

The front and back matter that began to accrete around these different editions, as well as the "updating" of maps, transformed the way in which readers might read the text. For example, Francesco Berlinghieri's vernacular verse adaptation of Ptolemy was the first edition (Florence, 1482) to include *tabulae novellae*, or updated maps, in this instance for Spain, France, Italy, and the Holy Land. Berlinghieri's edition also included new front matter that aided the reader's navigation through the Ptolemaic text. On folio 2r of this edition the Ptolemaic regions were alphabetized (from Achaia to Vindelicia), after which the relevant book, chapter, and map number were listed for each regional name. This edition also alphabetized the place-names of each region at the end of each book and then listed the respective longitude and latitude. The maps for each region were placed after each book. This editorial apparatus thus used the different chapter or "book" divisions as its basic organizational unit and alphabetized information with reference to each of its books.[25]

My study of Ptolemy's *Geography* concentrates on the 1486 edition printed at Ulm, the second edition to be printed North of the Alps. This edition is notable for several reasons. First, like all previous editions, including its prototype, the 1482 Ulm edition, it is printed in roman type, the typeface of choice for "scientific" texts.[26] (The mathematician Regiomontanus and Hermann Schedel of Nuremberg had just introduced the typeface to German presses north of the Alps.)[27] In addition, the printer of the 1486 Ptolemy recycled the woodcut maps of the 1482 edition but made significant additions to the front and back matter of the volume. Thenceforth, editions of the *Geography* would travel with other appended texts. Most importantly, elaborating on and significantly rearranging the editorial aids of Berlinghieri, the 1486 Ulm Ptolemy included an alphabetized register of places, *Registrum alphabeticum super octo libros Ptolomaei*, as prefatory material to the *Geography*. This *Registrum* was extracted from each of the regional books (books 2–4) and was accompanied by cross-listings of the number of the map on which the place could be located. A brief descriptive annotation accompanied many of the alphabetized places.

This seemingly mundane *Registrum alphabeticum* had powerful, if unintended, effects as an editorial apparatus. By alphabetizing all places without regard to the textual divisions of the "books," this edition stripped the *Geography* of time, the timing of reading, and superimposed instead an alphabetic list, or grid, onto a cartographic grid of longitude and latitude. Readers could locate the name of a place in the alphabetic list at the front of the volume and then they could simply turn to the relevant map at the back of the volume to verify its cartographic location. The alphabetical list of places and map references meant that it was no longer necessary, as it had been, to peruse the text of the *Geography* in order to link a place with a map. By the publication of the Strassburg edition of 1513, this editorial tool had reached its empirical minimalism—a long list of alphabetized places on the Ptolemaic maps with a list of the maps on which they could be found, along with their longitude and latitude (Figure 12.5). The effect of this apparatus was to make the *Geography* work like an atlas before the production of atlases (a phenomenon of the mid-sixteenth century).

The 1486 Ptolemy also introduced back matter to the *Geography*. It was the first edition to append a short treatise after the maps entitled "on three parts of the world and the various men, portents and transformations with rivers, islands and mountains." Using excerpts from the work of Isidore and Vincent of Beauvais, it offered readers familiar encyclopedic fare typically associated with *mappae mundi*.[28] The 1486 Ptolemy layers a range of complex material: roman typeface as signifier of the "scientific" content of the *Geography*, an alphabetized register of places cross-referenced to their respective maps (a tool that enables the book to work more like an atlas), and finally a seemingly atavistic encyclopedic tract on the wonders of the world.

The *Registrum* marks the use of alphabetization as an increasingly effec-

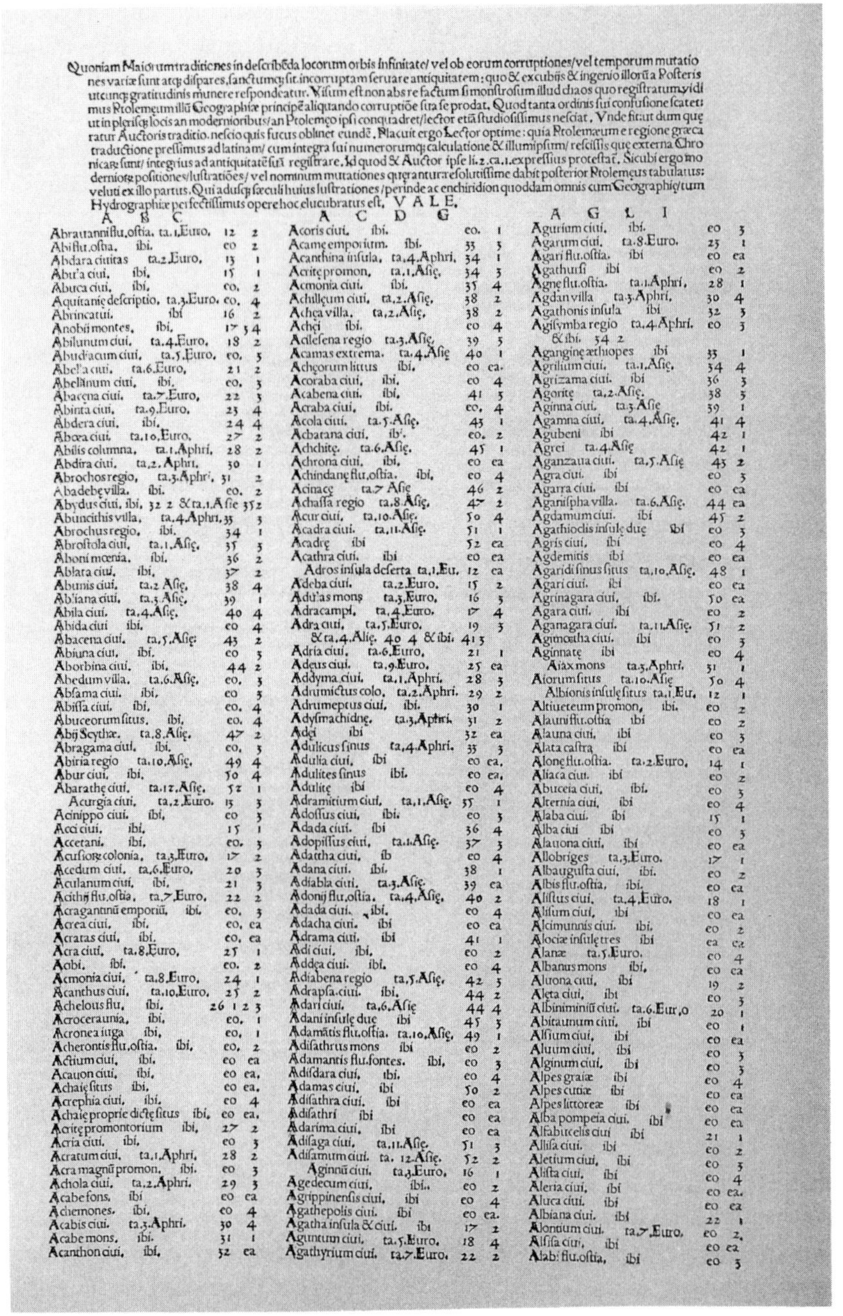

Quoniam Maiorum traditiones in describēda locorum orbis infinitate/ vel ob eorum corruptiones/vel temporum mutatio nes variæ sunt atq; dispares, sanctumq; sit incorruptam seruare antiquitatem: quo & excubijs & ingenio illorū a Posteris utcunq; gratitudinis munere respondeatur. Visum est non abs re factum si monstrosum illud chaos quo registratum vidi mus Ptolemęum illū Geographiæ principē aliquando corruptiōe sua se prodat. Quod tanta ordinis sui confusione scatet: ut in plerisq; locis an modernioribus/an Ptolemęo ipsi conquadret/lector etiā studiosissimus nesciat. Vnde fit ut dum quę ratur Auctoris traditio. nescio quis fucus oblinet eundē. Placuit ergo Lector optime: quia Ptolemæum e regione græca traductione pressimus ad latinam/ cum integra sui numerorumq; calculatione & illum ipsum/ rescissis quę externa Chro nicarū sunt/ integrius ad antiquitatē suā registrare. Id quod & Auctor ipse li.2.ca.1.expressius protestat. Sicubi ergo mo derniorū positiones/lustratiōes/ vel nominum mutationes quęrantur: resolutissime dabit posterior Ptolemęus tabulatus: veluti ex illo partus. Qui adusq; sæculi huius lustrationes/perinde ac enchiridion quoddam omnis cum Geographię/tum Hydrographiæ perfectissimus opere hoc elucubratus est. V A L E.

A B C		
Abrauannis flu. ostia. ta.1.Euro.	12	2
Abis flu. ostia. ibi.	eo	2
Abdara ciuitas ta.2.Euro.	13	1
Abu'a ciui. ibi.	15	1
Abuca ciui. ibi.	eo.	2
Aquitanię descriptio. ta.3.Euro.	eo.	4
Abrincatui. ibi	16	2
Anobii montes. ibi.	17	54
Abilunum ciui. ta.4.Euro.	18	2
Abudiacum ciui. ta.5.Euro.	eo.	3
Abel'a ciui. ta.6.Euro.	21	2
Abellinum ciui. ibi.	eo.	3
Abacęna ciui. ta.7.Euro.	22	3
Abinta ciui. ta.9.Euro.	23	4
Abdera ciui. ibi.	24	4
Abœa ciui. ta.10.Euro.	27	2
Abilis columna. ta.1.Aphri.	28	2
Abdira ciui. ta.2.Aphri.	30	1
Abrochos regio. ta.3.Aphri.	31	2
Abadebę villa. ibi.	eo.	2
Abydus ciui. ibi. 32 2 & ta.1.Asie	35	2
Abuncithis villa. ta.4.Aphri.	33	3
Abrochus regio. ibi.	34	1
Abrostola ciui. ta.1.Asię.	35	3
Aboni mœnia. ibi.	36	2
Ablata ciui. ibi.	37	2
Abunis ciui. ta.2 Asię.	38	4
Ab'iana ciui. ta.3.Asię.	39	1
Abila ciui. ta.4.Asię.	40	4
Abida ciui ibi.	eo	4
Abacena ciui. ta.5.Asię:	43	2
Abiuna ciui. ibi.	eo	3
Aborbina ciui. ibi.	44	2
Abedum villa. ta.6.Asię.	eo.	3
Absama ciui. ibi.	eo	3
Abissa ciui. ibi.	eo.	4
Abuceorum situs. ibi.	eo.	4
Abij Scythæ. ta.8.Asię.	47	2
Abragama ciui. ibi.	eo.	3
Abiria regio ta.10.Asię.	49	4
Abur ciui. ibi.	50	4
Abarathę ciui. ta.12.Asię.	52	1
Acurgia ciui. ta.2.Euro.	13	3
Acinippo ciui. ibi.	eo	3
Acci ciui. ibi.	15	1
Accetani. ibi.	eo.	3
Acusiorū colonia. ta.3.Euro.	17	2
Acedum ciui. ta.6.Euro.	20	3
Aculanum ciui. ibi.	21	3
Acithij flu. ostia. ta.7.Euro.	22	2
Acragantinū emporiū. ibi.	eo.	3
Acrea ciui. ibi.	eo.	ea
Acratas ciui. ibi.	eo.	ea
Acra ciui. ta.8.Euro.	25	1
Acobi. ibi.	eo.	2
Acmonia ciui. ta.8.Euro.	24	1
Acanthus ciui. ta.10.Euro.	25	2
Achelous flu. ibi.	26 1	2 3
Acroceraunia. ibi.	eo.	1
Acronea iuga ibi.	eo.	1
Acherontis flu. ostia. ibi.	eo.	2
Actium ciui. ibi.	eo	ea
Acauon ciui. ibi.	eo	ea.
Achaię situs ibi.	eo	ea.
Acrephia ciui. ibi.	eo	4
Achaię proprie dictę situs ibi.	eo	ea.
Acritę promontorium ibi.	27	2
Acria ciui. ibi.	eo	3
Acratum ciui. ta.1.Aphri.	28	2
Acra magnū promon. ibi.	eo	3
Achola ciui. ta.2.Aphri.	29	3
Acabe fons. ibi	eo	ea
Achemones. ibi.	eo	4
Acabis ciui. ta.3.Aphri.	30	4
Acabe mons. ibi.	31	1
Acanthon ciui. ibi.	32	ea

A C D G		
Acoris ciui. ibi.	eo.	1
Acamę emporium. ibi.	33	3
Acanthina insula. ta.4.Aphri.	34	1
Acritę promon. ta.1.Asię.	34	3
Acmonia ciui. ibi.	35	4
Achillęum ciui. ta.2.Asię.	38	2
Achęa villa. ta.2.Asię.	38	2
Achęi ibi.	eo	4
Acilesena regio ta.3.Asię.	39	3
Acamas extrema. ta.4.Asię	40	1
Achęorum littus ibi.	eo	ea.
Acoraba ciui. ibi.	eo	4
Acabena ciui. ibi.	41	3
Acraba ciui. ibi.	eo.	4
Acola ciui. ta.5.Asię.	43	1
Acbatana ciui. ibi.	eo.	2
Achchitę. ta.6.Asię.	45	1
Achrona ciui. ibi.	eo	ea
Achindanę flu. ostia. ibi.	eo	4
Acinacę ta.7 Asię	46	2
Achassa regio ta.8.Asię.	47	2
Acur ciui. ta.10.Asię.	50	4
Acadra ciui. ta.11.Asię.	51	1
Acadrę ibi	52	ea
Acathra ciui. ibi	eo	ea
Adros insula deserta ta.1.Eu.	12	ea
Adeba ciui. ta.2.Euro.	15	2
Adu'as monş ta.3.Euro.	16	3
Adracampi. ta.4.Euro.	17	4
Adra ciui. ta.5.Euro.	19	3
& ta.4.Asię. 40 4 & ibi.	41	3
Adria ciui. ta.6.Euro.	21	1
Adęus ciui. ta.9.Euro.	25	ea
Addyma ciui. ta.1.Aphri.	28	3
Adrumictus colo. ta.2.Aphri.	29	2
Adrumeptus ciui. ibi.	30	1
Adysmachidnę. ta.3.Aphri.	31	2
Adęi ibi	32	ea
Adulicus sinus ta.4.Aphri.	33	3
Adulia ciui. ibi	eo	ea.
Adulites sinus ibi.	eo	ea.
Adulitę ibi	eo	4
Adramitium ciui. ta.1.Asię.	35	1
Adossus ciui. ibi.	eo	3
Adada ciui. ibi	36	4
Adopissus ciui. ta.1.Asię.	37	3
Adattha ciui. ib	eo	4
Adana ciui. ibi.	38	1
Adiabla ciui. ta.3.Asię.	39	ea
Adonij flu. ostia. ta.4.Asię.	40	2
Adada ciui. ibi.	eo	4
Adacha ciui. ibi	eo	ea
Adrama ciui. ibi	41	1
Adi ciui. ibi.	eo	2
Addęa ciui. ibi.	eo	4
Adiabena regio ta.5.Asię.	42	3
Adrapsa ciui. ibi.	44	2
Adari ciui. ta.6.Asię	44	4
Adani insulę duę ibi	45	3
Adamātis flu. ostia. ta.10.Asię.	49	1
Adisathrus mons ibi	eo	2
Adamantis flu. fontes. ibi.	eo	3
Adisdara ciui. ibi.	eo	4
Adamas ciui. ibi	50	2
Adisathra ciui. ibi	eo	ea
Adisathri ibi	eo	ea
Adarima ciui. ibi	eo	ea
Adisaga ciui. ta.11.Asię.	51	3
Adisamum ciui. ta. 12.Asię.	52	2
Aginnū ciui. ta.3.Euro.	16	1
Agedecum ciui. ibi.	eo	2
Agrippinensis ciui. ibi	eo	4
Agathepolis ciui. ibi	eo	ea.
Agatha insula & ciui. ibi	17	2
Aguntum ciui. ta.5.Euro.	18	4
Agathyrium ciui. ta.7.Euro.	22	2

A G L I		
Agurium ciui. ibi.	eo	3
Agarum ciui. ta.8.Euro.	23	1
Agari flu. ostia. ibi	eo	ea
Agathursi ibi	eo	2
Agnę flu. ostia. ta.1.Aphri.	28	1
Agdan villa ta.3.Aphri.	30	4
Agathonis insula ibi	32	3
Agisymba regio ta.4.Aphri.	eo	3
& ibi. 54 2		
Agangine æthiopes ibi	33	1
Agrilium ciui. ta.1.Asię.	34	4
Agrizama ciui. ibi	36	3
Agoritę ta.2.Asię.	38	3
Aginna ciui. ta.3.Asię	39	1
Agamna ciui. ta.4.Asię.	41	4
Agubeni ibi	42	1
Agrei ta.4.Asię	42	1
Aganzaua ciui. ta.5.Asię	43	2
Agra ciui. ibi	eo	3
Agarra ciui. ibi	eo	ea
Aganispha villa. ta.6.Asię.	44	ea
Agdamum ciui. ibi	45	2
Agathiodis insulę duę ibi	eo	3
Agris ciui. ibi	eo	4
Agdemitis ibi	eo	ea
Agaridi sinus situs ta.10.Asię.	48	1
Agari ciui. ibi	eo	ea
Agrinagara ciui. ibi.	50	ea
Agara ciui. ibi	eo	2
Aganagara ciui. ta.11.Asię.	51	2
Agimœtha ciui. ibi	eo	3
Aginnatę ibi	eo	4
Aiax mons ta.3.Aphri.	31	1
Aiorum situs ta.10.Asię	50	4
Albionis insulę situs ta.1.Eu.	12	1
Altiueteum promon. ibi.	eo	2
Alauni flu. ostia ibi	eo	2
Alauna ciui. ibi	eo	3
Alata castrą ibi	eo	ea
Alonę flu. ostia. ta.2.Euro.	14	1
Aliaca ciui. ibi	eo	2
Abuceia ciui. ibi.	eo	3
Alternia ciui. ibi	eo	4
Alaba ciui. ibi	15	1
Alba ciui ibi	eo	3
Alauona ciui. ibi	eo	ea
Allobriges ta.3.Euro.	17	1
Albaugusta ciui. ibi.	eo	2
Albis flu. ostia. ibi.	eo	ea
Alistus ciui. ta.4.Euro.	18	1
Alisum ciui. ibi	eo	ea
Alcimunnis ciui. ibi.	eo	2
Alociæ insulę tres ibi	ea	ea
Alanæ ta.5.Euro.	eo	4
Albanus mons ibi.	eo	ea
Aluona ciui. ibi	19	2
Alęta ciui. ibi	eo	3
Albiniminiū ciui. ta.6.Eur.o	20	1
Abitaunum ciui. ibi	eo	1
Alsium ciui. ibi	eo	ea
Aluum ciui. ibi	eo	3
Alginum ciui. ibi	eo	3
Alpes graiæ ibi	eo	4
Alpes cutiæ ibi	eo	ea
Alpes littoreæ ibi	eo	ea
Alba pompeia ciui. ibi	eo	ea
Alfabucelis ciui ibi	21	1
Allisa ciui. ibi	eo	2
Aletium ciui. ibi	eo	3
Alista ciui. ibi	eo	4
Aleria ciui. ibi	eo	ea.
Aluca ciui. ibi	eo	ea
Albiana ciui. ibi	22	1
Alontium ciui. ta.7.Euro.	eo	2.
Alsisa ciui. ibi	eo	ea
Alabi flu. ostia. ibi	eo	3

Figure 12.5. First page of alphabetical register of places and coordinates from *Claudius Ptolomaeus Cosmographia*, Strassburg, 1513. From R. A. Skelton, *Claudius Ptolomaeus Cosmographia* (facsimile) (Amsterdam: Theatrum Orbis Terrarum, 1966).

tive indexing tool for cartography, joining the alphabet directly to longitude and latitude.[29] These intersections have ramifications for the processes of detemporalization. It might be argued that since Ptolemaic maps do not grid apocalyptic space, and, since they relied on the newly constructed self-generating and "timeless" typeface of the roman alphabet, these maps and their alphabetic indexes arrest the process of detemporalization under consideration here. Indeed, by "cleansing" cartographic space of the apocalypse and by cleansing the alphabet of the overdetermined territorial coding seen in the *Travels*, Ptolemaic maps might be understood as agents of amnesia that erased evidence of a troubling history of detemporalizing Jews—the problems of Gog and Magog, the Hebrew alphabet, and the Hebrew language. Ptolemaic maps, it is important to remember, did not circulate in isolation from other humanist mapping projects. I now turn to Christian-Hebrew studies to trace the borders of Ptolemaic cartography with philology.

Classical Christianity and the "Old Talmudic Jew"

The project of alphabetizing space and using the alphabet as a tool to map places coincided significantly within another humanist project, that of Christian-Hebrew studies. The mid-fifteenth century saw a renewed interest in the philological study of Hebrew scriptures and Kabbala among humanist scholars. These humanists were especially interested in the classicizing notion of a "prisca theologia," a search for an original Jewish antiquity recuperable prior to Jewish refusal of Christ as Messiah. In an early defense of Christian-Hebrew studies in response to the serious accusation of judaizing, the Florentine Hebraist Giannozzo Manetti (1396–1459) wrote polemically that he had to undertake his translation of the Psalter from the Hebrew to Latin because of the ignorance of the Jews who did not have the appropriate philological skills in Latin and Greek to deal with their own sacred text. The work of Christian-Hebrew studies would, according to Manetti, save the Psalter from the obstinacy of the Jews.[30] Manetti's defense marked one strand of Christian-Hebrew studies as imperial and appropriating rather than cooperative and tolerant—let humanist Christians undertake what contemporary rabbis were too philologically benighted to do properly. Thus Christian-Hebrew studies as a rationalized humanistic undertaking honed a sharp edge against the Jews, using Hebrew as a weapon against them.

Translation of the Old Testament from the Hebrew to Latin was not the only strand of Christian-Hebrew studies. The encounter of humanist philologists with Jewish mysticism was also compelling. Just as the Ulm 1486 edition of Ptolemy appeared, Pico della Mirandola finished his nine hundred conclusions on the Kabbala. In a theological family tree Kabbala provided for Pico the "missing link" between "prisca theologica," that is, pre-Crucifixion Judaism, and Christian revelation.[31] Pico thus sought to map a new "missing link" for Christendom, that of an "old Talmudic" Jewish body, infused with wisdom and untainted by the obstinacy of refusing to recognize Christ.[32] Pico constructs this phantasmatic body just as coeval medieval Jews were expelled at last from medieval mapping practices and, increasingly, from medieval territories as well.

What is the significance of this "old talmudic" body, a missing Jewish link, imagined and possessed by Christian-Hebrew studies in the latter half of the fifteenth century—a body that is invented as editions of Ptolemy's *Geography* roll off the press? It is not possible to answer such a question exhaustively here, but in the spirit of this essay, I turn to an exemplary moment to illustrate the crucial stakes at issue. In the city of Trent in 1475, town magistrates arrested all eighteen resident Jewish men and one Jewish woman to investigate the purported ritual murder of a two-year-old Christian boy, Simon. The inquest, torture, and executions of these Jews occurred at the crossroads of Italy and Germany, of humanist and scholastic thought, of local and papal contests, coincidentally at the very time that editions of Ptolemy's *Geography* were coming to press. Supporters of the trial and the cult of the boy-martyr Simon used the press (Latin and vernacular) to disseminate their propaganda. The extracted narrative of the trial record and the popular, printed iconography of Simon dwell on his circumcision at the hands of these Jews (Figure 12.6).[33]

The executed bodies of these Trent Jews, who died as persecution of Jews intensified in northern Italy and southern Germany in the latter part of the fifteenth century, need to be joined with the missing Jewish link, the old talmudic Jew, imagined by philologists such as Pico. Medieval Christians had relied on the body of the Jew to authorize the integrity of their chief ritual, the Eucharist. The Christian believed that the Jews' handling of the host could make it bleed, testimony of its cultic holiness. Moreover, only Jews could ritually circumcise a Christian boy to produce a facsimile of a little Christ for cultic, and very lucrative, Christian relic worship (Biddick, "Genders"). Christian-Hebraists changed these rituals of verification. Rather than have living Jews guarantee the optical efficacy of the Eucharist as a sacrament, instead these philologists—in an act of excessive philological mimesis that guaranteed their philology as a new textual sacrament—circumcised the Hebrew alphabet. In surgically reterritorializing the study of the Hebrew alphabet as a mathematical and philological science, philologists drained it of its blood, so to speak, just at the moment that their counterparts prosecuted Jews in inquisi-

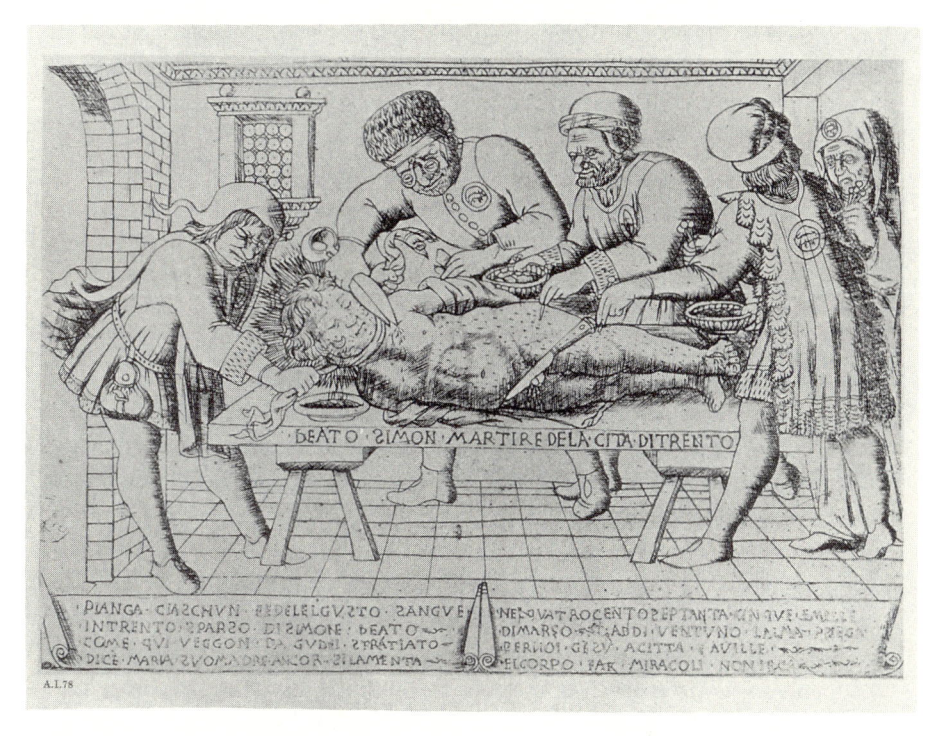

Figure 12.6. Engraving of the ritual murder of Simon of Trent, 1475. From Arthur M. Hind, ed., *Florentine Engravings and Anonymous Prints of Other Schools*, part 1 of *Early Italian Engraving*, vol. 11 (1938; reprint, Krauss, 1970), plate 74.

torial courts for draining young, male Christians—and Christendom itself—of blood.

In this way printing helped constitute, although it did not technologically determine, the further detemporalization of European Jews. As humanistic studies shifted its anxious need for origins to print-related activities, it diminished its need for sacramental presence to authorize symbols. Thus, the dissemination of a *printed* Christendom further enabled the expulsion and persecution of contempory Jews, since the antique "old talmudic" Jew, as a graphic phenomenon, could be much more reliably constructed, reproduced, and disseminated through print. Jews were becoming reduced to "paper Jews" for Christians. Hence the corporeal expulsion of Jews from humanist spaces has much to do with the mechanical reproduction and, more importantly, with the dissemination of print media during the first print-century. This media provided the opportunity to construct a seemingly timeless antique Jewish origin that could be controlled, circulated, and reproduced. Thus guaranteed of origin, cartographic space could become timeless, as it did in the Ulm 1486 edition of Ptolemy's *Geography*. Such a totalizing gesture, is, however, never truly verifiable. Perhaps, too, that is why the 1486 edition anxiously appends to itself the small tract on marvels and wonders. Perhaps, too, that is why the world map by John Ruysch, which was published among the *tabulae novae* of the Rome Ptolemy of 1508, located "iudei inclusi" in northern Greenland. The apocalyptic Jews return for a moment on the Ruysch map, which A. E. Nordenskiöld describes as "not a copy of the map of the world by Ptolemy, nor a learned master-piece composed at the writing-table, but a revision of the old maps of the known world, made on a Ptolemaic, i.e. on a scientific basis" (64).

Just as Petrus Alfonsi would colonize the place of the geographic observer by excluding Jews from it, just as Mandeville declared their language "not quite, not right" among "Western" alphabets, thus excluding Jews from the scriptural territory of civilization, so did a strand of humanist philology expel Jews from the expertise of Christian-Hebraic studies. Their Hebrew language could be turned against them through a philological technology. Ptolemy's widely disseminated *Geography*, published in northern Europe with its apparatus of alphabetized places in roman font, "cleansed" the space of the medieval world map and produced through the alphabet a territory that would refigure space, old and new, for colonization. Thus it can be said that the modernist fiction of the stand-alone map stands on displaced and dead bodies, real (such as the dead Jews of the Trent ritual murder trial) and phantasmatic (the medieval Jew). The chastening of space in the Ptolemaic project did the cultural work that paved the way for the intensification of Jewish expulsions in the late fifteenth century.

This double-barreled technology, alphabet as territory, cartography as alphabet, helped to spread the carnage so notable in that mid-millennium. Upon its export to the New World this cartographic technology produced, yet again, catastrophic effects, as the work of Walter Mignolo and others in an important book, *Writing without Words*, has taught us (also *Darker Side*; also Rafael). The power of alphabetic cartography persists even today, albeit very much embedded, in the Human Genome Project, a scriptural mapping technology par excellence (Fox Keller; Hall). Indeed, taking a cue from the film *Pulp Fiction* (1994), there are ways in which the Human Genome Project, as hegemonically conceptualized and funded, is very much about "getting medieval." An understanding of this cartographic genealogy, as I have tried to outline here, can contribute to the urgent political task of refiguring power in contemporary cartographies.

Notes

My deepest thanks to James Clifford, Donna Haraway, and colleagues at the Center for Cultural Studies at the University of California-Santa Cruz where, with the generous support of the Rockefeller Foundation, I undertook the research for this project. I am grateful to the editorial support of Sealy Gilles and Sylvia Tomasch who first invited me to present this essay in their session "Text and Territory" at the International Congress on Medieval Studies, Kalamazoo, in May 1995. Mary B. Campbell, the commentator of that session, has continued to provide me with invaluable inspiration, both scholarly and poetic. Meeting and talking with Marcia Kupfer was also one of the great boons of revising this paper. I remain indebted, as ever, to Kerry Walk for her wisdom.

1. On *mappae mundi*, see Kupfer; and Woodward.

2. I use the word "colonize" to think about systemic domination and subordination whereby "to colonize" means to disempower psychically as well as corporeally. Suleri has called this undoing, with its disavowed crisscrossing of identification and desire, colonialism's "intimate terror" (28). Many medievalists either reject the notion of medieval colonialism as oxymoronic, indeed anachronistic, or they draw sharp differences between modern and medieval colonialism (see Bartlett, 306–14). Such arguments frequently rely uncritically on the work of Anderson, who has linked colonialism with the project of nation. Such linkage is too rigid, I argue, for it dehistoricizes colonial processes and colonized peoples. The periodization of colonialism and ethnography begins to look very different if one includes Jews. On this important point, see Efron; Daniel Boyarin; Jonathan Boyarin, 52–76.

3. On astrolabes, see Sarton; Hartner; North; Gandz; Gunther, *The Astrolabes of the World*, and *Chaucer and Messahalla*. The main part of the astrolabe, its inner surface is called the "mother" ("mater" in Latin; "umm" in Arabic). The first Latin account of the astrolabe appears in *De mensura astrolabii* (1040) by Hermann Contractus, of the monastery school of Reichenau (Hartner, 290); second was Adelard of Bath's treatise, circa 1142–46 (Sarton, 2.1668).

4. "Et hoc ergo certe non abnego, tuo namque ipsius gladio occidere te multum cupio" (*Patrologia Latina* 157.539h; hereafter cited as PL followed by volume and column numbers) [I (Petrus) certainly do not deny this, for I strongly desire to kill you with your own sword].

5. On Christian-Jewish polemic, specifically those of Petrus Alfonsi and Gilbert Crispin, see Funkenstein; Abulafia, "Jewish-Christian Disputations," and "Bodies in the Jewish-Christian Debate"; Dahan, *La Polémique chrétienne*, and *Les Intellectuels chrétiens*; Grabois; Tolan; and Blumenkranz, *Disputatio*. Alfonsi's popular polemic (PL 157.527–672) continued to be copied through the fifteenth century, traveling alone in only 14 percent of the instances; of the sixty-eight medieval copies bound with other material, eight (12 percent) occurred with texts of the Victorine canons.

6. See Barkai; Levy; Goldstein. The earliest surviving astrolabe dates from 984. I am interested in the proliferation of astrolabes after this date in cross-cultural spaces of Islamic-Christian-Jewish contact. Gunther describes six astrolabes from the eleventh century; astrolabes inscribed with Hebrew lettering postdate the twelfth century (Gunther, *Astrolabes*, 302–4).

7. Alfonsi is not known to have written a treatise on the astrolabe, but his English student, Walcher of Malvern, used the astrolabe, and another, Adelard of Bath, wrote a treatise on its use (Tolan, 42, 47).

8. On the fetish, see de Lauretis. The technologies that I am discussing dispossess and in so doing become fetish effigies "with no past and no future" (266). Through disincarnation of historical subjects, these technologies pretend to incarnate the "real" as object.

9. On "mappings" among the Victorines, see von den Brincken, "Mappa mundi"; Dalché; Flint, "World History," and "Honorius Augustodunensis"; also Kupfer.

10. Like the Eucharist, *mappae mundi* reminded Christians that they were making "progress"; see Southern, "Hugh of St. Victor."

11. In this essay, I am interested only in the intertwining of an apocalyptic tradition of Gog and Magog with the identification of Jews as the enclosed peoples of Gog and Magog. On the Beatus tradition, see Williams, *The Illustrated Beatus*. Andrew Runni Anderson offers a survey of the complicated medieval tradition of the enclosed peoples of Gog and Magog; but see Westrem, this volume, for other traditions as well as for some problems with this work.

12. See Goldberg, "The History That Will Be."

13. Important studies of the *Travels* include Campbell, *Witness*; Deluz; Greenblatt; Hanna; and Higgins, "Imagining Christendom."

14. On "astrological" theology, see T. Gregory; Flint, "World history"; Pomian; Smoller; McGinn; and North.

15. See Gow; DiMarco, n. 23.

16. No comprehensive study of the occurrence of the alphabets in Mandeville-texts exists, though some discussion occurs in J. W. Bennett, 65–66 and throughout; Letts, *Sir John Mandeville*, 151–60; and Deluz, 162–73. By circa 1390, Otto von Diemeringen's German translation includes alphabets for the Chinese and for Prester John; a Dutch version, copied in 1430, has seventeen alphabets (J. W. Bennett, 5). In this essay, I am interested in alphabetic allusions in the Hamelius edition (citations from this edition). On fonts in printed versions, see Marx, who notes that no movable Hebrew types were used in Christian books of the fifteenth century despite their availability.

17. On thirteenth-century Christian representations of cannibalism, see Guzman; and Tattersall. These texts frequently conflated the enclosed tribes of Gog and Magog with cannibals, as an inscription on the Hereford *mappae mundi* makes explicit: "[H]ere there are savages who feed on human flesh and drink human blood, accursed sons of Cain. God shut them in through the agency of Alexander the Great" (quoted from Guzman, 49). An intensifying anti-Semitic tradition identified Jews with cannibalism and European stories of Jewish blood-libel with the things of the last days associated with Gog and Magog.

18. A mid-fourteenth-century English astrolabe used the Gothic capitals of the alphabet to mark every fifteenth interval of the 360 degrees at the border of the astrolabe (see Gunther, *Astrolabes*, no. 299, for a photograph of the Painswick astrolabe). The alphabet begins, then, to mark important increments on the astrolabe; that is, the alphabet is colonizing the astrolabe itself at the same moment that the *Mandeville*-author oscillated between the astrolabe and the alphabet.

19. I am drawing on notions of deterritorialization in Deleuze and Guattari.

20. The traveler notes that the Arabic alphabet has four more letters than Latin, and English two more than Latin (Hamelius, 92); the implication is that the Latin

alphabet is exemplary, in comparison to which other alphabets have fewer or more letters.

21. I am drawing upon Taussig's notions of mimetic excess in European colonialism.

22. The Brussels manuscript is a copy of a late-fifteenth-century alphabet misattributed to Marie de Bourgogne. On fifteenth-century alphabets, see Dumon; Feld, "Constructed Letters," and "The First Roman Printers"; and Damiano da Moille, whose roman alphabet is the first printed version.

23. On the return of Ptolemy's *Geography* to the West and its printing history, see Babicz; Durand; Edgerton; Geanakoplos; Nordenskiöld; and Weiss. The first printed edition of the *Geography* with a definite date appeared in Vicenza (without maps) in 1475; the date of the Bologna edition is debated. There followed a Rome edition in 1478, a metrical version, Florence, 1480; Ulm, 1482, 1486; Rome, 1490, 1507; 1508; Venice, 1511; Strassburg, 1513, 1520, 1522, 1525. See Skelton for facsimiles of *Ulm 1482, Strassburg 1513, Florence 1482*. The *Geography* was retranslated and also published with other geographical treatises after 1500; see Stevens; also Stahl.

24. Jardine encourages the reader not to view the "edition" as an enclosed, self-contained entity but rather to question how we have arrived at such a modernist fiction of the book (175).

25. See Skelton's intro. to the facsimile of Berlinghieri's work. The Ulm 1482 version does not provide the reader with any editorial tools, such as alphabetized lists of provinces or of places within each of the regional sections; see Tedeschi.

26. For a very general introduction to typeface, see Martin, 303–5.

27. Regiomontanus used roman type fonts for printing scientific works, notably the *Astronomica* of Manlius.

28. This mini-encyclopedia, composed primarily of excerpts from Isidore, traveled with subsequent editions of Ptolemy's *Geography* to the Strassburg 1513 edition.

29. On alphabetization, see Daly; Illich; Illich and Sanders; and Miethaner-Vent.

30. On Renaissance Christian-Hebrew studies, see Bonfil, 145–78; Hsia, *Myth*; and Ruderman. On Manetti, see Dröge. On Pico, see Wirszubski.

31. It important to note that Pico relied on the translations of Flavius Mithridates, a Jewish convert, for his study of Kabbala. On Good Friday 1481, Mithridates preached a sermon to the popes and cardinals in the Vatican in which he presented "secret Jewish evidences from a pre-Christian 'old Talmud' confirming the mysteries of Christ's Passion" (Wirszubski, 106). See also Jerome Friedman; and McGinn, "Cabalists."

32. The "technological" means of arriving at this "old talmudic body" involved procedures through which the Hebrew language was converted into a number code. In his important study of Pico and Kabbala, Wirszubski has shown how the translations of Mithridates interpolated these "ciphering" practices during translation. Hsia has called Christian-Hebrew studies the "disenchantment" of Hebrew (*Myth*). According to Wirszubski, this disenchantment paradoxically involved its technologization through philology and natural magic: "Pico viewed Kabbala from an entirely new standpoint: he is the first Christian who considered Kabbala to be simultaneously a witness for Christianity and an ally of natural magic" (151).

33. On this trial, engravings, and the problem of inscription in Christian-Jewish ethnic conflict, see Biddick, "Paper Jews; and Hsia, *Trent 1475*, and *Myth*.

Bibliography

Abu-Lughod, Janet. *Before European Hegemony: The World System A.D. 1250–1350*. New York: Oxford University Press, 1989.
Abulafia, Anna. "Bodies in the Jewish-Christian debate." In Kay and Rubin, 124–37.
———. "Jewish-Christian Disputations and the Twelfth-Century Renaissance." *Journal of Medieval History* 15 (1989): 105–25.
Acta Sanctorum. Brussels: Culture et civilisation, 1965– .
Adamnan. *De locis sanctis*. Ed. and trans. Denis Meehan. Scriptores Latini Hiberniae 3. Dublin: Dublin Institute for Advanced Studies, 1958.
Adler, Alfred. "Enéas and Lavine: *Puer et Puella Senes*." *Romanische Forschungen* 71 (1959): 73–91.
Ælfric's Lives of Saints. Ed. Walter W. Skeat. Early English Text Society original series 82. 1885. Reprint, Oxford, 1996.
Ahmad, S. Maqbul. "Cartography of al-Sharīf al-Idrīsī." In Harley and Woodward, vol. 2, book 1, 156–74.
Aïtoff, Sr. Marie-Serge. *Ste. Françoise Romaine*. Bec-Hellouin, 1983.
Alan of Lille. *Anticlaudianus, or The Good and Perfect Man*. Trans., with commentary, James J. Sheridan. Toronto: Pontifical Institute of Mediaeval Studies, 1973.
Alberti, Leon Battista. *I Libiri della Familia*. Trans. R. N. Watkins as *The Family in Renaissance Florence*. Columbia: University of South Carolina Press, 1969.
Alfred. *King Alfred's West-Saxon Version of Gregory's Pastoral Care*, part one. Ed. Henry Sweet. Early English Text Society original series 45. 1871. Reprint, Kraus, 1978.
Almqvist, Bo. *Norrön niddiktning: Traditionshistoriska studier i versmagi*. 1. *Nid mot furstar*. 2.1–2 *Nid mot missionärer. Senmedeltida nidtraditioner*. Nordiska texter och undersökningar 21 and 23. Stockholm: Almqvist and Wiksell, 1965, 1974.
Ambrosiani, K. *Viking Age Combs, Comb Making and Comb Makers in the Light of Finds from Birko and Ribe*. Stockholm, 1981.
Anderson, Andrew Runni. *Alexander's Gate, Gog and Magog, and the Legend of the Inclosed Nations*. Cambridge, Mass.: Medieval Academy of America, 1932.
Anderson, Benedict. *Imagined Communities: Reflections on the Origin and Spread of Nationalism*. London: Verso, 1991.
Andersson, T., and K. I. Sandred, eds. *The Vikings*. Proceedings of the Symposium of the Faculty of Arts of Uppsala University, June 6–9, 1977. Uppsala: Almqvist and Wiksell, 1978.
Angeli, Giovanna. *L'"Enéas" e i primi romanzi volgari*. Milan: Riccardo Ricciardi, 1971.
Anglo-Saxon Minor Poems. Vol. 6 of *The Anglo-Saxon Poetic Records*. Ed. Elliott Van Kirk Dobbie and George Philip Krapp. New York: Columbia University Press, 1942.
Appel, Carl, ed. *Provenzalische Chrestomathie*. 6th ed. Leipzig: Reisland, 1930.
Aquinas, Thomas. "Utrum anima separata pati possit ab igne corporeo." *Summa theologica* (edition *a Leone XIII P. M.*). Vol. 5. Rome: Typographia Senatus, 1887.

---. "Whether the Separated Soul Can Suffer from a Bodily Fire?" *Summa theologica*. Trans. Fathers of the English Dominican Province. Vol. 3. New York: Benziger Brothers, 1948.
Arentzen, Jörg-Geerd. *Imago Mundi Cartographica: Studien zur Bildlichkeit mittelalterlicher Welt- und Ökumenekarten unter besonderer Berücksichtigung des Zusammenwirkens von Text und Bild*. Münstersche Mittlelalter-Schriften 53. Munich: Wilhelm Fink, 1984.
Asad, Talal. *Genealogies of Religion: Discipline and Reasons of Power in Christianity and Islam*. Baltimore: Johns Hopkins University Press, 1993.
Asser. *Alfred the Great: Asser's "Life of Alfred" and Other Contemporary Sources*. Ed. Simon Keynes and Michael Lapidge. New York: Penguin, 1983.
Atiya, Azia Suryal. *The Crusade of Nicopolis*. London: Methuen, 1934.
Augustine. *Basic Writings of Saint Augustine*. Vol. 1. Ed. Whitney J. Oates. New York: Random House, 1948.
---. *The City of God*. Trans. Marcus Dods. New York: Modern Library, 1950.
Babicz, József. "Donnus Nicolaus Germanus: Probleme seiner Biographie und sein Platz der Rezeption der ptolemäischen Geographie." In Koeman, 9–42.
Bacon, Roger. *Opus majus*. 2 vols. Trans. Robert Belle Burke. 1928. Reprint, New York: Russell and Russell, 1962.
Baetke, Walter. "Christliches Lehngut in der Sagareligion." In *Kleine Schriften: Geschichte, Recht und Religion in Germanischem Schrifttum*, 319–50.
Bakhtin, M. M. *Rabelais and His World*. Trans. Helen Iswolsky. Cambridge, Mass.: MIT Press, 1968.
Baldwin, John W. *The Government of Philip Augustus: Foundations of French Royal Power in the Middle Ages*. Berkeley: University of California Press, 1986.
Bammer, Angelika, ed. *Displacements: Cultural Identity in Question*. Bloomington: Indiana University Press, 1994.
Barkai, Ron. "L'Astrologie juive médiévale: Aspects théoriques et pratiques." *Le Moyen Âge* 43 (1987): 323–48.
Barlow, Frank. "The Effects of the Norman Conquest." In *The Norman Conquest: Its Setting and Impact. A Book Commemorating the Ninth Centenary of the Battle of Hastings*, 125–61. London: Battle and District Historical Society, 1966.
Barnes, Trevor J., and James S. Duncan, eds. *Writing Worlds: Discourse, Text and Metaphor in the Representation of Landscape*. New York: Routledge, 1992.
Barolini, Teodolinda. *The Undivine Comedy: Detheologizing Dante*. Princeton, N.J.: Princeton University Press, 1992.
Barry, Phillips. Review of Andrew Runni Anderson, *Alexander's Gate, Gog and Magog, and the Inclosed Nations*. *Speculum* 8 (1933): 264–70.
Barthélemy, Dominique. "The Aristocratic Households of Feudal France—Kinship." In Duby, *Revelations*, 85–155.
Bartlett, Robert. *The Making of Europe: Conquest, Colonization and Cultural Change, 950–1350*. Princeton, N.J.: Princeton University Press, 1993.
Bately, Janet M. "King Alfred and the Latin MSS of Orosius' History." *Classica et Mediaevalia* 22 (1961): 69–105.
---. "King Alfred and the Old English Translation of Orosius." *Anglia* 88 (1970): 433–60.
---. "Those Books That Are Most Necessary for All Men to Know: The Classics and Late Ninth Century England: a Reappraisal." In Bernardo, 45–78.

Beck, H., D. Ellmers, and K. Schier, eds. *Germanische Religionsgeschichte: Quellen und Quellenprobleme*. Berlin: Walter de Gruyter, 1992.

Beckwith, Sarah. *Christ's Body: Identity, Culture and Society in Late Medieval Writings*. London: Routledge, 1993.

Bede. *Historia Ecclesiastica Gentis Anglorum*. Vol. 1 of *Baedae Opera Historica*. Trans. J. E. King. Cambridge, Mass.: Harvard University Press, 1971.

Benediktsson, Jakob. "Markmið Landnámabókar: Nýjar rannsóknir." *Skírnir* 148 (1974): 207–15.

———. "Some Problems in the History of the Settlement of Iceland." In Andersson and Sandred, 161–65.

———, ed. *Íslendingabók. Landnámabók*. 2 vols. Íslenzk fornrit 1.1–2. Reykjavík: Hif Íslenzka fornritafelag, 1968.

Benjamin, Walter. *Illuminations*. Trans. Harry Zohn. New York: Harcourt, Brace and World, 1968.

Bennett, Josephine Waters. *The Rediscovery of Sir John Mandeville*. MLA Monograph Ser. 19. New York: MLA, 1954.

Bennett, Judith. "The Village Ale-Wife: Women and Brewing in Fourteenth-Century England." In Hanawalt, 20–35.

Bernard of Clairvaux. *Sermones super Cantica Canticarum. Patrologia Latina* 183. Rome: 1957.

Bernardo, Aldo, ed. *The Classics in the Middle Ages*. Binghamton, N.Y.: Medieval and Renaissance Texts and Studies, 1990.

Berryman, John. *77 Dream Songs*. New York: Farrar, Strauss and Giroux, 1964.

Bevan, W. L., and H. W. Phillott. *Mediaeval Geography: An Essay in Illustration of the Hereford Mappa Mundi*. 1873. Reprint, Amsterdam: Meridian, 1969.

Bezzola, Reto R. *Les Origines et la formation de la littérature courtoise en Occident (500–1200)*. 3 vols. in 5 parts. Paris: Champion, 1944–63.

Biddick, Kathleen. "Genders, Bodies, Borders: Technologies of the Visible." *Speculum* 68 (1993): 389–418.

———. "Paper Jews: Inscription/Ethnicity/Ethnography." *Art Bulletin* 78 (1996): 594–99.

Bigalli, Davide. *I Tartari e l'Apocalisse: Ricerche sull'escatalogia in Adamo Marsh e Ruggero Bacone*. Florence: La Nuova Italiana, 1971.

Birns, Nicholas. "The Trojan Myth: Postmodern Reverberations." *Exemplaria* 5 (1993): 45–78.

Bleeth, Kenneth. "Narrator and Landscape in the Commedia: An Approach to Dante's Earthly Paradise." *Dante Studies* 88 (1970): 31–50.

Bloch, R. Howard. *Etymologies and Genealogies: A Literary Anthropology of the French Middle Ages*. Chicago: University of Chicago Press, 1983.

———. *Medieval Misogyny and the Invention of Western Romantic Love*. Chicago: University of Chicago Press, 1991.

Blumenfeld-Kosinski, Renate. "Old French Narrative Genres: Towards the Definition of the *Roman Antique*." *Romance Philology* 34 (1980): 143–59.

Blumenkranz, Bernhard. *Disputatio Iudei et Christiani Gilberti Crispini*. Antwerp: Spectrum, 1956.

———. *Juden und Judentum in der mittelalterlichen Kunst*. Stuttgart: Kohlhammer, 1965.

———. *Le Juif médiévale au miroir de l'art chrétien*. Paris: Études Augustiniennes, 1966.
———. "Synagoga méconnue, Synagoga inconnue." *Revue des Études Juives* 125 (1966): 35–49.
Blunt, Alison, and Gillian Rose, eds. *Writing Women and Space: Colonial and Postcolonial Geographies*. New York: Guilford Press, 1994.
Bonfil, Robert. *Jewish Life in Renaissance Italy*. Berkeley: University of California Press, 1994.
Boone, Elizabeth Hill, and Walter D. Mignolo, eds. *Writing Without Words: Alternative Literacies in Mesoamerica and the Andes*. Durham, N.C.: Duke University Press, 1994.
Boorstin, Daniel J. *The Discoverers*. New York: Random House, 1983.
Borges, Jorge Luis. *A Universal History of Infamy*. New York: Dutton, 1972.
Boswell, John. *Christianity, Social Tolerance, and Homosexuality: Gay People in Western Europe from the Beginning of the Christian Era to the Fourteenth Century*. Chicago: University of Chicago Press, 1980.
Bosworth, Joseph, trans. and ed. *A Description of Europe, Africa, etc., by Alfred the Great*. London: Longmans, 1855.
Boyarin, Daniel. "'Épater l'embourgeoisement': Freud, Gender and the (DE)Colonized Psyche." *Diacritics* 24 (1994): 17–41.
Boyarin, Jonathan. *Storm from Paradise: The Politics of Jewish Memory*. Minneapolis: University of Minnesota Press, 1992.
Bray, Alan. *Homosexuality in Renaissance England*. London: Gay Men's Press, 1982.
Breisach, Ernst, ed. *Classical Rhetoric and Medieval Historiography*. Studies in Medieval Culture. Kalamazoo, Mich.: Medieval Institute, 1985.
Bremer, Ernst. "Mandeville, Jean de (John, Johannes von)." In *Die deutsche Literatur des Mittelalters: Verfasserlexikon*. Vol. 5. 2d ed. Ed. Kurt Ruh, et al. Col. 1201–14. Berlin: Walter de Gruyter, 1985.
Brincken, Anna-Dorothee von den. "Die Ausbildung konventioneller Zeichen und Farbgebungen in der Universalkartographie des Mittelalters." *Archiv für Diplomatik Schriftgeschichte Siegel- und Wappenkunde* 16 (1970): 325–49.
———. *Fines Terrae: Die Enden der Erde und der vierte Kontinent auf mittelalterlichen Weltkarten*. Monumenta Germaniae Historica, Schriften 36. Hanover: Hahn, 1992.
———. "Mappa mundi und Chronographia: Studien zur imago mundi des abendländischen Mittelalters." *Deutsches Archiv für Erforschung des Mittelalters* 24 (1968): 118–86.
———. "'... Ut describeretur universus orbis': Zur Universalkartographie des Mittelalters." In Zimmermann, 249–78.
Brooks, Peter. *Reading for the Plot: Design and Intention in Narratives*. New York: Knopf, 1984.
Brown, Peter. *The Cult of the Saints: Its Rise and Function in Latin Christianity*. Chicago: University of Chicago Press, 1981.
———. *Religion and Society in the Age of Augustine*. London: Faber and Faber, 1972.
Brownlee, Marina S., Kevin Brownlee, and Stephen G. Nichols, eds. *The New Medievalism*. Baltimore: Johns Hopkins University Press, 1991.
Brundage, James A. *Law, Sex, and Christian Society in Medieval Europe*. Chicago: University of Chicago Press, 1987.

Bullough, Vern L. *Sex, Society, and History*. New York: Science History Publications, 1976.
Burgwinkle, William E. "Ethics and the Courtly Lady." *Hawaii Review* 30 (1990): 72–129.
———. "Knighting the Classical Hero: Homo/Hetero Affectivity in *Enéas*." *Exemplaria* 5 (1993): 1–43.
Buridant, Claude, ed. *La Lexicographie au Moyen Âge*. Lille: Presses Universitaires, 1986.
Burns, E. Jane. "The Man behind the Lady in the Troubadour Lyric." *Romance Notes* 25 (1984): 254–70.
Butler, Judith. "Desire." In Lentricchia and McLaughlin, 369–86.
———. "Imitation and Gender Insubordination." In Fuss.
Bynum, Caroline Walker. "The Female Body and Religious Practice in the Later Middle Ages." In Feher, Naddaff, and Tazi, 160–219.
———. *Fragmentation and Redemption*. New York: Zone Books, 1992.
———. *Holy Feast and Holy Fast: The Religious Significance of Food to Medieval Women*. Berkeley: University of California Press, 1987.
———. *Jesus as Mother*. Berkeley: University of California Press, 1982.
Byock, Jesse. *Medieval Iceland: Society, Sagas, and Power*. Berkeley: University of California Press, 1988.
Caesarius of Arles. *Regula sanctarum virginum*. Vol. 2 of *Opera Omnia*, ed. G. Morin, 101–27.
Camille, Michael. *The Gothic Idol: Ideology and Image-making in Medieval Art*. Cambridge: Cambridge University Press, 1989.
Campbell, Mary B. " 'The Object of One's Gaze': Landscape, Writing, and Early Medieval Pilgrimage." In Westrem, 3–15.
———. *The Witness and the Other World: Exotic European Travel Writing, 400–1600*. Ithaca, N.Y.: Cornell University Press, 1988.
Campbell, Tony. *The Earliest Printed Maps, 1472–1500*. Berkeley: University of California Press, 1987.
———. "Portolan Charts from the Late Thirteenth Century to 1500." In Harley and Woodward, vol. 1, 371–463.
Cary, George. *The Medieval Alexander*. 1956. Reprint, Cambridge: Cambridge University Press, 1967.
Caviness, Madeline H. "Patron or Matron? A Capetian Bride and a Vade Mecum for Her Marriage Bed." *Speculum* 68 (1993): 333–63.
Cervigni, Dino. "The Muted Self-Referentiality of Dante's Lucifer." *Dante Studies* 107 (1989): 45–74.
Chekin, Leonid. "Christian of Stavelot and the Conversion of Gog and Magog: A Study of the Ninth-Century Reference to Judaism Among the Khazars." *Russia Mediaevalis* 9 (1997): 13–36.
Cheyette, Fredric L., ed. *Lordship and Community in Medieval Europe*. New York: Holt, Rinehart and Winston, 1968.
Cholakian, Rouben, *The Troubadour Lyric: A Psychocritical Reading*. New York: Manchester University Press, 1990.
Christian of Stavelot [Christianus Druthmarus]. *Expositio in Matthæum Evangelistam*. PL 106:1259–1504.

Clover, Carol J. "Regardless of Sex: Men, Women and Power in Early Northern Europe." *Speculum* 68 (1993): 364-88. Reprinted in *Studying Medieval Women: Sex, Gender, Feminism*, ed. Nancy F. Partner, 61-85. Cambridge, Mass.: Medieval Academy of America, 1993.

Clunies Ross, Margaret. "The Development of Old Norse Textual Worlds: Genealogical Structure as a Principle of Literary Organisation in Early Iceland." *Journal of English and Germanic Philology* 92 (1993): 372-85.

———. "Hildr's Ring: A Problem in *Ragnarsdrápa*." *Mediaeval Scandinavia* 6 (1973): 75-92.

———. "The Myth of Gefjon and Gylfi and Its Function in Snorra Edda and Heimskringla." *Arkiv för nordisk filologi* 93 (1978): 149-65.

———. "Þórr's Honour." In Uecker, 48-76.

Cohen, Jeremy. *The Friars and the Jews: The Evolution of Medieval Anti-Judaism*. Ithaca, N.Y.: Cornell University Press, 1982.

Cohen, Sherrill. *The Evolution of Women's Asylums Since 1500: From Refuges for Ex-Prostitutes to Shelters for Battered Women*. New York: Oxford University Press, 1992.

Conner, Patrick W., ed. *The Abdingdon Chronicle: AD 956-106*. Vol. 10 of *The Anglo-Saxon Chronicle: A Collaborative Edition*. Cambridge: D. S. Brewer, 1996.

Copeland, Rita. *Rhetoric, Hermeneutics, and Translation in the Middle Ages: Academic Traditions and Vernacular texts*. Cambridge: Cambridge University Press, 1991.

———. "Rhetoric and Vernacular Translation in the Middle Ages." *Studies in the Age of Chaucer* 9 (1987): 41-75.

Cormier, Raymond J. *One Heart One Mind: The Rebirth of Virgil's Hero in Medieval French Romance*. University, Miss.: Romance Monographs, Inc., 1973.

Crane, Susan. *Gender and Romance in Chaucer's "Canterbury Tales."* Princeton, N.J.: Princeton University Press, 1994.

Crew, Raymond, and Nicholas H. Steneck, eds. *Society and History: Essays by Sylvia Thrupp*. Ann Arbor: University of Michigan Press, 1977.

Crone, Gerald P. "New Light on the Hereford Map." *Geographical Journal* 131 (1965): 447-62.

———. *The World Map of Richard of Haldingham in Hereford Cathedral*. Reproductions of Early Manuscript Maps 3. London: Royal Geographical Society, 1954.

Dahan, Gilbert. "Exégèse et polémique dans les commentaires de la *Genèse* d'Étienne Langton." In Dahan, *Les Juifs*.

———. *Les Intellectuels chrétiens et les juifs au moyen âge*. Paris: Cerf, 1990.

———. *La Polémique chrétienne contre le judaïsme au moyen âge*. Paris: Albin Michel, 1991.

———, ed. *Les Juifs au regard de l'histoire: Mélanges en l'honneur de Bernhard Blumenkranz*. Paris: Picard, 1985.

Dalché, Patrick Gautier, ed. *La "Descriptio Mappe Mundi" de Hughes de Saint-Victor*. Paris: Études Augustiniennes, 1988.

Daly, Lloyd W. *Contributions to a History of Alphabetization in Antiquity and the Middle Ages*. Collection Latomus 90. Brussels: Berchem, 1968.

Damiano da Moille. *The Moyllus Alphabet: A Newly Discovered Treatise on Classic Letter Design Printed at Parma, c. 1480*. Ed. Stanley Morison. New York: Pegasus, 1927.

Dante Alighieri. *The Divine Comedy*. 3 vols. Trans., with commentary, Charles S.

Singleton. Bollingen Ser. 79–81. Princeton, N.J.: Princeton University Press, 1970–75.

Davis, Charles. "The Florentine 'Studia' and Dante's Library." In di Scipio and Scaglione, 339–61.

Davis, R. H. C., and J. M. Wallace-Hadrill, eds. *The Writing of History in the Middle Ages: Essays Presented to Richard William Southern*. Oxford: Clarendon, 1981.

Deferrari, Roy J. *Hugh of Saint Victor on the Sacraments of the Christian Faith*. Cambridge, Mass.: Medieval Academy of America, 1951.

Deleuze, Gilles, and Félix Guattari. *Anti-Oedipus: Capitalism and Schizophrenia*. Minneapolis: University of Minnesota Press, 1983.

Deluz, Christiane. *Le Livre de Jehan de Mandeville: Une "géographie" au XIVe siècle*. Vol. 8. Louvain-la-Neuve: Publications de l'Institute d'Études Médiévales de l'Université Catholique de Louvain, 1988.

Demaray, John. "Pilgrim Text Models for Dante's 'Purgatorio.'" *Studies in Philology* 66 (1969): 1–24.

Depping, G. B., ed. *Règlements sur les arts et métiers de Paris rédigés au XIIIe siècle et connus sous le nom de Livere des Métiers d'Etienne Boileau*. Paris, 1937.

Devic, C., and J. Vaissette. *Histoire générale du Languedoc*. 16 vols. Toulouse, 1872–76.

DiMarco, Vincent. "The Amazons and the End of the World." In Westrem, 69–90.

di Scipio, Giuseppe, and Aldo Scaglione, eds. *The Divine Comedy and the Encyclopedia of Arts and Sciences*. Amsterdam: John Benjamins, 1988.

Donahue, Charles Jr. "What Causes Fundamental Legal Ideas? Marital Property in England and France in the Thirteenth Century." *Michigan Law Review* 78 (1979): 83–84.

Donoghue, Daniel. "Laʒamon's Ambivalence." *Speculum* 65 (1990): 537–63.

Dröge, Christoph. "'Quia Morem Hieronymi in Transferendo Cognovi . . .': Les Débuts des études hébraïques chez les humanistes italien." In Zinguer, 65–88.

Duby, Georges. *The Chivalrous Society*. Trans. Cynthia Postan. Berkeley: University of California Press, 1980.

———. "Dans la France du nord-ouest au XIIe siècle: Les 'Jeunes' dans la société aristocratique." *Annales: Economies, Sociétés, Civilisations* 19 (1964): 835–64.

———. *Hommes et structures du Moyen Âge*. Paris: Mouton, 1973.

———. "In Northwestern France: The Youth in Twelfth Century Aristocratic Society." In Cheyette, 268–90.

———. *Medieval Marriage: Two Models from Twelfth-Century France*. Trans. Elborg Forster. Baltimore: Johns Hopkins University Press, 1978.

———. *The Three Orders: Feudal Society Imagined*. Trans. Arthur Goldhammer. Chicago: University of Chicago Press, 1982.

———, ed. *Revelations of the Medieval World*. Trans. Arthur Goldhammer. Vol. 2 of *A History of Private Life*, ed. Philippe Ariès and Georges Duby. Cambridge, Mass.: Harvard University Press, 1988.

Dufournet, Jean, ed. *Relire le "Roman d'Enéas"*. Paris: Champion, 1985.

Dumon, Pierre. *L'Alphabet Gothique dit de Marie de Bourgogne: Reproduction du codex Bruxellensis II 845*. Antwerp: De Nederlandsche Boekhandel, 1973.

Dumville, David. "Genealogies and Regnal Lists." In Sawyer and Wood, 72–104.

Duncan, James, and David Ley, eds. *Place/Culture/Representation*. London: Routledge, 1993.

Durand, Dana Bennett. *The Vienna-Klosterneuburg Map Corpus of the Fifteenth Century: A Study in the Transition from Medieval to Modern Science*. Leiden: Brill, 1952.
Durling, Robert M. "Deceit and Digestion in the Belly of Hell." In Greenblatt, 61–93.
Earnshaw, Doris. *The Female Voice in Medieval Romance Lyric*. New York: Peter Lang, 1988.
Edgerton, Samuel Y. "Florentine Interest in Ptolemaic Cartography as Background for Renaissance Painting, Architecture, and the Discovery of America." *Journal of the Society of Architectural Historians* 33 (1974): 274–92.
Edwards, A. S. G., ed. *Middle English Prose: A Critical Guide to Major Authors and Genres*. New Brunswick, N.J.: Rutgers University Press, 1984.
Efron, John M. *Defenders of the Race: Jewish Doctors and Race Science in Fin-de-Siècle Europe*. New Haven, Conn.: Yale University Press, 1994.
Egeria. *Egeria: Diary of a Pilgrimage*. Ed. and trans. George E. Gingras. Ancient Christian Writers: The Works of the Fathers in Translation, 38. New York: Newman Press, 1970.
———. *Egeria's Travels*. Trans. John Wilkinson. London: Society for the Propagation of Christian Knowledge, 1971.
Eibl-Eibesfeldt, Irenäus. *Ethology: The Biology of Behaviour*. 2d ed. Trans. E. Klinghammer. New York: Holt, Rinehart and Winston, 1975.
Eisenstein, Zillah, ed. *Capitalist Patriarchy and the Case for Socialist Feminism*. New York: Monthly Review Press, 1979.
Eliade, Mircea. *The Sacred and the Profane: The Nature of Religion*. Trans. Willard R. Trask. New York: Harcourt Brace Jovanovich, 1959.
Elliott, Dyan. *Spiritual Marriage: Sexual Abstinence in Medieval Wedlock*. Princeton, N.J.: Princeton University Press, 1993.
Ellis, Roger, ed. *The Medieval Translator: The Theory and Practice of Translation in the Middle Ages*. Cambridge: D. S. Brewer, 1989.
Emmerson, Richard K. *Antichrist in the Middle Ages*. Seattle: University of Washington Press, 1981.
Emmerson, Richard K., and Bernard McGinn, eds. *The Apocalypse in the Middle Ages*. Ithaca, N.Y.: Cornell University Press, 1992.
Enéas: Roman du XIIe siècle. Ed. J. J. Salverda de Grave. 2 vols. Paris: Champion, 1983, 1985.
Ennen, Edith. *Frauen im Mittelalter*. Munich: C. H. Beck, 1985.
"En un vergier sotz fuella d'albespi." In Appel, 90.
Eusebius of Caesarea. *History of the Church*. Trans. George Williamson. Harmondsworth: Penguin, 1965.
Fabian, Johannes. *Time and the Other: How Anthropology Makes Its Object*. New York: Columbia University Press, 1983.
Faral, Edmond. *La Légende arthurienne: Études et documents*. 3 vols. Paris: Bibliothèque de l'École des Hautes Études, 1929.
———. *Recherches sur les sources latines des contes et romans courtois du moyen âge*. Paris: Champion, 1913.
Feeley-Harnik, Gillian. *The Lord's Table: Eucharist and Passover in Early Christianity*. Philadelphia: University of Pennsylvania Press, 1981.
Feher, Michael, Ramona Naddaff, and Nadia Tazi, eds. *Fragments for a History of the Human Body, Part One*. New York: Zone, 1989.

Feld, M. D. "Constructed Letters and Illuminated Texts: Regiomontanus, Leon Battista Alberti, and the Origins of Roman Type." *Harvard Library Bulletin* 28 (1980): 357–79.
———. "The First Roman Printers and the Idioms of Humanism." *Harvard Library Bulletin* 36 (1988): 10–91.
Ferrante, Joan. "Male Fantasy and Female Reality in Courtly Literature." *Women's Studies* 11 (1984): 67–97.
Fischer, Joseph. *Géographie de Ptolémée: Traduction latine de Jacopo d'Angiolo de Florence*. Paris: Bibliothèque Nationale, 1926.
Fisher, D. J. V. *The Anglo-Saxon Age*. London: Longman, 1973.
Fisher, Elizabeth. *Woman's Creation: Sexual Evolution and the Shaping of Society*. Garden City, N.Y.: Anchor Press, 1979.
Flint, Valerie. "Honorius Augustodunensis: Imago Mundi." *Archives d'histoire doctrinale et littéraire du Moyen Âge* 49 (Année 57) (1982): 7–153.
———. *The Imaginative Landscape of Christopher Columbus*. Princeton, N.J.: Princeton University Press, 1992.
———. "World History in the Early Twelfth Century: The Imago Mundi of Honorius Augustodunensis." In Davis and Wallace-Hadrill, 211–38.
Fontette, Micheline de. *Les Religieuses à l'âge classique du droit canonique*. Paris: J. Vrin, 1967.
Foote, Peter. Preface to Margaret Cormack, *The Saints in Iceland: Their Veneration from the Conversion to 1400*, ix–xvi. Brussels: Society of Bollandists, 1994.
———. "Wrecks and Rhymes." In Andersson and Sandred, 57–66.
Fox Keller, Evelyn. "From Secrets of Life to Secrets of Death." In Jacobus, Fox Keller, and Shuttleworth, 177–91.
Frank, Roberta. *Old Norse Court Poetry: The Dróttkvætt Stanza*. Islandica 42. Ithaca, N.Y.: Cornell University Press, 1978.
Freccero, John. *Dante: The Poetics of Conversion*. Ed. Rachel Jacoff. Cambridge, Mass.: Harvard University Press, 1986.
French, Dorothea R. "Journeys to the Center of the Earth: Medieval and Renaissance Pilgrimages to Mount Calvary." In Sargent-Bauer, 45–81.
Freud, Sigmund. *Civilization and Its Discontents*. New York: W. W. Norton, 1961.
Friedman, Jerome. "The Myth of Jewish Antiquity: New Christians and Christian Hebraica in Early Modern Europe." In Popkin and Weiner, 35–56.
Friedman, John Block. "Medieval Cartography and 'Inferno' XXXIV: Lucifer's Three Faces Reconsidered." *Traditio* 39 (1983): 447–56.
———. *The Monstrous Races in Medieval Art and Thought*. Cambridge, Mass.: Harvard University Press, 1981.
Froissart, Sir John. *Chronicle*. Vol 6. Trans. Sir John Bouchier. London: David Nutt, 1903.
Fuss, Diana, ed. *Inside/Out: Lesbian Theories, Gay Theories*. New York: Routledge, 1991.
Funkenstein, Amos. "Basic Types of Christian Anti-Jewish Polemics in the Later Middle Ages." *Viator* 2 (1971): 373–82.
Gallez, Paul. "Walsperger and His Knowledge of the Patagonian Giants, 1448." *Imago Mundi* 31 (1981): 91–93.
Gandz, Solomon. *Studies in Hebrew Astronomy and Mathematics*. New York: Ktav, 1970.

Gardiner, Eileen, ed. *Visions of Heaven and Hell before Dante.* New York: Italica Press, 1989.
Gaunt, Simon. "From Epic to Romance: Gender and Sexuality in the *Roman d'Enéas*." *Romanic Review* 83 (1992): 1–27.
———. "Gay Studies and Feminism: A Medievalist's Perspective." *Medieval Feminist Newsletter* (1992): 3–8.
———. *Gender and Genre in Medieval French Literature.* Cambridge: Cambridge University Press, 1995.
Geanakoplos, Deno J. "Italian Humanism and the Byzantine Émigré Scholars." In Rabil, 350–81.
Gennep, Arnold van. *The Rites of Passage.* Trans. M. B. Vizedom and G. L. Caffee. 1909. Reprint, Chicago: Routledge and Kegan Paul, 1960.
Geoffrey of Monmouth. *Historia regum Britanniae.* Ed. Jacob Hammer. Medieval Academy of America Publication 57. Cambridge, Mass.: Medieval Academy of America, 1951.
Gibb, Hamilton. "The Influence of Islamic Culture on Medieval Europe." In Thrupp, *Change*.
Gildas. *De Excidio Britanniae.* 1838. Reprint, Kraus, 1964.
Goldberg, Jonathan. "The History That Will Be." *GLQ* 1 (1995): 385–404.
———. *Sodometries: Renaissance Texts, Modern Sexualities.* Stanford, Calif.: Stanford University Press, 1992.
Goldin, Frederick. *The Mirror of Narcissus in the Courtly Love Lyric.* Ithaca, N.Y.: Cornell University Press, 1967.
———, ed. *German and Italian Lyrics of the Middle Ages: An Anthology and a History.* New York: Doubleday, 1973.
———, ed. *Lyrics of the Troubadours and Trouveres: An Anthology and a History.* New York: Doubleday, 1973.
Goldstein, Bernard R. *Theory and Observation in Ancient and Medieval Astronomy.* London: Variorum Reprints, 1985.
Goodich, Michael. *The Unmentionable Vice: Homosexuality in the Later Medieval Period.* Santa Barbara, Calif.: ABC-Clio, 1979.
Gow, Andrew Colin. *The Red Jews: Antisemitism in an Apocalyptic Age, 1200–1600.* Studies in Medieval and Reformation Thought 55. Leiden: Brill, 1995.
Grabois, Aryeh. "The *Hebraica Veritas* and Jewish-Christian Relations in the Twelfth Century." *Speculum* 50 (1975): 613–34.
Gravdal, Kathryn. "Camouflaging Rape: The Rhetoric of Sexual Violence in the Medieval Pastourelle." *Romanic Review* (1985): 361–73.
———. *Ravishing Maidens: Writing Rape in Medieval French Literature and Law.* Philadelphia: University of Pennsylvania Press, 1991.
Grayzel, Solomon. *The Church and the Jews in the XIIIth Century.* 1922. Rev. ed., New York: Hermon Press, 1966.
Greenberg, David F. *The Construction of Homosexuality.* Chicago: University of Chicago Press, 1988.
Greenblatt, Stephen. *Marvelous Possessions: The Wonder of the New World.* Chicago: University of Chicago Press, 1991.
———, ed. *Allegory and Representation: Selected Papers from the English Institute, 1979–80.* Baltimore: Johns Hopkins University Press, 1981.

Greenfield, Stanley, and Daniel Calder. *A New Critical History of Old English Literature*. New York: New York University Press, 1986.
Gregory, Derek. *Geographical Imaginations*. Cambridge: Blackwell, 1994.
Gregory, T. "Temps astrologique et temps chrétien." In Leroux, 557–73.
Grillo, Peter R. "The Courtly Background in the *Romance d'Enéas*." *Neuphilologische Mitteilungen* 69 (1968): 688–702.
Grosjean, Georges, ed. *Mapamundi: The Catalan Atlas of the Year 1375*. Trans. B. M. Charleston. Zürich-Dictikon: Graf, 1977.
Guibert de Nogent. *Autobiography: Self and Society in Medieval Europe*. Ed. and trans. John Benton. New York: Harper and Row, 1970.
Guidebook to Palestine. Trans. J. H. Bernard. Vol. 6 of Library of the Palestine Pilgrims' Text Society.
Guiraud, Jean. *L'inquisition médiévale*. Paris: J. Tallandier, 1978.
Gunther, Robert William T. *The Astrolabes of the World*. 2 vols. 3d ed. London: Holland Press, 1972.
———. *Chaucer and Messahalla on the Astrolabe*. Vol. 5 of *Early Science in Oxford*. Oxford: Oxford University Press, 1929.
Gurevich, A. I. *Medieval Popular Culture: Problems of Belief and Perception*. Trans. Janos M. Bak and Paul A. Hollingsworth. Cambridge: Cambridge University Press, 1988.
Guzman, Gregory G. "Reports of Mongol Cannibalism in the Thirteenth-Century Latin Sources: Oriental Fact or Western Fiction." In Westrem, 31–68.
Hakluyt, Richard, ed. *The Principall Navigations, Voiages and Discoveries of the English Nation (London, 1589): A Photo-lithographic Facsimile*. Hakluyt Society extra ser. 39. 2 vols. Cambridge: Cambridge University Press, 1965.
Hall, Stephen S. *Mapping the Next Millennium: How Computer-Driven Cartography Is Revolutionizing the Face of Science*. New York: Vintage, 1993.
Hallberg, Peter. "The Ship—Reality and Image in Old Norse Poetry." In Andersson and Sandred, 42–56.
Halperin, David M. *One Hundred Years of Homosexuality and Other Essays on Greek Love*. New York: Routledge, 1990.
Hanawalt, Barbara A., ed. *Women and Work in Preindustrial Europe*. Bloomington: Indiana University Press, 1986.
Hanna, Ralph, III. "Mandeville." In Edwards, 121–33.
Hanning, Robert W. *The Vision of History in Early Britain*. New York: Columbia University Press, 1966.
Hansen, Elaine Tuttle. *The Solomon Complex*. Toronto: University of Toronto Press, 1988.
Harksen, Sibylle. *Women in the Middle Ages*, trans. Marianne Herzfeld. Abner Schram, dist. by Universe Books, n.d.
Harley, J. B., and David Woodward, eds. *The History of Cartography*. Vol. 1: *Cartography in Prehistoric, Ancient, and Medieval Europe and the Mediterranean*. Vol. 2, book 1: *Cartography in Traditional Islamic and South Asian Societies*. Chicago: University of Chicago Press, 1987, 1992.
Hartmann, Heidi. "Capitalism, Patriarchy, and Job Segregation." In Eisenstein, 206–47.
Hartner, Willy. *Oriens-Occidens*. Hildesheim: Georg Olms, 1968.

Hastrup, Kirsten. *Culture and History in Medieval Iceland: An Anthropological Analysis of Structure and Change*. Oxford: Clarendon Press, 1985.

Hawkins, Peter. "Divide and Conquer: Augustine in the Divine Comedy." *PMLA* 106 (1991): 471–82.

Heers, Jacques. *Le Clan familial au moyen âge: Étude sur les structures politiques et sociales des milieux urbains*. Paris: Presses Universitaires de France, 1974.

Heffernan, Thomas. *Sacred Biography: Saints and Their Biographers in the Middle Ages*. New York: Oxford University Press, 1988.

Helgason, Jón, ed. *Skjaldevers*. Nordisk filologi 1. Copenhagen: Munksgaard, 1962.

Herlihy, David. *Medieval Households*. Cambridge, Mass.: Harvard University Press, 1985.

Higgins, Iain. "Imagining Christendom from Jerusalem to Paradise: Asia in Mandeville's Travels." In Westrem, 91–114.

———. *Writing East: The Fourteenth-Century "Travels" of Sir John Mandeville*. Philadelphia: University of Pennsylvania Press, 1997.

Higgonet, Margaret. "Mapping the Text: Critical Metaphors." In Higgonet and Templeton.

Higgonet, Margaret, and Joan Templeton, eds. *Reconfigured Spheres: Feminist Explorations of Literary Space*. Amherst: University of Massachusetts Press, 1994.

Hindman, Sandra, ed. *Printing the Written Word: The Social History of Books, circa 1450–1520*. Ithaca, N.Y.: Cornell University Press, 1991.

Hocquenghem, Guy. *Homosexual Desire*. Trans. Daniella Dangoor. 1978. Reprint, Durham, N.C.: Duke University Press, 1993.

Hodgen, Margaret T. *Early Anthropology in the Sixteenth and Seventeenth Centuries*. 1964. Reprint, Philadelphia: University of Pennsylvania Press, 1971.

Hollis, Stephanie. *Anglo-Saxon Women and the Church: Sharing a Common Fate*. Woodbridge: Boydell Press, 1992.

Holtsmark, Anne. "Vitazgjafi." *Maal og minne* (1933): 111–33.

Homer. *Odyssey*. Trans. Richmond Lattimore. New York: Harper and Row, 1967.

Howard, Donald. "The World of Mandeville's Travels." *Yearbook of English Studies* 1 (1971): 1–17.

Howe, Nicholas. *Migration and Mythmaking in Anglo-Saxon England*. New Haven, Conn.: Yale University Press, 1989.

———. *The Old English Catalogue Poems*. Copenhagen: Rosenkilde and Bagger, 1985.

Howell, Martha C. *Women, Production and Patriarchy in Late Medieval Cities*. Chicago: University of Chicago Press, 1986.

Hsia, Po-chia R. *The Myth of Ritual Murder: Jews and Magic in Reformation Germany*. New Haven, Conn.: Yale University Press, 1988.

———. *Trent 1475: Stories of a Ritual Murder Trial*. New Haven, Conn.: Yale University Press, 1992.

Huchet, Jean-Charles. "The Romances of Antiquity." *A New History of French Literature*, ed. Denis Holier et al. Cambridge, Mass.: Harvard University Press, 1989.

———. *Le Roman médiéval*. Paris: Presses Universitaires de France, 1984.

Hueffer, Francis. *The Troubadours*. 1878. Reprint, New York: AMS, 1977.

Hughes, Diane O. "Domestic Ideas and Social Behavior: Evidence from Medieval Genoa." In Rosenberg, 115–43.

Hughes, Robert. *Heaven and Hell in Western Art*. New York: Stein and Day, 1968.

Hultkrantz, Åke. *The Supernatural Owners of Nature: Nordic Symposium on the Religious Conceptions of Ruling Spirits (Genii Loci, Genii Speciei) and Allied Concepts*. Acta Universitatis Stockholmiensis. Stockholm Studies in Comparative Religion 1. Stockholm: Almqvist and Wiksell, 1961.
Ibn-Muqidh, Usamah. *An Arab Syrian Gentleman and Warrior in the Period of the Crusades: Memoires of Usamah Ibn-Muqidh*. Trans. Philip K. Hitti. Princeton, N.J.: Princeton University Press, 1987.
Illich, Ivan. *In the Vineyard of the Text: A Commentary to Hugh's "Didascalicon."* Chicago: University of Chicago Press, 1993.
Illich, Ivan, and Barry Sanders. *ABC: The Alphabetization of the Popular Mind*. New York: Vintage, 1988.
Ingledew, Francis. "The Book of Troy and the Genealogical Construction of History: The Case of Geoffrey of Monmouth's *Historia Regum Britanniae.*" *Speculum* 69 (1994): 665–704.
Isidore of Seville. *Etymologiarum sive originum libri xx*. Ed. W. M. Lindsay. 2 vols. Oxford Classicals Texts. 1911. Reprint, Oxford: Clarendon Press, 1985.
Itinera et relationes fratrum minorum saeculi XIII et XIV. Vol. 1 of *Sinica Franciscana*, ed. Anastasius van den Wyngaert et al. Florence: Collegium S. Bonaventura, 1929.
Itineraria et alia geographica. Corpus Christianorum Series latina 175. Turnhout, Belgium: Brepols, 1965.
Jacobus, Mary, Evelyn Fox Keller, and Sally Shuttleworth, eds. *Body/Politics: Women and the Discourses of Science*. New York: Routledge, 1990.
Jacques de Vitry. *The History of Jerusalem. A.D. 1180 by Jacques de Vitry*. Trans. Aubrey Stewart. Palestine Pilgrims' Text Society 11. 1896. Reprint, New York: AMS Press, 1971.
Jardine, Lisa. *Erasmus, Man of Letters: The Construction of Charisma in Print*. Princeton, N.J.: Princeton University Press, 1993.
Jerome [Hieronymus]. *Hebraicae Quaestiones in Libro Geneseos*. Ed. P. de Lagarde. Corpus Christianorum Series latina 72. Turnholt: Brepols, 1959, 1–56.
Jerome [Paula]. "Epistola CVIII" ("Ad Eustochium virginem"). In *Patrologia latina*, vol. 22, cols. 878–906.
Jesch, Judith. *Women in the Viking Age*. Woodbridge: Boydell Press, 1991.
Jóhannesson, Jón. *Gerðir Landnámabókar*. Reykjavík: Hif Íslenzka bókmenntafelag, 1941.
Jones, Thomas. "The Black Book of Carmarthen 'Stanzas of the Graves.'" *Proceedings of the British Academy* 53 (1967): 97–137.
Jones, W. Powell. *The Pastourelle: A Study of the Origins and Tradition of a Lyric Type*. Cambridge, Mass.: Harvard University Press, 1931.
Jónsson, Finnur, ed. *Den norsk-islandske skjaldedigtning*. Vols. 1A–2A (Tekst efter håndskrifterne), 1B–2B (rettet tekst). Copenhagen: Villadsen and Christensen, 1908–15.
Jónsson, Guðni, ed. *Grettis saga Ásmundarsonar*. Íslenzk fornrit 7. Reykjavík, 1936.
Jordan, William Chester. *Women and Credit in Pre-Industrial and Developing Societies*. Philadelphia: University of Pennsylvania Press, 1993.
Kaske, Carol V. "Mount Sinai and Dante's Mount Purgatory." *Dante Studies* 89 (1971): 1–18.

Kay, Sarah. *Subjectivity in Troubadour Poetry*. Cambridge: Cambridge University Press, 1990.
Kay, Sarah, and Miri Rubin, eds. *Framing Medieval Bodies*. Manchester: Manchester University Press, 1994.
Keith, Michael, and Steve Pile, eds. *Place and the Politics of Identity*. London: Routledge, 1993.
Kermode, Frank. *The Sense of an Ending: Studies in the Theory of Fiction*. New York: Oxford University Press, 1967.
Kilgour, Maggie. *From Communion to Cannibalism: An Anatomy of Metaphors of Incorporation*. Princeton, N.J.: Princeton University Press, 1990.
Kimble, George H. T. *Geography in the Middle Ages*. London: Methuen, 1938.
Klapisch-Zuber, Christiane. *Women, Family and Ritual in Renaissance Italy*. Chicago: University of Chicago Press, 1985.
Kleiner, John. "Mismapping the Underworld." *Dante Studies* 107 (1989): 1–21.
Kleine Schriften: Geschichte, Recht und Religion in Germanischem Schrifttum. Weimar: Bohlau, 1973.
Koch, Gottfried. *Frauenfrage und Ketzertum im Mittelalter*. Berlin: Akademie-Verlag, 1962.
Koeman, Cornelis, ed. *Land- und Seekarten in Mittelalter und in der frühen Neuzeit*. Wolfenbütteler Forschungen 7. Munich: Kraus, 1980.
Köhler, Erich. *L'Aventure chevaleresque*. Paris: Gallimard, 1974.
———. "Sens et fonction du terme 'jeunesse' dans la poésie des troubadours." In *Mélanges Crozet*.
Kolodny, Annette. *The Land before Her: Fantasy and Experience of the American Frontiers, 1630–1860*. Chapel Hill: University of North Carolina Press, 1984.
———. *The Lay of the Land: Metaphor as Experience and History in American Life and Letters*. Chapel Hill: University of North Carolina Press, 1975.
The Koran. Trans. N. J. Dawood. 1956. Reprint, Harmondsworth: Penguin, 1977.
Kowaleski, Maryanne. "Women's Work in a Market Town: Exeter in the Late Fourteenth Century." In Hanawalt, 145–64.
Kretschmer, Konrad. "Eine neue mittelalterliche Weltkarte der Vatikanischen Bibliothek." *Zeitschrift der Gesellschaft für Erdkunde zu Berlin* 26 (1891): 381–406.
Kupfer, Marcia. "Medieval World Maps: Embedded Images, Interpretative Frames." *Word and Image* 10 (1994): 262–88.
Kyng Alisaunder. Ed. G. V. Smithers. 2 vols. Early English Text Society original series 227, 237. London: Oxford University Press, 1947, 1953.
Lane, Frederic C. *Venice: A Maritime Republic*. Baltimore: Johns Hopkins University Press, 1973.
Langland, William. *A Vision of Piers Plowman: A Complete Edition of the B-Text*. Ed. A. V. C. Schmidt. London: Dent, 1978.
Langmuir, Gavin. *Toward a Definition of Anti-Semitism*. Berkeley: University of California Press, 1990.
Latour, Bruno. *We Have Never Been Modern*. Cambridge, Mass.: Harvard University Press, 1993.
Laurent, J. C. M., ed. *Peregrinatores Medii Aevi Quatuor*. Leipzig: Hinrichs, 1864.
Lauretis, Teresa de. *The Practice of Love: Lesbian Sexuality and Perverse Desire*. Bloomington: Indiana University Press, 1994.

Laurie, Helen C. R. "'Enéas' and the Doctrine of Courtly Love." *Modern Language Review* 64 (1969): 283–94.
Lawman. *Brut*. Trans. Rosamund Allen. London: Dent, 1992.
Layamon. *Brut*. 2 vols. Ed. G. L. Brook and R. F. Leslie. Early English Text Society new series 250, 277. London: Oxford University Press, 1963, 1977.
Lees, Clare A., ed. *Medieval Masculinities*. Minneapolis: University of Minnesota Press, 1994.
Lefebvre, Henri. *The Production of Space*. Trans. D. Nicholson-Smith. 1974. Reprint, Oxford, 1991.
Le Goff, Jacques. *The Birth of Purgatory*. Trans. Arthur Goldhammer. Chicago: University of Chicago Press, 1984.
Lejeune, Rita. "Jean de Mandeville et les Liégeois." In *Mélanges de linguistique romane et de philologie médiévale offerts à Maurice Delbouille*, 2.409–37.
Lentricchia, Frank, and Thomas McLaughlin, eds. *Critical Terms for Literary Studies*. Chicago: University of Chicago Press, 1995.
Leporace, Tullia Gasparrini, ed. *Il mappamondo di Fra Mauro*. Rome: Istituto Poligrafico dello Stato, 1956.
Lerer, Seth. *Literacy and Power*. Lincoln: University of Nebraska Press, 1991.
Lerner, Robert E. *The Power of Prophecy: The Cedars of Lebanon Vision from the Mongol Onslaught to the Dawn of the Enlightenment*. Berkeley: University of California Press, 1983.
Leroux, Jean-Marie, ed. *Le Temps chrétien de la fin de l'Antiquité au Moyen Âge—III-XIII siècle*. Paris: Centre National de la Recherche Scientifique, 1984.
Le Saux, Françoise. *Laʒamon's "Brut": The Poem and Its Sources*. Wolfeboro, N.H.: D. S. Brewer, 1989.
The Letters of Abelard and Heloise. Trans. Betty Radice. Baltimore: Penguin Books, 1974.
Letts, Malcolm. *Sir John Mandeville: The Man and His Book*. London: Batchworth Press, 1949.
Levy, Raphael. *The Astrological Works of Abraham Ibn Ezra*. Johns Hopkins Studies in Romance Literatures and Languages 8. Baltimore: Johns Hopkins University Press, 1927.
Lewis, Suzanne. *The Art of Matthew Paris in the "Chronica Majora."* California Studies in the History of Art 21. Berkeley: University of California Press, 1987.
Library of the Palestine Pilgrims' Text Society. 13 vols. 1887–97. Reprint, New York: AMS Press, 1971.
Lid, Nils. "Eldviging I." Kulturhistorisk lexikon for nordisk middelalder 3, cols. 579–81. Copenhagen: Rosenkilde og Bagger, 1958.
Liebermann, Felix, ed. *Die Heiligen Englands: Angelsächsisch und Lateinisch*. Hanover: Hahn'sche Buchhandlung, 1889.
The Life of Christine of Markyate: A Twelfth-Century Recluse. Ed. C. H. Talbot. New York: Clarendon Press, 1987.
Liggins, E. "The Authorship of the Old English Orosius." *Anglia* 88 (1970): 289–322.
Lindemann, Rolf. "A New Dating of the Ebstorf Mappamundi." In Pelletier, 45–49.
Lindow, John. "The Social Semantics of Cardinal Directions in Medieval Scandinavia." *Mankind Quarterly* 34 (1994): 209–24.
Lindow, John, L. Lönnroth, and Gerd Wolfgang Weber, eds. *Structure and Meaning*

in Old Norse Literature: New Approaches to Textual Analysis and Literary Criticism. The Viking Collection 3. Odense: Odense University Press, 1986.
Livingston, Charles H. "Fragment d'un roman de chevalrie." *Romania* 66 (1940–41): 85–93.
Lönnroth, Lars. "Dómaldi's Death and the Myth of Sacral Kingship." In Lindow, Lönnroth, and Weber, 73–93.
Lopez, Robert S., and Irving W. Raymond, eds. and trans. *Medieval Trade in the Mediterranean World.* New York: Norton, n.d.
Lowe, Lisa. *Critical Terrains: French and British Orientalisms.* Ithaca, N.Y.: Cornell University Press, 1991.
Lugano, Placido Tommaso, ed. *I Processi Inediti per Francesca Bussa dei Ponziani (Francesca Romana), 1440–1453.* Vatican City: Biblioteca Apostolica Vaticana, 1945.
Lyotard, Jean-François. *Heidegger and "the jews."* Trans. Andreas Michel and Mark S. Roberts. Minneapolis: University of Minnesota Press, 1990.
Maalouf, Amin. *The Crusades through Arab Eyes.* New York: Schocken Books, 1985.
Magerøy, Hallvard. *Omstridde spørgsmål i Nordens historie. 3. Norsk-Islandske problem.* Oslo: Universitetsforlaget, 1965.
Malone, Kemp. "On King Alfred's Geographical Treatise." *Speculum* 8 (1933): 67–78.
Mandeville, John. *The Bodley Version of Mandeville's Travels from Bodleian MS. e Musaeo 116 with Parallel Extracts from the Latin Text of British Museum MS. Royal 13 E. ix.* Ed. M. C. Seymour. Early English Text Society original series 253. London: Oxford University Press, 1963.
———. *The Buke of John Maundeuill being the Travels of Sir John Mandeville, Knight 1322–56. A Hitherto Unpublished English Version from the Unique Copy (Egerton MS. 1982) in the British Museum edited together with the French Text, Notes, and an Introduction.* Ed. George F. Warner. Westminster: Roxburghe Club, 1889.
———. *Liber Ioannis Mandevil.* Ed. Hakluyt, I:23–79.
———. *Mandeville's Travels.* 2 vols. Ed. P. Hamelius. Early English Text Society original series 153 and 154. Reprint, Millwood, N.Y.: Kraus, 1974.
———. *Mandeville's Travels.* Ed. M. C. Seymour. Oxford: Oxford University Press, 1967.
———. *Mandeville's Travels: Texts and Translations.* 2 vols. Ed. Malcolm Letts. Hakluyt Society 2d ser. 101–2. London: Hakluyt Society, 1953.
———. *The Metrical Version of Mandeville's Travels from the Unique Manuscript in the Coventry Corporation Record Office.* Ed. M. C. Seymour. Early English Text Society original series 269. London: Oxford University Press, 1973.
Mansi, J. D. *Sacrorum conciliorum nova et amplissima collectio.* 31 vols. Venice, 1959– .
Marcabru. *Poésies complètes du troubadour Marcabru.* Ed. J. M. L. Dejeanne. 1909. Reprint, New York: Johnson, 1971.
Marchello-Nizia, Christiane. "Amour courtois, société masculine et figures du pouvoir." *Annales: Economies, Sociétés, Civilisations* 36 (1981): 969–82.
Marci, Marcus, of Kronland. *Idearum operaticium idea.* Prague, 1635.
Margolis, Nadia. "Flamma, Furor, and Fol'amors: Fire and Feminine Madness from the *Aeneid* to the *Roman d'Enéas.*" *Romanic Review* 78 (1987): 131–47.
Martianus Capella. *The Marriage of Philology and Mercury.* Vol. 2 of *Martianus Capella and the Seven Liberal Arts.* Trans. William Harris Stahl and Richard Johnson, with E. L. Burge. New York: Columbia University Press, 1977.

Martin, Henri-Jean. *The History and Power of Writing*. Trans. Lydia G. Cochrane. Chicago: University of Chicago Press, 1994.
Martin Saint-Léon, Etienne. *Histoire des Métiers*. Paris: Guillaumin, 1897.
Marx, Alexander. "Some Notes on the Use of Hebrew Type in Non-Hebrew Books, 1475–1520." In *Bibliographic Essays: A Tribute to Wilberforce Eames*, 381–408. 1924. Reprint, Freeport, N.Y.: Books for Libraries Press, 1967.
Massey, Doreen. *Space, Place, and Gender*. Minneapolis: University of Minnesota Press, 1994.
Mayer, Anton. *Mittelalterliche Weltkarten aus Olmütz*. Vol. 8 of *Kartographische Denkmäler der Sudetenländer*. Prague: K. André, 1932.
McGinn, Bernard. "Cabalists and Christians: Reflections on Cabala in Medieval and Renaissance Thought." In Popkin and Weiner, 11–34.
———. "Portraying Antichrist in the Middle Ages." In Verbeke, Verhelst, and Welkenhuysen, 1–49.
McNamara, Jo Ann. "Canossa: The Ungendered Man and the Anthropomorphized Institution." In Ramet and Treadgold, 131–50.
———. "The Herrenfrage: The Restructuring of the Gender System, 1050–1150." In Lees, 3–30.
———. "Muffled Voices." In Nichols and Shank, 11–29.
Meissner, Rudolf. *Die Kenningar der Skalden; Ein Beitrag zur skaldischen Poetik*. Bonn: Schroeder, 1921.
Mélanges Crozet. 2 vols. Poitiers: CESCM, 1966.
Mélanges de linguistique romane et de philologie médiévale offerts à Maurice Delbouille. Gembloux: J. Duculot, 1964.
Mellinkoff, Ruth. "Judas's Red Hair and the Jews." *Journal of Jewish Art* 9 (1983): 31–46.
Menocal, Maria Rosa. *The Arabic Role in Medieval Literary History*. Philadelphia: University of Pennsylvania Press, 1987.
Meulengracht Sørensen, Preben. "Freyr in den Isländersagas." In Beck, Ellmers and Schier, 720–35.
———. *Saga and Society: An Introduction to Old Norse Literature*. Trans. J. Tucker. Studia Borealia, Nordic Studies 1. Odense: Odense University Press, 1993.
———. "Sagan um Ingólf og Hjörleif: Athugasemdir um söguskoðun Íslendinga á seinni hluta Þjóðveldisaldar." *Skírnir* 148 (1974): 20–40.
———. *Saga og samfund*. Copenhagen: Berlingske Forlag, 1977.
———. *The Unmanly Man: Concepts of Sexual Defamation in Early Northern Society*. Trans. J. Turville-Petre. Viking Collection 1. Odense: Odense University Press, 1983.
Michael, Ian. "Typological Problems in Medieval Alexander Literature: The Enclosure of Gog and Magog." In Noble, Polak, and Isoz, 131–47.
Michelant, Henri, and Gaston Raynaud, eds. *Itinéraires à Jérusalem et descriptions de la Terre Sainte rédigés en français aux XIe, XIIe et XIIIe siècles*. Publications de la Société de l'Orient Latin. Série géographique 3. Geneva, 1882.
Miethaner-Vent, Karin. "Das Alphabet in der mittelalterlichen Lexikographie: Verwendungsweisen, Formen und Entwicklung des alphabetischen Anordnungsprinzips." In Buridant, 83–112.
Mignolo, Walter D. *Darker Side of the Renaissance: Literacy, Territoriality, and Colonization*. Ann Arbor: University of Michigan Press, 1995.

———. "Signs and Their Transmission: The Question of the Book in the New World." In Boone and Mignolo, 220-70.

Miller, Konrad. *Die Ebstorfkarte.* Vol. 5 of *Mappaemundi: Die ältesten Weltkarten.* Stuttgart: Roth, 1896.

Mitchell, Stephen A. "On the Composition and Function of Guta Saga." *Arkiv för nordisk filologi* 84 (1984): 151-74.

Monneret de Villard, Ugo. *Il Libro della Peregrinazione nelle Parti d'Oriente di Frate Ricoldo da Montecroce.* Rome: Istituto Storico Domenicano, 1948.

Montclos, Jean de. *Lanfranc et Bérenger: La Controverse Eucharistique du XIe siècle.* Louvain: Spicilegium Sacrum Lovaniense, 1971.

Moore, R. I. *The Formation of a Persecuting Society: Power and Deviance in Western Europe, 950-1250.* New York: Blackwell, 1987.

Morgan, Alison. *Dante and the Medieval Other World.* Cambridge: Cambridge University Press, 1990.

Moseley, C. W. R. D. "Behaim's Globe and 'Mandeville's Travels.'" *Imago Mundi* 33 (1981): 89-91.

Mulholland, Mary Ambrose. *Early Gild Records of Toulouse.* New York: Columbia University Press, 1941.

Mundy, John H. *Europe in the High Middle Ages, 1150-1300.* 2d ed. London: Longmans, 1991.

———. *Men and Women at Toulouse in the Age of the Cathars.* Toronto: Pontifical Institute of Medieval Studies, 1990.

Neckel, Gustav, and Hans Kuhn, eds. *Edda. Die Lieder des Codex Regius nebst verwandten Denkmälern.* 5th ed. Heidelberg: Carl Winter Universitatsverlag, 1983.

Needham, Joseph. *A History of Embryology,* 2d ed. 1959. Reprint, New York: Arno Press, 1975.

Newman, Barbara. *Sister of Wisdom: St. Hildegard's Theology of the Feminine.* Berkeley: University of California Press, 1987.

Nichols, John A., and Lillian T. Shank, eds. *Distant Echoes.* Kalamazoo, Mich.: Cistercian Publications, 1984.

Nichols, Stephen, ed. *The Songs of Bernart de Ventadorn.* Chapel Hill: University of North Carolina Press, 1962.

Nicolaus of Lyra. *Postillae perpetuae super totam Bibliam.* Venice: Franz Renner, 1482-83.

Noble, David F. *A World without Women: The Christian Clerical Culture of Western Science.* New York: Random House, 1992.

Noble, Peter, Lucie Polak, and Claire Isoz, eds. *The Medieval Alexander Legend and Romance Epic: Essays in Honour of David J. A. Ross.* Millwood, N.Y.: Kraus, 1982.

Nordal, Sigurður, ed. *Egils saga Skallagrímssonar.* Íslenzk fornrit 2. Reykjavík: Hif íslenzka fornritafelag, 1932.

Nordenskiöld, A. E. *Facsimile Atlas to the Early History of Cartography.* 1889. Reprint, New York: Dover, 1973.

North, J. D. "Astrology and the Fortune of Churches." *Centaurus* 24 (1980): 181-211.

O'Faolain, Julia, and Lauro Martines, eds. *Not in God's Image: Women in History from the Greeks to the Victorians.* New York: Harper and Row, 1973.

Odo of Deuil. *De profectione Ludovici VII in orientem.* Ed. and trans. Virginia Gingerick Berry. New York: Norton, 1948.

Old English Exodus. In *The Junius Manuscript*, ed. George Philip Krapp. Anglo-Saxon Poetic Records 7. New York: Columbia University Press, 1931.

The Old English Orosius. Ed. Janet Bately. Early English Text Society supplementary series 6. London: Oxford University Press, 1980.

Olsen, Magnus. *Farms and Fanes of Ancient Norway: The Place-Names of a Country Discussed in Their Bearings on Social and Religious History*. Instituttet for sammenlignende kulturforskning, ser. A: Forelesninger, 9. Oslo: Aschehoug (W. Nygaard), 1928.

Orosius. *Pauli Orosii: Historiarum adversum paganos libri VII*. Ed. C. Zangemeister. Corpus Scriptorum Ecclesiasticorum Latinorum 5. Vienna, 1882.

———. *The Seven Books of History against the Pagans*. Trans. Roy J. Deferrari. Vol. 50 of *Fathers of the Church*. Washington, D.C.: Catholic University Press, 1964.

Otis, Leah L. *Prostitution in Medieval Society: The History of an Urban Institution in Languedoc*. Chicago: Chicago University Press, 1985.

Otter, Monika. "'Gaainable Tere': Symbolic Appropriation of Space and Time in Geoffrey of Monmouth and Vernacular Historical Writing." In Westrem, 157–77.

———. *Inventiones: Fiction and Referentiality in Twelfth-Century English Historical Writing*. Chapel Hill: University of North Carolina Press, 1996.

Overing, Gillian R., and Marijane Osborn. *The Landscape of Desire: Partial Stories of the Medieval Scandinavian World*. Minneapolis: University of Minnesota Press, 1994.

Paden, William D. "Rape in the Pastourelle." *Romanic Review* 80 (1989): 331–49.

———. "Reading Pastourelles." *Tenso* 4 (1988): 1–13.

———. "The Troubadour's Lady: Her Marital Status and Social Rank." *Studies in Philology* 72 (1975): 28–50.

———, ed. *The Medieval Pastourelle*. New York: Garland, 1987.

Pagden, Anthony. *European Encounters with the New World: From Renaissance to Romanticism*. New Haven, Conn.: Yale University Press, 1993.

Palmer, J. J. N. *England, France and Christendom, 1377–99*. Chapel Hill: University of North Carolina Press, 1972.

Pálsson, Hermann, and Paul Edwards, eds. and trans. *The Book of Settlements: Landnámabók*. Winnipeg: University of Manitoba Press, 1972.

Parker, Andrew, Mary Russo, Doris Sommer, and Patricia Yaeger, eds. *Nationalisms and Sexualities*. London: Routledge, 1992.

Parkes, Malcolm B. "The Paleography of the Parker Manuscript of the *Chronicle*, Laws and Sedulius, and Historiography at Winchester in the Late Ninth and Tenth Centuries." *Anglo-Saxon England* 5 (1976): 149–71.

Partner, Nancy F. *Serious Entertainments: The Writing of History in Twelfth-Century England*. Chicago: University of Chicago Press, 1977.

Paschasius Radbertus. *De Corpore et Sanguine Domini*. Ed. Bedae Paulus O. S. B. Corpus Christianorum Continuatio Medievalis 16. Turnhout: Brepols, 1969.

Patch, Howard. *The Other World According to Descriptions in Medieval Literature*. Cambridge, Mass.: Harvard University Press, 1950.

Patience. In *The Works of the "Gawain"-Poet*, ed. Charles Moorman. Jackson, Miss.: University Press of Mississippi, 1977.

Patrologie cursus completus . . . Series latina. Ed. J. P. Migne. Paris: Migne, 1844–55.

Patterson, Lee. *Negotiating the Past: The Historical Understanding of Medieval Literature*. Madison: University of Wisconsin Press, 1987.

Paula. *The Pilgrimage of the Holy Paula*. Trans. Aubrey Stewart. Vol. 1 of Library of the Palestine Pilgrims' Text Society. Reprint, New York: AMS Press, 1971.

Paxson, James J. "A Theory of Biblical Typology in the Middle Ages." *Exemplaria* 3 (1991): 359–83.

Pelletier, Monique, ed. *Géographie du monde au Moyen Âge et à la Renaissance*. Editions du Comité des Travaux Historiques et Scientifiques, Mémoires de la Section de Géographie 15. Paris, 1989.

Peter Comestor. *Historia scholastica*. PL 198:1045–1722.

Philippe de Mézières. "L'Épistre lamentable et consolatoires." In *Oeuvres de Froissart*. Vol. 16. Ed. Kervyn de Lettenhove. Brussels: Victor Devaux, 1872.

———. *Le Songe du vieil pèlerin*. 2 vols. Ed. G. W. Coopland. Cambridge: Cambridge University Press, 1969.

Phillips, J. R. S. *The Medieval Expansion of Europe*. Oxford: Oxford University Press, 1988.

Pipping, Hugo, ed. *Gutalag och Gutasaga jämte ordbok*. Samfund til udgivelse af gammel nordisk literatur. Copenhagen: Miller, 1905–7.

Plummer, Charles, ed. *Two of the Saxon Chronicles Parallel*. 1929. Reprint, Oxford: Clarendon Press, 1952.

Poerck, Guy de. "La Tradition manuscrite des 'Voyages' de Jean de Mandeville: À propos d'un livre récent." *Romanica Gandensia* 4 (1955): 125–58.

Poirion, Daniel. "De l'Enéide à l'Enéas: Mythologie et moralisation." *Cahiers de Civilisation Médiévale* 19 (1976): 213–29.

Poliakov, Léon. *The History of Anti-Semitism*. Vol. 1. Trans. Richard Howard. New York: Vanguard, 1965.

Polo, Marco. *Marco Polo: Il Milione*. Ed. Luigi Foscolo Benedetto. Florence: Olschki, 1929.

———. *The Travels*. Trans. Ronald Latham. 1958. Reprint, Harmondsworth: Penguin, 1979.

Pomian, Krzystof. "Astrology as Natural Theology of History." In Zambelli, 29–43.

Poole, Austin Lane. *From Domesday Book to Magna Carta, 1087–1216*. Oxford History of England. Oxford: Oxford University Press, 1955.

Popkin, Richard H., and Gordon M. Weiner, eds. *Jewish Christians and Christian Jews: From the Renaissance to the Enlightenment*. Boston: Kluwer Academic Publishers, 1994.

Postan, M. M., E. E. Rich, and Edward Miller, eds. *Cambridge Economic History of Europe*. Cambridge: Cambridge University Press, 1963.

Rabil, Albert, ed. *Renaissance Humanism: Foundations, Forms, Legacy*. Vol. 1. Philadelphia: University of Pennsylvania Press, 1988.

Rafael, Vicente. *Contracting Colonialism: Translation and Christian Conversion in Tagalog Society under Early Spanish Rule*. Durham, N.C.: Duke University Press, 1993.

Rafnsson, Sveinbjörn. *Studier i Landnámabók: Kritiska bidrag til den isländska fristatstidens historia*. Bibliotheca Historica Lundensis 31. Lund: Gleerup, 1974.

Ramet, Sabrina Petra, and Donald Treadgold, eds. *Render unto Caesar*. Washington, D.C.: American University Press, 1995.

Rauf Coilyear. In *Three Middle English Charlemagne Romances*, ed. Alan Lupack, 161–207. Kalamazoo: Western Michigan University Press, 1990.

Reiter, Rayna, ed. *Toward an Anthropology of Women*. New York: Monthly Review Press, 1975.

Renard, G. *Guilds in the Middle Ages.* New York, 1918.
Rich, Adrienne. "Compulsory Heterosexuality and Lesbian Existence." *Signs* 5 (1980): 631–60.
Richards, Jeffrey. *Sex, Dissidence and Damnation: Minority Groups in the Middle Ages.* London: Routledge, 1990.
Ridder, Klaus. *Jean de Mandevilles "Reisen": Studien zur Überlieferungsgeschichte der deutschen Übersetzung des Otto von Diemeringen.* Münchener Texte und Untersuchungen zur deutschen Literatur des Mittelalters 99. Munich: Artemis, 1991.
Ridyard, S. J. "*Condigna Veneratio*: Post-Conquest Attitudes to the Saints of the Anglo-Saxons." In *Anglo-Norman Studies IX: Proceedings of the Battle Conference, 1986,* ed. R. Allen Brown (1986): 179–206.
Roesdahl, Else, et al. *Viking og Hvidekrist: Norden og Europa, 800–1200.* Copenhagen: Nordisk Ministerrad, 1992.
Röhricht, Reinhold, and Heinrich Meisner, eds. "Ein Niederrheinischer Bericht über den Orient." *Zeitschrift für Deutsche Philologie* 19 (1886): 1–86.
Rollason, D. W. "Lists of Saints' Resting Places in Anglo-Saxon England." *Anglo-Saxon England* 7 (1978): 61–93.
Roper, Lyndal. *The Holy Household: Religion, Morals and Order in Reformation Augsburg.* Oxford: Oxford University Press, 1989.
Rose, Gillian. *Feminism and Geography: The Limits of Geographical Knowledge.* Minneapolis: University of Minnesota Press, 1993.
Rosenberg, Charles, ed. *The Family in History.* Philadelphia: University of Pennsylvania Press, 1975.
Ross, Alan S. C. "Ohthere's 'Cwenas and Lakes.'" *Geographical Journal* 120 (1954): 337.
———. *The Terfinnas and Beormas of Ohthere.* Leeds Texts and Monographs 7, 1940.
Ross, David J. A. *Alexander Historiatus: A Guide to Medieval Illustrated Alexander Literature.* Beiträge zur klassischen Philologie 186. 1963. Reprint, Frankfurt: Athenäum, 1988.
Rousse, Michel. "Le Pouvoir, la prouesse et l'amour dans l'*Enéas*." In Dufournet.
Rubin, Gayle. "The Traffic in Women: Notes Toward a Political Economy of Sex." In Reiter, 157–210.
Rubin, Miri. *Corpus Christi: The Eucharist in Late Medieval Culture.* Cambridge: Cambridge University Press, 1991.
Ruderman, Daniel B. "The Italian Renaissance and Jewish Thought." In Rabil, 383–483.
Ruggiero, Guido. *The Boundaries of Eros: Sex Crime and Sexuality in Renaissance Venice.* New York: Oxford University Press, 1985.
Russell, Jeffrey Burton. *Lucifer: The Devil in the Middle Ages.* Ithaca, N.Y.: Cornell University Press, 1984.
Russell, Josiah Cox. *Late Ancient and Medieval Population Control.* Philadelphia: Memoirs of the American Philosophical Society 160, 1985.
Sargent-Bauer, Barbara N., ed. *Journeys toward God: Pilgrimage and Crusade.* Studies in Medieval Culture 30, 1992.
Sarton, George. *From Rabbi Ben Azra to Roger Bacon.* Vol. 2 of *Introduction to the History of Science.* Washington, D.C.: Carnegie Institution, 1931.
Sawyer, P. H., and I. N. Wood, eds. *Early Medieval Kingship.* Leeds: Editors, 1977.
Schachterle, Lance, and Mark Greenberg, eds. *Literature and Technology.* Lehigh, Pa.: Associated University Presses, 1992.

Schiller, Gertrud. *Iconography of Christian Art.* 2 vols. Trans. Janet Seligman. Greenwich: New York Graphic Society, 1971.
Schulenburg, Jane. *Forgetful of Their Sex.* Chicago: University of Chicago Press, 1995.
Schwartzberg, Joseph E. "Geographical Mapping." In Harley and Woodward, vol. 2, book 1, 388–493.
Searle, Eleanor. *Predatory Kinship and the Creation of Norman Power, 840–1066.* Berkeley: University of California Press, 1988.
Sedgwick, Eve Kosofsky. *Between Men: English Literature and Male Homosocial Desire.* New York: Columbia University Press, 1985.
———. *Epistemology of the Closet.* Berkeley: University of California Press, 1990.
Seiferth, Wolfgang S. *Synagogue and Church in the Middle Ages: Two Symbols in Art and Literature.* Trans. Lee Chadeayne and Paul Gottwald. New York: Ungar, 1970.
Seymour, M. C. "The Scribal Tradition of *Mandeville's Travels* in England." In Mandeville, *Metrical Version,* 193–97.
———. "The Scribal Tradition of Mandeville's *Travels*: The Insular Version." *Scriptorium* 18 (1964): 34–48.
Shapiro, Susan E. "Ecriture judaïque: Where Are the Jews in Western Discourse?" In Bammer, 182–201.
Sigal, Gale. *Erotic Dawn-Songs of the Middle Ages: Voicing the Lyric Lady.* Gainesville: University Press of Florida, 1996.
Sinclair, John D., trans. *Purgatorio.* Vol. 2 of *The Divine Comedy of Dante Alighieri.* Oxford: Oxford University Press, 1961.
Skelton, R. A. *Claudius Ptolomaeus Cosmographia. Strassburg 1513* (facsimile). Amsterdam: Theatrum Orbis Terrarum, 1966.
———. *Claudius Ptolomaeus Cosmographia. Ulm 1482* (facsimile). Amsterdam: Theatrum Orbis Terrarum, 1963.
———. *Francesco Berlinghieri Geographia: Florence 1482.* (facsimile). Amsterdam: Theatrum Orbis Terrarum, 1966.
Smalley, Beryl. *The Study of the Bible in the Middle Ages.* Notre Dame, Ind.: University of Notre Dame Press, 1964.
Smith, Barbara Herrnstein. *Poetic Closure: A Study of How Poems End.* Chicago: University of Chicago Press, 1968.
Smith, Joshua Toulmin, ed. *English Gilds: The Original Ordinances of More than 100 English Gilds.* London: Early English Text Society, 1924.
Smith, Neil, and Cindi Katz. "Grounding Metaphor: Towards a Spatialized Politics." In Keith and Pile, 67–83.
Smoller, Laura Ackerman. *History, Prophecy and the Stars.* Princeton, N.J.: Princeton University Press, 1994.
Soja, Edward. *Postmodern Geographies: The Reassertion of Space in Critical Social Theory.* London: Verso, 1989.
Southern, R. W. "Aspects of the European Tradition of Historical Writing: 2. Hugh of St. Victor and the Idea of Historical Development." *Transactions of the Royal Historical Society* 21 (1971): 159–79.
———. *Western Views of Islam in the Middle Ages.* 1962. Reprint, Cambridge, Mass.: Harvard University Press, 1980.
Speer, Mary B. "Wrestling with Change: Old French Textual Criticism and Mouvance." *Olifant* 7 (1979/80): 311–26.

Spiegel, Gabrielle M. "Genealogy: Form and Function in Medieval Historical Narrative." *History and Theory* 22 (1983): 43–53.

———. *Romancing the Past*. Berkeley: University of California Press, 1993.

Stahl, William Harris. *Ptolemy's Geography: A Select Bibliography*. New York: New York Public Library, 1953.

Staley, Edgcumbe. *The Guilds of Florence*. London: Methuen, 1906.

Starr, Joshua. "The Mass Conversion of Jews in Southern Italy (1290–1293)." *Speculum* 21 (1946): 203–11.

Stein, Robert M. "Signs and Things: The Vita Heinrici IV Imperatoris and the Crisis of Interpretation in Twelfth Century History." *Traditio* 43 (1987): 105–19.

Stevens, Henry N. *Ptolemy's Geography: A Brief Account of All the Printed Editions down to 1730*. London, 1908.

Stock, Brian. *Listening for the Text: On the Uses of the Past*. Baltimore: Johns Hopkins University Press, 1990.

Strömbäck, Dag. "Att helga land: Studier i Landnáma och det äldsta rituella besittningstagandet." In *Festskrift tillågnad Axel Hägerström den 6 september 1928 av filosofiska och juridiska föreningarna i Uppsala*, 198–220. Uppsala: Almqvist and Wiksell, 1928.

Stuard, Susan Mosher. "To Town to Serve: Urban Domestic Slavery in Medieval Ragusa." In Hanawalt, 39–55.

Suleri, Sara. *The Rhetoric of English India*. Chicago: University of Chicago Press, 1992.

Sumption, Jonathan. *Pilgrimage: An Image of Medieval Religion*. Totowa, N.J.: Rowan and Littlefield, 1975.

Sveinsson, Einar Ól., and Matthías Þórðarson, eds. *Eyrbyggja saga*. Íslenzk fornrit 4. Reykjavík: Hif íslenzka fornritafelag, 1935.

Sweet, Henry, ed. *King Alfred's Orosius, Part One: Old English Text and Latin Original*. Early English Text Society original series 79. 1883. Reprint, New York: Kraus, 1974.

Switten, Margaret, ed. *The Medieval Lyric: Anthology I*. South Hadley, Mass.: Mount Holyoke College, 1988.

Tanner, Marie. *The Last Descendent of Aeneas: The Hapsburgs and the Mythic Image of the Emperor*. New Haven, Conn.: Yale University Press, 1993.

Tatlock, J. S. P. *The Legendary History of Britain: Geoffrey of Monmouth's "Historia Regum Britanniae" and Its Early Vernacular Versions*. Berkeley: University of California Press, 1950.

Tattersall, Jill. "Anthropophagi and Eaters of Raw Flesh in French Literature of the Crusade Period: Myth, Tradition, and Reality." *Medium Aevum* 57 (1988): 240–53.

Taussig, Michael. *Mimesis and Alterity: A Particular History of the Senses*. New York: Routledge, 1993.

Tedeschi, Martha. "Publish and Perish: The Career of Lienhart Holle in Ulm." In Hindman, 41–67.

Theoderich. *Guide to the Holy Land*. 2d ed. Trans. Aubrey Stewart. New York: Italica Press, 1986.

Thorndike, Lynn, ed. *University Records and Life in the Middle Ages*. 1944. Reprint, New York: Norton, 1975.

Thrupp, Sylvia L. "The gilds." In Postan, Rich, and Miller, 230–80.

———. "Comparison of Cultures in the Middle Ages: Western Standards as Applied to Muslim Civilization in the 12th and 13th Centuries." In Crew and Steneck, 67–88.

———, ed. *Change in Medieval Society*. New York: Appleton-Century-Crofts, 1964.

Tibbetts, Gerald T. "Later Cartographic Developments." In Harley and Woodward, vol. 2, book 1, 137–55.

Tolan, John. *Petrus Alfonsi and His Medieval Readers*. Gainesville: University of Florida Press, 1993.

The Tollemache Orosius. BM Additional Manuscript 47967. Ed. A. Campbell. Early English Manuscripts in Facsimile 3. Copenhagen: Rosenkilde and Bagger, 1953.

Tomasch, Sylvia. "*Mappae mundi* and the 'Knight's Tale': The Geography of Power, the Cartography of Control." In Schachterle and Greenberg, 66–98.

Topsfield, L. T. *Troubadours and Love*. Cambridge: Cambridge University Press, 1975.

Townsend, David. "Anglo-Latin Hagiography and the Norman Transition." *Exemplaria* 3 (1991): 385–433.

Trachtenberg, Joshua. *The Devil and the Jews: The Medieval Conception of the Jew and Its Relation to Modern Antisemitism*. 1943. Reprint, Philadelphia: Jewish Publication Society of America, 1983.

Trexler, Richard C. "The Foundlings of Florence." *History of Childhood Quarterly* 1 and 2 (1973): 259–84.

Turner, Ralph V. "Changing Perceptions of the New Administrative Class in Anglo-Norman and Angevin England: The *Curiales* and Their Conservative Critics." *Journal of British Studies* 29 (1990): 93–117.

Turville-Petre, E. O. G. *Scaldic Poetry*. Oxford: Clarendon Press, 1976.

Turville-Petre, Gabriel. "The Cult of Freyr in the Evening of Paganism." *Proceedings of the Leeds Philosophical and Literary Society* 3 (1935): 317–33.

Turville-Petre, Thorlac. *Alliterative Poetry of the Later Middle Ages*. London: Routledge, 1989.

Twain, Mark. *Innocents Abroad*. 1869. Reprint, London: Century, 1988.

Uecker, H., ed. *Studien zum Altgermanischen. Festschrift für Heinrich Beck*. Berlin: Walter de Gruyter, 1994.

Vance, Eugene. "Semiotics and Power: Relics, Icons, and the *Voyage de Charlemagne à Jérusalem et à Constantinople*." In Brownlee, Brownlee, and Nichols, 226–49.

Van Den Abbeele, Georges. *Travel as Metaphor from Montaigne to Rousseau*. Minneapolis: University of Minnesota Press, 1992.

Vaughan, Richard, ed. and trans. *The Illustrated Chronicles of Matthew Paris: Observations of Thirteenth-Century Life*. Cambridge: Alan Sutton, 1993.

Verbeke, Werner, Daniel Verhelst, and Andries Welkenhuysen, eds. *The Use and Abuse of Eschatology in the Middle Ages*. Louvain: Mediaevalia Lovaniensia. Ser. 1. Studie 15 (1988).

Verduin, Kathleen. "Dante and the Sin of Satan: Augustinian Patterns in *Inferno* XXXIV.22–27." *Quaderni d'italianistica* 4 (1983): 208–17.

Vincent of Beauvais [Vincentius Bellovacensis]. *Speculum historiale*. Vol. 4 of *Bibliotheca Mundi. seu Speculi Maioris*. Douai, 1624. Reprint, facsimile, Graz: Akademische Druck- und Verlagsanstalt, 1965.

Vita S. Umilianae de Cerchi. In *Acta Sanctorum*. May 21.

Vita s. Godelevae. In *Acta Sanctorum*. July 6.

Wace. *Le Roman de Brut*. 2 vols. Ed. Ivor Arnold. Paris: Société des Anciens Textes Français, 1938, 1940.

Walter, J. von. *Die ersten Wanderprediger Frankreichs: Robert von Arbrissel*. Leipsig: Studien zur Geschichtes der Theologie und Kirche 9, 1903.

Walters, Jonathan. "No More than a Boy: The Shifting Construction of Masculinity from Ancient Greece to the Middle Ages." *Gender and History* 5 (1993): 20–33.

Warner, Michael. "From Queer to Eternity: An Army of Theorists Cannot Fail." *The Village Voice Literary Supplement*. June 1992, 18–19.

Wars of Alexander. Ed. Hoyt N. Duggan and Thorlac Turville-Petre. Oxford: Oxford University Press, 1989.

Weiss, Robert. "Jacopo Angeli Da Scarperia (c. 1360–1410–11)." In *Medioevo e Rinascimento: Studi in Onore di Bruno Nardi*, 801–27. Sansoni: Firenze, 1955.

Westrem, Scott, ed. *Discovering New Worlds: Essays on Medieval Exploration and Imagination*. New York: Garland, 1991.

Whitelock, Dorothy, ed. *The Anglo-Saxon Chronicle*. New Brunswick, N.J.: Rutgers University Press, 1961.

Wickler, W. "Ursprung und biologische Deutung des Genitalpräsentierens männlicher Primaten." *Zeitschrift für Tierpsychologie* 23 (1966): 422–37.

Wilkinson, John, ed. and trans. *Jerusalem Pilgrimage, 1099–1185*. Hakluyt Society. 2d ser. 167. London: Hakluyt Society, 1988.

William of Malmesbury. *Chronicle of the Kings of England*. Ed. J. A. Giles. Bohn's Library. London: George Bell, 1895.

———. *De gestis regum Anglorum*. Ed. William Stubbs. Rolls ser. Reprint, London: Kraus, 1964.

William of Rubruck. "The Journey of William of Rubruck." Trans. by a nun of Stanbrook Abbey. In *Mission to Asia*, ed. Christopher Dawson. Reprint, Toronto: University of Toronto Press, for the Medieval Society of America, 1980.

Williams, John. *The Illustrated Beatus*. London: Harvey Miller, 1991.

———. "Purpose and Imagery in the Apocalypse Commentary of Beatus of Liébana." In Emmerson and McGinn, 217–33.

Wilson, Stephen, ed. *Saints and their Cults: Studies in Religious Sociology, Folklore, and History*. Cambridge: Cambridge University Press, 1985.

Winnett, Susan. "Coming Unstrung: Women, Men, Narrative, and Principles of Pleasure." *PMLA* 105 (1990): 505–19.

Wirszubski, Chaim. *Pico della Mirandola's Encounter with Jewish Mysticism*. Cambridge, Mass.: Harvard University Press, 1989.

Wolf, Armin. "News on the Ebstorf World Map: Date, Origin, Authorship." In Pelletier, 51–68.

Woodward, David. "Medieval *Mappaemundi*." In Harley and Woodward, vol. 1, 286–370.

Woolf, Virginia. *A Room of One's Own*. New York: Harcourt Brace Jovanovich, 1929.

———. *To the Lighthouse*. New York: Harcourt Brace Jovanovich, 1927.

Wrede, Henning. *Die antike Herme*. Trierer Beiträge zur Altertumskunde 1. Mainz am Rheim: P. von Zabern, 1985 [1986].

Wright, John Kirtland. *The Geographical Lore of the Time of the Crusades: A Study in the History of Medieval Science and Tradition in Western Europe*. New York: American Geographical Society, 1925.

Young, Robert J. C. *Colonial Desire: Hybridity in Theory, Culture and Race*. New York: Routledge, 1995.
Yunck, John A., trans. *Enéas: A Twelfth-Century French Romance*. New York: Columbia University Press, 1974.
Zacher, Christian K. *Curiosity and Pilgrimage: The Literature of Discovery in Fourteenth-Century England*. Baltimore: Johns Hopkins University Press, 1976.
Zaleski, Carol. *Otherworld Journeys: Accounts of Near-Death Experiences in Medieval and Modern Times*. New York: Oxford University Press, 1987.
Zambelli, Paola, ed. *Astrologi hallucinati: Stars at the End of the World in Luther's Time*. New York: Walter De Gruyter, 1986.
Zimmermann, Albert, ed. *Methoden in Wissenschaft und Kunst des Mittelalters*. Miscellanea Mediaevalia 7. Berlin: Walter de Gruyter, 1970.
Zinguer, Ilana, ed. *L'Hébreu au temps de la Renaissance*. New York: Brill, 1992.
Zink, Michel. "Une Mutation de la conscience littéraire: Le Langage romanesque à travers des exemples français du XIIe siècle." *Cahiers de Civilisation Médiévale* 24 (1981): 3–27.
Zumthor, Paul. *Essai de poétique médiévale*. Paris: Seuil, 1972.
———. "Intertextualité et mouvance." *Littérature* 41 (1981): 8–16.

List of Contributors

Kathleen Biddick is associate professor of history at the University of Notre Dame and director of the Gender Studies Program. Her forthcoming book, *Medievalism in Fragments* (Duke University Press), considers political links among disciplinary categories, periodization, and pleasure in medieval studies.

Mary Baine Campbell is associate professor of English and American literature at Brandeis University. Her publications include *The Witness and the Other World* (Cornell University Press, 1988), and a book of poems, *The World, the Flesh, and Angels* (Beacon Press, 1989). Her current book in progress, *Wonder and Science*, studies the mutual emergence of anthropology and prose fiction in early modern Europe.

Christine Chism is an assistant professor of English at Rutgers University. She is currently finishing a book on medieval alliterative poetry called *Historical Rivals: Alliterative Revivals*.

Margaret Clunies Ross, McCaughey Professor of English language and early English literature at the University of Sydney, is the author of six books, including *Skáldskaparmál: Snorri Sturluson's Ars Poetica and Medieval Theories of Language* (Odense, 1987) and *The Myths*, vol. 1 of *Prolonged Echoes: Old Norse Myths in Medieval Northern Society*, (Odense, 1994). Her present research projects include the second volume of *Prolonged Echoes* and an edited volume for Cambridge University Press, *Medieval Icelandic Literature and Society*.

Sealy Gilles is assistant professor of English at Westchester Community College. She has published on the Old English "Wanderer" and is currently working on a study of the performance of mortality and morbidity in Chaucer's *Troilus and Criseyde*.

Iain Macleod Higgins is associate professor of English at the University of British Columbia. He is the author of *Writing East: The Fourteenth-Century "Travels" of Sir John Mandeville* (University of Pennsylvania Press, 1997), and is currently preparing an annotated anthology documenting the reception of *The Book of John Mandeville* between 1375 and 1900.

Vincent A. Lankewish recently received his doctorate in English from Rutgers University. He is preparing a book-length analysis of representations of marriages between men, entitled *Strange Nuptials: Male-Male Desire, Marriage, and Genre in Victorian England*.

Jo Ann McNamara is professor of history at Hunter College and the Graduate Center of the City University of New York. She is the author of numerous articles on women in the Middle Ages and of *Sisters in Arms: Catholic Nuns through Two Millennia* (Harvard University Press, 1996).

Gale Sigal is the Zachary T. Smith Professor at Wake Forest University where she teaches in the English department and directs its Master's degree program. She is author of *Erotic Dawn-Songs of the Middle Ages: Voicing the Lyric Lady* (University Press of Florida, 1996) and coeditor of *Voices in Translation: The Authority of "Olde Bookes" in Medieval Literature: Essays in Honor of Helaine Newstead* (AMS Press, 1992).

Robert M. Stein is associate professor of languages and literature at Purchase College of the State University of New York and adjunct professor of English and comparative literature at Columbia University. He is working on a book-length study of the emergence of historical chronicles and chivalric romances in the twelfth century.

Sylvia Tomasch is associate professor in the English Department at Hunter College and advisor of its Master's degree program. Her book, *The Medieval Geographic Imagination*, is forthcoming from Stanford University Press.

Scott D. Westrem is associate professor of English and comparative literature at Lehman College and the Graduate School of the City University of New York. He has edited a collection of essays on exploration and travel literature, *Discovering New Worlds: Essays on Medieval Exploration and Imagination* (Garland, 1991), and his book *Johannes Witte de Hese's Itinerarius: An Extension of the Fourteenth-Century Pilgrim's Horizon* will be published by the Medieval Academy of America.

Index

abacus board, 1–3
Adamnan, *De locis sanctis*, 18, 35, 37–38
Ælfric, *De auguriis*, 171
Africa, 3, 112
al-Andalus, 121, 123
Alan of Lille, *Anticlaudianus*, 11 n.1
Alexander the Great, 116–39; as embodiment of chivalry, 136; as iconoclast, 117, 128–29; celestial, 135–36; Egyptian origins of, 116, 118; *Historia de preliis Alexandri Magni*, 57, 138 n.2; hybrid nature of, 119, 126, 136; *Iskandarnâmah*, 60; *Kyng Alisaunder*, 57; legends, 57, 60; oriental origins of, 116, 127; Walter of Châtillon, *Alexandreis*, 57
Alfred (king of England), 81–83, 85–86, 88–89, 92–94
Alliterative Revival, 116, 131, 136, 138 n.1
Almqvist, Bo, 168–69, 180
alphabet: as technology of dispossession, 276–81, 288; as territory, 290; cartography as, 290; Hebrew, 271, 276, 277, 279–81, 290; in *Book of John Mandeville*, 277–79; Latin, 281; print, 283–84
Amazons (Amasona), 54, 61, 65, 69, 71, 207
ancestor(s), 79, 85, 95; Alexander as, 136; as legitimizing land claims, 161; denial of, 128–29; Norse, spirits of, 160, 172; search for English, 106
Anderson, Andrew Runni, 56–57, 68
Anectanabus (in *Wars of Alexander*), 117–18, 127; death of, 128–29
Anglo-Saxon Chronicle, 80–81, 94–95
Anglo-Saxons, 79, 84–85, 88, 92, 109; and Normans 108–9
antipodes, 39, 43, 44, 47
anti-Semitism, 55, 65–71, 247–93
Aquinas, 24, 27–28 n.9; *Summa theologica*, 19
Ari Þorgilsson, 165, 174, 176
Arthur, King, 109–12
Asser, 92
astrolabe, 271–74, 276, 278; and alphabets, 279–81; and astronomy, 271; as fetish, 271
astrology: apocalyptic strain of, 273; as technology of dispossession, 276

Athelstan, 108
audience: Anglo-Saxon, 88, 91; for *Wars of Alexander*, 126, 136–37; invocation of, 173; of *Divine Comedy*, 247, 262–64; values of, 92
Auðr Ketilsdóttir (Unnr) (in *Landnámabók*), 160, 175–77
Augustine, 55, 67–68; on circumcision, 257; theory of evil, 256, 261

Bacon, Roger, *Opus majus*, 66
Baltic, 83, 85, 90, 95
Barolini, Teodolinda, 247, 263–64
Bately, Janet M., 81, 84
Bayezid (Lamorabaquy) (in Froissart), 119
Beatrice (in *Divine Comedy*), 15, 16, 26; body of, 19
Bede, 35, 37, 59, 83–85
Benjamin, Walter, 16, 26
Berengar of Tours, 102
Berryman, John, 26
Bevan, W. L., and H. W. Phillott, 30, 31
biology, Aristotelian, 144, 145, 151
Bleeth, Kenneth, 28 n.14
bodies: and family luck, 175; and souls, 19, 23–24; as metaphors, 23; fragments of, 100–103; monstrous, 101–3; of kings, 175; of nations, 104; of saints, 104, 106; of the wicked, 100–101; unbroken, 99
body: of Christendom, 125, 289; of fetus, 23, 26; of Jews, 255, 257, 288–90; of Satan, 255–58; of women, 186; signifying land, 237, 242; translation of, 114
Book of John Mandeville, The, 20; and astrology, 276; as analogue of *Catalan Atlas*, 49–50; as analogue of world maps, 31, 49, 50; as medieval multitext, 31–53; authorship of, 32; Behaim globe as analogue, 53 n.24; composite nature of, 32; interpolations in, 45–46; Jerusalem in, 33–51; Jews in, 68–70, 276–81; linearity of, 50; manuscript versions of, 32, 33, 40–49; printed versions of, 32, 33; redactions of, 45–48; related genres, 31; sources, 45–48; translations of,

Book of John Mandeville, The (continued) 32, 33; use of alphabets, 277–79. See also *Mandeville*-author
Borges, Jorge Luis, 4–5, 10, 11–12 n.8
Boswell, John, 221
Brahmans, 19, 117; as innocents, 132–33, 136, 139 n.15
Brincken, Anna-Dorothee von den, 59
Britons, 108–14
Brittany, 101, 110
Brooks, Peter, 16, 25
Brundage, James A., 221, 242 n.4
Burgwinkle, William E., 212
Butler, Judith, 10, 11 n.2, 12 nn. 9, 15, 213, 237–38
Bynum, Caroline Walker, 102

Cadwathlader (Cadwallader), 108, 112–14
Camille (Amazon queen) (in *Roman d'Enéas*), 207–8, 233–34, 218–19
Camille, Michael, 251–52
Campbell, Mary Baine, 5, 79, 90–91, 120
Campbell, Tony, 52 n.20
Candace (queen of Prasiaca) (in *Wars of Alexander*), 126, 133–35
cannibalism, 259; and castration, 257, 260, 264; and Eucharist, 102
canso, 185–206; lady (*domna*) in, 185, 198–205; nonreciprocal love in, 199–203; vs. *pastourelle*, 185–206
cartographic technologies, 268–93
cartography: christianized, 49; medieval European, 3, 268; political, 3–5; Ptolemaic, 269–70; temporal ideology of, 270. See also *Mappae mundi*
Catalan Atlas. See Cresques, Abraham
center: of Dante's cosmos, 254, 258, 260, 263; of world maps (*see* Jerusalem)
Cervigni, Dino, 259
chivalry: expectations of, 116, 125; failure of, 118–19; fourteenth-century English, 136; need for others, 117; relationship to the East, 119
Christendom: England as part of, 99; margins of, 90; universal, 44–45, 50
Christian of Stavelot, *Expositio in Matthæum Evangelistam*, 65
Christian-Hebrew studies, 270, 281, 287–90; and humanism, 287–90
christianism, 249, 261, 262–64, 265 n.5
Christianity: and its others, 254; and other monotheisms, 124; Christians vs. Jews, 251, 262; in Iceland, 174; parallels with paganism, 174; triumphant, 110–11
Christians: anamnesis, 251; anxiety, 251; apologetic, 81, 90; attitude toward pagan customs, 162, 171, 175; aversion to the East, 121; corruption, 124–25; historiography, 60; readers, 278; settlement in Iceland, 163; vs. Jews, 251, 262
city. *See* Urbanization
Clover, Carol J., 160
conquest: and insecurity, 116; as patricide, 131; impact on language, 108; interpretation of, 112; of Asia, 116, 119; of England, 98, 101, 104; of land, 161; of Latium, 224; sexual, 133–35, 186–93, 222–36; vs. assimilation, 124
Constantine (of Brittany), 110–11
Copeland, Rita, 81–82
Cormier, Raymond J., 212, 237, 243 n.7
court vs. country, as places for women, 185–206
Crane, Susan, 212, 213, 237
Cresques, Abraham, *Catalan Atlas*, 49–50, 61–62
crusades, 118–19; chronicles of, 121; effects on *mappae mundi*, 49; failure of, 123, 125; motives for, 122; promoted by monarchs, 137

Dante, *Divine Comedy*: absence of Jews, 248–55; corporeality of, 19, 23, 24, 25; cosmic system, 254; eros in, 16, 26–27; materiality of, 26; mosques in, 253; Muslims in, 253; readings of, 247, 262–64; topography of, 21–22
Dante, *Inferno*, 247–67; Christian culture of, 249; Satan in, 248, 249; walls of Dis, 252–54
Dante, *Purgatorio*, 15–28; and related genres, 17–19; as fiction, 23, 25; as love story, 26; as suspense, 16; as travel account, 15, 16, 24; bodies in, 21–22, 24; emphasis on body, 19–25; fires of, 19, 23, 24; middleness of, 15–25; models for, 17
Dante-pilgrim, 15, 17, 26; body of, 20–22, 24; journey of, 255, 259, 261–64; sleep of, 21–22
Dante-poet: as eyewitness travel writer, 18, 26; as reader, 27 n.3; narrative strategy of, 247, 248, 249, 251, 253, 256, 258, 261, 262–64
Darius (of Persia) (in *Wars of Alexander*), 129–31
Demaray, John, 17

Index

desire: geographical, 3–12, 224; heterosexual, 213, 238; sodomitical, 211–13, 236–42
Dis (in *Divine Comedy*), 249, 252, 253, 254
Duby, Georges, 106
Durling, Robert M., 261

earth: and burial of wicked, 101; beneath throne, 130–32; personification of, 182 n.4; sacred, 183 n.20; sphericity of, 44; symmetrical, 44
East/West. *See* Orient
Edmund (saint), 100
Edward (king of England), 101
Egill Skalla-Grímsson, 166–67
Enéas (in *Roman d'Enéas*), 207, 209–10, 214–19, 223–28, 231, 233–42
England: fragmented, 101; history of, 97–115; hybrid nature of, 102–3
Estonia, 83, 85, 89–90; burial practices, 88–89, 97
Eucharist, 102–3, 106, 275, 288; and Passover, 259–62; crisis of belief, 260; parody of, 248, 259, 261; theology of, 115 n.6
exploration, 83, 85; motives for, 86–87, 90–91

Fabian, Johannes, 269
Felix, Fabri, 38–39
Faral, Edmond, 211
fathers: acknowledgment of, 128; conflict with, 117–18; inherited power from, 217; multiple, 127; patricide, 117–19, 128–29, 131; secret, 127
Ferenczi, Sandor, 221–22
Fisher, D. J. V., 92
Flint, Valerie I. J., 58, 277
Foote, Peter, 160
Foucault, Michel, 219
fragmentation: of bodies, 100–103, 175; of conqueror, 126; of England, 101; of manuscripts, 137, 138 n.1; of territory, 106–7
Freud, Sigmund, 143
Friedman, John Block, 40
Froissart, Sir John, *Chronicle*, 119

Gardner, John, 25–26
Gaunt, Simon, 210–12
gaze: Christian, 271; deadly, 133; male, 271
gender: and class, 144–45, 186–98; and place names, 176; and topography, 186, 195; battles, 212–17; in land claims, 160; norms, disrupted, 218–19
genealogy, 85; and land claims, 165; Angevin descent model, 106; as history, 105; as ideological, 106; Capetian descent model, 106; discontinuity, 107; Icelandic, 161; Norman descent model, 106–7; of Alexander, 119; of aristocratic families, 115 n.7
Gennep, Arnold van, 172
Geoffrey of Monmouth, *Historia regum Britanniae*, 58, 83, 104–5, 107, 112
geography: and history, 79, 85; as writing of the world, 5, 10–11; astral, 278; classification in, 123; delusions of geographers, 5; of England, 100; on abacus board, 1–3; political, 44–45; Ptolemaic, 38, 39, 269, 284–87; theological, 30, 41; tribal, 84–85
Geometry (allegorical figure), 1–2, 11 n.1
Germanic peoples, 81, 83–84, 94–95, 114 n.3
ghetto, 248, 251, 253, 254, 257
Gog/Magog, 54–75: and Antichrist, 56, 62, 66, 69, 275, 277; as internal threat, 67; as semantic cipher, 55, 59; as unclean, 61; cannibalism and, 61, 66, 70; enclosed by Alexander, 56, 60, 61, 62, 66, 68, 69, 276; ethnic identifications, 55, 56–57, 62, 65–71, 72 n.4; in Alexander-legends, 57–58; in *Book of John Mandeville*, 68–70; in classical texts, 59; in fiction, 58; in Qur'an, 56; in theological texts, 67–68; on Arabic maps, 31, 59–60; on maps and in geographical texts, 58–62, 66–68, 70–71, 74–75 n.30, 275, 277, 278; on nautical charts, 61; on the *Catalan Atlas*, 61–62; sinister implications of, 55; unclean, 61; unstable meaning of, 56; variations of names, 57–60, 62, 67, 72 n.7, 74 n.30, 75 nn. 31, 39. *See also* Amazons; Jews; Magog; Mongols; others
Goldberg, Jonathan, 212, 219–20
Gow, Andrew Colin, 74 n.29
Gravdal, Kathryn, 191–92
Greenblatt, Stephen, 40, 276, 279
Gregory, Derek, *Geographical Imaginations*, 5–9

Halperin, David M., 221
Hanning, Robert W., 98
Hereford map. *See* Richard of Haldingham
heterosexuality: as means of closure, 236–37; as origin, 238; compulsory, 212; in romance, 211
historiography, 97–115; and romance, 105; Anglo-Norman, 98, 105
history (histories): in chronicles, 79–80; insular, 80–81, 83; local, 94–95; narratives of,

history (histories) *(continued)* 98, 106–7; of England, 97–115; of salvation, 37, 105, 112; Virgilian, 105
Hocquenghem, Guy, 213, 221–22, 227, 230, 234
Hofgarða-Refr, 166
Holy Land: centrality of, 43–48; Christian control of, 122; Europeans in, 120; guidebooks, 17–18; *itineraria*, 17–19; topography of, 17–19
homophobia, 209–10, 220, 221
homosexuality, 180–81, 243 n.7; active vs. passive, 163, 208, 213, 219–23, 228–31, 233, 235–36, 243 n.11; and brothels, 151; and dishonor, 163; and eroticism, 230; and psychoanalytic theory, 221, 243 n.7; and the Church, 212; as parody, 238
Howard, Donald, 44
Howe, Nicholas, 85
Hugh of St. Victor: *De arca Noe*, 274; *Description mappe mundi*, 61, 274–76

Iceland: icons, 174; law code, Icelandic, 161, 168–69; settlement of, 159–83
Icelandic texts: *Egils saga*, 169, 175; *Hálfdanar saga svarta*, 175; *Haraldskvæð*, 167; *Íslendingabók*, 165, 174, 176; *Laxdæla saga*, 160; *Sigrdrífumál*, 165; *Vatnsdæla saga*, 175; *Víga-Glúms saga*, 175. See also *Landnámabók*
identity: cultural, 97; hybrid, 104; loss of, 222; national, 83, 95, 104–5, 114; personal, 103–4
immigrants/emigrants, 181; relation to homeland, 159–61, 164–65, 171
Ingledew, Francis, 104–5
Ingólfr, Arnarson, 170, 172–73
Irish: as heathen, 110–11; in Iceland, 174
Isidore of Seville, *Etymologiae*, 34, 285
Islam, 122; influence on Europe, 120–21; relationship to Christianity, 123–25; scriptures, 121
Íslendingasögur (family sagas), 159, 165
itineraries (*itineraria*). *See* Travelers and travel literature

Jacques de Vitry, *Historia orientalis*, 35, 66, 70
Jardine, Lisa, 284
Jerome, 37, 67; *Commentary on Ezekiel*, 34
Jerusalem: as infidel city, 3, 44; cartographic displacement of, 11, 38, 49; centrality of, 11, 30–51, 52 n.9; descriptions of, 41, 54; in *Book of John Mandeville*, 41–49; in pilgrimage texts, 35–39; on Walsperger map, 3; proofs of centrality, 30, 37, 38–39
Jews, 102–3, 117, 120; absence from *Divine Comedy*, 247–67; absence of, 269–70; and Gog/Magog, 65–71; and Muslims, 253; and Old Testament, 275; as center, 254, 258; as origins, 249, 251, 254, 288; circumcision of, 257; conversion of, 102–3; detemporalization of, 269–70, 274, 275, 287; dispossession of, 270–71, 276; distinguished from Hebrews, 248, 249–51, 254; exodus and Passover of, 259–62, 263; in Italy, 252, 265–66 n.11; international colonization of, 271; knowledge of Hebrew, 69, 70, 278–79; medieval, 266 n.13; negative depictions of, 250, 257, 259, 260; "Old Talmudic," 287–90; polemics against, 270; Red, 67; ritual murder accusations against, 288; silencing of, 262–63; synagogues of, 253; Ten Tribes, 66, 69, 70, 276
Johannes Witte de Hese, *Itinerarius*, 54–55, 71
Judas (in *Divine Comedy*), 248, 251, 253, 254; eating of, 260–61
Judecca (*guidecca*), 247–67
Jupiter (in Marriage of Philology and Mercury), 2, 10

Kabbala, 287–88
Kenelm, Saint, 100, 104
knights: as predators, 186–198; landless, 211
Kola Peninsula, 83, 86

Lamory (Lamary), 43–44, 278
land: acquisition of, 211; and gender, 179–80; and marriage, 227–28, 237, 239, 241–42; anthropomorphizing of, 165; as homosocial bond, 213, 223; as virginal, 182 n.4; boundaries of, 165; feminized, 162, 182 n.4, 222; infidel, 3; inheritance of, 106, 115 n.9, 164, 182 n.7; sacred, 183 n.18; uninhabited, 86–87, 162; violation of, 163
land-taking, 161–65, 172; and luck, 170–77, 181, 183 n.17; and sacrifice, 170–73; as sexual, 162, 181; Christian objects used in, 174; gendered, 160, 162, 165, 175–79; legitimacy of, 159–60; phallic objects used in, 167–69, 172–81, 183 n.18; rituals of, 161–62, 164, 172–75, 177–79, 180; sacred objects used in, 173–74; supernaturally sanctioned, 175, 177, 181
Landnámabók (Book of Settlements), 159–61, 164–65, 167–69, 174–79

Langland, William, *Piers Plowman*, 124–25
Langmuir, Gavin, 254
Latinus (in *Roman d'Enéas*), 213, 214–17, 219, 222–26, 228–30, 235, 237, 240–42
Latium, Queen of (in *Roman d'Enéas*), 207–10, 212, 214–19, 221–24, 226–28, 230, 236–40, 242, 243 n.9
Lavine (in *Roman d'Enéas*), 209–10, 213, 217, 219–20, 223–24, 227–29, 236–42
Laȝamon, *Brut*, 58, 105–15
Le Goff, Jacques, 26
Liggins, Elizabeth, 81
Lud (king of Britain) (in Laȝamon's *Brut*), 109

Magog, 55–56, 62; as Saracen, 58; son of Japheth, 55, 59
Mamluk sultanate, 122–23
Mandeville's Travels. See *Book of John Mandeville*
Mandeville-author, 39, 44–45, 48–49, 51, 69–70, 124–25, 290
Manetti, Giannozzo, 287
mappae mundi, 3, 49, 59, 71; and Ptolemaic cartography, 269; as technology, 275; Christian perspectives in, 60; circularity of, 50–51; ideology of, 50; lack of coordinates on, 58; orientation of, 3, 62; T-O form, 3. See also maps and geographies
maps and geographies: Andreas Bianco, 11 n.6, 74 n.30; Anglo-Saxon ("Cotton"), 60; Beatus of Liebana, *Commentary on the Apocalypse*, 59; Borgia, 74 n.30; Ebstorf, 61, 70; Fra Mauro, 68, 11 n.6; Geneva Sallust, 72–73 n.13; Hans Rüst, 75 n.30; Henry of Mainz, 61; Honorius Augustodunensis, *Imago mundi*, 60, 274, 277; Jerome, 59, 72 n.10; Johann of Udine, 62; John Ruysch, 290, 75 n.30; Lambert of Saint-Omer, *Liber floridus*, 60; Nicholas of Lyra, 68, 75 n.33; Olmütz, 62; Pierre d'Ailly, *Imago mundi*, 277; Pirrhus de Noha, 11 n.6. See also Cresques, Abraham; Hugh of St. Victor; Matthew Paris; Ptolemy; Richard of Haldingham; Walsperger, Andreas
maps: Arabic, 59–60; portolans, 49–50
Marcabru, "L'autrier jost'una sebissa," 186–98
Marci, Marcus, 23
marriage: and land, 176, 210, 236–37; as political, 223; exogamy vs. endogamy, 211, 216; medieval practices, 210–11; regulation of, 211; tensions within, 214

Martianus Capella, *The Marriage of Philology and Mercury*, 1, 5, 6
Matthew Paris, *Chronica majora*, 36, 49, 59
Maxims II, 80–81, 94
McNamara, Jo Ann, 204
medieval studies, 5, 10–11, 262–64, 269
men: and courtly code, 186, 187, 195, 198, 203; and Latin, 145; and power, 143; competition for women, 153; homosociality of, 144, 151, 152, 155, 181, 218, 220, 223, 237, 211; male dominance, 186; mastery of household, 152; myth of male nature, 146; patriarchy, 146–47, 152, 175, 217, 218; phallus, 220, 230, 232; relationships between, 237–39; ungendering of, 145. See also Fathers
Menocal, Maria Rosa, 121
Menologium, 80–81, 94
Meulengracht Sørensen, Preben, 160, 170, 176, 180
middles: as boring, 26; pleasures of, 16; *Purgatorio* as, 16, 22, 25; vs. endings, 1, 25
Mongols: alliance with, 45; and Gog/Magog, 65–67; and Jews, 66–67; and Muslims, 67; invasions of, 65
monsters, 70, 117, 120, 126; basilisk, 133; female, 101–3; multiple, 135
Moore, R. I., 114
Morte Arthure, 120, 136

Nicopolis, Battle of, 119, 123, 125–26, 136–37
Normandy, 101–2, 106
Norway, 83, 86, 159, 161, 169, 171–73

oceans, coiled, 135–36
Óðinn, 175, 178
Odo of Deuil, 121, 123, 138 n.5
Odysseus (in *Odyssey*), 15, 24
Ohthere, 83, 85–91
Old English Orosius, 80–82, 85–86, 90, 93–94
Orient, 116–39: as enemy, 129–31; as exotic, 120–21; as origin, 127; as pagan, 111; conflict with, 117–21, 127; dependence on, 123, 126; wealth of, 118
origins, 119; genealogical, 106; of Anglo-Saxons, 81, 85, 90, 94–95; of Christianity, 249, 251, 254; of Jews, 287–89
Ørlygr Hrappson (in *Landnámabók*), 174
Orosius, *Historia adversum paganos* (*History against the Pagans*), 80–85, 93–95, 275
others, 87–88, 110–11; African, 112; anxiety about, 56; attitudes toward, 80, 89–92, 120; eastern, 112, 118, 121; encounters with, 79,

others (*continued*)
83, 86–87, 95; identified with Gog/Magog, 56–57; internalization of, 254; multiplicity of, 98, 112, 114, 126; persecution of, 114
Otter, Monika, 115 n.4
Ottoman Turks: crusade against, 137; empire of, 119, 124

Paden, William D., 192
Pagden, Anthony, 55
Parliament of Three Ages, 131
Partner, Nancy F., 98
Paschasius Radbertus, *De corpore et sanguine domini*, 102
pastourelle, 185–206; class relations in, 190; gender relations in, 186–98; language of *pastora*, 196–97; shepherdess (*pastora*) in, 185–98; vs. *canso*, 185–86
periodization, 268–74, 291 n. 2
Peter Comestor, 65, 276
Peter the Venerable, 121
Petrus Alphonsi, *Dialogue against the Jews*, 270–74, 278, 290
Philip of Macedon, 127–28
Pico della Mirandola, 288
pilgrimage, 17–18, 26; Christian, 30; plot of, 27. *See also* Travelers and travel literature
Poliakov, Léon, 257
Prester John, 44, 54, 278
printing: and alphabets, 281–84; and Jews, 288–89
prophecy, 101, 112–14, 226; and prophet, 118; by the father, 128–29
Ptolemy, *Geography*: alphabetization, 284–87; detemporalization in, 285; maps in, 284–85, 287, 290; printed editions, 284–87; typeface, 284–85. *See also* geography, Ptolemaic

race, 110–12, 114 n.3
rape, 146–47; homosexual, 163, 180–81, 220; in *pastourelles*, 191–93, 205 n.7; metaphor for invasion, 220
rationalism, power of, 268, 279, 281
Rauf Coilyear, 58
Richard of Haldingham, Hereford map of, 3, 46, 70–71
Roman d'Enéas, 207–44
Ross, A. S. C., 86
Rustichello, 48

saints, 99–100, 104; burial lists of, 114–15 n.4;

lives of, 103; miracles of, 99–100; relics of, 113
Satan (in *Divine Comedy*), 248, 251, 254; and defecation, 261–62; and Jews, 247–67; as lack, 255; carnality of, 255; eating of, 259–62; genitals of, 255–58, 264; silencing of, 262–63, 264
Scandinavia, 81, 83, 84–86, 93, 95
Schulenburg, Jane, 204
sea voyages, 83, 85–87, 89, 165, 169–70, 172–73
Sedgwick, Eve Kosofsky, 238
settlement: and kinship, 164; as male activity, 160; of Iceland, 159–84. *See also* Land
Siege of Jerusalem, 116, 120
Simon of Trent, 288–89
Singleton, Charles S., 28 n.11
Siren: in *Divine Comedy*, 22–25; in *Odyssey*, 24, 25
sodomy: and eroticism, 221–22, 235; and foreign invasion, 212–13, 235, 220, 222–23; and land contests, 163, 168, 236; and Trojans, 209–11; as anal intercourse, 207–44; as assault, 226; as humiliation, 213, 221, 230; as source of pleasure, 223; as unnatural, 210; shifting definitions of, 212–13, 219, 242 n.4; symbolic, 180–81
Southern, R. W., 122–23
space: alphabetization of, 281–87; and narrative, 17; domestic, 160; gendered, 160, 185–206; public, 160; supernatural, 160; womanless, 143, 155
Stock, Brian, 268
Strömbäck, Dag, 161, 169, 177, 178, 184 n.24
supernatural beings: aid in battle, 97; aid in land taking, 159–63, 172–73, 176, 178; and sacred objects, 172, 181; female, 166, 180; guardians of land, 179–80; interaction with humans, 160; *landvættir*, 162–63, 168–71; nearness to, 135; presence in history, 98; support for patriarchy, 218
syneisactic communities, 144–46

Tatlock, J. S. P., 211–12
territory, 5, 10–11; and male-male desire, 219; and race, 110–12; as Christian, 174; invasion of, 212–13, 220, 222, 228, 230–31, 235; occupation of, 105; territorialization, 5. *See also* Land
texts, 5, 10–11; accuracy of, 71; and land claims, 161; and patriarchy, 161; and reality, 17; as cultural inscription, 81, 95; as para-

digm for settlement, 171; as record of settlement, 162; canonical, 81; compilation of, 80–81, 93–95, 161; endings, 16, 25; integrity of, 93; interpolations in, 82–85, 90–92; miraculous, 104; *mise en page*, 107; multi-textuality, 32–53; production of, 81, 92, 161; textualization, 5
Theoderich, *Booklet on the Holy Places* (*Libellus de locis sanctis*), 36
toponyms, movement of, 58
topography, Christian, 30, 37, 47–48
totems, 167–69, 172–75, 178–81
trade, 91, 123; silk, 122; spice, 123
translation, 81–86, 88, 92, 100; miraculous, 104; of history, 105, 107; of Islamic texts, 121; vernacular, 82, 91, 98
travel literature, 16–19, 25, 80, 85, 89, 91–92; as deferral, 24; sacramental moments of, 18; secular, 17, 19–20
travelers and travel literature: Antoninus Martyr, *Itinerary*, 35; Arculf, 35, 37 (*see* Adamnan); Bede, *On the Holy Land*, 35, 37; Bernard the Wise, *Itinerary*, 35; Burchard of Mt. Sion, *Description of the Holy Land*, 35; Egeria, 18, 35; *Guidebook to Palestine*, 18; *Hodoeporicon*, 35; John of Plano Carpini, 74 n.27; Marco Polo, *Description of the World*, 32, 72 n.20; Marino Sanudo, *Secrets for True Crusaders*, 35; Paula, 19; Philippe de Mézières, *Le Songe de vieil pelerin*, 36; Ricold of Monte Croce, 66–67; Saewulf, 36–37; *St. Patrick's Purgatory*, 17; *The Breviary of Jerusalem*, 35; *The Epitome of Certain Holy Places*, 35; Theodosius, *Topography of the Holy Land*, 35; William of Boldensele, *Liber de quibusdam partibus ultramarinis*, 40–41; William of Tripoli, *De statu Saracenorum*, 59. *See also Book of John Mandeville*; Dante; Fabri, Felix; Jacques de Vitry; Johannes Witte de Hese; Ohthere; Theoderich; William of Rubruck; Wulfstan
Trojans (in *Roman d'Enéas*): invaders of Latium, 207–10, 212–13, 215–20, 222–35; privileging male bonds, 237–38; significance of, 243 n.13
troubadour lyrics: Bernart de Ventadorn, "Be m'an perdut lai enves Ventadorn," 203; "Era·m cosselhatz senhor," 199–201; "Lancan vei la folha," 202–3; Cercamon, "Quant l'aura doussa s'amarzis," 201–2; Anon., "Et un vergier sotz fuella d'albespi," 199. *See also* Marcabru

Turnus (in *Roman d'Enéas*), 210, 213–14, 217, 222, 227–37, 239, 242
Twain, Mark, *Innocents Abroad*, 29–31, 37
typology, 98, 249, 253, 254

Þórr, 173, 177, 178, 180, 183 n.18

urbanization, impact on women, 143–58
Usamah Ibn-Mugidh, 120
Uthred of Boldon, 124

Verduin, Kathleen, 262
Victorine school, 274–76, 281
Vincent of Beauvais, *Speculum historiale*, 65–66, 285
Virgil (in *Divine Comedy*), 21, 22, 24, 255, 258, 259

Wace, *Le Roman de Brut*, 58, 107
Walsperger, Andreas, world map of, 3
Warner, Michael, 235
Wars of Alexander, 116–39
Westrem, Scott D., 79
White Sea, 83, 85, 86
William the Conqueror, 95, 97, 101
William of Malmesbury, *De gestis regum Anglorum*, 94, 97–106
William of Rubruck, "Journey," 20, 35, 36, 66
Wirszubski, Chaim, 293 nn. 31, 32
women: and apostolic orders, 145; and cities, 143–58; and marriage, 153–55, 158; armed, 110–11; as marriage brokers, 177; body of, 187–88; challenging patriarchy, 218–19; claustration of, 145–46, 148, 204; controls on behavior, 147; dichotomous image of, 185–206; enclosure of, 143, 145, 154, 155–56, 185–86, 198–204; enforced dependence of, 146; exclusion from education, 145; exclusion from work, 147–48, exclusion from public life, 148–49; hatred of, 145; heads of families, 160; heresy and, 147; holy, 100; in troubadour lyrics, 185–206; monstrous, 101; mothers, 217; position in Norse society, 162; power of, 134–35, 214, 217–19; prostitutes, 150–51, 192–93; servants, 150; settlers, 175–77; speech vs. safety of, 186; threats against, 147; transvestism, 110–11; unmarried, 150; violence against, 191–93; wicked, 100–101; widows, 155; work, 144, 147–52, 192
Woodward, David, 49, 59
Woolf, Virginia, 16, 186

Wulfstan, 83, 85, 89–90, 92–93; as ethnographer, 89–91
Wycliffe, John, 124–25

Zacher, Christian K., 40
Zumthor, Paul, 31